Y0-DWH-788

Language Skills in Elementary Education

Language Skills in Elementary Education

Fourth Edition

PAUL S. ANDERSON

DIANE LAPP

San Diego State University

MACMILLAN PUBLISHING COMPANY

New York

COLLIER MACMILLAN PUBLISHERS

London

Printed in the United States of America

Macmillan Publishing Company
866 Third Avenue, New York, New York 10022

Collier Macmillan Canada, Inc.

Library of Congress Cataloging-in-Publication Data

Anderson, Paul S.
Language skills in elementary education.

Includes bibliographies and index.
1. Language arts (Elementary) I. Lapp, Diane.
II. Title.
LB1576.A616 1987 372.6'044 86-16363
ISBN 0-02-303170-0

Printing: 2 3 4 5 6 7 Year: 8 9 0 1 2 3 4

ISBN 0-02-303170-0

Acknowledgments

AMHERST COLLEGE, TRUSTEES OF Reprinted by permission of the publishers and the Trustees of Amherst College from *The Poems of Emily Dickinson,* edited by Thomas H. Johnson, Cambridge, Mass.: The Belknap Press of Harvard University Press, Copyright 1951, (c) 1955, 1979, 1983 by the President and Fellow of Harvard College.

BARKER, BRANDON "Quiet Giants," by Brandon Barker; with permission of the author.

BENNETT, JOAN "Locomotive" by Rodney Bennett, copyright 1941 by Rodney Bennett.

CCM PROFESSIONAL MAGAZINES, INC. "Soft Is the Hush of the Falling Snow," by Emily Carey Alleman, from *Grade Teacher,* March 1953. This article is copyrighted C1953 by Macmillan Professional Magazines, Inc. All rights reserved.

CHRISTIAN SCIENCE MONITOR "Clouds," by Helen Wing. Reprinted by permission of the publisher.

CURRICULUM ASSOCIATES "Bocca-Wacca-Wattamus" and "Have You Met . . . Katy Cassandra Kadidilly Klup???" Selections from "Choral Reading Program" by Maurice Poe and Barbara Schmidt, reprinted with permission of Curriculum Associates, Inc.

FALLIS, EDWINA "The Grant Shoes," by Edwina Fallis.

FISHER, AILEEN "Coffeepot Face," by Aileen Fischer; by permission of the author.

HARCOURT BRACE JOVANOVICH, INC. "Good Night" from *Smoke and Steel* by Carl Sandburg, copyright, 1920, by Harcourt Brace Jovanovich, Inc.; copyright, 1948, by Carl Sandburg. Reprinted by permission of the publisher; "The Secret

Caverns" from *Little Boy and Girl Land* by Margaret Widdemer, copyright 1924, by Harcourt Brace Jovanovich, Inc.; copyright, 1952, by Margaret Widdemer Schauffler. Reprinted by permission of the publisher.

HARPER & ROW, PUBLISHERS, INC. "A Letter Is a Gypsy Elf," from *For Days and Days: A Year-Round Treasury of Child Verse,* by Annette Wynne (J. B. Lippincott). Copyright 1919 by Harper & Row, Publishers, Inc. Renewed 1947 by Annette Wynne. Reprinted by permission of Harper & Row, Publishers, Inc.

THE HORN BOOK, INC. "One Day When We Went Walking," by Valine Hobbs.

THE INSTRUCTOR PUBLICATIONS, INC. "Three Cheers for Peter," by Alice Hartich, *Instructor Magazine.*

JACOBS, DR. LELAND "Teaching the Language Arts" by Leland B. Jacobs

BERTHA KLAUSNER INTERNATIONAL LITERARY AGENCY, INC. "Funny the Way Different Cars Start," by Dorothy Baruch; permission granted by Bertha Klausner International Literary Agency, Inc.

LAIDLAW BROTHERS, PUBLISHERS "Song of the Pop-Corn," by Louise Abney, from *On the Way to Storyland,* c. 1961, by Laidlaw Brothers; "The American Flag," by Louise Abney, from *From Every Land,* Book 6, c. 1961, by Laidlaw Brothers, reprinted by permission of the publisher.

THE PERFECTION FORM CO. "Onceuponatime," reprinted with permission of The Perfection Form Company, Logan, Iowa 51546

RECREATION MAGAZINE "My Mother Read to Me." by E. H. Frierwood, from *Recreation,* February 1950.

REINER, MARIAN "Counting," from *Windy Morning* by Harry Behn. Copyright 1953 by Harry Behn. Copyright renewed c 1981 by Alice Behn Goebel, Pamela Behn Adam, Prescott Behn and Peter Behn. Reprinted by permission of Marian Reiner.

UNIVERSITY OF MINNESOTA "Finger Plays for Young Children," Leaflet No. 11, reprinted by permission of University of Minnesota. Institute of Child Development.

YALE UNIVERSITY PRESS "Bundles," by John Farrar, from *Songs for Parents,* Yale University Press. Add copyright notice; reprinted by permission of the publisher.

Dedicated to Mary Lapp

Lover of language, whose use of stories, poems, jokes and metaphors has been my model of language development.

Preface

This book is designed for you, the language arts teacher, as you plan learning experiences that will make a difference in the lives of your students. If you are questioning the fact that you are a "language arts teacher," remember that regardless of your content specialization you will be required to teach the language arts—which consist of language, listening, writing, and reading—because learning in any content area is dependent on prior acquisition of one or more of these skills. *All* teachers at *all* grade levels in *all* content areas are inevitably language arts teachers.

Teaching in the elementary schools involves hundreds of tasks. No one has ever tried to list all of them. Teachers acquire skill in much the same way that good parents learn to care for a family or physicians learn to treat their patients. Part of teaching proficiency comes from the memory of the way we were taught, part comes by learning from the experience of others, and part is based on our own willingness to work at tasks that we feel must be accomplished. A methods course in the language arts is designed to prepare you to teach by having you relate your own childhood efforts to speak, read, and write to those of young learners; to inform you about what others have learned who have worked in this area; and to present ways of working with problems that you will face. Some of these problems will have rather specific solutions, whereas others are predicaments that are never completely resolved. But with better teacher training and greater teacher awareness of child psychology, more and more children are learning to read well, to write with ease, to speak expressively, and to think efficiently.

Understanding and *teaching* the language arts skills are the basic concepts around which this book is organized. Early chapters describe the participants in the language arts program, the place of the language arts in the school curriculum, the interrelationships of language and culture, and the development of a managed language arts curriculum. Several chapters emphasize the many and varied ways in which teachers accomplish their goals. Do not hesitate to evaluate the ideas and procedures presented in these chapters. Select those that are most appropriate for your students.

Because this is the fourth edition of the text, there are numerous similarities between this and earlier versions. The original topics have all been extended and updated by exploration of current theories regarding language development, the writing process, the reading/writing relationship, children's literature, and the effective use of computers in the language arts classroom.

Throughout the text specific techniques, exercises, and activities are suggested. What happens in these classroom experiences must be something read, something written, something learned. Theory is practical in that it helps a teacher to decide which of many available activities and techniques to use. But no theoretician outside your classroom can know the individual child with whom you work as well as you can. It is your ability to know this child and to combine this knowledge with the information you acquire from a methods course that will determine your success as a teacher. The complexity of this task is an indication of how very important your role as a teacher will be.

Special thanks are extended to Anita Archer,

Monnie Barker, Jean Beebe, Jacqueline Collins, Nancy Curlett Farnan, James Flood, Linda Lungren, Carla Mathison, Lynne Thrope, and Cynthia Wagner for their assistance in the preparation of this text. The helpful reviews of this text during its preparation made by Jane Davidson, Northern Illinois University, Edward Hakanson of Drake University, Carolyn Meigs of Western Carolina University, Dennis Adams of The University of Northern Colorado, Marilyn Peterson of Iowa State University, Daniel Paul of Hope College, Rowena Paiz Lopez of IDRA, and Emmaline Henricksen of Kent State University are also greatly appreciated.

D. L.
P. S. A.

CONTENTS

PART I
YOU AND YOUR STUDENTS

PART II
FOUNDATION OF ALL LEARNING: THE LANGUAGE ARTS

Chapter 3 The Heritage of Language 47

Chapter 4 Acquiring and Using Our Language 62

PART III

COMPONENTS OF THE LANGUAGE ARTS PROGRAM

Chapter 5 Gaining Information Through Listening 81

Chapter 6 Oral Communication 101

Chapter 7 Learning to Read/Reading to Learn 130

Chapter 8 Exploring the World Through Literature 153

Chapter 9 Effective Spelling Instruction 188

Chapter 10 Handwriting Instruction 237

Chapter 11 The Conventions of Writing: Grammar, Usage, and Mechanics 283

Language Skills in Elementary Education

PART I

YOU AND YOUR STUDENTS

Chapter 1

Who Are Your Students?

(Photo by Linda Lungren)

OBJECTIVES

After reading this chapter, the student will be able to:

1. understand that a variety of students' learning strengths and needs exist in one classroom.
2. understand the needs of students who are second-language English speakers.
3. understand the needs of the special learners who are mainstreamed into the regular classroom.

Did You Know . . .?

1. Social class (income level) is the main criterion in determining how much and what kind of education a child will receive.
2. On the average, a child from a family in the lowest one-fourth income level will receive four fewer years of education than a child in the highest one-fourth income level.
3. Districts often provide more resources to schools in the middle- and upper-socioeconomic levels than to schools that serve poor children.
4. Social class can directly affect teacher expectations.
5. Black students are three times more likely to be misplaced in classes designed for children with mental disabilities.
6. The dropout rate for black students is twice that of white students.
7. Although 25 percent of all teachers will have children with limited English-speaking skills, only 3 percent of the teaching population is equipped to instruct these students.
8. Special education funding pressures schools to label children as being disabled inappropriately in order to "make up the numbers" to qualify.
9. Misuse and overemphasis of standardized test scores can label young children as failures and affect exactly what is taught in a district and how it is taught.
10. Sex discrimination exists in public schools, with the result that female students develop lowered expectations both educationally and vocationally.

These points of information relate to children who, Cardenas and First (1985) suggest, are at risk of not receiving the education necessary to function as literate members of society. Among these "children at risk" you will find many of your students. This chapter is designed to help you overcome these barriers to educating your students. By understanding who are in your classroom, where they come from, and what they can expect from the system, you may effectively shape your students for success.

Who Are Your "Regular" Students?

"Usual," "average," "normal," "everyday," "ordinary," "regular"—these are not effective adjectives to use when discussing human individuals. "Regular" students are usually those individuals who have no *extraordinary* educational needs as measured by intelligence scores; levels of emotional, developmental, academic, or social competence; or physical disabilities. Given individual variations, these are students who fit into the mainstream of the American educational system.

All students need to be treated as people of importance, and as individuals. As students, they need to have their intellectual, creative, and experiential horizons broadened. Enlightened exposure to as many different experiences as possible is the key to a successful start in education. The main body of teaching ideas in this book is designed for use with "regular" students. They may all be adapted to meet the needs of students whose abilities (in whichever area) fall outside this "normal" range. Of course, because there is great variation of ability within the given normal range, a section on individualizing for specific problems, or *adaptive education,* is provided. Before progressing to a discussion of teaching techniques, we need first to consider the students themselves.

> I have taught school for ten years. During that time I have given assignments, among others, to a murderer, an evangelist, a pugilist, a thief, and an imbecile.
>
> The murderer was a quiet little boy who sat on the front seat and regarded me with pale blue eyes; the evangelist, easily the most popular boy in school, had the lead in the junior play; the pugilist lounged by the window and let loose at intervals a raucous laugh that startled even the geraniums; the thief was a gay-hearted Lothario with a song on his lips; and

the imbecile, a soft-eyed little animal seeking the shadows.

The murderer awaits death in the state penitentiary; the evangelist has lain a year now in the village churchyard; the pugilist lost an eye in a brawl in Hong Kong; the thief, by standing on tiptoe, can see the windows of my room from the county jail; and the once gentle-eyed little moron beats his head against a padded wall in the state asylum.

All of these pupils once sat in my room, sat and looked at me gravely across worn brown desks. I must have been a great help to these pupils—I taught them the rhyming scheme of the Elizabethan sonnet and how to diagram a complex sentence.

White, 1937, pp. 151, 192

How Do You Work with Very Young Children in School?

At the nursery school and kindergarten level, each day is one of wonder and discovery. There are new things to see, new words to use, and new ideas to try. No day is long enough to see it all, and tomorrow seems so far away. As a teacher, you will be amazed at children's energy and constant need for activity.

In order to work well with very young children, you must learn to use a very different technique from that suitable for a group of young adults. In the Orient, a form of wrestling called judo has been developed. It is a method of using an opponent's strength and energy so that it reacts against him. When the opponent makes a rushing attack, the matter of judo estimates his force and momentum and instead of meeting them with an opposite force, attempts to direct them so that the opponent is thrown to the floor. Although the analogy is a bit strained, it suggests how you can manage the energy of young children. You should not try to stop it or even keep up with it; instead you should attempt to understand it and provide ways for directing this energy so that the child's needs are met.

A visit to a kindergarten will reveal the physical characteristics of the age. Children are active and must move their large muscles. There are room centers where movement is possible because of the play equipment. Because this is the age of chickenpox, measles, and mumps, there are frequent physical checkups and absences. Because vision is not yet mature, the child is protected from activities that call for frequent refocusing of the eyes. Rest periods and quiet times alternate with periods of activity because fatigue is a natural result of expending so much energy.

Intellectually, children of this age are beginning to understand time patterns, follow simple directions, and see differences more readily than similarities. They are not quite certain about the distinction between reality and fantasy and are able to tell or retell simple stories. The teacher provides opportunities to talk about and distinguish between imaginary and real things. The group shares experiences in order to build a common background. There is freedom to ask questions. Perhaps most important of all, children have an opportunity to listen and to be aware of things they have learned through listening.

Emotionally, the young child demands affection and attention. The desire to please is powerful, and many ways are used to gain status. Some show evidence of fear of the unknown, and the wise teacher is careful about phobic response to punishment. At this age the threat of being sent to the principal's office can become, in the imagination of a child, almost equal to that of capital punishment for an adult. On the playground, children become combative but are beginning to substitute language for force, using name calling or verbal quarreling instead of hitting and kicking.

In the classroom, there are outlets for emotions through dramatic play, listening to verse, and creative use of paints, clay, and paper. There is freedom to express opinions without fear of criticism, and there is freedom from pressure to work beyond abilities. Encouragement is given to children to enable them to recognize themselves as individuals and to respect the individuality of others. Limits to behavior are clearly defined so that the child is aware of how things are done while sitting on the rug, while tinkering with toys or equipment, or while playing outdoors or moving in single file through the halls.

Socially, children of this age are self-centered in their contacts with others. They must learn how to work in a group, they find sharing of prized objects a bit difficult, and they look to adults for approval.

In the classroom, children are given an opportunity to participate in group activities and to be creative in social situations by dictating stories, poems, and experiences to the teacher, who records them. Opportunities to look at the work or behavior of the group, or of other small groups, provide occasions to define limits and expectations.

The children are also taught such specifics as what to reply when a visitor comes to our room and says, "Good morning, girls and boys." How may we show a visitor what we are doing? How can this block house be made better? What might we do to improve the way we played at the swing today?

Much of what is done in school at this age is important to the immediate needs of the child, but teachers must anticipate as well the future needs that must be satisfied as the child masters reading, writing, and other skills needed by educated persons in our society. The term used to describe this is *promotion of readiness.* Among the many factors involved in language readiness are the following:

- Broad, rich experience
- Vocabulary development
- Ability to attend (stories, completion of work, participation)
- Recognition of visual likeness and difference
- Recognition of auditory likeness and difference
- Organization through sequence
- Ability to classify and generalize
- Ability to follow instructions
- Ability to speak clearly
- Interest in books and experience of others
- Ability to draw conclusions
- Ability to recall details

A wise teacher looks at the language needs of children at the kindergarten level and asks two questions: "What skills do they need now as they live and work together in this room?" and "What later needs will be influenced by what we do now?" These children may not have a formal reading, spelling, or writing program; however, nearly every activity will be related to later development of these skills. As children learn to identify their own clothes hangers, as they watch the teacher put labels on objects in the room or write the day of the week on the chalkboard, they begin to understand the meaning of reading. When a particular sound appeals to a child who repeats it in a song or verse, that child is mastering the phonetic elements of our language that will later help in learning to spell. The pictures made with great concentration at the easel are expressive experiences almost identical with later writing in that they both express an idea or experience visually.

From the moment children enter the room and are greeted in a friendly manner until they leave with a satisfactory feeling about the day, they have many language experiences. As Patrick makes an airplane, he enjoys using the words that he has heard: *jet, pilot, hostess, fuel,* and maybe *supersonic.* As he paints the plane, color words take on meaning. A feeling of orderliness, neatness, and appropriateness accompanies his activities throughout the day. In cleanup, he uses words like *over, under, behind, beside,* which have indefinite associations. Dramatic play in the home, store, and other interest centers in the classroom calls for conversations that explain sentence structure, choice of words, and organization of ideas. On Marty's walks he learns to see, listen to, and appreciate the sights and sounds of nature. When his sensory experiences are vivid, he bubbles over with ideas and loves to talk about what he saw, what he did, the way things look, and the emotions he feels.

Throughout the day you may find the right moment to bring literature either to one child alone or to a group of children. As a child works with others to build a play road, church, or bridge, you may find an occasion to read to the group such poems as James Tippet's "Trains," "Trucks," "Tugs," and "The River Bridge." A teacher who can go to her file and find "My Dog" and read, "His nose is short and stubby, his ears hang rather low," ending with the thought,

"Oh, puppy, I love you so," has given the children an expression for their inner feelings. If she teaches them the action play or finger play that starts "My dog, Duchess, knows many tricks" and substitutes the name of Shannon's dog, a new experience is shared.

At times, the teacher is wisest who remains silent and waits for children to react. She realizes that truly educative experiences mean not only active presentation of ideas, questions, and materials, but also a quiet alertness to and observation of the child's responses to the environment and to the teacher.

There is much "planned" listening for these children. While they close their eyes, they listen to the sound of the fire crackling, a truck passing, or an object being tapped. They listen to you read and to each other tell about the events at home. It has been said that "the child who listens is one who has been listened to." In order to serve the child's listening needs, we establish standards not only for what children will tell us, but also for the way they will learn. The group decides that today we will only tell about happy things, beautiful things, pets, or things that make sounds. The very shy may tell only the teacher; the very vocal must limit themselves to only one incident of the vacation.

The child leaves the kindergarten with the beginnings of many skills. Among those closely related to language, one should note these:

Beginning Language Skills

Ability to listen:
- when a story is read aloud
- when a speaker is telling of an experience
- to different sounds and tones
- to directions
- to hear likenesses and differences
- to rhythms
- to gain ideas

Ability to speak:
- in complete thoughts
- by repeating sounds
  - and imitate good speech patterns
- in a pleasant voice
  - and tell of a personal experience
  - and show feeling in manner of expression

Abilities related to future reading:
- recognizing simple sequence
- recognizing likenesses and differences in letter forms
- connecting symbols with ideas
- using care in handling picture books
- interpreting the events in a picture

Abilities related to future writing:
- learning to use paintbrush, chalk, pencil
- putting teacher-made signs and labels on objects
- expressing oral ideas that the teacher records
- experimenting with paint, chalk, crayon, and pencil in imitating writing

What Will Children in the Primary and Middle Grades Be Like?

As children progress through the first and second grades, their standards often exceed their abilities. There is much dissatisfied crumpling of paper and erasing. One writer describes this as the "eraser" age. Teachers sometimes make it a rule that all erasing will be done by the teacher in order to keep children from rubbing holes through the paper. This behavior is only one aspect of the child's awareness of criticism from peers or age mates. The world is no longer made for a student alone, but for the group or gang with whom the child identifies. What others think, the praise or punishment that others receive, and other children's opinions now have much greater influence on children's conduct than they did previously.

There is a loss of personal freedom of expression in art and story. Whereas the childlike Daryl once wanted to paint simply what he felt or saw, he is now concerned about the effect his work will produce on others. Group judgment or practice will also influence his clothes, eating habits, book choices, language use, and personal conduct.

By the age of eight, definite speech patterns have developed. The eye is more adapted to the tasks of reading and writing. There is a sense of hurry and untidiness that is related to a tendency toward accidents. These accidents are also associated with curiosity and interests that outdistance caution. Exploring the unknown is a favorite activity.

Emotionally, primary school children desire and seek prestige. The Cub Scout and Brownie uniform is worn with pride. Some who do not belong show jealousy, and, because feelings are still near the surface, violent outbursts or sullen withdrawal can be expected at times. Boy-girl relationships are either at the companion level or ignored. These children look for recognition from adults through use of social courtesies and individual association, but at the same time they seek independence through peer group approval. Most want adults to keep hands off, literally and figuratively.

The older children of this age range are sometimes described as being in the latency period rather than in preadolescence. Because they have already mastered the basic skills, they can follow their interests in all directions. Teachers of these groups are true generalists from the educational point of view. One day they may be learning how humans can breathe in outer space, the next how the United Nations is organized, and the next how the Aztecs told time.

In the sixth grade many of the girls have entered adolescence. They find emotions difficult to control. A trivial sight or event can cause a major crisis. Some overt emotional display may belie underlying causes. Sometimes these children cry when happy and show antagonism toward persons they admire. Ordinarily, the girls are taller and weigh more than the boys throughout the intermediate grades.

Intermediate grade students like to plan and organize. Clubs are organized almost solely for the fun of organizing them, although such activity may express a yearning for great achievement. There is little regret when nothing of much significance happens in a club meeting. The important point seems to be that the meeting takes place. Close friends also constitute an aspect of this period, and new friendships explain some of the changed classroom behavior. Elections are often little more than popularity contests. New students go through a period of popularity as individuals seek them as friends. Note passing, and in a few cases, actual flaunting of a boy- or girlfriend are other common forms of social behavior at this time.

Working with these children requires a fine balance of permissiveness and control. At times free rein must be given to permit maximum use of abilities and extension of interest. At other times the control of the adult leader must be exercised to prevent immature judgments and emotional actions. This control requires a knowledge of each individual and of the nature of group interaction.

Although beginning teachers are usually unprepared for the wide range of abilities encountered in groups of children, there are many common interests and needs toward which teaching energies can be directed, but no effort or magic can produce common achievement such as "fifth-grade work" or "sixth-grade norms" with a total class. We have not failed as teachers, nor have some children failed as students. Although teaching and learning take place, the responses are influenced by the individual abilities of those with whom we worked.

Previous studies of growth patterns of individual children (Piaget, 1963) reveal that although all children engage in the same stages of development, the ages of entering and exiting a stage are somewhat flexible. Some start early and continue to grow rapidly; others start late and are always behind their age mates. Yet we cannot be certain that children who start early will be always ahead of his group.

Piaget asserts that cognitive developmental changes are related to biological developmental processes. Thus, each stage of cognitive growth, with its concomitant changes, emerges logically, and inevitable connections stem from each of the preceding stages. The stages are not reversible, and no stage is avoidable.

Flexible developmental patterns are to be expected. Parents sometimes say, "My boy did not like reading until he had Miss Lungren in the third grade." With all due credit to Miss Lungren, the child was probably "not ready" for the experience prior to this time. However, it may have been the efforts of a Miss Lungren that prevented this child from accepting a self-image of being slow to learn or poor in scholarship.

Children move through a sequence of language growth in the elementary school, no two at the same rate or in the same way. The following is an approximate age sequence of the developmental stages of growth of preschool and elementary-school-age children.

Kindergarten (four and a half to six years)

Listening: Listen to peers in play groups. Develop an increasingly long attention span to stories. Can remember simple directions and messages.

Speaking: A few will still be developing speech sounds, using them correctly in some words and not in others. Use simple direct sentences. The vocabulary ranges from two thousand to more than ten thousand words.

Reading: Interpret books; explore books. Can identify some signs such as STOP or displayed words on television. About one in six hundred can read children's books.

Writing: Like to watch adults write. Experiment with crayons and paints.

Grade One (five and a half to seven years)

Listening: Listen to clarify thinking or to get answers to questions. Can repeat accurately what is heard. Listen for specific sounds in words and the environment.

Speaking: Can share experiences before the group in an established way. Use compound and complex sentences. Use the grammar patterns of the home. Some speech repetition takes place as they try to remember words for ideas they wish to express.

Reading: Read charts, preprimers, and primers and master a vocabulary of three hundred to six hundred words. Understand the use of many consonant and vowel sounds.

Writing: Write names, labels for pictures, and stories to illustrate art work. The spelling applies the phonics of reading.

Grade Three (six and a half to eight years)

Listening: Listen with increasing discrimination. Make suggestions and ask questions to check their understanding. Are aware of situations when it is best not to listen.

Speaking: Have mastered all sounds of speech and use them correctly. Use some of the shock words of our language without complete understanding.

Reading: Read with increasing attention to meaning, enjoy selecting their own stories, read their own writing. Usually start the year in a first reader of a commercial reading series.

Writing: Write well with print script. Use dictionary books or notebooks as references for spelling. Seek to correct misspellings.

Grade Three–Four (seven and a half to ten years)

Listening: Are increasingly aware of the value of listening as a source of information and enjoyment. Listen to the reports of others, tapes of their own reports, and radio broadcasts with purpose and pertinent questions. Display arrogance with words or expressions they do not understand.

Speaking: Reenact and interpret creative radio, movie, and story situations as they play. Speak fairly well to adults and able to make themselves understood. Are praised in most school-associated social situations. Vocabulary of some children may be as high as sixty thousand words.

Reading: Read with interpretive expression. Grow in reading speed as they read silently. Most children succeed in using reading as a study skill.

Writing: Reports are written in all subject areas. Creative stories and poems are written. Write rough copies with a willingness to recopy to improve legibility, ideas, and punctuation.

Grade Four–Six (nine and a half to twelve years)

Listening: Listen critically for errors, propaganda, false claims. Listen to a wide variety of stories, poetry, rhyme, and find pleasure in exploring new types.

Speaking: Show an increasing awareness of the social value of conversation and try to get what they want through persuasion. Become increasingly competent in the use of inflections, modulation, and other methods of voice control. Employ singing, yelling, whispering, and talking. Can conduct club meetings and present organized talks or dramatic recitations.

Reading: Show increased interest in factual material and how-to-do-it books. Many read independent of instruction. Use reading with greater purpose, such as getting information for a trip, checking references, or following a personal interest. Adapt method and speed of reading to the content and purpose.

Writing: Make between one and a half and two errors in each sentence at first. Find new uses for writing as they answer advertisements and do creative work. Are interested in the writing techniques of others and note good and poor composition in the newspapers. Like to see their writing in print. Use the dictionary as a spelling aid.

Although a general age range of language arts development has been suggested, a wide spectrum of skill development will be obvious in any elementary classroom, because you are working with *individuals,* all with varying degrees of experience and readiness. You may group them for instruction, but do not for one moment lose sight of the dimensions and needs of *each individual*. Each child, for ten months, will be dependent on you to provide learning experiences that nuture both cognitive and emotional growth. Indeed, teaching is a task that entails many elements.

Socially, children of this age are self-centered in their contacts with others. They learn how to work in a group, find sharing of prized objects a bit difficult, and look to adults for approval. (Photo by Linda Lungren)

Although many children in your classroom will demonstrate these general characteristics, some of your students may exhibit linguistic differences or special learning needs. Since the major portion of this book has been designed to provide you with information needed to teach the majority of your "regular" students, we will at this time provide you with some insights regarding your linguistically different children and those with special needs.

Who Are Your Bilingual Students?

As Lapp and Flood (1986) suggest, in many American schools, there are students who are proficient speakers, readers, and writers of both their native language (L_1), which may be Spanish, Portuguese, Chinese, or Italian, and English (L_2), which is their second language. These students are referred to as *balanced bilinguals*. There are also other students who exhibit a range of competency in speaking, writing, and reading both in their native language (L_1) and in English (L_2). There are many issues to consider when faced with the task of developing the language/reading/writing skills of all these students. For the sake of simplicity, we will refer to them collectively as *bilingual* students since the goal of the curriculum in the schools which they attend must be to develop balanced bilingual education.

Although it may seem obvious, it is important to remember that bilingual students are *not* disadvantaged. In fact, they have the ability to understand two languages. This language abundance sometimes calls for instruction in the native language, English only, or both.

Children come to school with a variety of language skills in reading, writing, listening, and speaking. The teacher's task is to help them to develop and extend these skills. It is in the nature of human development that all children learn to listen and speak before they learn to read and write. If a speaker and a listener share the same set of oral symbols for objects and relationships in their experience, oral language conveys meaning. Written language also conveys meaning if its symbols, based on these oral symbols, are shared by the reader and the writer. Therefore, the language arts teacher must build on the child's oral language base in order to enhance both the reading and writing processes. Without a strong oral language base, reading and writing are senseless to a student.

The topic of bilingual education is extremely important for the rapidly expanding bilingual population in the United States. These students need educators to answer such questions as (1) How do we educate language minority students who come to school speaking a language other than English? (2) How do we help these students grow in content area concepts while learning English and maintaining facility with their own language?

Most reading programs being developed today for bilingual students support the need for a strong oral language base. They are designed to teach children to read in their native language while doing oral work in the second language. Reading in the second language is not introduced until the child requires an oral base sufficient to support the development of other skills. In order to develop literacy in all of the language arts, an oral language base must precede learning to read and write. Students who first learn to read in the vernacular will make better progress, even in the second-language reading programs, than students who spend the same length of time working only on reading in a second language.

The bilingual approach has developed out of the frustration and ineffectiveness of attempts to educate limited-English-proficient (LEP) students through English-only instruction. Eleanor Thonis, a consultant in bilingual education for the Marysville, California, schools and the author of numerous publications on bilingual literacy (1976, 1983), describes the effects of pushing students into English reading:

> The sooner we had pupils with books in hand, the more virtuous we felt and the more reading proficiency we thought we were offering our pupils. It was disappointing to us that many of our best efforts failed. A few hardy pupils did learn to read well, several survived in spite of us, and an overwhelming number of pupils gave up and left us as soon as they were old enough (p. 10).

Although many still believe that the more basic skills instruction students receive in English, the greater will be their yield in scholastic achievement, low test scores, high dropout rates, and rampant unemployment for limited-English-proficient students who have been schooled in an English-only manner provide ample evidence that the monolingual method is not an effective mode of instruction.

Time Is a Major Factor in Language Development

Although socioeconomic considerations and cultural differences contribute to lack of performance in English, there is yet another factor. This is the problem LEP students have when they confront English print and are forced to deal with a symbol of a symbol—a graphic representation of speech sounds with which they are simply not familiar. These students do have many meanings based on their experiences in their own language, but they cannot attach meaning to the sounds, graphemes, and structures that they encounter in English. It is unrealistic for educators to expect students to learn to listen, to understand, to speak, to read, and to write in English while they are struggling to learn new ideas, concepts, and content through the medium of the same new language. Although it is true that within two or three years most of these students are able to learn a "survival English" that has lots of context to support it, they have not yet had sufficient time to master the abstract cognitive English required for academic success.

As Thonis (1983, p. 235) suggests, the development of literacy skills takes time for *any* student in *any* language. Ordinarily, monolingual students have had five years of oral language practice at home before entering the reading classroom. After a period of readiness for reading, students are offered reading instruction for the next five or six years. Usually, when they leave the fifth or sixth grade they have the necessary fluency and literacy skills to use in their junior and senior high school years. From this point on, there is little attention given to the teaching of reading as a subject. The curriculum emphasis shifts to subject matter, and students are expected to acquire content, knowledge, and skills. In terms of chronological age, students have enjoyed approximately eleven or twelve years in which to acquire the fluency and literacy skills that will serve them well the rest of their lives. Teachers recognize that skill acquisition takes appropriate instruction, guided practice, and time.

For students who spend the first five years of their lives in a Spanish environment, for example, their oral language in Spanish may be adequate for supporting a program of reading readiness in Spanish but is most inadequate for an English reading readiness program. When the next few years of schooling provide opportunities for instruction in Spanish reading and writing, these students at the end of their fifth or sixth grades should have literacy skills comparable to those of their English-speaking peers. During the oral English lessons along with the opportunities to acquire English through the many informal contacts with English-speaking classmates, comprehension of speech should be coming right along. As students *add* the literacy skills of English, they are building *balanced* skills in both languages and are moving toward the oral and written control of English as well as Spanish. These valuable proficiencies take time and patience.

How Can Literacy in One Language Be Transferred to Literacy in a Second Language?

As Thonis (1983), Cummins (1981), and Krashen (1981) suggest, learning a second language should be guided by the principles of learning a first language. Students should learn to listen, understand, and speak English in a natural way before they learn to read and write it.

Learners often transfer the forms and meanings of their native language and culture to the second language and culture. Lado (1976) suggests that learners do this both when attempting to speak and when trying to understand the new language.

Lado (1976), Thonis (1983), and others have compared the speech and print systems of Spanish and English and have concluded that there is tremendous opportunity for transfer of language, literacy, and thinking skills. Students who are already reading in Spanish bring a wealth of techniques, habits, and concepts from their successful experiences with Spanish directly into English.

As teachers, we can assume that once students have facility with one language, they have stored many meanings that they can refer to both when they are receiving and when they are sending messages. In addition to this competency, the students have also added the written system of their language. They have made the associations between print and speech, and they are able to represent their speech in print. Because these students can express and receive written language, Thonis (1983) reminds us, they are literate and they only learn to read once. Literate students have experienced their language proficiency across all language processes. They can understand, speak, read, and write. Their auditory symbol system—speech—supports their visual symbol system—print.

These bilingual speakers value their ability to function well in oral and written language. This successful functioning in communication has caused them to value themselves. Success and the expectation of success transfer into English in the same way that language elements that are shared between the two languages transfer.

The thinking strategies associated with reading comprehension are exactly the same in any language. The cognitive skills of identifying the main idea, recalling story details, understanding cause and effect, making inferences, sequencing, making judgments, making predictions, differentiating between reality and fantasy, and identifying an author's point of view are all part of the student's intelligence once they have been developed in the first language. To effect these same skills in English, Thonis (1983) suggests, simply requires the learning of the appropriate terminology and vocabulary in English.

This is not to say that transfer from one language to another takes place automatically. Transfer requires careful planning and organization by the teacher. Thonis (1983) further suggests that teachers must know how to make transfer happen by assisting students to recognize transfer possibilities and by consciously working transfer teaching into the curriculum whenever it seems appropriate and wise. Teachers are the best resource for the transferability of skills as they arrange instruction for transfer to take place and tell the students about skill transfer whenever a possibility exists. Thus we move toward the goal of dual literacy.

Can All Bilingual Students Be Taught in a Similar Manner?

Children who speak English as their second language have specific problems learning to read in English. Lapp and Flood (1986) suggest many possible sources of difficulty for the second-language students as well as many insights into the contrasts between the student's language and English.

SPANISH. Spanish is the second most frequently spoken language in the United States. It is possible that you will eventually work with Spanish-speaking students. In the next few pages, you will find information useful for teaching these students to read English.

Obviously, there is no reading methodology for all bilingual and ESL students. A matrix similar to the following one, which was developed by Lapp and Flood (1986), can help you to understand some of the differences among bilingual students with regard to reading and writing ability. Five different combinations are represented:

	Student 1	*Student 2*	*Student 3*	*Student 4*	*Student 5*
Speaks	Spanish	Spanish,	Spanish	Spanish,	Spanish,
	—	English	—	English	English
Reads	—	—	Spanish	—	Spanish,
	—	—	—	English	English

You will note that students 3, 4, and 5 have no problem per se, because each of them speaks and reads at least one language. Teaching student 3 to read in English or student 4 to read in Spanish depends upon several factors: age, the student's progress in English at the present time, and the need for reading in a second language. The following is an example of a prescriptive approach for teaching each of these students.

Student No. 1. Teach oral English before reading instruction in either language. Begin reading instruction in Spanish (if desired by student or parents).

Student No. 2. Begin reading instruction in one of the two languages, depending on the following factors:

a. Student preference
b. Local expertise
c. Age
d. Cultural factors
e. Family preference

Student No. 3. Begin oral instruction in English. Begin reading instruction in English.

Student No. 4. Begin reading instruction in Spanish (if desired by student).

Student No. 5. Continue. You are doing an excellent job.

Planning a Language Arts Program for Bilingual Students

ASSESSMENT. As suggested by Lapp and Flood (1986), the first question you will ask when you are working in English with a second-language student is "How much English does the student know?"

In asking this question, you are beginning to assess English proficiency. Remember that students have different proficiencies within their language ability. In most cases, it may be advantageous for you, as the teacher, to conduct a structured, but informal, nonthreatening interview to determine the student's proficiency and ease in speaking English.

Most tests that have been designed to assess language dominance have ignored the fact that students have variations in their language abilities. Sometimes their native language is their dominant, preferred language for a particular task, but sometimes it is not. This seems eminently logical because many adults experience the same phenomenon; that is, a Spanish-speaking adult who studied advanced statistics in England may prefer to use English when he is discussing statistics. Therefore, before globally assessing a student's language dominance, we need to ask, "What is the specific task that the person is being asked to perform?" and "What is the language of the person to whom the student will speak during the instructional period?" The answers to these questions will provide a great deal of useful information that will enable you to begin your instructional program.

In determining language proficiency, you will want to extract information about several aspects of language so that you can build a program for each student. An example of such a test that gathers information about the reading, writing, speaking, and listening skills of the bilingual student is the Marysville Test, which is administered in English and Spanish. Other tests are also available in other languages on a variety of reading levels. Many of these tests are available through the following sources:

Bilingual Syntax Measure, 1975 (grades K–2), Harcourt Brace Jovanovich, Inc., Testing Department, 757 Third Ave., New York, N.Y. 10017

Dos Amigos Verbal Language Scales, 1974 (grades 1–4), Academic Therapy Publications, 1539 Fourth St., San Rafael, Calif. 94901

James Language Dominance Test, 1974 (grades K–1), Learning Concepts, Speech Division, 2501 N. Lamar, Austin, Tex. 78705

Northwest Regional Educational Laboratory Assessment Instruments in Bilingual Education, 1978 (grades K–8), National Dissemination and Assessment Center Los Angeles, Calif.

Oller, J. and Perkins, K. (1980). *Research in language testing,* Rowley, MA; Newbury House Publishers.

Pletcher, B. et al. (1978). *A guide to assessment instruments for limited English speaking students.* Northvale, N.J. Santillana.

Sanchez, R. (1976). Critique of oral language assessment instruments. *NABE Journal, 1, 2.*

Sanchez, R., Romo, H., Santos Rivera, I., and Williams, B. (1978). *Issues in language proficiency assessment. San Diego: National Origin Desegregation Center.*

Spanish-English Language Dominance Assessment, 1972, Professor Bernard Spolsky, The University of New Mexico, 1805 Roma N.E., Albuquerque, N.M. 87106

PROGRAM FEATURES. As suggested in a 1984 editorial (*San Diego Union,* June 10, 1984, p. A-12), effective bilingual programs seem to have several features in common. These programs often have a strong emphasis on language development, and utilize staff members who are competent and who are sensitive to the needs of students from language minority populations, and have the necessary resources to carry out effective instruction. Another key element common to successful bilingual programs is that strong skills are developed through a developmentally sequenced curriculum. Furthermore, there is a strong emphasis on developing a solid oral language base as preparation for reading in English through an English-as-a-second-language component.

You may not have any bilingual students at the present time, but it is likely that at some point you will have one or more of them in your classroom. An entire English-as-a-second language curriculum cannot, of course, be condensed into a few pages, but we hope these suggestions help you to think about student differences.

MATERIALS SELECTION. In planning a bilingual program, you will need to purchase materials for use in your own classroom or in your school, and you will probably want to establish criteria for their selection. The following checklist is designed to help accomplish this.

	Yes	No
1. Teacher competency		
a. Must you be a content specialist to use the materials successfully?	____	____
b. Must you be bilingual to use the materials?	____	____
c. Are the materials usable by inexperienced teachers?	____	____
d. Does the publishing company or the school system provide consultants to instruct you in the use of the materials?	____	____
2. Learners		
a. Do the materials provide for student differences in intelligence, experience, and language fluency?	____	____
b. Do the materials contain stories of equal interest to both males and females?	____	____
c. Do the materials contain high-interest, low-vocabulary selections?	____	____
3. Program sequence		
a. Does the developmental sequence of the program closely parallel the natural development of language learning?	____	____
b. Does the program build on the natural language strengths of the student?	____	____
c. Does the program make provisions for the development of all of the language arts?	____	____
d. Do the materials provide for individualizing instruction?	____	____
e. Are the materials free from cultural stereotyping?	____	____

	Yes	No
f. Can the materials be integrated within an existing program?	____	____
4. Program packaging		
a. Do the materials contain charts, filmstrips, flashcards, and other supplementary materials?	____	____
b. Are the supplementary aids easily used by students?	____	____
c. Are materials for reinforcement, review, and evaluation provided?	____	____
d. Are the costs consistent with available program funds?	____	____
e. Are program constraints consistent with time allowances for classroom implementation?	____	____

As you plan programs for your bilingual students it is important to remember that there is ample evidence to indicate that high-quality bilingual programs can help to develop English academic proficiency for language minority students who come to school speaking languages other than English. An emphasis on language development, competent and sensitive staff members, ample resources, strong skill development in their native language, a solid oral base in English, and instructional strategies that maximize the transfer potential between languages are essential for success.

What Is an Appropriate Instructional Sequence for Bilingual Learners?

The question "How do I proceed in the task of teaching English structures to nonnative speakers?" is certainly complex. Again, researchers and teachers are not in total agreement on an appropriate sequence of instruction. The sequence you choose will probably reflect the individual differences of your students. The following scope and sequence chart, designed by Lapp and Flood (1986), can serve as *one* model for you. You will probably adjust this within your own classroom.

A Scope and Sequence Chart for Use in Teaching English to Speakers of Other Languages

Vocabulary Development

Beginning Level

A basic flexible-content vocabulary should include items relevant to the students' everyday experiences, e.g.:

Eating and cooking utensils	Colors
Common foods	Names of occupations
Parts of the body	Days of the week
Articles of clothing	Months of the year
Furniture	Seasons
Telling time	Holidays
Numbers: cardinal, ordinal	Various materials: wood, plastic, etc.
Family relationships	Most important geographic names
Common animals	
Words used to ask directions	

Pictures and/or objects should be used to explain all of the above.

In addition:

Several basic two-word verbs (verbs + particle): pack up, wait for, hang up, get up, etc.
Concepts of directionality: in front of, behind, before, after, etc.
Countable and noncountable nouns: *cup* as to *cereal,* etc.
Following simple directions
Simple synonyms, antonyms, especially adjectives and prepositions such as good-bad, on-off, etc.

Intermediate Level

Extension of vocabulary introduced above, plus:
- Shopping expressions
- Further occupations and reponsibilities
- Health and health practices
- Further synonyms and antonyms
- Family—names of more distant relatives
- Government agencies
- Clothing, materials

Intermediate-Advanced level

Daily living skills
- Purchasing suggestions
- Driving
- Traffic regulations
- Postal procedures
- Insurance procedures

Music, literature, the arts
Educational opportunities
Leisuretime activities
Travel
Government
Directions involving choice
Derivations
Structural analysis: prefixes, suffixes, hyphenation of words
Synonyms, antonyms, homonyms (more advanced)

Advanced Level

Study skills information—locating and organizing information, synthesizing information, and making cross-comparisons
Propaganda techniques—discerning fact and fiction
The human body and its actions
  Evening and morning activities
Special problems: Idiomatic expressions
  Multiple meanings of words
Advanced descriptive terminology
  Attributes of objects (size, shape, etc.)
  Attributes of people (including personality, etc.)
Buying and selling
Transportation and communication
Personal and professional contacts (job applications, etc.)
Further government interaction (law, courts, taxes, etc.)
Oral and written reports: books, movies, trips, etc.
Discussions on American history, geography, climate

Syntactic Structure

Beginning Level

A. Declarative and question sentence structures
   1. Word order of declaratives contrasted with different word order of questions with *be* verbs (*They are leaving, Are they leaving?*)
   2. Use of contracted forms of *be* verbs (*he's, they're, I'm*)
   3. Use of *be* verbs to show action:
      a. in progress
      b. of repetitive nature
   4. Use of determiners (*the, a, an*)
   5. Affirmative and negative short answers to questions with *be* verbs (*I'm going, He's not going*)

B. Verbs other than *be*
   1. Word order for declaratives compared to order for questions with *do* and *does*
   2. Affirmative and negative short answers to questions with *do* and *does*
   3. *-s* forms of third-person singular used with pronouns (*he, she, it*) and other singular nouns in declaratives, contrasted to plural nouns (*he runs, we run*)

C. Expression of time (tense)
   1. Use of *be* in expressions of past tense in statements and questions. (*I was walking, Were they singing?*)
   2. Irregular verbs which form past tense without *-ed* (use of vowel and consonant contrast)
   3. Formation of verbs other than *be* to express past tense using regular rule (*-ed*)
      a. Past tense forms and placement of verbs other than *be* in declaratives and questions
   4. Forms of short responses to questions asked in past tense (use of *be* or *do* appropriately)
   5. Use of *be* verbs + *going to* to express future tense. (*She is going to ride home, They are going to sing*)

D. Formation of questions with interrogative words or word order

E. Negatives
   1. Use and placement of *not* in declaratives (past, present, future) with verb *be*
   2. Use of *not* in questions with *be*
   3. Use of *not* in sentences (declarative and question) with *do* and verbs other than *be*
   4. Use of *any, rarely, seldom, few,* etc.

F. Frequency words
   1. Different positions of frequency words with *be* contrasted with positions with verbs other than *be* (*He sometimes walks, He is always late*)
   2. Use of *ever* in question patterns; *never* in declarative sentences

Articulation

A. Contrasted intonation contours of declarative sentences, questions, and short answers
B. Stress and accent patterns of requests
C. Articulation of contracted forms of *be* with pronouns: *he, she, we, you, it, there*
D. Articulation of the /s/, /z/, and /-əz/ of third-person singular verbs and plurals as in words such as *eats, wins, smashes* and contractions such as *it's, there's*
E. Unstressed forms of *a, an, the*
F. Articulation of /k/, /g/, /ŋ/: *kick, go, sing*
G. Stress and accent patterns of compound words
H. Articulation of /t/, /d/, and /-ed/ endings as in *foot, wood, hunted*
I. Articulation of /p/ and /b/ as in *pay, boy*
J. Articulation of /f/ and /v/ as in *calf, move*
K. Articulation of /θ/ and /ə/: *thin, those*
   1. Contrasting /t-/ with /θ/: *boat, both*
   2. Contrasting /d/ with /ə/: *day, they*

L. Articulation of /š/, /ž/, /č/, and /ǰ/: *mash, pleasure, choose, fudge*
M. Articulation of /m/ and /n/: *moon, no*
N. Articulation of /l/ and /r/: *lose, read*
O. Articulation of /w/ and /y/: *wood, yellow*
P. Articulation of front vowels:
  1. /i/ and /I/: *seat, sit*
  2. /e/ and /ɛ/: *say, pet*
  3. Contrast of /ɛ/ with /I/: *set, sit*
  4. Contrast of /I/, /ɛ/, and /i/: *sit, set, seat*
  5. /æ/: *hat*
Q. Articulation of middle vowels:
  1. /ə/ and /a/: *nut, hot*
  2. Contrast of /a/ and /æ/: *hot, hat*
  3. /ai/: *tie*
  4. /ər/: *hurt*
R. Articulation of glides and back vowels:
  1. /u/ and /U/: *food, foot*
  2. /aU/: *cow*
  3. /o/ and /ɔ/: *boat, bought*
  4. /oi/: *toy*

Intermediate Level

A. Review of patterns introduced at beginning level
B. Modification constructions: use of substitute words:
  1. How *other* and *another* can be substituted for nouns, contrasted with their use as modifiers of nouns
  2. Use of objective forms of personal pronouns in object position
C. Structures in which *me, to me,* and *for me* are used with certain verbs
D. Patterns of word order when expressing manner (*John runs quickly*)
E. Modals: use of *must, can will, should, may,* and *might* in appropriate place in sentence
F. Techniques for connecting statements:
  1. *and . . . either* contrasted with *and . . . too*
  2. Use of *but*
G. Structures with two-word verbs (verb + particle): *call up, put on*
  1. Structures in which they are unseparated
  2. Structures in which they are separated
H. Patterns for answers to *Why* and *How* questions
I. Special patterns for using *to* and *for:*
  1. *for* and *to* + other words as modifiers following some terms of quality
  2. Placement of *very, too, enough*
  3. Patterns in which nouns or pronouns are used after certain action words
J. *It* or *there* as subject of the sentence
K. *-'s* as a contraction and as a possessive marker
L. Comparisons:
  1. Structures for comparisons with *different from, same as, like, the same as, as . . . as*
  2. Patterns of comparison using *-er than* and *more than, of the, -est,* and *the most*

Articulation

A. Articulation of consonant cluster: /sp/ as in *special*
B. Articulation of consonant cluster: /st/, /sk/, /sn/, /sm/, /sl/, and /sw/ as in *step, skip, snap, smell, slip, swap*
C. Articulation of final consonant clusters: Consonant + /s/, consonant + /t/, consonant + /d/, as in *cats, dropped, flags, used*
D. Articulation of final consonant clusters: two consonants + /s/, as in *helps*
E. Articulation of final consonant clusters: two consonants + /t/, as in *jumped*
F. Intonation patterns used in comparisons

Intermediate-Advanced Level

A. Review of structures introduced at earlier levels
B. Word order pattern and use of relative clauses or embedded sentences to modify nouns:
  1. Words used as subject of the embedded sentence (*that, which, who,* etc.)
  2. *that* and related words in other positions
C. *what, when, who,* etc., in object position
D. Embedded sentences of different statement pattern type used in object positions
E. Patterns with *have* and *be* in the auxiliary:
  1. Present perfect complete *have* (*has*) + -ed/-en form of verb
  2. *be* + *-ing* verb form (used with *yet, anymore, still,* etc.)
  3. *have* + *been* + *-ing* verb forms in continuous present perfect structures
  4. Using *be* + *-ed/-en* verb forms
  5. Using *be* + *-ed/-en* and *-ing* in descriptions
  6. Special cases:
    a. *be* + two-word verbs and *-ing* form
    b. Use of *had* in the preceding structures

Special structural patterns

A. Verb modification:
  1. *wish* / *hope* } (*that*) + declarative sentence
  2. *to* omitted after certain verbs
B. Conditionals:
  1. Patterns with *should, might, could, must*
  2. Cause and effect sentence structures

C. Object structures and modification:
   1. Use of *-ing* endings of verbs
   2. Patterns for verbs followed by an object and one or more describing words, and/or an *-ing* form
   3. Verbs followed by two nouns with the same reference
   4. *-ing* endings used in subject position contrasted to their use at the beginning of sentences (referring to the subject)

D. Logical order of sentences in sequence:
   1. Ordering for sentences related by *however, therefore, also, but*
   2. Ordering for sentences related by terms of time or place (*before, after that, then*)

Advanced Level

A. Review of all preceding levels
B. Review of function words:
   1. auxiliaries: *will, may, can, could, should, might, would, must, have, be, shall, do*
   2. Preposition adverbs:
      a. Frequently used: *at, by, in, into, for, from, with, to, on, of, off*
      b. *Location*
      c. *Direction*
      d. *Time*
      e. *Comparison*
C. Conjunction patterns with *but* and *or*
D. Other complement structures:
   1. *believe* / *want* / *think* / *expect* } + declarative sentence
   2. Use of appropriate complementizer words in the preceding.

Articulation

A. Articulation of final consonant cluster: two consonants + /z/ as in *holds*
B. Articulation of final consonant cluster: two consonants + /d/ as in *solved*

Advanced Level

Articulation

A. Intonation and stress patterns used with comparisons, manner and time words, and prepositions
B. Intonation patterns for modals: *could, would, must, should,* etc.
C. Conjunction and intonation pattern with *or* and *but*
D. Words for degree and for generalizing
E. Articulation of *to* and *too*

Reading and Writing

Beginning Level

In beginning English, writing is quite limited. It should be directly related to the student's understanding and use of vocabulary and structures in the class. At this level, the comma, period, question mark, and apostrophe should be taught in order to develop proper intonation. The use of capital letters at the beginning of sentences should be introduced.

The following is a suggested guide for allotting time for the teaching of language skills at this level: listening—40%; speaking—40%; reading—15%; and writing—5%.

Intermediate Level

As in the beginning, writing should be a direct outgrowth of the student's mastery of the spoken word in class. Simple dictation and writing answers to questions generated by reading and conversation materials can be used as effective exercises.

Reading activities should include silent reading, group oral reading, and individual oral reading, with emphasis on the intonation patterns of language, such as rhythm and stress.

Proportions of time that might be spent in developing skills: listening and speaking—45%; reading—35%; writing—20%.

Intermediate–Advanced Level

At this stage, more time should be devoted to reading and writing. Advanced reading comprehension should be evaluated both orally and in written form and should include knowledge of literal, interpretive, and critical levels of cognition.

Writing skills should be directly related to the needs of daily living as well as the more formal requirements of education. Reference and study skills should also be emphasized.

Suggested proportions of time: listening and speaking—40%; reading—40%; writing—20%.

Advanced Level

At this stage, emphasis should be on the expansion of the material introduced at previous levels. The student should be encouraged to use his reading and writing skills to enable him to gain insight into all realms of our society.

It must be one of our goals as teachers of all grade levels to be cognizant of the origins of the language of our students if we are to engage in language expansion.

Who Are Your Gifted Students?

Before you can provide special instruction to gifted children, they must be identified. Since the term *gifted* is defined very broadly to refer to people who have intellectual gifts, many such students are never identified. Such intellectual gifts may be obscured because the students have, through boredom, become discipline problems or dropouts. Other gifted children may not score high on verbal identification measures because they are members of subcultures or economic classes that place little value on verbal ability. Unfortunately many gifted children are never identified; in fact, it is believed by many that from 10 to 50 percent are not.

During the last twenty years much attention has been directed toward clarifying the concept of giftedness. Marland (1972) offers a definition that, although often modified, still describes the stratification of this population.

> Gifted and talented children are those identified by professionally qualified persons who, by virtue of outstanding abilities, are capable of high performance. These are children who require differentiated educational programs and services beyond those normally provided by the regular program in order to realize their contribution to self and society. Children capable of high performance include those with demonstrated achievement and/or potential ability in any of the following areas:
>
> *1.* General intellectual ability
> *2.* Specific academic aptitude
> *3.* Creative or productive thinking
> *4.* Leadership ability
> *5.* Visual and performing arts

Although this definition encourages that special attention be directed toward children who excel in one of many areas, it is quite difficult to provide adequate identification because of limited assessment practices.

How Can You Identify Your Gifted Students?

Clarify Your Purpose for Identification. A process of identification must begin with clarification of purpose since by specification appropriate measurement becomes a reality. For example, you will need to ask, "Are we attempting to identify students with special talent in writing, mathematics, visual or performing arts, language, etc?" As language arts teachers you may be most interested in identifying those students who exhibit talent in any or all of the language areas (e.g., speaking, writing (essays, poems, stories)).

Once this question has been answered, you will need to determine why these children are being identified. And, once identified, is it possible to adjust programs and requirements to complement their needs? These are important issues that must receive careful attention since most existing school curricula have not been designed to meet the individual needs of all of these children.

Identification Measures. An effective process of identification should include both formal and informal measures. Formal measurements may be made through standardized tests; informal measures will include teacher and parent judgments. Many aspects of creativity and accelerated fluency in the language arts can best be identified in a classroom or informal setting. Unfortunately, some children who are not being challenged by the existing curriculum may go unnoticed.

Table 1–1 is an informal rating scale that can be used by teachers to help in the identification process.

If you believe you have gifted students in your classroom, scores from group intelligence and achievement tests can provide further information. It is important to be cautious about using such scores because group tests are often less reliable than individual tests and often do not adequately differentiate abilities in

Table 1–1
Sample Scale Items: Teacher Ratings for Behavioral Characteristics of Superior Students

Learning characteristics	1. Has unusually advanced vocabulary for age or grade level; uses terms in a meaningful way; has verbal behavior, characterized by "richness" of expression, elaboration, and fluency.
	2. Is a keen and alert observer; usually "sees more" or "gets more out of" a story, film, poem, etc., than others.
Motivational characteristics	1. Strives toward perfection; is self-critical; is not easily satisfied with own speed or products.
	2. Is quite concerned with right and wrong, good and bad; often evaluates and passes judgment on events, people, and things.
Creativity characteristics	1. Displays a great deal of curiosity about many things; is constantly asking questions about anything and everything.
	2. Displays a keen sense of humor and sees humor in situations that may not appear to be humorous to others.
Leadership characteristics	1. Is self-confident with children his own age as well as adults; seems comfortable when asked to show work to the class.
	2. Tends to dominate others when they are around; generally directs the activity in which he is involved.
Visual and performing arts characteristics	1. Incorporates a large number of elements into art work; varies the subject and content of art work. (Art)
	2. Is adept at role playing, improvising acting out situations, "on the spot." (Dramatics)
	3. Perceives fine differences in musical tone (pitch, loudness, timbre, duration)

Source: From Renzulli, J., Smith, L., White, A., Callahan, C., and Hartman, R. (1976). *Scales for Rating Behavioral Characteristics of Superior Students.* Mansfield Center, Conn.: Creative Learning Press, Inc. Used with permission.

the upper range. Also many children do not test well in timed situations.

Are you beginning to believe that the identification of gifted students is an involved process? If so, you are correct. Although you may believe that identification is not the most important step in working with gifted students, test scores may be the means of determining eligibility for state or federal funding. We must be careful to expend equal time and resources in program planning once we have satisfied existing local identification guidelines.

What Should Be the Characteristics of a Program for the Gifted?

Although you may attempt to meet the needs of students who have been identified as gifted within the regular classroom, special programs for these children should also be provided. Program modification should be made in *content* to be learned, *processes* for learning, and *environment* for learning.

CONTENT. The content of the curriculum for the gifted student should be *accelerated* so that more complex sets of information may be explored. It should be *enriched* to provide students with in-depth study of curriculum topics. It is possible to add *acceleration* and *enrichment* to regular classroom assignments. For example, if all students are required to study the history and culture of past generations, the gifted students in the class can be asked to select one invention (the chimney) and discuss the way it influenced cultural changes. Burke (1978) provides an example of the work of one gifted student who was given this topic.

1. The chimney produced structural changes in houses. With a flue to conduct sparks, a fire no longer had to be in the center of a room and the chimney could be used as a spine against which to support more than one room, allowing the structure to be divided into a number of rooms, upstairs and downstairs.
2. The new house structure led to a separation

of social classes: the privileged took the better, warmer rooms upstairs, leaving the workers downstairs. This may have been the beginning of the upstairs-downstairs separation of social classes in England.

3. The development of the chimney also had an effect on business. By providing enough warmth for paperwork to be continued in cold weather, it improved the commercial status of farms.
4. The chimney and fireplace improved personal hygiene by making bathing more comfortable.
5. Finally, romantic love was stimulated and encouraged by the fireplace. It introduced the concept of privacy, by dividing the hall into separate rooms. Lovemaking became a private, romantic activity.

The work of this student illustrated the far-reaching societal influence of an invention. Certainly this assignment encouraged the gifted student to investigate the topic creatively.

Content for the gifted should also be *sophisticated* in order to encourage students to explore abstraction in topics such as scientific laws, values, and ethics. Novelty of content is also a characteristic of the gifted curriculum. Students are encouraged to identify relationships across content and language arts areas.

PROCESSES. One common objective held by those who work with gifted students is that their learning experiences should enhance their capability to become productive thinkers. Treffinger (1980) has proposed a set of tasks that teachers of the gifted can apply to any content area.

1. "Just suppose that . . . (any unreal or 'contrary to fact' situation)." What would be the results? What if it were against the law to smile? What if the Loyalists had won the Revolutionary War? What if a child from Mars enrolled in our class?
2. "Product improvement." There are plenty of things it might be fun to make better. Our desks at school. The classroom. Our yard at home or the playground at school. Toys. Books. Tests. Chalkboards. Overhead projectors.
3. "Incomplete beginnings." Create pictures, designs, or stories from incomplete beginnings. Here are some interesting shapes. What can you make from them? Here are some polygons. What can you do with them?
4. "New uses for common objects." Usually, we use the ruler to measure things. What else might it be used for? How else might we use desks? Chairs? Calendars? Pencils? Books? Window shades? Bulletin boards?
5. "Alternate titles or endings." For a story, a picture, or any situation, can you think of many possible titles? From a picture or the beginning of a story, think of (write down, act out, tell to others, etc.) many different endings. Can we all begin to make up a story, each person adding a line, or a character, or an event? (Each might finish it in his or her own way.)

In addition to these activities, another process that is often encouraged when working with the gifted is guiding problem-solving activities. Parnes, Noller, and Biondi (1977) have suggested that the following five steps be used by gifted students when engaging in creative problem solving.

1. Fact finding: collecting data about the problem.
2. Problem finding: restating the problem in solvable form.
3. Idea finding: generating many possible solutions.
4. Solution finding: developing criteria for the evaluation of alternatives.
5. Acceptance finding: convincing the audience who must accept the plan that it can work.

As teachers we can easily apply these steps to language arts activities in any of the content areas. You might pose the following problem to your students. Problem: "Let's explore what might happen if we expended all of our now renewable natural resources."

Their responses could be presented in written or oral text.

As in any classroom, housing any children, gifted students have successful learning experiences in environments that encourage exploration. Callahan (1978) offers us a few suggestions for creating such an environment.

1. "Provide a nonthreatening atmosphere." The classroom environment should be structured in such a way that students' ideas and opinions are respected and questions are encouraged.
2. "Don't be the judge of the worth of all products in the classroom." An open, nonjudgmental attitude in the teacher allows more freedom for divergent thinking as well as for the evaluative skills necessary to complete the creative process. Encourage students to develop criteria to judge their own work and that of their peers.
3. "Model creative thinking, or introduce others who can illustrate the creative-thinking process for the students." It's important for the teacher to model creative problem-solving procedures as much as possible, not just during "creativity time."
4. "Provide stimuli for as many of the senses as possible." A variety of stimuli encourages students to view a problem from different perspectives. It also seems to enhance the sense of openness and psychological freedom.

Who Are Your Special Needs Students?

With the implementation of P.L. 94–142, the Education for All Handicapped Children Act, all classroom teachers must have some understanding of special education, the teaching of special students. In addition to the ever-present disparity of reading levels within one classroom, you now must also integrate or mainstream into your instructional framework mildly retarded students, learning-disabled students, and those with speech disorders. The task certainly appears awesome, but with the proper use of personnel, facilities, and funds, plus an understanding of the handicaps afflicting these special students, teaching strategies can be devised to meet this challenge. This section provides a brief overview of information about the students with handicapping conditions who are most likely to be mainstreamed into the regular classroom, as well as techniques and educational considerations that apply to each group of special needs children.

The Hearing Impaired

DEFINITION. Individuals with a hearing impairment are generally classified as either deaf or hard-of-hearing. A *deaf* person is one whose hearing disability precludes successful processing of linguistic information through auding, with or without a hearing aid.

A *hard-of-hearing* person is one who, generally with the use of a hearing aid, has residual hearing sufficient to enable successful processing of linguistic information through auding (Report of the Ad Hoc Committee to Define Deaf and Hard of Hearing, 1975, p. 509). This is the type of hearing impaired student who may be mainstreamed into the regular classroom.

CLASSROOM CONSIDERATIONS. Perhaps the most devastating aspect of a hearing impairment is its effect on communication abilities, including language acquisition, speech production, and reading skills. The lack of adequate auditory feedback both from oneself and from others, coupled with the inability to hear an adult model speak the language, contributes greatly to a difficulty with language acquisition. Since the language arts are essentially the same translation of a printed code into the sounds that make up language, a hearing impairment that has resulted in reduced language skills usually interferes with learning to read. Perhaps the most important consideration for hearing impaired students is that they are all individuals and cannot be expected to perform in the same way just because they share a common difficulty. With this in mind, there are some general suggestions for making mainstreaming easier for the hearing impaired.

1. *Seating arrangement:* Allow the student to experiment with his or her seating arrangement, within reason, always providing the seat near the front if necessary.
2. *Talking to the student or addressing the class:* Try to refrain from moving about; keep your hands, pencil, paper, and so on, away from your mouth to provide as clear a sound and image as possible. Write on the board first and then talk about it, rather than speaking with your back to the class. Enunciate clearly and speak at a moderate pace, but do not exaggerate speech.
3. *Attending and comprehending skills:* Be sure that the hearing impaired student is not just looking attentive, but is actually understanding what is going on in class. Verify that he understands instructions and assignments and is following class discussion as much as possible. Do not, however, expect him to attend all of the time, as it is extremely hard work and very tiring.
4. *Integration into the classroom:* Natural classroom opportunities (for example, a unit of the senses, science lesson, discussion pertaining to broadcasting or sound waves) can foster an understanding of the nature of a hearing impairment so that other students will be more at ease with a handicapped classmate's disability. An understanding of why a deaf or hard-of-hearing student may sound unusual or hard to comprehend when he or she speaks may help the other students try harder to listen and be friendly. Above all, set reasonable goals for the hearing impaired; it is better to err on the side of high expectations.

INSTRUCTIONAL METHODS. It is highly unlikely that any classroom teacher would be faced with the very specialized task of teaching reading to a hearing impaired student who has no communication skills at all. Here are some suggestions for teaching the low incidence of hearing impaired students in the regular classroom.

1. Present new vocabulary words by writing them, pronouncing them, and using them in sentences. New words may also be written for the student to take home to study with outside help.
2. Provide "previews" of the topics to come by listing the main points and new words so that the student may prepare in advance and be more familiar with the material when the class discusses it.
3. Create a "buddy" or "notetaker" system to aid the handicapped student with details missed during class. Notetakers are especially useful because it is very difficult to watch the speaker intently and write at the same time. Notetakers themselves benefit by taking more complete notes.
4. Photographs and illustrations from magazines provide excellent stimuli for vocabulary development. Scrapbooks and photograph albums compiled by the student (using pictures he or she has taken) with written captions are an excellent way to improve language skills. Make this an ongoing journal of day-to-day experiences. Some journal entries could be expanded into essays in which the students practice more refined writing skills by making rough, intermediate, and final drafts.

The Speech Impaired

DEFINITION. As Lapp and Flood (1986) suggest, speech is the action of vocally reproducing the sounds, in proper sequence, of a language; a speech impairment, then, is a condition that interferes with this sound-producing process.

A speech impairment can have many causes (for example, a cleft palate, cleft lip, or cerebral palsy), but it generally falls into (or overlaps) three categories: articulation disorders, voice disorders, and fluency disorders.

Articulation Disorders. These generally consist of errors of sound production involving *omissions* (for example, *ru* for *run; ift* for *lift*), *substitutions* (*bery* for *very*), *additions* (*puraple* for *purple*), and *distortions* (consistently mispronouncing /r/) (Perkins, 1971). Misarticulation is common in young children, but by the age of seven or eight these mistakes should disappear naturally unless a speech problem exists.

Voice Disorders. Although it is very difficult to quantify voice qualities, problems generally fall into these areas:

Pitch: High or low, depending on age and sex of the individual

Intensity: Loudness or volume

Quality: The way the voice "sounds": sweet, rough, mellow, and so on. Problem qualities are hoarseness, breathiness, and nasality. These may indicate the need for medical treatment.

Flexibility: The ability to modulate pitch and intensity to put expression in the voice. Monotone and singsong voices indicate a problem with flexibility.

Fluency Disorders. When the flow of speech is interrupted to such a degree that it becomes unintelligible or unpleasant to hear, the speaker is suffering from a fluency disorder, commonly known as *stuttering*. The interruptions consist of repetitions and prolongations of sounds, hesitations, and interjections ("uh, uh . . .").

There is no conclusive evidence as to what causes stuttering, although many theories have been advanced, ranging from underlying emotional conflicts to organic dysfunctions (for discussion of these theories, see Van Riper, 1972; Bloodstein, 1969; Ainsworth, 1970). Although the problem of stuttering is a familiar disorder, the actual number of stutterers constitutes only 1 percent of the population (Hull, Miekle, Timmons, and Willeford, 1969), and it seems to disappear as mysteriously as it comes on (Van Riper, 1972).

Classroom Considerations. As suggested by Lapp and Flood (1986) speech impairments can cause social and emotional trauma if afflicted persons are not made to feel accepted. Academic problems may result if the student does not participate in class discussions or ask questions about concepts that are not understood or becomes so uncommunicative that language ability itself begins to degenerate. The primary role of the classroom teacher is to put the student at ease in the group and make speaking experiences pleasant and nonthreatening.

Instructional Methods. Speech pathologists generally believe that disorders of voice and misarticulation are learned behaviors, not inherent qualities (Schiefelbusch and Lloyd, 1974; Sloane and MacAulay, 1968). Consequently, it becomes the clinician's job to use learning techniques to teach the appropriate new speech skills. Many of these teaching strategies are highly structured, programmed learning systems that incorporate behavior modification techniques as well as generally relying on modeling (that is, imitation) and positive reinforcement.

As Lapp and Flood (1986) suggest, making speech and language occasions pleasant may be the most important part of your job when working with mainstreamed speech impaired students. Fortunately, that objective is equally important for all students in the class, so most of these activities can be readily used for everyone.

1. Stimulate discussion by having students create and present a reader's theater production. Rehearsals should stress good articulation and expressive use of voice.
2. Allow students to use a camera for taking slides on a subject of their choice, then have them arrange and present a slide show with either live narration or tape-recorded narrative.
3. Make a game out of using descriptive language by blindfolding a student, handing him an object, and asking him to describe its qualities.

Individual or team points could be scored on the basis of the number of adjectives used or qualities mentioned, as well as whether the student guesses what the item is. As an individual venture, a "touch" box into which various items are placed can be constructed; the student is asked to describe into the tape recorder the way each item feels.

4. A file of pictures and photographs that serves as a stimulus to creating stories about events or emotions can be useful not only for written assignments (that could be read orally), but for spontaneous or prepared oral stories that can be taped or read to the class.
5. A group story can be formulated from one of the pictures by asking one student to begin a story with a statement and then asking each student to contribute to the story another statement based on the preceding one. Stories become quite outrageous, and language experience can be enhanced further by doing this in small groups so students can have more than one chance to participate in a given story.

The Visually Impaired

DEFINITION. As suggested by Lapp and Flood (1986), the category of the visually impaired includes individuals who are referred to as *partially sighted,* which indicates a visual acuity of 20/70 after correction, and *blind,* indicating a visual acuity of 20/200 after correction. As with most definitions regarding individuals, these terms are almost useless as educational criteria for assessing student abilities and needs. The scores that form the basis for this definition are from the Snellen Chart, which measures only distance reading ability. Since reading instruction is given at a close range and since individuals use their residual vision with differing degrees of competency, the numbers 20/70 and 20/200 indicate very little (Gearheart and Weishahn, 1976). Other classification and measurement scales of visual ability that have been proposed essentially stress that teachers should not base any instruction strictly on test scores but on observation of the student's functional abilities (Genensky, 1970; Barraga, 1970; Harley, Spollen, and Long, 1973).

CLASSROOM CONSIDERATIONS. Since reading is largely a visual process, it is obvious that visually impaired students may encounter many difficulties, including concept development, left-to-right orientation, and clarity of the word image itself (Degler and Risko, 1979). They may be behind their peers in reading level because of a slower reading rate or inappropriate instructional methods (Turnbull and Schulz, 1979), but visually handicapped students, whether partially sighted or blind, are easily accommodated into the regular classroom with minimal adaptations.

Putting a student at ease in the school environment is essential to successful instruction. Two key words when working with visually handicapped youngsters are *orientation,* which refers to a person's spatial placement in relation to objects in the environment, and *mobility,* which refers to the ability to move about in the environment. Mobility and orientation instruction are special skills, and most students will receive this training from a specialist before entering the regular classroom.

INSTRUCTIONAL METHODS. The classroom teacher must, however, assist in orienting the student to the classroom and school environment. Suggestions for accomplishing this follow.

1. Spend time with the student in the classroom before the school year begins, or, if this is not possible, make time available before or after school. Make sure he is comfortable with the surroundings and knows how to find the appropriate desk, books, and materials. Similarly, acquaint the student with the layout of the entire school, including the cafeteria, library, restrooms, and so on. When appropriate, ask other students to perform this orientation to help

the student become acquainted with some of his classmates.

2. Discuss and practice the fire drill procedure and route.
3. Arrange for extra traveling time for the visually impaired student either before or after the other students.
4. Encourage these students to ask for help when they need it, and instruct sighted students to assist when called upon. Special training provided by a mobility instructor in guiding a blind or partially sighted person might be both useful and interesting for the other students.
5. Provide ample work space for extra equipment, such as braille books, magnifying devices, typewriter, or tape recorder.
6. Be sure to call the student by name and encourage classmates to identify themselves until the student learns their voices.
7. Include the visually handicapped student in as many of the regular class activities as possible, as all the students will profit from this interaction.
8. Include prereading activities such as discussion of new vocabulary words and concepts, using the concrete multisensory approach outlined earlier in this section. For low vision students, large, clear pictures are useful for explaining ideas, as well as promoting creative language experience stories. To illustrate such concepts as "velvety" or "corrugated," cards can be covered with any number of substances to provide the desired tactile response. Sound effects and the objects themselves are also useful for presenting new ideas to visually impaired students.
9. To develop listening skills for the visually impaired, the teacher can use tape-recorded material, sighted readers, and everyday classroom activity. Tape recorders are essential and may be used in the following ways: Record sentences or passages from stories and ask the student to repeat them into the tape and play back for correction. On tape, record a series of sounds using bells, drums, and so on. This can be used as a game by several students, awarding points for the longest correct series recalled.
10. Reader's Theater is very beneficial to visually handicapped students because it gives them a chance to participate in oral, expressive reading with their classmates. Although their reading rate may be slower than that of other students, with practice an accomplished production can be performed.

The Orthopedically and Other Health-Impaired

DEFINITION. As emphasized by Lapp and Flood (1986), the category of orthopedically and other health impaired students covers a wide range of disabilities, from cerebral palsy to diabetes to missing limbs. The common link among these persons is that the primary difficulty is the result of a nonsensory physical handicap. There are few common learning problems associated with this group, as many physical impairments have no real effect on cognitive ability or learning potential, whereas others such as cerebral palsy and spina bifida may have significant neurological complications that contribute to severe communication problems. Perhaps the most common characteristic of this group is the psychological aspect of coping with a very obvious, disfiguring, or life-threatening disability. In this context, as with all handicapping conditions, the individual ability to adapt to a given condition or disease has a dramatic impact on the functional severity of the disability, regardless of the medical prognosis.

CLASSROOM CONSIDERATIONS. Federal law (P.L. 93–112, section 502) now provides architectural access and adequate toilet facilities for wheelchairs; therefore your major environmental concern should be for proper placement of the physically handicapped student in the classroom. Where the student sits should depend on any accompanying sensory handicaps and accessibility (for instance, maneuvering space) to various parts of the classroom (the student's desk, free reading center, individual study carrels, media center, games, and so on) so that the disabled student is as free to participate in all learning options as the other students with as little special help as possible.

After the student is physically at ease in the class environment, your main concern must be to help him attain a positive self-concept, this process for the physically impaired, involves, to a large extent, fostering independence and an acceptance of the handicapping condition (Bigge and O'Donnell, 1977).

Instructional Methods. The learning problems of the physically impaired may range from those of the mentally retarded to those of the gifted; therefore it is impossible to offer specific techniques unique to this class of handicap. Suggestions offered in the other sections of this chapter as well as in other chapters can help you to plan appropriate instruction. Emphasis should always be first on self-help, survival, and social skills, with more academic pursuits based on these initial skills. As with all special students, never underestimate them! A challenge should always be presented, keeping a close watch on frustration levels.

The Learning Disabled

Definition. In 1963, Samuel Kirk coined the term *learning disabilities,* which has since been used to describe a whole group of problems that affect an individual's ability to learn. The most important aspect of a definition of learning disabilities is that it is not one single condition and consequently cannot be treated in one single way. Any definition of learning disabilities provokes great controversy, but there is professional agreement about two of the most common components of these definitions.

1. A learning disabled student does not achieve at the level of his academic potential. This potential is usually measured by comparing scores on a standardized achievement test; however, other methods using formulas for ratio discrepancy (Mykelbust, 1968) may provide a more accurate picture of expected achievement versus actual achievement.
2. A learning disabled student has a wide range of achievement, which spreads across the academic spectrum. He may be strong in reading but weak in spelling or math, or have excellent oral communication skills but be unable to write a coherent sentence.

Although there is no universally acceptable definition of learning disabilities, we believe that "a learning disabled child is simply not achieving up to his potential" (Hallahan and Kauffman, 1975) and that it is your job as a teacher to teach that student.

Classroom Considerations. Since learning disabilities are very complex, a wide variety of teaching strategies must be employed to meet the needs of affected students in the regular classroom. Ranging from the hyperactive child who creates general chaos to the quiet student who cannot seem to follow directions, learning disabled students ideally should have individualized programs to meet their specific educational requirements; at the same time allow them to participate with the rest of the class whenever possible to encourage correct socialization. The approaches and suggestions described in the following sections may be adapted for use either in an individual or in a class situation.

1. Never *assume* that they have understood directions even if the instructions are perfectly clear to everyone else.
2. Try to make class exercises short and success-oriented. Team games are especially useful when there is no direct individual pressure on the members (for example, Blackboard Scrabble) and if the student can cope with the excitement.
3. Alternative teaching and response methods (for example, a typewriter, computer, or tape re-

corder) may be useful with some learning disabled students for completing assignments.

4. Structure the time into small segments with varying activities—quiet independent work, work with a tutor or aide, classroom work, physical work (filing, board games, and so on).

Remember that you are a crucial person in the life of a learning disabled student and that your relationship with the student must be as close and understanding as possible.

Instructional Methods. Since learning disabilities are a composite of many difficulties that are unique to each individual, no one method of teaching will satisfactorily meet the needs of all students. Many theories or methods for teaching learning disabled students exist, and it is necessary to compose a *comprehensive instructional framework* (CIF) for each student. This consists of selecting those methods (or aspects of them) that will best remediate the deficiencies exhibited by a particular individual. Once the theoretical methods of instruction are chosen, an *individualized educational program* (IEP), pinpointing specific goals, techniques, and exercises, can be developed. After an educational outline based on the major instructional approaches to learning disabilities is established, the actual teaching techniques and the rest of the classroom program will easily and naturally build up around this theoretical framework.

Any method of language arts with which the teacher and student are comfortable can be used to teach learning disabled students. Certain modifications of the material are necessary for certain types of problems. Suggested techniques for adapting existing academic material are presented here.

1. Exaggerate the item being taught, causing the student to focus all of his or her attention on the task. For example:
   - When teaching new vocabulary words in context, highlight the new word with larger print or color.
   - When teaching minimal pairs, highlight the distinguishing letter as above.
2. Break up stories, lessons, worksheets, and other assignments into small parts that culminate in success-oriented tasks. For example:
   - Determine how much the student can read before frustration sets in, and divide the stories into sections that can be handled successfully. Ask questions after each section to reinforce the skill being taught, aid in recall, and spark interest in continuing.
   - The use of a typewriter, tape recorder, computer, or other audio-visual tool provides useful diversions between reading tasks; assignments can be related to what was just done or can preview what is coming up.
3. If a restricted environment is indicated for certain activities, create an "office" from carrels, partitions, or appliance crates that are free from distracting stimuli. Students may be assigned "office hours" when the space is for their own private use. Behavior modification principles can be applied to "buy" more or less office time (depending on which is considered more desirable by student and teacher).

How Can You Meet All Your Students' Needs?

Adaptive Education

Instruction designed for individuals who often function as members of larger groups has always consisted of *adapting* existing curriculum to meet the specific needs of specific students. Thus adaptive education has been a major focus of productive teaching techniques for the last twenty years. Various researchers (Rothrock, 1982; Fenstermacher and Goodlad, 1983; Wang and Walberg, 1985) have found that although interest in adaptive instruction has lost some of its momentum in recent years, it continues to be one of the most effective means to educate students.

A wide variety of curriculum, materials, and strategies have been used successfully with students who have diverse socioeconomic and educational backgrounds. Included in this array are mastery learning, cooperative team learning, individual tutoring, and large- and small-sized group instruction. If all of these approaches are effective, how can the teacher decide what to do in his or her classroom?

Flexibility may be the key ingredient for successfully matching individuals and instruction. As we will emphasize throughout all of the chapters of this book, effective instruction that is designed for the individual needs of students who may work independently or in group situations has the following characteristics:

1. The *strengths* and *needs* of *all* learners have been assessed.
2. Instruction is based on these assessed *strengths* and *needs* of learners.
3. The materials and procedures for learning permit each student to master the curricular goals at a pace related to his or her assessed strengths, needs, and interests.
4. All students are considered equal members of the team environment and are actively involved in individual and group decision making.
5. Evaluation is a continuous process that results in program planning.
6. *Testing* and *teaching* are not confused.

When students live in a school environment that adheres to the principles of this philosophy, they cooperate in the learning experience. They view themselves as team members who are supported in their learning efforts. When you provide cooperative, adaptive conditions for learning, the potential of each of your students will be met.

Summary

Teachers are always concerned with meeting the needs of *all* of their students. Throughout this chapter, instructional strategies were presented for use with

regular students in the primary and middle school years.
bilingual and limited-English-speaking students.
gifted students.
special-needs students.

The characteristics of each population and techniques for assessing specific needs were also presented.

Suggested Classroom Projects and Questions for Discussion

Projects

1. Select from the library three articles that deal with the concept of cooperative learning (refer to Slavin, 1980, in the Bibliography). After reading these articles, prepare a lesson for any content area and grade level of your choice that illustrates this philosophy of learning.
2. Plan several classroom projects (trips, panel discussions, community volunteers) that encourage interaction of regular students, bilingual students, and students with special needs.
3. Read five articles concerning strategies for teaching bilingual students. Plan a lesson that shares the language of the ESL student with the English-speaking students.
4. Plan a classroom festival that encourages students to show customs, beliefs, rituals, and so on, from their ancestral heritage.
5. Design a classroom map that displays the ancestral heritage of your students. Discuss the languages that were spoken by their ancestors.
6. Read several articles that discuss the emotional needs of mainstreamed children. Plan strategies to encourage emotional security for all of your students.
7. Visit the library and select several readings on the topics of the gifted. While reading, try to determine (a) Who are the gifted? (b) How you will be able to identify them? (c) How you can facilitate their learning?
8. Select several of the teaching suggestions discussed throughout this chapter. Use these ideas to plan a common lesson for the gifted, "regular," and special students who may be in your classrooms.
9. Prepare a list of *Classroom Rules for Courtesy* that will encourage mutual student respect for all.

10. After reading and thinking about a classroom composed of bilingual, regular, gifted, and special students, prepare a list of your concerns about your ability to meet all of their needs. Attempt to answer your concerns by selected readings from the Bibliography.

Questions

1. If you peeked into classrooms around the United States, what types of students might you find? Discuss your comfort in teaching these various groups.
2. Why are students with special needs being mainstreamed into regular classrooms?
3. Why do many educators and legislators believe that the composition of a classroom should be similar to that of "the regular world"?
4. How, as a teacher, can you find time to plan instruction for students with diverse backgrounds, experiences, and needs?
5. What types of experiences can you plan to encourage classroom cooperation and respect among and for all students?
6. What can the regular classroom teacher do to ensure second-language learning?
7. How can you prepare yourself to work with children who are unlike the way you were as a child?
8. What are your beliefs regarding an environment that integrates *all* children?
9. What do you believe elementary teachers can do to combat the high dropout rate?
10. How will you keep a check on yourself to see that your instructional practices do not favor some of your students at the expense of others?

PART II

FOUNDATION OF ALL LEARNING: THE LANGUAGE ARTS

Chapter 2

The Wonderful World of Communication

(Photo by Linda Lungren)

OBJECTIVES

At the end of this chapter students should be able to:

1. describe the complexity of the communication process.
2. discuss the role of language arts in the curriculum.
3. explain the principles of effective language arts instruction.

We'll begin with a box, and the plural is boxes.
But the plural of ox should be oxen, not oxes.

The one fowl is a goose, but two are geese,
Yet the plural of mouse should never be meese.

You may find a lone mouse or a whole set of mice,
Yet the plural of house is houses, not hice.

If the plural of man is always called men,
Why shouldn't the plural of pan be called pen?

If I speak of a foot and you show me your feet,
And I give you a boot, would a pair be called beet?

If one is a tooth and the whole set are teeth,
Why should not the plural of booth be called beeth?

Then one may be that and three would be those,
Yet hat in the plural wouldn't be hose.
And the plural of cat is cats and not cose.

We speak of brother and also of brethren,
But though we say mother, we never say methren.

Then the masculine pronouns are he, his, and him,
But imagine the feminine she, shis, and shim.

So English, I fancy, you all will agree,
Is the funniest language you ever did see.

Author Unknown

Language—The Art of Communication

Language is something more than a system of communicating; it is also a social convention which one must observe under penalty of being misjudged. Ignorance or improper use of language can easily interfere with your success or advancement.

Mario Pei, *Language for Everybody*. (1965, pp. 4–5.)

The world of communication is a truly dynamic one. Language as communication is the one attribute that sets humans apart from all other creatures and binds humans together across all geographic barriers. A word can cause us to sink into the deepest despair or lift us to inspired action. Language can be the tool for great achievement in art, engineering, and social progress or for confusion, war, and destruction. The choice is ours, and the tool is powerful.

As Emily Dickinson so adequately told us in 1872

A Word is dead
When It is said,
Some say.

I say it just
Begins to live
That day.

The mere sound of poetry gives intense pleasure, to which form and the various levels of meaning can only add. The story of the tower of Babel tells symbolically how a civilization without communication must fall. Without language there is no way to accumulate or pass on cultural knowledge.

Whose life may not be changed by the utterance of either a single sentence of promise or perjury? How many civilizations are now only memories because they failed to understand the importance of signing or failing to sign a treaty or because they could not express their intentions clearly to an opponent? After the atomic explosion at Hiroshima, the Japanese were warned to surrender. It is said that their carefully worded response asked for a delay but was mistakenly interpreted by the Allies as a refusal. So the city of Nagasaki paid dearly for a misunderstood phrase.

Yet whole civilizations, their palaces and city walls long since crumbled, are still alive through songs, poems, and histories. Through the poetry of Homer, we can today feel the crushing despair of the people of Troy when their hero Hector died.

When he discovered a way to write words, man was no longer dependent on the memory of listening. Meanings became clearer and understanding more certain. Written words are a link with all generations to come and with all past generations. If there are no written clues, relics and ruins can only hint at lost civilizations. Other cultures, although buried under desert sands, seem almost contemporary because of written records that tell us about their religion, education, businesses, and even the intimate gossip of their times.

The Content of Communication

If we separate the ideas communicated from the means of communication (the reading, speaking, writing, or listening), we have the content of communication. It is sometimes claimed that language arts instruction must use social studies, science, or other information in order to assemble ideas to share. This notion has at times resulted in the tendency of some teachers to teach facts and neglect instruction in language skills. Their logic seems to be that skills will develop without planned instruction if the student has enough to talk and write and think about.

Another belief is that students need skill mastery in order to deal competently with the world's ever-increasing body of knowledge. An individual who reads with ease and expresses himself clearly and comfortably will continue to learn and share throughout life. But if the goal is to master many volumes of facts during the elementary school years, the pressure on teachers and students may result in inadequate competence in language skills.

One guiding principle of a language arts curriculum is that language skills, like motor skills, are best developed in an integrated fashion. Learning experiences should involve several or all language skills instead of one at a time. Plays, games, and class presentations are multidimensional activities that can involve the whole language system.

"Our talk show idea isn't panning out. Hardly anybody knows how to talk yet."

Figure 2–1. © 1986; Reprinted courtesy of Bill Hoest and *Parade* Magazine.

The Symbolic Nature of Language

Sounds and symbols *mean* nothing unless we agree to use them as representations of objects and concepts. Lip movements and handspelling meant nothing to Helen Keller until she could conceive of them as naming something specific. Language requires agreement about the specific connections between the symbols and the things or ideas to which they refer.

The use of language as a symbolic system is more than the manipulation of abstractions. A language can be seen as behavior, a set of activities with a much broader nature than that of other systems. Language is an habitual, even unconscious, response instead of something new and unfamiliar in each situation. To a greater degree than the visual or the performing arts, language arts are anchored in a set of shared conventions. Unlike mathematical expression, language carries emotional connotations and expresses subjective feelings. Mastery of language requires complex and sophisticated effects. Just as a parent is proud of the first words a child speaks, so is the teacher justly proud of the child's first written vocabulary, first written story, and comprehension of written discourse. Teachers must realize that the child who does not develop the language skills demanded by the modern world is at a disadvantage, because this weakness will limit his options for work and narrow his horizons for learning.

Communication is an interesting word. When two or more individuals have a successful communication, they share an understanding or feeling; normally, this communion is an exchange of ideas grounded on a common basis of understanding.

Language is the foremost means of communicating most ideas and feelings. It can speak to us from the far distant past, but it can also travel around the planet and into space. Communication today can be almost instantaneously transmitted everywhere on earth electronically. Through television, telephone, and radio, as well as the printed and spoken word, language is humanity's common bond.

The capacity for language is a specific human trait; any language may theoretically be learned by any child or adult. Communication is therefore always a possibility, if not a reality. A child's earliest babbling is nonnationalistic; there is no initial predisposition to one language or another. Instead, exposure, practice, and maturity seem to be the determinants of speech. Increased language arts skills increase the individual's power to learn and to share, whichever language is employed.

Language Learning in the Curriculum

> "Well then," the Cat went on, "you see a dog growls when it's angry and wags when it's pleased. Now I growl when I'm pleased and wag my tail when I'm angry. Therefore I'm mad."
>
> "I call it purring, not growling," said Alice.
>
> "Call it what you like," said the Cat.
>
> Lewis Carroll, *Through the Looking Glass*

In view of the state of the world, communication is vital but not easy to achieve. As a thinking individual, one is always concerned with communication. For you, as a teacher, the concern is paramount. Just as you may remember a college teacher who seemed at times incomprehensible, students can find you hard to follow if you take too much for granted. (Do you say "certainly" when something is not at all certain for a first grader?) Sometimes we compromise meaning and communication by using words in ways others do not. Past a certain degree of imaginative novelty this creates trouble instead of interest. However, two individuals would have to have exactly the same experiences, moods, and memories of words between them to have the same response to a situation, and in that case, why would they need communication? Because we are not mechanical in the way we think and speak, our words are not limited to rigid, universal meanings that never change. Without the great connotative richness of language, we would lose metaphor, allegory, and the other "figures" of speech. Fortunately, language has the flexibility to operate at almost any level of meaning.

Defining "Language Arts"

> It took me a long time to learn where he came from. The little prince, who asked so many questions, never seemed to hear the ones I asked him. It was from words dropped by chance that, little by little, everything was revealed to me.
>
> Antoine de Saint-Exupéry, *The Little Prince*

Art is something expressive, creative, original, and usually personal. The term *skill* is reserved for an acquired ability that is mechanical, exact, and impersonal. Learning the proper spelling of a word is certainly learning a skill, whereas writing a poem or personal letter is considered the expression of a language art. Since both are part of language instruction, any modern language curriculum must show concern for both skills and arts. In reality and in practice, they are not as separate as they might seem.

The word *teach* is derived from the Anglo-Saxon *taecean* and from the German *zeigen,* meaning "to show." The teacher's role is to show, to make available, to open, and to point the way. This introduces a second important principle of the language arts curriculum, which is the necessity for active involvement of the learner in the process of education. Gone, we hope, is the image of the stern pedagogue enumerating facts that the students must commit to memory or fail. George Orwell says he was taught in school that "Disraeli brought peace with honor," but was never allowed to wonder to whom or how this was done. Memories and instances of this kind of teaching remain, although research in educational psychology since the time of John Dewey has stressed the need for the learner to participate actively in the learning process. A language arts curriculum should compel the teacher to match the level of the child's learning to the task, instead of insisting that the child get in stride with the teacher's teaching. In this way the student must be active and responsive, and so must the teacher.

Language arts describes a major portion of the elementary curriculum, which includes the communication processes of listening, speaking, reading, and writing. The development of these interrelated communication processes serves the learner when *gaining* (intake) information as well as when *giving* (output) information.

Integrating the Language Arts

We must view the art of communication as an interrelated process, for more often than not we utilize more than one of the processes (listening, speaking, reading, writing) at a time. Loban (1976) found that students evidencing low abilities in oral language also evidenced difficulty in reading and writing, and further that students with adequate language abilities evidenced little if any difficulty in acquiring other communication skills.

As a classroom teacher, you have the task not only of integrating the language arts among themselves, but also of integrating them throughout the entire curriculum. When a student engages in a science, math, or social studies activity, is he not required to employ all the language arts processes? Doesn't he often *listen* to instructions of shared ideas? Isn't he often required to *speak* about his ideas? He may be involved in the *reading* of these content materials as well as the *writing* of detailed reports to express his ideas. Throughout the curriculum, students are employing the language arts. Therefore, it seems quite unrealistic to believe that for forty minutes each day we can have one separate period devoted to teaching the communication processes.

Teaching the Language Arts

The teacher asked of the child,
"What would you have of me?"
And the child replied,
"Because you are you, only you know some of the
  things
I would have of you.
But because I am I,
I do know some of what I would have of you."

The teacher asked again,
"What would you have of me?"
And the child replied,
"I would have of you what
You are and what you know.
I would have you speaking and silent,
Sure and unsure, seeking for surety,
Vibrant and pensive.
I would have you talking and letting me tell,
Going my way with my wonderings and enthusiasms,
And going your way that I may know new curiosities,
I would have you leading step by step.
You letting me step things off in my own fashion."

"Teach me," said the child,
"With simplicity and imagination—
Simply that the paraphernalia and the gadgets
Do not get between us;
Imaginatively that I may sense and catch your
  enthusiasm,
And the quickening thrill of never having been
  this way before.
Too, I would have you watching over me,
  yet not too watchful,
Caring for me, yet not too carefully,
Holding me to you, yet not with bindings,
So when the day comes, as it must,
  that we, each, go our separate ways,

I can go free.
Let me take you with me not because
  I must, but because I would have it so.
Let me take you with me because you have become,
  in me,
Not just today—
Tomorrow!"

Leland B. Jacobs

Your desire to teach can open the doors to an exciting adventure, the adventure of learning. Each day offers many new dimensions for you and for those you teach. You and your students can be stimulated by each other's ideas and experiences, feelings of success and satisfaction, and constant desire to grow in many cognitive and affective areas. The rewards of teaching, and of learning, are many.

Teaching is an art. Techniques and materials can be shared, but the human relationships of the teaching-learning process cannot be assimilated through words alone. In recent years paint-by-number kits have been designed for do-it-yourself painters, using key numbering to indicate which areas are to be painted a certain color. If one follows the directions, one can produce something that resembles the original painting, but at best it is only a copy of another's creative expression and planning. One's first efforts at original painting will perhaps betray uncertainties of line and form. However labored, it is a creation rather than an imitation. With talent, training, and determination, the amateur painter may in time produce a genuine work of art. In teaching, some start with great talent and seem to know not only how to work with children but also how to use suggestions for the best results. Others start with nothing more than interest and must master the skills by hard work. The rewards are worth the effort since few professionals are ever offered the satisfactions that a teacher knows as students develop the communication processes that will help them face with confidence their responsibilities as adults. Well-defined principles of teaching will aid you in helping your students develop such processes.

Teacher-Student Interaction

The first principle is that teaching effort is most effective when the learner has a basic understanding of established goals and sees the relationship between what is taught and those goals. A visit to an elementary classroom will reveal that the teacher knows a great deal about each child. One of her concerns is interest. As she plans she asks, "What will interest Eric?" Or she will remember, "Lynne is very interested in insects." She knows that students follow patterns of interests as they develop. Home, parents, babies, and fun are universal interests of the beginners. As their environment expands, interests will include neighbors, children far away, and foods of different countries. Schools often plan their curriculum units around these common interests. Such interests establish purposes for reading, writing, and research; they therefore provide goals for the child in undertaking certain tasks.

When children have rather limited interests, the effective elementary teacher plans situations that will arouse curiosity and generate questions. Sometimes a film will awaken interest in volcanoes or animals. An exhibit of pioneer objects that can be handled may lead to further study of history. When this is accomplished, the teacher has instilled an interest. Sometimes a teacher is criticized for forcing interests on students rather than developing those that already exist. The problem faced by most teachers is one of working with a large group of students rather than with just one or two. With a few a teacher could well teach language in association with the emerging interests of each student. With a total class, a teacher faces such practical problems as meeting certain expected achievement standards and having enough material on hand to achieve certain objectives, as well as the social responsibility of controlling youthful energy so that learning can receive some direction. Motivation that results only in acceptance by students of teacher-determined goals will never be as effective as goals mutually desired by teacher and pupil. At times during the day motivation can come from each individual student; at other times it must be group-determined.

The word *attainable* is significant with respect to goals. The student who is constantly asked to do more than he can accomplish is in a difficult position. An adult can simply walk away from such a situation by resigning from a job, changing courses, or moving to another town. The student cannot meet frustrating conditions in the same way. Children may misbehave or move into a dream world and ignore what is happening around them. Some will put forth extra effort to master a task for a time if they feel the pressure from home or the teacher. Eventually, for the sake of relieving tension, these students create for themselves an acceptable self-image that does not value the specific skill. It is safe to say that few children are motivated for any length of time by continuous failure. Of equal importance in considering the word *attainable* is the student who achieves without effort. For some students, the tasks of education present little challenge. In almost any classroom there is one child who is completely bored by the situation. Frequently we exploit these children by making "little teachers" out of them. This action at least recognizes their superior knowledge, although it seldom helps them toward their own greater educational growth. The most effective effort is expended by students when they attempt tasks that fall into the "range of challenge"—not too easy and not too hard—where success, given good instruction, seems quite possible.

Personalized Learning

A second basic understanding about directing the learning of students is that you as a teacher must consider individual differences. A college classroom of future teachers studying the language arts is a fairly homogeneous group. Not only have the students passed through a number of education filters so that they all must be good learners, but also they have made a common vocational choice. No elementary classroom can be made this homogeneous. Yet there are still differences within the college classroom: some students are married and have children; others have traveled widely; others belong to campus organizations. Although they may have a common interest in teaching, their other interests may vary widely.

A classroom of students will reveal differences in rate of learning, interests, social and economic backgrounds, and dozens of other factors that must be recognized. The teacher knows that the *whole* child comes to school, not just a mind to be taught. Some of the differences that the teacher considers are the student without a breakfast, the student who is worried because he heard his parents quarreling the night before, the student who speaks English as a second language, and the student who had a nightmare after seeing a TV movie. These differences have a direct influence on the goals established for each student.

It should not be assumed that all instruction must be individualized because of these differences. There are common needs that might be considered with respect to the group. Many similar interests based on ages and years in school form the basis for group instruction. The important thing to remember is that a competitive rating is not appropriate in many elementary classrooms. To let a student who reads very well set the expected standard for the class would be as foolish as to let the one who sings best establish the only acceptable vocal standard for all. Yet we sometimes act as if we were saying that unless you read as well as Daryl, you cannot get an *A* in reading.

It is especially important that as a teacher you accept individual differences as well as recognize them. Some teachers spend a career trying to make people alike in the area of reading and writing. One hears them say, "If Harold would only try as hard as Shannon!" the inference being that with more effort Harold could be like Shannon. As students advance through the school years, the differences in the skills taught at school will become greater. For a teacher it is important to be careful in making predictions about students based on present performance or potential level of achievement. Some "late bloomers" may eventually surpass pupils who seem far ahead of them in grade school. It is well to remember that it is only in school that success is limited to success in reading.

Simulated Learning Situations

A third basic principle of teaching students is to present the learning processes or information in situations similar to those in which they will be used. Language is functional when it is used in conversation, reports, letter writing, listening to the radio, viewing television, telling a story, or any other of the communicative acts of daily life. Effective expression, legibility in writing, correctness in usage, or thoughtfulness in listening and reading will develop only to the extent that children discover these skills to be of value in their daily, functional use of language. To stress instruction of any aspect of language without this understanding on the part of the learner produces very limited results.

This does not mean that drill is entirely out of place in a language arts program. But to be effective, the drill of a particular process must be presented in context. Drill on a specific word in spelling may involve writing the word many times, just as drill in basketball may involve shooting toward the basket over and over again.

The same is true of worksheets, which are true learning devices only when the student who does them understands why he has made an error and desires to correct it. Some students, filling in blanks on worksheets, make the same errors year after year, and the teachers carefully record scores made on these assignments. Some teachers have the students correct their errors and think that they are doing a good job of teaching. Teachers may defend this procedure by saying that all judgments concerning the language arts are based on standardized test results. These teachers feel that they are preparing the children for this measurement by such drills, and in that respect they are correct. But it should also be recognized that they are teaching for testing rather than for any functional use of the language.

An example of an effective application of this learning principle can be found in association with letter writing. During the school year the need to write a business letter will arise in connection with the curriculum of the students. At that time, instruction should be given concerning the form of such letters, and careful attention directed to their content. If the letter is actually mailed, children will welcome the experience and remember the information that was taught.

Related to this is the care that must be taken to insure that something once taught will be used when needed. After a new language skill is taught, it becomes a standard to be used by the students in all their work. Throughout the year, students will add to the list of standards that they are expected to maintain as they write and speak; as their new knowledge is employed, habits become established.

Developing Concepts

A fourth basic principle of teaching is that concepts are best established by using many firsthand perceptual experiences. How easy our task would be if it were only a matter of "telling" things to the student. If concepts were built by lectures, an oral reading of the law would make good citizens of all of us. However, a concept is merely a *word* or *phrase* that identifies or classifies a group of objects, events, or ideas. Given any group of objects, we are concerned with finding distinguishing features that can be classified or given a concept label. A concept may be concrete—*cat* or *truck*—or it may be abstract—*friendship* or *maturity*. The concept may be more or less inclusive as well. *Animal* is more inclusive than *dog,* and *dog* is more inclusive than *German shepherd*.

CONCEPT FORMATION. *Concept formation* is the process of building an understanding of objects and experiences, particularly in relation to others. The product of concept formation, or conception, is a *concept*. We often refer to a concept as a *term*.

Concept formation, in its simplest form, consists of three basic steps:

1. Delineating global wholes into specific elements.
2. Grouping these elements on the basis of common characteristics.
3. Naming, labeling, or categorizing the elements.

Because young children are growing both mentally and physically, they need many opportunities to examine and reorganize the concepts they have developed. They need many experiences that will expose them to new objects, events, and ideas. The child's ability to comprehend what he reads and his ability to think evaluatively will be facilitated by his having carefully defined concepts.

Concept Attainment. Concept attainment is affected by several factors, including the nature of the concept (whether it is abstract or concrete), the child's developmental stage, and the kinds of experiences he has had in his lifetime.

Much of Piaget's work deals with how the individual attains concepts. He discusses *accommodation* and *assimilation* in the developing child. *Accommodation* refers to the individual's modification or reorganization of his existing mental structure. When he encounters something new that is not part of his existing mental structure, he must accommodate the new information to the old. *Assimilation* refers to the individual's internalization of the change. Once he can handle the new experience with ease, he has assimilated the new information.

The accommodation-assimilation process is a form of *adaptation*. The individual is learning to deal with new experiences and information and is therefore adapting to new elements in the environment.

Developmental Stages. In dealing with children, one must allow time for the accommodation process Piaget has discussed among the stages of thought development in the growing child. He suggests that the evolution of thought coincides *roughly* with age-developmental stages:

1. *Sensorimotor* stage or preverbal intelligence, roughly from birth to eighteen months or two years.
2. *Preoperational,* roughly from two to seven years. This is the stage in which children group and categorize according to function. For example, a child might group pencil with paper, or hat with coat. Another child might group a knife with a carrot and potato because "you can peel them with it."
3. *Concrete operations,* roughly from seven to eleven years. This is the stage of thinking while mentally or physically manipulating specific objects or concrete events.
4. *Formal operations,* from about eleven years on. This is the stage of conceptual or formal thought, during which the child likes to think in abstract terms and enjoys hypothesizing.

As a true developmental stage theorist, Piaget suggested that cognitive growth stages stem from the preceding stages and emerge in a logical pattern. The stages are irreversible and unavoidable. Therefore, a child cannot go through the concrete operations stage and then the preoperational stage, nor can he go directly from the sensorimotor stage to the concrete operations stage. The child must accomplish certain learning tasks before going on to more complex tasks. Thus, a child cannot skip or reverse stages.

Although the developmental stages are identified with certain age ranges, these ranges are only approximations. The rate at which children pass through the developmental processes is not fixed, but is an approximation that may be affected by intelligence, physical and mental health, social conditions, experience, and other variables. Throughout life, regardless of age, when little conceptual knowledge of a topic is held by the learner it may be necessary to begin learning through a concrete example.

Students can learn only what they have experienced. All meanings are limited by the experiences of the learner. The understanding of democracy may start from such basic behaviors as taking turns, participating in a group decision, acting as chairman of a group, or being on the school safety patrol. Eventually we hope that these experiences will aid the child in developing an understanding of our way of life.

Fortunately, the imagination of a child is so vivid that some concepts will develop as he identifies himself with characters in a story or with great persons in history. Some children can do this as they read, others as they participate in role-playing dramatizations, and still others through discussion of problems and situations.

It is important to remember that when a learner is presented with information that is not familiar, it will often be necessary to begin instruction at a very concrete level, regardless of age.

Retaining What Has Been Learned

A fifth basic principle has been implied in the other four, but for the purpose of emphasis it should be noted separately. Simply stated, learning must be used to be retained. Learning for a specific situation, such as memorizing a part in a play or studying Japanese while visiting Japan, disappears in a very short time if not reused. Nearly every college student reading this page once knew how to solve a problem involving square roots. Now, if you tried to obtain the square root of any four-digit number without referring to the tables, you would probably find you have completely forgotten how to do it, simply because the knowledge has not been used recently. Usually we plan instruction with respect to specific learning in what might be called a spiral organization. We start with the known, go to the new, and then return to the known. We call this process teaching, reinforcing knowledge, integration of knowledge, and rehearsal. Much rehearsal is necessary if information is to be retained in long-term memory.

This principle places a responsibility on the teacher. The teacher, as the mature individual in the teaching-learning situation, is expected to plan and select experiences that are useful to the child at his present stage of development. Application of this principle means that teachers must first find a way in which the language skills we teach children can be of immediate service to them, and then see that they are used with frequency to prevent forgetting.

External Learning Stimulants

A sixth basic principle that greatly influences learning involves external learning stimulants such as the family, home environment, and parental involvement.

The student's oral language experiences are a vital factor in his reading success. Oral language provides a foundation on which the child is able to build many other language skills. To encourage optimal language development, parents need to talk a great deal even to their youngest child. This will provide the child with the language model needed for learning. The family, therefore, begins influencing the child's attitude toward the language arts as early as the child is able to hear and respond to language.

One of the most valuable experiences that the parent can provide is reading stories aloud to the maturing child. The parent can hold the book so the child can see both the illustrations and the printed page; this establishes and reinforces an understanding of the relationship between the spoken word and the printed page. This also serves to promote discussions of the story and pictures by the parent and child and may introduce new words into the child's vocabulary. Enjoyment of good literature also offers the child new language models and may initiate a growing interest in becoming an independent reader.

Family influences and verbal interaction have been discussed as factors related to the student's reading success. Children also need books and materials (toys, chalkboards) in order to prepare for reading (Bernstein, 1967; Beck, 1973; Durkin, 1974). The availability and use of reading materials and organizational opportunities by the child in the home environment are important to the development of reading skills.

Television viewing may very well be the single greatest home environmental influence on the child's later cognitive abilities, including reading ability. Today's

One of the most valuable experiences that the parent can provide is reading stories aloud to the maturing child. (Photo by Linda Lungren)

question is not whether educational television *is* effective, but rather to what degree it affects the growing child. In response to the need for updated norms to account for the influence of television, there has been a great deal of research on the social and cognitive effects of television on children (Raffa, 1985; Pezdek and Stevens, 1984; Fakouri, 1984). Television can be a vehicle of tremendous potential in children's learning. Our concern should not be only with reading via the printed page, for it can also be facilitated by television. The world of television is here to stay, and we should explore the many possibilities it offers for the development of language skills. We attempt to offer specific suggestions regarding the role of television in the classroom in Chapter 14.

As teachers we must have as one of our primary objectives to expose children to the excitement of language so that "once they glimpse the excitement of words they will never again say that English is a dull subject" (Boiko, 1967, p. 37). This text is designed to help you accomplish this objective.

Summary

The view of language arts as the base and means of integrating all facets of curriculum was the primary theme of this chapter. Language as a process of communication that can be personalized and expanded through such an integrated curriculum was also thoroughly discussed. Six basic principles of good teaching and role of the teacher as the catalyst for the success of such a program were also explored in this chapter.

Suggested Classroom Projects and Questions for Discussion

Projects

1. Find examples that show how history has been altered because of a lack of communication.
2. Prepare a collection of poems, quotes and essays that illustrate the wonderful world of communication.
3. Select two minority cultures and study the sociological differences exhibited through their languages.
4. Select two educational psychology textbooks from the library and read the sections on memory. Discuss the role of rehearsal in long-term memory.
5. Prepare a sequence of lessons that move the student from the concrete to the formal operations stage of development.
6. Prepare a list of ways by which you can involve parents in home extension learning activities that will benefit their children.
7. Plan a series of activities that demonstrate the effective use of television viewing.
8. Collect headlines which have more than one meaning (Example: REAGAN BEATS MONDALE).

9. Read several of the word books in Appendix A and prepare a list of the ways you could use them in your classroom.
10. Plan a series of lessons that involve the middle-school-aged learner in language, listening, reading, and writing activities.

Questions

1. Why can the language arts be viewed as the foundation of the curriculum?
2. How are cultural differences exhibited through the sociology of language?
3. Why is it important to attempt to personalize your classroom curriculum?
4. What should be the student's role in curriculum planning?
5. How does the prior learning of a student affect your curriculum?
6. Why do all learners need to return to the *concrete operations* stage of learning when they encounter unfamiliar material?
7. What should be the parent-school relationship?
8. How do parents and the home affect student learning?
9. Why is it impossible to foster a language arts curriculum in a silent classroom?
10. How can television be an aid to your classroom curriculum?

Chapter 3

The Heritage of Language

(Photo by Linda Lungren)

OBJECTIVES

After reading this chapter the student should be able to:

1. understand the relationship between culture and language.
2. understand the components of a language system.
3. understand the origins of the English language.
4. understand the role of the teacher in extending the language of every student.

Cultural Influences on Language

> Linguistically speaking, man is not born free. He inherits a language full of quaint sayings, archaisms, and a ponderous grammar; even more important, he inherits certain fixed ways of expression that may shackle his thoughts. Language becomes man's shaper of ideas rather than simply his tool for reporting ideas.
>
> Peter Farb, "Man at the Mercy of His Language"

Do you realize that the simplest words in our language are items in a vast chronicle that tell the story of a dynamic people and their language? Have you ever wondered why surnames seem to fall into groups, some ending in *-ton* and others in *-son?* Why there are Latin words where English ones might do as well, such as *post meridian* and *ante meridian?* Why we don't have the profusion of verb and noun endings that French, German, Italian, and other languages have?

"No, No! How many times do I have to tell you? It's before except after !"

Figure 3–1. © 1986; Reprinted courtesy of Bill Hoest and *Parade* Magazine.

Why we hear the Greek *hoi polloi* and the French *savoir faire?* Why there are so many "little" words in English? How "good" a language English is, and what it means for a language to be "good"?

The purpose of this chapter is to illustrate the historical development and cultural significance of the English language. It is important for you as a language arts teacher to have a broad understanding of the forces that have shaped our language in order to share with your students a sense of its dynamic qualities.

Language abilities in speaking, listening, thinking, reading, and writing are not developed independently of each other; neither is any individual's language ability developed independently of a group life in which he can find his securities, his values, and his language patterns. This group life is what we call a culture: the sum total of all the material achievements, customs, beliefs, and values of any group of people. Culture includes the people themselves and their ways of communicating and interacting with each other within their institutions. A culture cannot be viewed merely as an aggregate of parts, but must be seen as a functionally integrated whole. Art, literature, and philosophy emerge from the group's social experiences and provide more experience and a cultural heritage. Thus a culture is a dynamic and changing pattern, always being created by its members and in turn influencing the behavior of its creators and participants.

The American culture furnishes the context in which all American schools function. Together with democratic values and methods, a common basic language makes it possible for the United States to be a national, cultural unit.

Culturally determined goals in language teaching make language a social tool for such purposes as understanding oneself and other people, relating oneself to the world through literature, finding personal satisfaction through expressive and creative use of language to solve personal and group problems, developing discriminative power to detect the purposes behind the written or spoken symbols, and evaluating the reliability of the spoken and printed messages. These goals have grown out of the modern setting of cultural activities. The conditions of living in today's world make it important to listen to and evaluate a radio or TV broadcast, to read and interpret a newspaper intelligently, and to speak, write, read, and listen with concern for integrity, logic, and honesty of expression.

It is the culture which forms the values that determine the opportunities for learning in the schools. Such questions as who will go to school, for how long, in what kind of building, and with which teacher are answered in different ways by different cultures. Laura Ingalls Wilder in *These Happy Golden Years* describes a culture that felt that a few weeks of school in midwinter were adequate.

The culture determines what the interests and experiences of schoolchildren will be. What a child reads, speaks, and writes about is influenced by the family and community in which he lives. Children are most interested in the learning activities they can experience in their learning environments.

The culture determines the meanings that children attach to words and statements. A child raised on the prairies of eastern Colorado has limited, if any, experience to relate to the word *woods*. Eventually, through pictures and descriptions he finds a meaning, but it will never be as complete as that of a child who has watched a forest change through the seasons, known the fun of seeking wild fruit and nuts, or participated in the gathering of maple sap. The Navajo child whose dwelling has always been a hogan does not use, hear, or read the word *house* with the same meaning as the child who has lived in a brick bungalow.

The culture also determines when learning experiences shall be introduced and the sequence in which skills shall be developed. As knowledge from the fields of child development and social anthropology has accumulated, leaders in education are finding that the cultural patterns of age and grade expectations in a middle-class society do not always agree with what is known about children's initimate growth patterns; the culture often expects learning to occur before the child is ready for it. However, cultural expectations provide a strong stimulus for learning, and when the timing of the expectation is synchronized with the individual's growth pattern, this cultural influence may enhance educational achievement.

It is unfortunate that our culture has defined types of speech that are expected of boys and of girls. The little boy has often been respected for speaking like a "male" but scolded, teased, or otherwise punished for speaking like a "female." The father serves as a sex model of the culture that the boy is encouraged to learn. The works of Key (1975), Lakoff (1975), and Kelly (1986) provide us with many insights regarding sex stereotyping in our language.

Children speak the way their family and members of their neighborhood speak because this is the group with which they have made first identifications. To *identify* with a person or group means to form a strong emotional attachment. Children's first identifications are the result of their human need for love and membership in the group. When children identify with someone, they unconsciously imitates that person's speech patterns. Children are prone to retain these early speech habits, for they give them identification badges; they are the symbols by which children prove that they belong to a group. The extent to which children speak correctly or according to the school standards indicates the patterns that are in the security-giving group life surrounding them.

It is significant to note that the social group, even more than the family, provides the pattern for speech imitations after early childhood—more specifically, the peer group to which an individual belongs during later childhood and adolescence. The school must then *accept* as well as *extend* the language of the child.

When teachers begin to understand the middle-class expectations for rapid training, they will more clearly see why early reading and writing have become symbols of status. Children who learn to read early prove their and their parents' worthiness by this important cultural achievement. Teachers, too, are sometimes sensitive to their status position and exert similar pressures on children for early reading performance.

The cultural expectation for learning to read during the first year of school experience was established at a time when children were beginning the first reader at the age of seven, eight, or even nine years. It has persisted in the cultural pattern, although the age for beginning first grade has been lowered. It also was once culturally acceptable to leave school without having mastered reading.

Language instruction is dependent not only on children's inner maturational pattern but also on their experience background and opportunities for learning. A teacher must respect every child's commonplace experiences. The teacher should dignify some of the everyday incidents of life and thereby help children feel comfortable about their own home life and group experiences. An example of how this may happen is related by a teacher at a small school. Ten-year-old Denny, who seemed active and interested outside the schoolroom but who had never volunteered to share any of his interests in writing, said that he "didn't want to write anything." Denny had never been to a circus. His only experience with airplanes had consisted of watching them fly overhead. He did not have a horse or a pet. The teacher's concern for Denny's lack of interest in sharing experiences led her to the discovery that she had asked children to write about the unusual, or the exciting, or the very, very new experiences that only certain children had had. She now changed her approach and encouraged them to write about such everyday occurrences as skinning a knee, getting wet in the rain, or running a race; Denny then made some attempts to write about these "commonplace" experiences. Later, he wrote rather well about "Hurting My Thumb."

Language instruction is dependent not only on students inner maturational pattern but also on their experiential background and opportunities for learning. The skills of oral reading are most naturally developed in the reading of plays. (Photo by Linda Lungren)

Similarly, a child who comes from a home where a foreign language is spoken may not be ready to read English. The school program must both supplement and complement the cultural nurturing of language growth.

We must understand language and language history to foster language growth. Human language is certainly unique among communicative systems. Aside from the sound in a handful of onomatopoetic words such as *buzz* and *clang,* there is little within the sounds or shapes of words and phrases to indicate the idea being communicated; yet through language we can examine cultures thousands of years old or thousands of miles away, we can send astronauts into space, and we can provide education and legal protection for billions of individuals. What makes language so flexible for different needs, so precise in a specific case, and so common that we take such a sophisticated system for granted?

The Language System

What Is a Word?

Can you answer this question? A word is simply a sound or a group of sounds that make sense to speakers of a particular language. People can make sounds that have no meaning. If people want to communicate, they make sounds that have meaning to other members of their language community. People spoke words long before they wrote them and a very long time before they developed machines to print them.

Linguists make the distinction between a sign system and a symbol system of communication. An arm raised with the palm outward is a passable symbol for "STOP!" and the sounds combined in /stop/ constitute a sign for the same notion. The language community of which you are a part has agreed to let both sign and symbol convey the meaning of *stop,* although this may not have been true a thousand years ago, nor may it continue to be the case for hundreds of years to come.

What Are the Characteristics of a Language?

A language is conventional, arbitrary, changeable and adaptable. If we see that language is *conventional,* we must also note that it is *arbitrary.* A four-wheeled freight-carrying vehicle is known as a truck in the United States and a lorry in much of Great Britain. This example of different naming conventions illustrates their arbitrary nature, yet people have chosen for any of a large number of reasons to use either *truck* or *lorry* or both if they travel. As we noted before, there is nothing inherent in the orthography or spelling of words to convey meaning. Symbol and sign systems are *conventional* and *arbitrary.*

Both of these aspects point to other features of language: it is *changeable* and *adaptable* over time. If convention and habit determine vocabulary, inflections and spelling, new conventions and new habits can determine new forms of language. This is, in fact, the process that has made our English language into the system we now use.

What Is the Difference Between Language Structure and Function?

It is helpful to distinguish between the *structure* and the *function* of language. This book is written in a language structure that all readers of English will be able to understand. It would succeed just as well in its function as a text about language arts instruction if it were translated to the structure of another language. Any language user may request, congratulate, daydream, hypothesize, describe, or interrogate. Linguists agree that all human languages perform much the same *functions* and are equally "good" at them. The *structure* is what varies from one language to another and within one language over time.

No one language or dialect is "best" either structurally or functionally, in the way German was once judged "best" for scientific communications, because language is dynamic and can change as its users and their world change. Classical Latin is one of the few examples to the contrary. It is called "dead" because it is not used in conversation and therefore is not susceptible to influences outside its written form. The language of Latin literature has a consistency that anyone who has studied the classical form can understand.

Because convention determines change, a language can develop irregularities and lapses in logic while it fulfills the needs of a speaking community. Irregular forms and the fact that some nouns can be verbs, whereas others cannot, illustrate that language and logic are not always partners in the English language. This does not mean that the language is not efficient, for it has changed to serve our purposes admirably.

What Cultural Influences Are Reflected in the History of the English Language?

Language is of major importance in our culture. Familiarity with the great literature of our language can help us with philosophical issues, but we must also concern ourselves with the historical development of language in order to comprehend orthography, sentence structure, and the changes in vocabulary and usage.

Similarities in vocabulary and structure among many languages of Europe and the Middle East were of great interest to linguists during the nineteenth century. It became apparent that these languages formed a group or family of languages, and it was hypothesized that there must have been a common parent language. Some characteristics of this prehistoric parent language, called Indo-European (Figure 3–2), can be reconstructed from the common characteristics of its offspring. Eleven major subgroups to the base language, believed to have originated in East Central Europe, have been postulated. Three language subgroups have particular relevance to English: Hellenic, Italic, and Teutonic or *Germanic.*

The Hellenic and Italic groups gave rise to Greek and Latin, respectively, from which many English words were borrowed directly, whereas others came indirectly via French. It is the Teutonic group, though, from which English has largely developed, as we shall soon see.

The original speakers of the tongue from which English arose were Germanic dwellers on the eastern

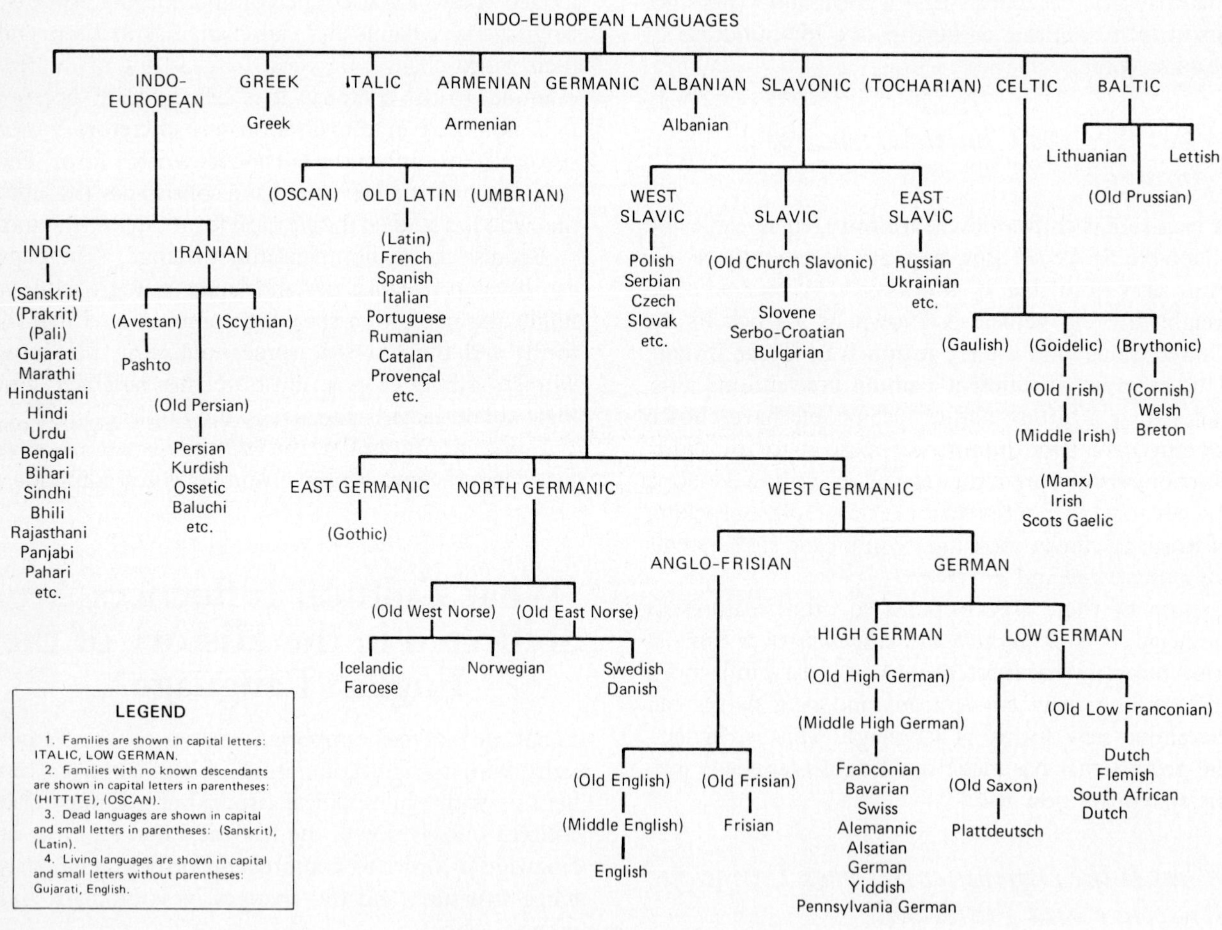

Figure 3–2. Indo-European languages.

or European coast of the North Sea from Denmark to Holland. These Anglo-Saxons and Jutes had undoubtedly raided the British shores even before the Roman departure in A.D. 410.

When the last legions were summoned back to defend their Italian homeland, the Britons started fighting among themselves. The Jutes were called in by the British King Vostigen to assist him, after which they settled in Kent. The Saxons did not arrive until 477 or the Angles until 547. Many of these came as mercenaries lured by the promise of land, which was divided as war booty.

A number of the early outside influences on the language of Britain came from Rome. As early as 54 B.C., Julius Caesar reconnoitered on British soil and established friendly contacts with various chieftains. The Roman conquest was not completed until a century later and was marked by periods of savage resistance. The completeness of the cultural impact on the Britons is not known; the many Roman ruins throughout Britain would indicate a thoroughgoing Romanization of the country. For a period of almost four hundred years the Romans were in complete control of Britain.

Later, the influence of Latin was extended by the activities of the Church. By the sixth century Christianity had spread throughout all of England. Christian converts were among the Anglo-Saxons, who conquered England after the Romans left; before this time, the majority of the Welsh and British inhabitants were Christians.

There are over 450 words of Latin origin found in Old English; these include *cheese* (caseus), *mint* (moneta), *seal* (sigillum), *street* (strata), *kitchen* (coquina), *cup, plum, inch, wine, abbot, candle, chapter, minister, noon, nun, offer, priest, inscribe* (scribere), *cap, silk* (sericus), *sack, pear, cook, box, school, master, circle, spend, paper, term,* and *title.*

The influence of Latin has continued through the years. Sometimes the borrowed words have come through French, Spanish, or Italian, but many retain their original form or drop an ending. One recognizes the Latin derivation of words like *censor, census, genius, inferior, quiet, reject, legal, history, individual, necessary, picture, nervous, lunatic,* and *interrupt.* The Latin prefixes *pre-, pro-, sub-, super-* and endings *-al, -ty, -ble, -ate, -tion, -ize* are often used with words from other sources. Of the twenty thousand words in full use today about twelve thousand are of Latin, Greek, or French origin.

During the Roman Empire, the Teutonic or Germanic tribes inhabited the forested area of present-day Germany. Their language can be divided into three dialects: *Eastern,* or Gothic, for which there is no remaining language; *Northern,* which gave rise to Danish, Swedish, and Norwegian; and *Western,* which was spoken by coastal tribes including the Angles, Saxons, and Jutes.

Old English: A.D. 600–1100

By the beginning of the seventh century, the Germanic language that we call Anglo-Saxon emerged from the confusion and turmoil of the British conquest to take its place among the modern tongues of Europe. Among the factors thought to have influenced this development were the wide acceptance of a single religion and the unity of the seven kingdoms to resist the Danish invasions.

The sounds of the language resembled those of modern German rather than those of modern English. The lowercase *c* always had the hard *k* sound. The letters *j, g, v* were not used; *f* suggested our *v* sound; *h* was more like the *ach* of German. One additional letter, þ, called *thorn,* was used for one of the *th* sounds; we still use the *u* sound, and *i* has replaced *y* in many words. Nouns had four cases: nominative, genitive, dative, and accusative. Adjectives were designed to agree with the word modified. Our little word *the* could assume any one of twelve different forms to show gender, number, and case. There were only present and past tenses.

Only a small percentage of our vocabulary today is Anglo-Saxon. If one were to take two thousand Anglo-Saxon words at random, one would find only a little more than five hundred still in use; however, these would include many of our most common words, such as *man, wife, child, horn, harp, coat, hat, glove, hall, yard, room, bread, fish, milk, house, home, hand, thumb, head, nose, ear, eye, arm, leg, eat, work,* and *play*.

The Anglo-Saxon ability to form compounds led to expressions in which the original elements are almost lost. For example, *good-by* or *good-bye* is a corruption of "God be with you."

Some words from the Anglo-Saxon have picturesque word origins. *Spider* means "spinner" and *beetle,* "biter." The "poll" in *poll tax* is the old word for *head. Strawberries* once were strung on a straw.

In spite of the Latin influence in the Church, such Anglo-Saxon words as *god, gospel, lord, Holy Ghost, sin,* and *doomsday* survived. In isolated dialects some Anglo-Saxon forms have resisted change; *larned* is used for *taught, hundreder* for *centurion, foresayer* for *prophet,* and *gainraising* for *resurrection.*

In the year 787, piratical rovers from Scandinavia first visited England, and for more than a hundred years they continued to make landings primarily for the sake of pillage. In 840, 35 shiploads of Danes landed in Dorset; in 851, 350 ships came up the Thames and apparently for the first time wintered in England. Eventually they became so numerous that, for the sake of order, Alfred the Great made a settlement in 986 whereby half of England had its own Danish king; at one time all of England was ruled by these Danish kings. (When you say "They are ill," you are speaking Old Norse, from which has descended modern Danish.) At least fourteen hundred localities in England have Scandinavian names.

Such words as *steak, knife, dirt, birth, fellow, guess, loan, sister, slaughter, trust, wart, window, odd, tight, skin, happy, ugly, wrong, scare,* and *though* are among our language heritage from the Danes. The *-son* of our family names replaced the *-ing* of the Saxon. *Washington* actually means "Wasa's children's farm."

Such doublets as *no—nay, rear—raise, fro—from, shatter—scatter, shirt—skirt, ditch—dike,* and *whole—hole* are a part of the divided language loyalties of the islanders. The first is Saxon, the second Norse. Because of language mixing and the Teutonic or Germanic stress on the first syllable or root word, English moved away from inflections to its largely noninflected present state. There has since been a steady decline in the number of English inflections.

The future tense that had hitherto been expressed by the present, "I go tomorrow"; the pronouns *they, their, them;* and the omission of the relative pronoun *that* in such expressions as "the house I saw" were Scandinavian introductions into our language.

The Scandinavian invasion was not limited to the British Isles. Just as the Danes were settling in England, other Norsemen were invading the coast of France. As the British secured peace by granting an area to the invaders, so those in France were granted the reign centering about Rouen. These Normans accepted both the religion and the customs of the Franks. Indeed, this acceptance was so rapid that the grandson of their Viking leader Rolf (or Rollo) could not learn his ancestral language at home but was sent away to learn Norse. Thus it was that when these Normans invaded England they brought with them not only the French language but vestiges of Scandinavian as well; indeed, other languages than these were spoken by the forces under William, Duke of Normandy. There were mercenaries from Spain, Italy, and Germany.

Middle English: A.D. *1100–1500*

The struggle between the hardy race that had been developed in England under the wise policies of Alfred the Great and this Norman force was a long and bitter one. The Anglo-Saxon nobility finally was reduced to the level of its own peasantry. Their language was scorned as being fit only for inferiors. With their defeat, the land was divided among the conquerors. William of Normandy displaced the Anglo-Saxon ruling class in 1066 and replaced it with French-speaking Normans.

At the dawn of the thirteenth century there were three languages in England: French was the literary and courtly tongue, Latin the language of the Church and legal documents, and Anglo-Saxon that of the marketplace.

Conquerors clung to their own ways since they planned eventually to return to their homeland. While the Normans were occupying England, their forces were defeated in France, in 1204, and most of them gave up all thought of returning to that land. This changed their attitude toward the Anglo-Saxons and the language they spoke. At the same time, the French spoken in England became mocked as provincial by Parisians. In 1349 English was reinstated in the schools, and in 1362 Parliament was reopened in English. During this time, hundreds of words came into the language. Some were words that one class might acquire from another, such as *baron, noble, dame, servant, messenger, story, rime, lay*. French law terms remain in use: *fee, simple, attorney general, body politic, malice aforethought*. In our kitchens we use *sauce, boil, fry, roast, toast, pastry, soup, jelly, gravy, biscuit, venison, supper, salad, saucer, cream*. The French words *beef, veal*, and *pork* remain along with the Saxon *ox, calf*, and *swine*. Our present word *island* represents a blend of Saxon *iegland* and the French word *isle*. Among our synonyms, we have French and Saxon words in *acknowledge, confess; assemble, meet; pray, beseech; perceive, know;* and *power, might*. The words associated with the arts are French, or Late Latin through French: *amusement, dancing, leisure, painting, sculpture, beauty, color, poetry, prose, study, grammar, title, volume, paper, pen, copy, medicine, grief, joy, marriage*, and *flower*.

Many of the terms of the modern square dance are French. When one "sashays to the corner," the word is an adaptation of *chasser*, which means to *chase;* and *do si do* is *dos-à-dos*, or *back-to-back*. Many military terms are French: *army, navy, enemy, arms, battle, siege, sortie, soldier, guard, spy, lieutenant, rank, vanquished*, and *conquer*.

But the most important thing that happened during these years was a tremendous simplification of the language. No longer were nouns and adjectives delineated. One form of each word emerged as that most frequently used. One authority says with a note of regret that if the language had remained neglected by scholars for another hundred years, it might have emerged with a great purity of expression and meaning determined on basic usefulness to a people blessed with considerable common sense.

In review, then, the English language contains words, patterns of speech, and spellings that were influenced by historical developments. Starting with the ancient Celtic, we next found the Latin influence of the Roman invaders. The basic language structure is Germanic as introduced to the British Isles by the Angles, Saxons, and Jutes. This in time was influenced by the Danes. With the Norman invasion, we have noted both the French and continuing Scandinavian influences. Because of the Church, the Latin influence continued through the years. Although trade with other lands has also influenced our vocabulary, these are the major historical sources of the English language we use today.

Modern English: A.D. 1500 to Present

With the development of printing, a number of important changes came into the language. The English printer William Caxton (1422–91) made the works of Chaucer (1343–1400) available to the general public beginning in 1477; he is famous for printing the first book in English in 1475 (*The Reccuyell of the Historyes of Troye*).

Something happens when words are reproduced in print; they achieve an importance and dignity they do not possess in speech form. The very act of duplication or making copies seems to grant authority to the printed word. The spelling of a word or the sentence structure that appears in such an important literary effort places the stamp of social and cultural approval on the form; at any rate, we can trace many of our instructional problems in language to these first printed books.

One of the problems was that of spelling. The word *guest* appears as *gest, geste, ghest; peasant* as *pesant* or *pezant; publicly* as *publickly, publikely, publiquely; yield* as *yeild, yielde*, and *yilde*.

Often it was a printer's effort to make words seem

more consistent or even more scholarly that determined the form used. The silent *b* in *debt* and *doubt* originated from the premise that the original Latin forms had *b*. An early form was *det* or *dette*. The *gh* in *delight* and *tight* is a result of analogy with *light* and *night*. A number of words such as *won* in which the *o* represents the sound of *u* were an effort toward spelling reform. When such words are spelled with *u*, the handwriting tends to become a confusing series of upstrokes.

Geoffrey Chaucer helped to take English from its fourteenth-century position as a major London dialect to the beginning of modern Standard English. Writers during the next two hundred years made conscious efforts to invest English with the range and flexibility to compete with French as the language of culture and with Latin as the language of scholarly instruction. Chaucer wrote in a composite of dialects that is fairly easily read by a modern reader. Here is a selection from the General Prologue to the *Canterbury Tales* (c. A.D. 1390, lines 43–46):

> A knyght ther was, and that a worthy man
> That fro the tyme that he first bigan
> To riden out, he loved chivalrie,
> Trouthe and honour, fredom and curteisie.

Chaucer's English contains many French words and spellings, but it is recognizable English.

Shakespeare's English is even more familiar, and it is truly Modern English, although it differs from what we use today, almost four centuries later. The fact that literature four hundred years old does not seem foreign to us points out the decelerated pace of change. There are several reasons for the slower rate of language change and for a different style of change. Here is one example to keep in mind: in Old English a new term was frequently the result of joining two older ones, such as *woruld* + *had* for *worldhood*. Our modern term *secular life* shows the French and Latin influence of a word borrowed directly from other languages, part of the Renaissance spirit.

Along with increased availability of books, the prominence of London as a cultural city and the increase of the reading public due to the rise of the middle class placed conservative constraints on the language. Two other events gave English its present shape. One is the "great vowel shift" in the years 1500 to 1650, when the sounds of English vowels underwent an extensive sound change.

The sounds of Middle English vowels shifted in length, with those that were already long becoming a combination of two vowel sounds. This difference gives the same word quite a different sound in Modern English from the one it had in Middle English. The other major influence in Modern English was the English Renaissance, which followed the Italian Renaissance by roughly one century. The sixteenth and seventeenth centuries were the age of humanism, and literary figures were much enamored of the Greek and Latin languages. These structures, it was thought, were more suitable for abstract thought. Dryden later claimed that it was necessary to translate his more significant thoughts from Latin, in which he could think more deeply. One result of the revival of classicism was a massive borrowing of Latin words. Of the thousands brought by scholars into English, many took hold; others—like *canicular, ossoany, diuturnity,* and *clenches* —did not.

It was during this time that English spawned a peculiar but predictable observer—the *purist,* the one who wishes to see the language cleansed and preserved from the ruin of foreign frills and corruptions. A purist, of course, is faced with a conundrum—English incorporates many influences, and without them it might not have developed into a distinct language. The people with whom the purists were largely at odds were the *classicists,* grammarians trying to fit English grammar into a Latin mold and including the apparently unnecessary declensions of English verbs in the lessons of English schoolchildren. The purist tradition is alive today in those who decry the use of Latinate constructions or technical jargon where simple English might do. The classicist tradition, which helps us make sense of language, is alive and well in the dicta regarding *lie, lay,* and *irregardless.* We call the codifying of the way people "ought" to use language *prescriptive grammar* as opposed to *descriptive grammar,* or the way people *do* use language.

It has been estimated that ten thousand words were added to the language during the Renaissance, and they became widespread through the press. Shakespeare added such words or expressions as *accommodating, apostrophe, dislocate, frugal, heartsick, needle-like, long-haired, green-eyed,* and *hot-blooded.* Words such as *capacity, celebrate, fertile, native, confidence,* and *relinquish* were called barbarisms and were understood by few readers.

No description of this time would be complete without reference to the King James Bible of 1611. It is estimated that fewer than six thousand different words are used in this translation and that fully 94 percent of these were part of the common speech of the day. The translators were apparently concerned with reaching the masses in a language that would be understood by all. Hence it was up to them to use the best-known words.

Some words are repeated with great frequency (*and* is used 46,277 times). Although there is monotony in some parts, the text is usually very clear in spite of the profound ideas expressed. Shakespeare shows us the range of thought that can be expressed with many (15,000 to 17,000) words, and the Bible demonstrates almost the same range with only 6,000.

Today a highly literate adult is not likely to have a recognition vocabulary of many more than 150,000 words. Of this number a few will be used over and over again. One-fourth of all our spoken vocabulary consists of repetitions of the words *and, be, have, it, of, the, to, will, you, I, a, on, that,* and *is.*

Since the invention of printing, new words have been added to English in many ways. Some are borrowed from other languages; others have been created for new products; and still others seem to be accidents or the results of misunderstanding foreign speech. If a person who spoke Anglo-Saxon were to listen to us today, he would have a very difficult task understanding all that we say.

From the Italian we find these words: *design, piazza, portico, stanza, violin, volcano, alto, piano, torso, cello, vogue, serenade, trombone, broccoli, boloney, confetti* (hard candy), *cash, carnival, cartoon, studio, solo,* and *opera.*

Spanish words include *alligator, banana, canoe, cocoa, hammock, hurricane, mosquito, potato, tobacco, rodeo, cockroach, cork, tornado,* and *sombrero.* In the western United States many towns, hills, and rivers are Spanish-named as a result of the early exploration and settlement in those states during the seventeenth and eighteenth centuries. The terms of ranch life and of the cowboy and his equipment are usually Spanish in origin: *hacienda, mustang, corral, lasso,* and *lariat.*

The Dutch are responsible for such words as *chapter, yacht, schooner, boor, drawl, deck, boom, cruiser, furlough, landscape, tub, scum, freight, jeer, snap, cookie, toy, switch, cole slaw,* and *yankee.*

The Arabic language gave us *candy, lemon, orange, spinach, sugar, algebra, alkali, alcohol, assassin, syrup, sofa, divan, mattress, magazine,* and *safari.*

From Hebrew we have *camel, ebony, sapphire, seraph, cherub, cabal,* and *rabbi.*

From India came *loot, pundit, rajah, punch, coolie, bungalow, calico, cot, polo, thug,* and *khaki.*

Kimono, samurai, and *kamikaze* are Japanese.

Malay gave us *caddy.*

The people of Africa gave us words for *gorilla, voodoo, zebra,* and probably *jazz.*

Native Americans are the creators of many of our words; among these are *moccasin, raccoon, skunk, totem, woodchuck, hominy, caucus,* and *tomahawk.* Every state contains Indian place names: *Chicago* means "a place that smells like skunks," *Peoria* "a place of fat beasts," and *Manhattan* "the place where all got drunk."

You may be wondering what changes have occurred recently in the English language. New words come into our language almost daily. Some are changes in the word root: *edit* from *editor, peddle* from *peddler, jell* from *jelly.* Others are abbreviations, such as *pub* from *public house, cad* from *cadet, pup* from *puppy.* Some imitate other words: *motorcade* and *aquacade* from *cavalcade, litterbug* from *jitterbug, telethon* from *marathon.* We combine words to make new ones, with *smoke* and *fog* becoming *smog, motor* and *hotel* becoming *motel,* and *liquid oxygen* becoming *lox* (used for fuel in rockets).

Old words are used in new ways or as different parts of speech. A master of ceremonies is abbreviated *emcee;* this in turn becomes a verb in such usages as

"Allen may emcee the show." An example of one word used to serve different parts of a sentence is the newspaper headline that reads, "POLICE POLICE POLICE SHOW."

Words change in meaning. *Harlot* once meant "servant," while *wanton* and *lewd* meant "untaught" or "ignorant." *Notorious* was simply "well known." A *governor* was a "pilot," *rheumatism* meant a "head cold," and a *nice person* was a "foolish person."

In the years since World War II many words have been added to our language: *cinerama, countdown, zoorama, fallout, readout, sonic boom,* and *astronaut* are examples.

Do You Speak a Dialect?

The term *dialect* refers to the form of a spoken language that is peculiar to a particular group of people. *American Speaking,* a National Council of Teachers of English recording (1967), provides samples of dialect variations. Each speaker who participated in making the record was from one of the major dialect regions of the United States. The map of English dialects in Figure 3–3 illustrates these regions.

Slang and technical jargon have also been mighty contributors to the language of late. Slang and other newly coined terms will survive or subside on their own merits; generally the mortality rate is very high. *Keen* and *super* have a hollow sound now, although they are not a generation old. *Blurb* and *go-getter* seem to be useful and have taken hold. Purists who object that slang is an empty-headed shortcut to nonthinking should remember that language itself is the decisive and deliberative judge of what will become part of its lexicon.

Another important influence on the language today is what might be called "hyperliteracy." As the efforts of Noah Webster suggest, a strange process seems to be occurring through which letters in a word come to be pronounced even if they generally had been omitted in speaking. *Often* is one example of this, in which the *t* is pronounced by some highly educated people. Even the second *c* in Connecticut is sometimes heard. This is a process that may be unique to our era.

Our language has systemically changed as a means to facilitate communication. As lexicons have been added or deleted, meanings have also changed. The following nine basic principles should enable you to understand our language heritage better.

1. *Language is a system.* It is a system of complex patterns and a basic structure. There are individual units that work together with other units. Thus linguistically we look at grammar not to identify parts of speech but to learn the forms and patterns within the system. Children learn a language by learning to *use* these structured patterns rather than by analyzing them.
2. *Language is vocal.* Only speech provides all the essential signals of a language. The unit parts of *phonemes* are those sounds that make a difference in meaning when used. Letters are an attempt to represent the sounds of a language. Reading is first of all a recoding of print to sound, then a decoding of the language to meaning. This is why a reading program should be based on the child's existing language knowledge.
3. *Language is composed of arbitrary symbols.* This means that the relationship between symbol and meaning is also arbitrary. It is wrong to argue that one should say *pail* rather than *bucket* or *shades* instead of *curtains* or *blinds* and that there should be only one correct pronunciation of a word. The recognition that language symbols are arbitrary may keep us from *being* arbitrary.
4. *Language is unique.* No two languages have the same set of patterns, sounds, words, or syntax. English is neither German nor Latin. For many years our school grammar has misled students by providing Latin grammatical statements as if they were true about English. It would be equally erroneous to insist that students follow the grammatical rules for German.

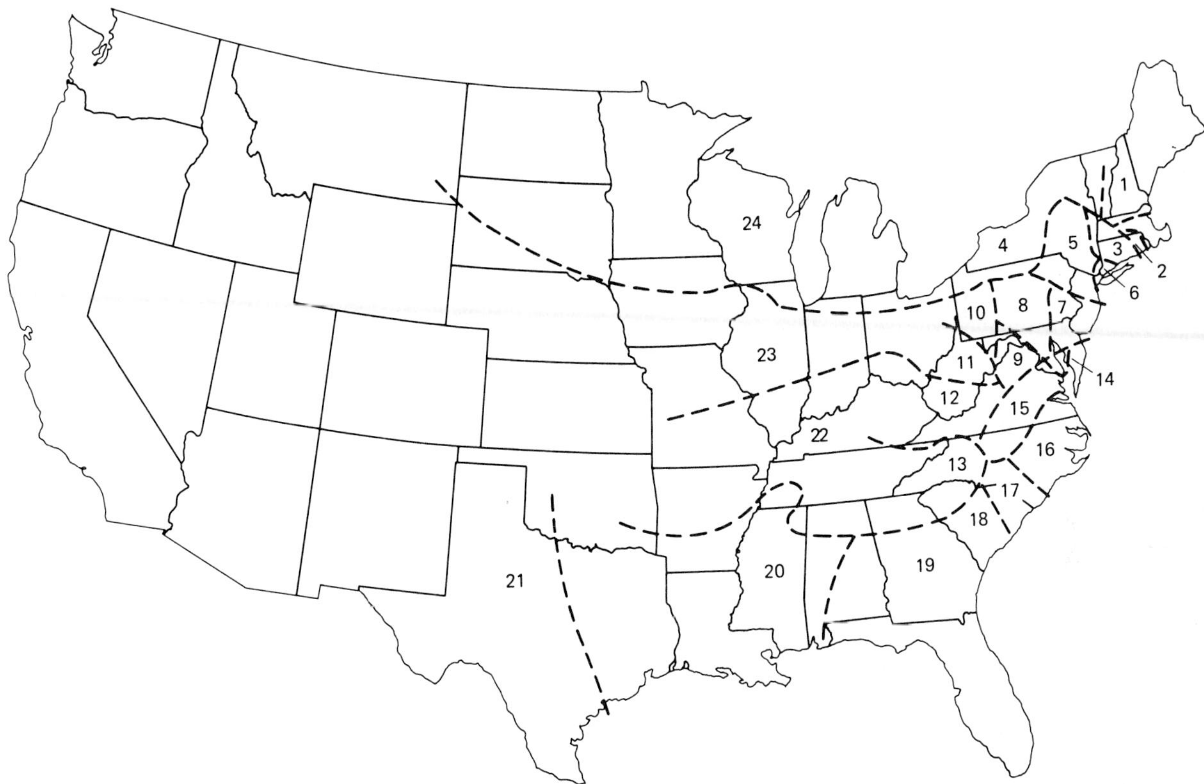

Figure 3–3. American English dialects. (1) N.E. New England; (2) S.E. New England; (3) S.W. New England; (4) Upstate New York and W. Vermont; (5) Hudson Valley; (6) Metropolitan New York; (7) Delaware Valley; (8) Susquehanna Valley; (9) Upper Potomac and Shenandoah valleys; (10) Upper Ohio Valley; (11) N.W. Virginia; (12) S.W. Virginia; (13) W. North Carolina and W. South Carolina; (14) Delmarva (E. shore of Maryland and Virginia and S. Delaware); (15) Virginia Piedmont; (16) N.E. North Carolina (Albemarle Sound and Neuse Valley); (17) Cape Fear and Peedee valleys; (18) South Carolina; (19) Eastern Southern; (20) Central Southern; (21) Western Southern; (22) South Midlands; (23) North Midlands; (24) Northern.

5. *Language is composed of habits.* Our use of the system itself is on the habit level. Our ways of pronouncing a sound or ordering words in a sentence are done as automatically as walking. Teachers are not going to get anyone to speak English by telling him about the language or having the learner memorize language forms. Learning a language is governed by situations that require its use. The situations control the vocabulary and the syntax.
6. *Language is for communication.* Language must first make sense to the user—but it must also make sense to others. If the pronunciation is misunderstood, or forms indicate a meaning other than the one intended, the language fails to communicate. This demands an analysis on

the part of the listener. If this is done, it is apparent why standard usage is essential, and at the scholarly level an exactness is necessary. Getting a job, participating in group discussions, and writing to be understood require a high quality of language. Although there is less concern about the best way to speak and write, there will always be a concern for grammatical adequacy to assure the exchange of meaning.

7. *Language is related to the culture in which it exists.* Language exists in speakers who are in certain places doing certain things. Almost every trade has words and expressions understood only by the in-group. Sometimes this is called jargon, a kind of occupational slang. At other times it is highly technical language requiring similar experiences to assure communication. And finally, as Pei (1965, p. 4) cautions us

> Language is something more than a system of communicating; it is also a social convention which one must observe under penalty of being misjudged. Ignorance or improper use of language can easily interfere with your success or advancement.

8. *Language changes.* Turns of phrases and newly coined words are constantly infiltrating the language through print and other media. Although expressions like *y'all* for the second-person plural are frowned on by many, they do find their way into common use. However, their meanings vary among the many regions of the country. The larger and more culturally diverse a land area, the more likely it is that subcultures, including sublanguages or dialects, will develop. The greater the differences among various environments, the greater will be the differences in language styles.
9. Language consists of many dialects with no one dialect being superior to another.

Summary

The etymology of the English language was extensively examined in this chapter. In addition, the importance of preserving culture through language, personalized variations in American dialects, second-language learning, and bilingualism were topics that also received major attention. In sum, the concept that language is a personal dimension of human beings characterized this chapter.

The following three major principles were presented:

1. Language is a living, changing entity.
2. Language is continuously changing.
3. Much of our present language has roots in the past.

Suggested Classroom Projects and Questions for Discussion

Projects

1. Select a specific cultural heritage of the students you may currently teach or ones you hope to teach someday. Study the culture to determine whether any current customs or behavior of this population are a result of their heritage.
2. Determine your cultural heritage. Try to trace the influence of your heritage on the development of the English language which is illustrated in Figure 2–1.
3. Prepare a list of ten current slang expressions. Try to trace their development.
4. After reading the section of this chapter on cultural influences reflected in the history of the English language prepare a chart for children that conveys some of this interesting information.
5. Prepare a variety of activities for students in grades 1 and 2, 3 to 5, and 6 to 7 that will encourage the sharing of their language heritage.
6. Prepare a classroom chart of words and their word origins. Ask your students to add words from their culture to the chart.
7. Study the "rules of etiquette" of three different cultures of the students in your classroom (for example, Hispanic, British, Japanese) to determine their differences.
8. Interview several bilingual speakers to determine what they believe to be effective strategies for learning a second language.
9. Develop several strategies for teaching English to non–English-speaking students.

10. Prepare a list of poems, plays, and songs from various cultures that you will be able to use in your classroom.

Questions

1. What personal cultural activities are a dimension of your language heritage?
2. What is the relationship between language and culture?
3. Do you speak a dialect?
4. What influences have caused people who live in various sections of the United States to speak different dialects?
5. Why does the English language continue to change?
6. What classroom activities will provide an atmosphere which encourages language expansion rather than language elimination?
7. What does it mean to say that "language is changeable and adaptable over time"?
8. What significant influences did the subgroups of East Central Europe have on English?
9. How have recent immigrants influenced the English language?
10. Why does it help us to understand people and their culture if we understand their language?

Chapter 4

Acquiring and Using Our Language

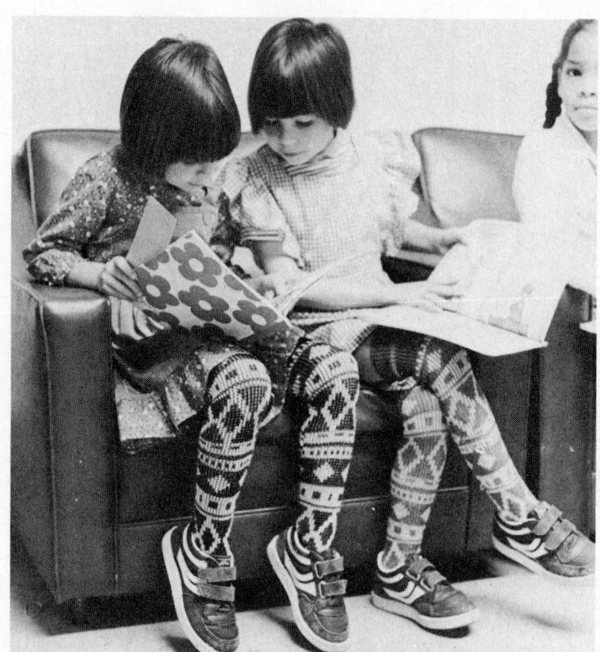

(Photo by Linda Lungren)

OBJECTIVES

At the end of this chapter students should be able to:

1. understand the way language is acquired.
2. understand factors that influence the development of language.
3. understand the teacher's goal in language expansion.

During a visit to a first-grade class, I observed a teacher in the following conversation with her students.

Teacher: We are going to be sharing many ideas this year. One of the ways we share ideas is through our *talk* or *communication* with each other. How did you learn to talk?

Eugene: I learned to talk because I went gaa-gaa, goo-goo.

Romeo: When my mother told me how to say "mama."

Aubrey: My mom taught me to talk and I just practiced. My mom showed me how to read words.

Regina: My mother told me how to say "cookie." . . . Because whenever I said "cookie" she gave me a cookie.

Mike: My mom taught me. She told me when you blow your breath you move your tongue and when you get used to doing it then you learn to talk. . . . She taught me how to learn to say words. . . . "May I go to the bathroom?" and "Please."

Elliott: My dad taught me. He sat me in a chair and taught me.

Adrian: When I was a little baby, my mother said, "I'm going to sit you on the floor and tell you how to speak." She taught me how to say my name, how to say her name and how to say my brother's name.

Maribell: I learned Spanish first. . . . I learned English at school. . . . English was easier.

As you can see from this example, it is a pleasant but difficult experience to attempt to explain how we learned to speak. Have you ever listened to two four-year-olds having a conversation and wondered how they know so much when they are so little? How did they *learn* to talk? Is language *learned* or does it *develop* naturally? Is the language acquisition process the same for everyone in every language? How much of what we remember about acquiring our language is fact? This chapter will explore such issues.

How Is Language Acquired?

From the field of physiology we have learned that all human infants are neurologically immature at birth, with the central nervous system, which includes the brain and spinal cord, more developed than the peripheral nervous system. As infants learn to control their muscles, this maturation enables them to discriminate among sets of sounds, shapes, and colors. By the end of a baby's first month of life, the mother or caregiver can often detect pain, rage, or mere exuberance in the vocalizations that are made. Just as the baby's random movements with the arms and legs are exercise and help the infant to gain control over his body, so are such vocalizations the baby's way of exercising the speech mechanism.

A newborn child is physically equipped to perceive and produce speech. However, many of the sounds made by infants are not directly related to the sounds of their later languages. According to Lenneberg (1966, 1967) and other investigators, there is an age range for the stages of language development, and these stages occur in a sequential order. Every physiologically "normal" child learns to talk, given a minimal amount of language input. Even mentally retarded children with IQs of 60 learn to talk, although often not as rapidly as the normal child, and often with more limited vocabulary.

A child entering first grade can send as well as receive spoken messages. These skills have been developed through the child's involvement in a language-rich environment. In exchanging messages within this environment, children evidence internalization of a working grammar of their native language. Children of this age have not acquired all of the structures of adult grammar, but they have developed the basic grammatical structures of their native language.

Modeling plays an important role in linguistic development. This is shown by the fact that the congenitally deaf children cannot learn normal speech because their inability to hear makes it impossible for them to imitate sounds. Of equal importance to the modeling of others are children's repetition of their own sounds. Nearly everyone is familiar with the "babbling" of an infant; it is thought that a desire to hear oneself talk contributes to this activity. When infants are in the presence of their parents and accidentally or purposely make a speechlike sound, they are likely to pronounce the word that approximates the sound they have just made. This is good training because it provides auditory strengthening and stimulates the child to remake the sound that was produced. So often these pleasant experiences are later retold to children. This accounts for the statements by children opening this chapter. We saw in these statements that children believe their parents were intricately involved in their language acquisition.

The nature and purpose of parental speech in the language acquisition process of the young child are explored in the works of Weber-Olson (1984) and Wells and Wells (1984). They suggest that the *quality* as well as *quantity* of parental speech interactions affect the development and linguistic interactions of children. Cahir and Shuy (1981) suggest that in most homes the father's influence on the child's language development may not be significant, and that analysis of the mother's language patterns is predictive of the language patterns of the children.

According to a report by Brown and Bellugi (1964) on the early language of two children, young speakers concern themselves with syntax (sentence arrangement) in remarkably efficient ways. Two children, a boy aged twenty-seven months and a girl aged eighteen months, imitated their mothers' sentences, and although they left out words, they never changed the original order of words they repeated. "Frazer will be unhappy" became "Frazer unhappy." "He's going out" became "He go out." Words and parts of words that carry meaning were retained in these and other samples. "No, you can't write on Mr. Cromer's shoe" was condensed to "Write Cromer's shoe." It was never, "Shoe write Cromer." The investigators remind us that in speaking such sentences as "Frazer will be unhappy," the adult spontaneously stresses the most important words, here *Frazer* and *unhappy*. This is an essential facet of our language; we do, indeed, stress the meaning-bearing words. Children learn the stress system as easily as they learn to talk. Innumerable repetitions make it automatic since, as Buss (1984) suggests, the melodic features of language play a major role in both oral and book language learning.

Loban (1976) presented a fascinating study of the language of a group of children from their entrance into kindergarten through their graduation from high school. In this study the pupils were asked in an interview to tell what they saw in a carefully selected group of pictures and what they thought about them. The responses were recorded and the language was analyzed according to a scheme devised by a panel of linguists.

One of the major problems in any such analysis is the presence in the speech of children and young people of certain "tangles" of language. There are hesitations, false starts, and meaningless repetitions that interrupt the sentence patterns. These tangles were extracted and studied separately from the remaining sentences. During kindergarten and the first three grades, the total group and the high subgroup showed a steady decrease in the number of tangles (35 percent) and the number of words per tangle (50 percent). The low group, on the other hand, increased both the number of tangles and the average number of words per tangle during the same four-year period. Throughout the study, the low group said less, had more difficulty saying it, and had a smaller vocabulary with which to say it. The high group was distinguished from the kindergarten group by the ability to express tentative thinking, as revealed by such words and phrases as *perhaps, maybe,* and *I'm not exactly sure.* The gifted children sensed alternatives, while the less gifted made flat, dogmatic statements. Although the pictures invited generalizations and figurative language, little of either strategy was used by any of the children.

Furrow and Nelson (1984) suggest that a mother's use of nouns and pronouns and their references to objects and persons when speaking to their young children relate to their children's use of such references in their language. They further suggest that environmental factors contribute significantly to stylistic differences in language acquisition. What do such findings suggest to us as teachers?

As teachers, we need to question whether the complexity and sophistication of the language structures used by children should be thought of solely as a measure of intellectual potential or also as a correlate to environmental influences. We must be careful as teachers to remember that we are the *developers* rather than simply the measurers of the potential that all children, from all types of environments, bring to the world of school. Early school performance illustrates the learning that happens in the home. Too often children in the primary grades may be mislabeled as lacking intellectual potential simply because such early learning is not closely related to behaviors needed for school success.

The importance of home environment in the development of language is stressed in the work of Cazden (1981), who studied the differences between the language development in middle-class children and children who were socially and economically lower than middle class. She found great differences in language development, even at an early age. Studies such as this tell us what exists at a given age, not what can exist if we as teachers provide extensive oral language experiences in the early years.

The Phenomenon of Language Acquisition

The notion of a *critical period* in language development refers to a stage in which the human organism is especially sensitive to a specific component of language. It is possible that there are certain periods that are extremely sensitive for the development of each of the language components of phonology, syntax, morphology, semantics, and pragmatics. These periods of heightened sensitivity may parallel Piaget's (1963) stages of cognitive development; for example, the first growth spurt between two and four years of age may be the most sensitive period for phonological development. It is important to note that *critical period* here refers to a time of particular sensitivity to language development, not a terminal point after which no language development will occur.

Let us look at some of the factors that affect a child's sensitivity to language development. Three of the major determinants are neurophysiology, psychology, and environment.

Neurophysiology

The critical period hypothesis is derived from behavior observed in animals such as geese (Lorenze, 1970). In applying this biological concept of critical period to the acquisition and development of language, Lenneberg (1966, 1967) and others have claimed that language cannot be learned as easily after the completion of the lateralization of the brain, a phenomenon that Lenneberg believes to occur at puberty.

Krashen (1972) claims that lateralization is complete by age five, but others such as Eimas and Corbit (1973) suggest that it occurs even earlier. Kinsbourne and Smith (1974) suggest that lateralization has much in common with Piaget's concept of the sensorimotor stage, a proposal that may lead researchers to an investigation of the relationship between the sensorimotor period and the critical period of language development.

Psychology and Environment

A second determinant of language development is the psychological composition of the individual. Psychology includes such factors as cognition, intellectual functioning, experience, attitude, motivation, and culture, all of which must be considered when proposing a theory to explain a sensitive stage of development.

One must also consider environmental influences such as auditory input/stimulation, semantic input, and syntactic input. DeVilliers and deVilliers (1979) suggest that infants pick up the "feeling-tone" transmitted by their parents' speech long before they learn individual words. The case of "Genie" (Curtiss et al., 1974; Fromkin and Robman, 1974)—a fictitious name—demonstrates the profound effect of environment on language. Genie was a thirteen-year-old girl who was brought to the Children's Hospital in Los Angeles in November 1970 after having been virtually locked in a closet for most of her life. The actual details of the case are unknown for the most part. But at the time of her entry into Children's Hospital she had no speech, had few signs of any nonverbal language, and was barely able to control the vocal muscles that allow speech production, chewing, and swallowing. After several years of life in a normal foster home and work with educators, psychologists, and speech pathologists, Genie has exhibited an incredible amount of growth. She is able to comprehend speech, use expressive speech, and understand cognitive relationships far beyond the expectations of many researchers who would hold to a strict critical period theory of development. Although her phonology is far from perfect, her syntax, in general, exceeds what is expected of a typical five- or six-year-old who has been learning English for that number of years. The case of Genie certainly is relevant to Lenneberg's theory of a critical period for language acquisition, which he suggests occurs between birth and puberty. Lenneberg's hypothesis may not be totally valid, because Genie's language acquisition *began* at the onset of puberty.

It should be emphasized that neurophysiological, psychological, and environmental factors are not separable in their effects on an individual's sensitivity to language development. It is simply not clear which factor may operate first or which is most significant for the acquisition of language.

Second Language Acquisition

There is much controversy among those linguists who study the learning of second languages, and the implications of this controversy are significant for educators. There are those who claim, along with Lenneberg, that the ability to acquire language is actually dependent on certain maturational stages, such as the range of two to three years old when a great deal of phonological information is acquired. As one matures, the theory runs, one loses the ability to learn a language in a "natural" way. Noam Chomsky and other linguists, however, hold that the language acquisition device has full potency throughout life. The implication of the former theory is that a second language can refer to rules from the first one, but that second-language acquisition can never be unconscious and natural. It must be very conscious, with intense drill and evaluation of rules, conjugation of verbs, and so on. The latter theory holds that unconscious acquisition of a second language is always possible and so an immersion, or language experience, approach is the more legitimate one. The contrast between these two approaches underscores the way our assumptions about language determine our teaching styles and points to the need for research on teaching effectiveness and on learning stages.

How Children Learn to Use Language

Have you ever been at a party and wondered why some people are so good at thinking of things to talk about? Have you ever run out of topics to discuss with a stranger?

Speech is often a social overture (for example, the asking of a question that requires no answer). Talking often accompanies action in other motor areas. The child appears to fill every waking moment with oral expression; indeed, it seems that talking is almost compulsive in nature.

For a child as young as three years, language serves the purpose of simple narration, with the related incidents usually being telescoped into a single sentence. For example, "We went downtown" may be used to cover all the exciting things that happened. Occasionally children of three can enlarge upon this, and some children of four can tell enough of an incident to hold the attention of other children. Imaginative elements often crop up, possibly reflecting the stories that are read to children of this age. For example, a child may relate, "Once there was a big engine. It came right up to the door and asked for breakfast."

Shirley (1933) found that in a single day her three-year-old child asked 376 questions and that her four-year-old child asked 397. This is probably somewhat high for average children but gives an idea of why this age is referred to as the "question age."

Blachowicz (1984) adds to our understanding of the sophistication of children's language by distinguishing the difference between linguistic insight and linguistic awareness. Most children are aware of and able to use sophisticated language structures but are often unable to express the "why" of their choices. The most complicated and advanced use of language is to express reasoning: "If I don't wear my mittens, I don't get them dirty" or "Where does my dinner go when I eat it?" As the children's experiences enlarge and as their mastery of vocabulary increases, their reasoning becomes increasingly complex. The more extensive and varied experiences one is exposed to contribute to the ability and ease of using language.

In the early years egocentricity predominates in language content. The six-year-old's insistent "Look at me" is familiar to every parent and teacher.

Almost all studies of children's language have noted the lateness with which pronouns are added to the child's vocabulary. It is not unusual to hear a three-year-old refer to himself as "Jimmy" instead of saying "I," "me," or "myself."

Developmental trends explain the peculiar flavor of the very young child's speech. For example, McCarthy's (1934) study of recorded responses from twenty children at each of seven age levels from eighteen to fifty-four months suggests nouns constitute about 50 percent of the total speech of very young children. Verbs increase from about 14 percent of the total speech at eighteen months to about 25 percent at fifty-four months. Adjectives increase over the same interval from about 10 to about 20 percent. Connectives do not appear until about two years of age; after that age they steadily increase in proportion. Therefore, the young child typically uses many nouns and verbs, very few pronouns, and practically no connectives. Young children's speech is thus direct, unadorned, and essentially disconnected.

Almost one-half of a century later, Berman (1983), in attempting to characterize the process of first-language acquisition, suggested that language learning involves the acquiring of both language knowledge and behavior, hence of the internalized representations underlying linguistic competence and also the ability to use such knowledge to interpret language and to speak the language.

For these reasons, measuring the vocabulary of a child presents many problems. The words used will be limited by the occasion or situation. Decisions must be made as to what constitutes a word. Should *chairs* be counted as a separate word from *chair?* Should *moo-moo* be accepted as a word for *cow?* Should each meaning of a word be counted as a separate vocabulary understanding?

Vocabulary studies have been conducted in a number of situations. Conversations have been recorded; the written material of an individual has been analyzed; children have been stimulated to write all the words they know by showing them pictures or giving them key words; lists have been used to check recognition.

One research study by Larrick (1959) used a pocket dictionary of 18,000 words to check vocabulary; it was concluded that a twelve-year-old knew 7,200 words. When another study used a dictionary of 371,000 words, it was concluded that a child that age knew 55,000 words. With respect to the vocabulary of first-grade children, some studies indicate that a vocabulary of 2,500 words is normal, whereas others indicate that 24,000 words is normal.

Repeated tests with college undergraduates indicate a vocabulary of over 100,000 words, and probably over 200,000. It seems likely that such vocabulary development must occur gradually throughout the individual's growth, so the evidence suggests that the vocabulary of children has probably been underestimated.

An additional consideration is the fact that children's speaking vocabularies differ from their listening and reading vocabularies. Children understand many words spoken to them that they never use in their own speech, and adults read and sometimes write words that they do not use in their spoken vocabulary.

The Nature of Language

Language has a fairly definite structure that can be described by a set of rules we call "grammar." These rules or statements about the nature of language meet with fairly wide agreement. In this section we will discuss these generalizations as they apply to the English language system.

Language is usually discussed in terms of four components:

1. Phonology (the sound system)
2. Morphology (the word-formation systems)
3. Syntax (the system of word relations)
4. Semantics (the meaning system for words and sentences)

Phonology

Young children, during their first year of life, develop consonantlike sounds from back to front in the mouth. For vowellike sounds, the direction of development is from front to back for the first part of the year but switches during the last part (McCarthy, 1934; Irwin, 1947a, 1947b, 1947c; Alyeshmerni and Tauber, 1975).

According to Jakobson (1941, translated to English in 1968), children establish a series of oppositions within a sound continuum in order to impose order on the speech sounds they hear. The first oppositions they produce are usually between a consonant and a vowel: usually between the vowel /a/ and the consonant /p/. The consonant-vowel opposition appears in the production of the syllable *pa,* which explains the frequency of /papa/ as a first syllable word sequence in young children. When there is less than optimal control over the larynx and the velum (the soft palate), the first syllable sequences are usually /bab/ or /mama/. This is why *papa, baba,* and *mama* are often the child's first quoted sequences and why these terms are used as parental names in many cultures.

Infants experiment with the vocal mechanism in producing various sounds. By about four months of age they have almost totally mastered the basic principles of its effective use. They can gurgle, chuckle, laugh, blow bubbles, and experiment with the use of breath control, the tongue, and the larynx. During this period, usually called the babbling stage, infants learn to modify the tension of their vocal cords and to vary the positions of tongue and lips in order to imitate sounds they hear. At this time they have command of most vowel sounds and a few of the consonants. Some children are able to produce all consonants and some diphthong sounds by six or seven months of age. At approximately nine months, children's babbling usually softens into the rhythm of the speech they hear in their environment. The child's first real word is usually uttered at between nine and fourteen months of age. The child's active vocabulary at eleven or twelve months usually consists of *mama, daddy,* and one or two other words. Stop and think for a second about how many hours of practice the child has had up to this point. It is no wonder that second language acquisition cannot be completed in a short time period.

The exact point at which actual words are substituted for babbling is unclear. We usually depend on parents for these records, and the data may not be reliable, for first words are so anxiously awaited by parents that word formation can be more imagined than real.

The child's first words, *holophrases,* usually monosyllables or repetitions of monosyllables such as *ma'* and *mama,* serve as interjections or nouns. The child, with gestures, can convey a variety of meanings with only one word. The single word *water* or *wa-wa* may mean "I want a drink," "See the pool," "It's raining," "I want that glass," and so on. Infants' first words usually have an emotional quality, as he expresses a wish, feeling, or need. Some authorities believe that the production of the word is secondary to the general emotional status of the child at that time. Words may often be used to supplement emotional expression, body movement, and other devices used to express wants.

Principles of Phonology. Phonology is a rule-bound system in which the smallest meaningful speech sound unit is called the *phoneme*. The English language is composed of approximately forty of these distinct speech sounds, which are related by the presence or absence of distinctive features. For example, the words *but* and *putt* are the same except for the voicing, or vocal cord involvement, of the initial phoneme. Both /b/ and /p/ are articulated in the same place, with the lips together, and in the same manner, with a slight puff of air when the lips are opened. In contrast, /k/ and /p/ are alike in being unvoiced and also are alike in manner of articulation because both involve an air stop, but they differ in place of articulation, with /k/ far back at the velum instead of at the lips.

Positions of Articulation. Most of the contrasts in the sounds of speech are made by modifying the relation of the lower jaw and tongue to the upper jaw. The generally stationary organs of the upper jaw are called points of articulation (Table 4–1). They are the upper lip and the teeth, the alveolar ridge, the (hard) palate, the velum (soft palate), and the uvula. The uvula and upper lip are the only organs in the upper jaw that move. The organs along the lower jaw are called articulators. They are the lower

Table 4–1
Major Positions of Articulation

Lip sounds (bilabial)	p	the *pop* sound (not *puh*)
	b	the *bubble* sound (not *buh*)
	m	the *humming* sound
	w	the *soft wind* sound
	y	the *smile* sound
Lip-breath sounds (glottal)	h	the *little puff* sound
	wh	the *big puff* sound
Tip-of-the-tongue sounds (apicoalveolar)	t	the *ticking watch* sound
	d	the *tapping* sound
	n	the *spinning* sound
Back-of-the-tongue sound (dorsovelar)	k	the *little cough* sound
	g	the *gurgle* sound
	l	the *bell* sound
	ng	the *ring* sound (ting-a-ling)
	r	the *rooster* sound
Lip-teeth sounds (labiodental)	f	the *cross kitty* sound
	v	the *airplane* sound
Tongue-teeth sounds (interdental)	the	(as *this*) the *flat tire* sound
	the	(as *the*) the *motor* sound
Teeth sounds (front palatal)	s	the *steam* sound
	z	the *buzz* sound
	sh	the *baby's asleep* sound
	zh	the *vacuum cleaner* sound
	ch	the *train* sound
	j	the *jump* sound

lip and teeth, and the apex (tip), front, and dorsum (back) of the tongue.

The glottal position occurs when no organs other than the vocal folds are used in producing a sound. The /h/ in *he* and the sound heard between the two parts of the colloquial negative *hunh-uh* are examples of this position of articulation.

Morphology

Morphology is the study of the smallest units of meaning in language, morphemes. Inflectional endings and tense markers, as well as the root words to which they are attached all represent types of morphemes. As teachers we often think we teach children these elaborate language procedures. As suggested by researchers (Berko-Gleason, 1958; Malstrom, 1977; Kuczaj, 1977) this is yet another feature of the English language that most children have mastered before entering school. Here we are interested in looking briefly at how the child demonstrates a growth of understanding about the effects that changes in inflectional endings and tense markers have on meaning in language.

The word *boy* is one morpheme, whereas *boys* is two: *boy* plus plurality conferred by the suffix *-s* (or *-es* in some words). In this example there are two classes of morpheme, the lexical *boy* and the grammatical *-s*. Lexical morphemes have inherent meaning, whereas grammatical morphemes structure the sentence or add meaning to lexical morphemes. The following examples (Table 4–2) further illustrate this difference:

Table 4–2
Morphemes

Lexical Morphemes	*Grammatical Morphemes*
boy	-s, -es
green	-d, -ed
swim	to (in infinitive)
chase	that (as in "the fact that")
soon	-'s
from	-ing

In one important study on the acquisition of morphology, Jean Berko-Gleason (1958) showed children a picture of a cartoon figure, telling them, "This is a *wug*." She then told the children that there were two animals, showed them a picture, and said: "There are two ________," expecting the children to supply the plural *wugs* (/wəgz/). She used nonsense words that took all three types of English plural morphemes into consideration (/-s/ as in *hats*, /-z/ as in *rugs*, /-iz/ as in *doses*). She found that children in the age range of four to five years made 6 percent errors with the /-iz/ forms but only 2 percent errors with /-z/ forms. She also found that the children did have /-iz/ forms

Table 4–3
Grammatical Morphemes

1. Present progressive	
-ing	Eric's sleep*ing*
2. Prepositions	
in	*in* house
on	*on* chairs
3. Plural	
-s	shoe*s*
4. Past irregular	
go	he *went*
break	it *broke*
5. Possessive	
's	Shannon'*s* ball
6. Uncontractible linking verb	
is	*Is* the dog brown?
7. Articles	
the	*the* wagon
a	*a* toy
an	*an* apple
8. Past regular	
-ed	snow*ed*
9. Third-person regular	
-s	play*s*
10. Third-person irregular	
-s	ha*s*
11. Uncontractible auxiliary verb	
is	*Is* Denise playing?
12. Contractible linking verb	
s	Stacy'*s* sleepy.
13. Contractible auxiliary verb	
s	Daryl'*s* smiling.

in their lexicons, for 91 percent had the correct plural for *glass*. Thus at a relatively early age, children are able to account for morphological changes in language.

The work of Brown and Frazer (1963) as well as others suggests that most English-speaking children acquire use of grammatical morphemes in a predictable sequence. Table 4–3 illustrates such a sequence.

A curious thing happens while the child is acquiring morphemic knowledge: the phenomenon of overgeneralization or inappropriate rule formation. An example will help to explain what happens. In learning the tense forms of the verb *to run*, children may use both *run* and *ran* appropriately for a while. After learning the regular past tense marker *-d*/*-ed*, however, they may begin to say *runned* or *runnded* before using both *ran* and *run* correctly again. The explanation for this phenomenon is that *ran* and *run* are originally learned as separate lexical items. When the regular past tense rule is learned later, it is overgeneralized in application to irregular verbs and *ran* is forgotten or ignored. The proper past tense forms are finally acquired as irregular instances. The significance of the process is that it demonstrates the tendency of the language learner to formulate, apply, and then modify rules. We will return to this important principle when we discuss grammar.

Syntax

Store I to go.
I have cookie may a?

In order to make sense of these words we must reorder them syntactically. How do we learn to apply the appropriate syntax?

Syntax is the structuring of language or the rules that order and relate words within a sentence. Adults have extensive sets of rules for their communications, but these are largely inappropriate for children's language. What is the structure of children's language? Let us review briefly.

Children produce their first words in the wide normal age range of nine to fourteen months. Before this age they have been able to produce many phonemes of all languages with their vocal apparatus, but not to convey meaning. The first words often have emotional and egocentric content, and early one-word utterances can also serve as what is called holophrastic speech. This kind of speech has a largely social function of labeling and pointing out objects in the environment, condensing into one word both the name of an object and the fact that it is noticed. Examples include *dada, doggy, car, go, gone, book.* At approximately twenty months, or when the vocabulary is about fifty words, two-word utterances begin as the individual words are combined. Most of these early combinations are "telegraphic." According to Brown and Fraser (1963), articles, prepositions, and auxiliaries are not used. Here are some samples of telegraphic speech: *mommy glass, baby book.*

Bohannon (1984) cautions teachers that children's awareness of word order or syntactic awareness in language may be important to reading because it helps them detect meaningful relationships between words.

QUESTIONS. English has two ways to form a question: (1) beginning the sentence with a verb or auxiliary (*do, did*), for example, "Does Big Boy have the salad?" and (2) beginning the sentence with a "*wh*-word" (*who, what, where, when, why, how*). Studies by Menyuk (1969) suggest that from the earliest stages of language development, children, through intonation, patterns, and simple transformations, learn to produce questions. The first type of question is called a yes/no question. *Wh-* questions are called information questions.

When children learn to ask questions, they do so first by incorporating the rising intonation typical of English questions into the same sentences they use for statements and demands, for example, "Lynne happy?" The second step in the acquisition process is the use of *wh-* questions. When yes/no questions occur for the first time, the auxiliary *do* takes on a unique function in inverted questions and in negatives. The system is similar to an adult system, but auxiliaries are still not inverted in *wh-* questions, for example,

"Does he say why?" There are no combinations of auxiliaries in the children's speech ("Has he had the operation?"), although these combinations can occur in adult English. The auxiliary form of *be* does not usually appear in early children's speech: "He has been having a good time in New Orleans."

Donaldson (1978) suggests that when children are presented with complex questions they often give inappropriate responses. For example, the question "No one can go without money?" can be easily misunderstood as a fact instead of a question. Children often rely on the situation if they have not developed sufficient knowledge of the language.

RELATIVE CLAUSES. Carol Chomsky (1969) showed that many children do not fully comprehend relative clauses until quite late; many eight-year-olds do not thoroughly understand sentences like "Tell Linda when to water the plants" and "Ask Nancy which chair to sit at." If pushed, some young children will say, "Nancy, which chair to sit at?"

Clark (1972), like Chomsky, suggests that most children who are five to ten years of age regard the first noun phrase in a sentence as the subject and the second noun phrase as the object, so that "The pie was eaten by Bob Hill" is thought of as subject—pie, object—Bob Hill.

Some psychologists have suggested that acquisition of grammar and modification of rules go on not just throughout childhood but rather throughout life. Carol Chomsky (1969) found that many children ten years old still adhere rigidly to the *minimal distance principle* that assumes that the subject of a verb is the noun phrase immediately before it. In the sentence "Harold promised Mary to make dinner" it is Harold who will be the chef, yet many school-age children will believe the chef to be Mary. These children have not learned to modify the often-correct minimal distance principle to accommodate verbs like *promise* that take indirect objects. Table 4–4 (Lenneberg, 1966) shows when certain linguistic performances are likely to occur in normally developing children:

Table 4–4
Linguistic Performances

Age	*Vocalization*
At birth	Crying
1–2 months	Cooing, crying
3–6 months	Babbling, cooing, and crying
9–14 months	First words
18–24 months	First sentences
3–4 years	Almost all basic syntactic structure
4–8 years	Almost all speech sounds correctly articulated
9–11 years	Semantic distinctions established

From Lenneberg, E. H. (1966). The natural history of language. In F. Smith & G. Miller (Eds.), *The Genesis of Language*. New York: John Wiley and Sons.

Semantics

Semantics is the study of word meanings, including phonology, syntax, and pragmatics. Single words can have multiple meanings, and "fixed" multiple meanings can be altered by syntactic and contextual constraints. A four-year-old child understands that a figurative meaning is being attached to the word *devil* when his mother says, "Jimmy, you're acting like a little *devil*." He also knows when *devil* is used in a positive or negative way by his mother's tone and by contextual considerations (his actions).

Using Jakobson's (1941, 1968) notion of binary oppositions, H. H. Clark (1970) has proposed a theory of distinctive features in phonology. Jakobson maintained that young children interpret *less* as though it means *more*. Clark argued that when young children learn polar adjectives and comparatives, they first learn that *more/less, big/little, near/far* refer to the same concept: having. Next, children learn that dimension is involved and proceeds to use both words positively—therefore, *big/little*. Finally, children realize that the dimension is polar, and they begin to use the words correctly.

Clark's semantic feature theory may look like this:

	CAT + animal + four legs	*COW* + animal + four legs
Later development:	+ little	+ big

Chomsky (1972), attempting to minimize semantics, claimed, "It has been found that semantic reference . . . does not apparently affect the manner in which acquisition of syntax proceeds; that is, it plays no role in determining which hypotheses are selected by the learner" (p. 33).

Disagreeing with Chomsky, E. V. Clark (1971) stated, "Semantic information does affect the manner in which the subject (or child) approaches the learning of syntactic rules, contrary to Chomsky's (1965) assumption. Without any semantic information, subjects simply tried to learn the relative positions of words" (p. 56).

Many researchers (Halliday, 1973; Stibbs, 1980) suggest that the way in which speakers encode meaning in language is extremely complex. For young children what they *mean* to say may be extremely more complex than what they are *able* to say. Halliday (1973) suggested the following seven functions of language.

1. *Instrumental*—The speaker uses language to state a material task he wishes to accomplish: "I want to wash my car."
2. *Regulatory*—The speaker uses language to control behaviors of other: "Finish the dishes, please." "Beginning at 10 A.M. I want you to (1) make the coffee; (2) sweep the office; (3) type the letters."
3. *Interactional*—The speaker uses language to mediate between self and others: "Let's finish our homework."
4. *Personal*—The speaker uses language as a form of individuality: "I like chocolate cake."
5. *Heuristic*—The speaker uses language to help himself understand the existing reality: "Do you think . . . ?"
6. *Imaginative*—The speaker uses language to expand or explore the environment. Games and storytelling are characteristic of this type of language: "Let's pretend that this stick is a magic wand. . . . If I were king, I'd wave my magic wand and make this street a field of strawberries."
7. *Representational*—The speaker uses language to convey a message or proposition. Adults are very aware of this dimension of language: "It's raining today."

The Nature of a Grammar

How do native speakers develop a language? It can be said somewhat simplistically that they gather information about language, form hypotheses about the underlying principles of the language's organization, and test those hypotheses in the world. Children, then, are striving to acquire the concepts that control language rather than merely the words that compose it. One's knowledge of the rules of a language and the concepts that underlie it is regarded as one's language competence. As suggested by Noam Chomsky (1965), a description of this linguistic competence possessed by the native speakers of a language is called a grammar. A *grammar* describes what is known, however unconsciously, by the speakers of a language. Chomsky (1965) as well as Lenneberg (1967) claim that the capacity to acquire language competence is an innate attribute of the human organism. There is considerable support for this position, but we will only say now that all humans in reasonable environments acquire language, and the possibility of forgetting how to use language seems unlikely. Before we treat the nature of the knowledge possessed by a natural language user, it may be worthwhile to explore the criteria used in evaluating grammar. A grammar must first of all be descriptively adequate, meaning that it must account for all the data that can be observed. When you call a friend in the evening and no one answers the phone, there are several theories to explain why, all of which are descriptively adequate. We will suggest three:

Theory 1: He has not come home.
Theory 2: He has gone out for the evening.
Theory 3: A marauding band of Martians swooped in and kidnapped him.

All theories account for the observed facts and are, in that sense, descriptively adequate. The second criticism, explanatory adequacy, requires that the theory makes as few assumptions as possible and at the same time expresses as many relevant generalizations as possible. Certainly theory 3 does not meet this criterion, because it makes unaccountable assumptions and fails to express the generalization that, in fact, people often are away from home of their own free will.

One grammar that attempts to satisfy the two criteria of descriptive and explanatory accuracy is transformational grammar.

Transformational Grammar

Most people agree that sentences such as

1. John loves Mary.
2. Mary is loved by John.

are pretty closely related. But how are they related, and what underlies their relationship? They seem to have the same meaning but a different structure. Now consider the sentences

1. The shooting of the hunters frightened us.
2. Sailing ships can be exciting.

Each of these sentences can be interpreted in two different ways. For example, in the first sentence it can be the hunters' use of guns or the hunters' having been shot that we find frightening.

One proposed explanation of the differing interpretations follows: Language has a meaning level (which is called its deep structure) and a level consisting of actual sentences used in communication (which is called its surface structure). Noam Chomsky (1957) originally suggested simple, active declarative sentences as the deep structures that are then subjected to certain transformations, such as the passive transformation through substitution of a reflexive pronoun and through conjoining. Transformation produces the surface structure we hear, which differs in construction but not in meaning from the original deep structure. The hearer can transform this sentence back into its deep structure and assimilate the intended meaning.

In the sentences "John loves Mary" and "Mary is loved by John" the deep structure and therefore the meaning are identical. The sentence "Sailing ships can be exciting" is ambiguous because it could arise from either of two different deep structures: "The sailing of ships can be exciting," or "Ships with sails can be exciting."

We have, then, meaning or semantics on one level and phonological form on the "surface" level above meaning. The link between these two is syntax—the vehicle for bringing meaning to the surface. Transformational grammar allows four basic kinds of operations on base sentences (deep structure). These operations can occur in any order, any number of times, and operate on specific elements in the sentence.

Transformation can

1. Move elements:
from "The chairman began the financial review after introducing the board members."
to "After introducing the board members, the chairman began the financial review."
The adverbial phrase has been shifted.

2. Delete elements:
from "He was stung on the arm by a bee."
to "He was stung on the arm."
The phrase "by a bee" has been deleted (called agent deletion).

3. Insert elements:
from "He is baking bread."
to "He is not baking bread."
Linguists do not entirely agree about negative insertion transformations.

4. Transpose elements:
   from "John loves Mary."
   to "Mary is loved by John."
   This passive transformation transposes the subject and object of the sentence.

The capacity for this linguistic behavior is innate, and therefore the child's language normally develops according to a conventional set of patterns. In transformational terms, a grammar is the set of rules for bringing meanings to the surface. We will borrow from transformational or T-grammar to explain much that is observed in children's language.

Rule Formation Theory

As has been previously noted, a child learns language by acquiring the concepts underlying language performance. The child wants to know not only how to form the plural of *candy* but also how to form the plurals of all words. This apparent fact contradicts the notion that children learn items one at a time and progress in a linear fashion. Children strive instead to learn the rules that will bring the ideas to the surface. Through these attempts language structure is learned.

The first item of support for this notion of the child's role as a systematic language processor is the presence of identifiable grammars in children. A pivot/open grammar is one example of a ruled grammar. Support also comes from the previously mentioned overgeneralization of learned structures in children. When a child acquires a new morphemic ending, it usually sweeps over all possible areas, whether correct or not. Most children cannot know or guess that *ox* comes from a dialect of southern England and is made plural with the addition of *-en*. They apply the rule they know, which is to add *-es* to a word that ends in a voiceless stop.

Support also comes from the behavior of children called on to repeat phrases that contain constructions too sophisticated for their current grammatical knowledge or contrary to whatever grammatical rules they have at the time. If asked to repeat "I haven't any candy," the child of two or three is likely to say "I got no candy." Neither shaping, correcting, nor rehearsing seems effective in eliciting an exact repetition. Obviously the child is incorporating what he hears into his rule system and expressing it via that same rule system. Although incorporation shares the same deep structure, expression takes a different surface structure.

The Teacher's Role in Language Expansion

Since language continues to develop beyond childhood, it is important to know how this happens. Here we shall discuss two important types of language development that occur long after the acquisition of a language's structuring in grammar. Both can be greatly influenced by education.

Pragmatic Development

Throughout life we use language, but clearly language can be used well, poorly, or indifferently. To expand, it can be used effectively, ineffectively, humorously, persuasively, deceptively, artistically, or in many other ways. The knowledge of how to use language is called pragmatics, and it is what a writer might call style. To say that we all differ in terms of command of style is to understate the case greatly. We may all possess the same basic knowledge of language structure, but we differ greatly in the way we use it. The language arts curriculum can and should be effective in giving students many styles of language use, including those for formal social expression, informal correspondence, spontaneous expression, logical argument, criticism, and diplomacy. Language arts teachers should explore the whole intriguing area of using language most effectively in particular situations. How would a letter written to a mail-order business be different from one written to the editor of a newspaper? If you were writing a repair manual, why would the style you used be different from that of a fairy tale?

Our goal as teachers of the language arts is to ensure that our students acquire language flexibility; that is, the ability to know how and when to use the multiple dimensions of their language. (Photo by Linda Lungren)

Our goal as teachers of the language arts is to ensure that our students acquire language flexibility, that is, the ability to know how and when to use the multiple dimensions of their language. Specific suggestions for accomplishing this goal may be found in Chapter 6, "Oral Communication."

Metalinguistic Development

Certainly we all possess some common knowledge of language—its basics of pronunciation, vocabulary, and grammar. However, another area where we differ greatly is in our knowledge of what we know. Think a minute; this merely means knowing what we are doing when we use language. The fact that some of us, more than others, can dwell on, analyze, criticize, subvert, or play with language is significant. This self-knowledge of one's linguistic processes is called metalinguistic awareness. The user of puns, riddles, and paradoxes is showing an acute knowledge of language that allows him to manipulate it. In *The Taming of the Shrew* a character orders his servant to "knock me soundly upon this door," and the servant is befuddled, not wishing to believe that he should swat his master against the door. In this example, Shakespeare is mocking an affected style of speech and at the same time playing with language. This is also true for "Jam every other day," which Alice is promised as wages from the Queen. She later learns that "every other day" means every day except today.

It is said that reading requires bringing to conscious awareness what we know *about* language; furthermore, what we know about language we must have learned, whether in the classroom or elsewhere. It can even be hypothesized that the differences in individuals' performance in school are ultimately differences in metalinguistic ability. Here there is much need for research and workable knowledge of how and what to teach people about language that will help them use it to increase their own knowledge of the world. Here, too, is where metalinguistics and pragmatics intersect. Knowledge about styles, modes, and structure of language is clearly connected to both metalinguistic and pragmatic knowledge. These areas of expertise can develop throughout life and must be given careful attention when one plans for language instruction. The teacher will never really provide anyone with language, but he or she can certainly help to provide an increased awareness of the way to use that language.

Summary

Language acquisition and development can be seen as rule-bound activities. Children strive to learn the grammar of their linguistic community by a process of forming linguistic hypotheses and testing them out on others. The claim has been made that this capacity is innate and coded in the gene structure of humans. This capacity for language is a uniform one possessed by all undamaged human beings and is unmatched by any other species. By and large, language everywhere is acquired via the same invariant stages and is processed by the same kinds of operations; this suggests that language production is dominated by some mechanism dependent on deep structures that undergo any number of transformations before an utterance is delivered in its surface form. Language comprehension works in the opposite direction, deriving deep structure from its surface forms.

Language arts teachers need to be aware of the effect they can have on the development of a child's language. They must make children aware of the power of language as a tool for personal, professional, and global communication. This knowledge is what linguists slightly mystify with the name *pragmatics,* which simply means the effective and appropriate use of language.

Another area in which teachers can make an impact is metalinguistic awareness. Increased familiarity with the workings of language makes its use that much more adept, in the same way that knowledge of the way a sewing machine or car works can improve a user's performance. There are, of course, many ways to approach metalinguistics in the classroom. Beware of the pedantic teacher who thinks children need to know tedious structural rules merely for their own sake. Language instruction can be a joy. For example, etymology is by nature fascinating, as is exercise of the human facility for punning and otherwise joking with words. Believing that language arts is a dull subject is like believing that the telephone's best use is as a paperweight.

Suggested Classroom Projects and Questions for Discussion

Projects

1. Observe children in classrooms to determine the types of language expansion activities that are provided.
2. Visit primary and intermediate classrooms to observe the different language structures that exist in the language of children at various age levels.
3. Analyze language lessons in language arts programs to determine the competencies that are being promoted.
4. Compare the language structures in basal readers to determine whether they are similar to those of the students who are reading them.
5. Listen to parents and their children to determine whether there are similar structures in their language patterns.
6. Listen to the language of those around you to determine which of Halliday's language functions they are employing.
7. Prepare language activities that will expand the language patterns of second language learners.
8. Listen to the television programs designed for children to determine the language expansion activities that are being presented.
9. Visit a local game store to determine whether there are appropriate language games available for your students.
10. Record your own language to become familiar with the way it sounds to your students.

Questions

1. How do language experts suggest that language is acquired?
2. What is the role of the parent and home environment in language development?
3. Are first and second languages acquired in a similar manner?
4. Why is it important that a grammar be both descriptive and explanatory?
5. Explain the way children develop morphemic knowledge.
6. When children enter school, is their language a reflection of experience or potential? Please explain through example.
7. Discuss the concept of language flexibility and its relation to Halliday's functions of language.
8. What are appropriate general goals for an elementary school language arts curriculum?
9. What is the role of the classroom teacher in the language expansion process?
10. Why should teachers encourage students to try out many types of language?

PART III

COMPONENTS OF THE LANGUAGE ARTS PROGRAM

Chapter 5

Gaining Information Through Listening

(Photo by Linda Lungren)

OBJECTIVES

After reading this chapter, the student will be able to:

1. understand the importance of specific instruction in listening comprehension.
2. describe the various processes involved in listening and the relation of these elements to classroom instructions.
3. understand the relationship of listening skills to reading comprehension.
4. organize and manage a listening comprehension component of a language arts program.

Listening and Nonlistening

"Listen to me when I speak to you." "You're not listening." "Listen to this!" "If you'll just listen . . ." "Listen here . . ."

As teachers, parents, or former children we have all used these phrases or had them used on us. Certainly from the minute we are born, and quite possibly even before we are born, sounds influence us in diverse ways. The primary learning mode for infants and young children is auditory. By listening to environmental sounds and, most importantly, to the sounds of language, children develop cognitive schemata to serve as the basis of all they will come to know. By listening to the naming of items or emotions, children learn the basis of the language they will eventually process into speech. Although this early listening is indiscriminate and the processing that takes place is unsophisticated, it is nevertheless an essential beginning to the development of the intellect.

No one questions the importance of listening as a means of learning for all of us. Paul Rankin's (1926) pioneering study showed that high school students in Detroit spent 30 percent of the time they devote to language each day in speaking, 16 percent in reading, 9 percent in writing, and 45 percent in listening. Miriam Wilt (1959) more recently found that elementary school children spent about two and one-half hours of the five-hour school day in listening. This was nearly twice as much time as their teachers estimated the children spent in listening. Are these amounts of time similar for students in classrooms today? Some feel that in the usual classroom the chances are about sixty to one against any given pupil's speaking, compared to the possibility of others' speaking and a pupil's listening.

Undoubtedly, there is as wide an individual difference in the area of listening as in other skills. We speak of some people as being auditory-minded and of others as visual-minded. Speech and music teachers have long been aware of the differences among students in hearing specific sounds.

It has been suggested that some of these differences are culturally determined. Some sociologists explained the fact that boys in the elementary school are apt to have more reading problems than girls by the observations that in many families the mother talks more frequently with the little girl than with the little boy. The result of such "preferential" talking, according to the theory, is that girls are more advanced in language than boys of the same age, especially in the primary grades. In Japan, the exact opposite has been noticed. Little girls were long considered academically "inferior" until it was realized that boy children were getting much more attention at home and at school. In some classrooms, over 80 percent of the questions were being directed to the boys until the inequity was brought to the attention of the teachers.

In homes where parents not only talk to their children but listen as well, the listening skills of the children tend to be well developed. A child's opportunity to acquire good listening skills is improved when parents themselves are good listeners and good providers of listening material. In this regard, another cultural influence on listening is provided by radio and television. Kindergarten teachers are reporting that children come to school with a much wider knowledge than the curriculum assumes. In India, where there is a high degree of illiteracy, one might assume that the population would be relatively uninformed about world events. This, however, is not the case. The availability of free radios in many community teahouses has resulted in a surprisingly well-informed adult population.

What Is Listening?

As early as 1954 Brown suggested that the terms *hearing* and *listening* were both limited in meaning, and that the gerund *auding,* based on the neologic verb *to aud,* more accurately described the skill that concerns teachers. "Auding is to the ears what reading is to the eyes." If reading is the gross process of looking at, recognizing, and interpreting written symbols, auding may be defined as the gross process of listening to, recognizing, and interpreting spoken symbols. More recently Pearson and Fielding (1982) have helped expand this definition by suggesting that *to aud* means to listen with comprehension and appreciation.

Children *hear* the whistle of a train, the chirp of a bird, or the noise of traffic. They *listen* either passively or actively to a popular song or news broadcast. But when they listen attentively to a teacher to get directions, or to get facts from a classmate's report, or to understand two sides of a debate, they may be said to be *auding,* for they are listening to verbal symbols with comprehension and interpretation. Throughout this discussion, the term *listening* will be used in referring both to the response that Brown describes as auding and also to the other styles of listening.

Although a model of listening comprehension is useful to conceptualize this complex process, it is misleading to believe that each step occurs sequentially and in isolation. In most situations, an individual cannot disassociate hearing from listening and auding. With this in mind, it is still helpful to examine each of the general categories of listening (hearing, listening, and auding) more closely to provide us with specific areas on which to focus in the teaching of listening skills.

HEARING. *Auditory acuity* refers to the actual physical ability to hear. A person who is limited or lacking in auditory acuity is considered hearing impaired or deaf. There is, of course, little a classroom teacher can do to improve a student's ability to hear; however, by being aware of the symptoms of hearing difficulty, a teacher can assist a child in obtaining the help of a qualified audiologist. Often schools provide routine hearing screenings, but by observing a student's daily behavior, a teacher may be able to anticipate a hearing problem. Some of the symptoms of deficient auditory acuity are:

1. Difficulty in following simple directions.
2. Mispronunciation of known words.
3. Abnormally soft or loud speech.
4. Confusion.
5. Need for excessive volume on a tape recorder, TV, or record player.
6. Turning the head to one side or the other when listening, standing close, or otherwise straining to hear.

Certain environmental factors may aggravate certain physical hearing problems. *Auditory fatigue* takes place when the ears are subjected to a continuous barrage of loud, monotonous sounds—the beat of rock music, traffic noise, or heavy machinery. Although this sort of hearing loss is temporary, prolonged exposure to these sounds on the naked ear may cause permanent damage. As well as loud sounds, too many sounds may be disturbing at this most basic level of listening, that is, hearing. *Masking* occurs when the general hubbub becomes so loud it overtakes the specific listening experience. The phrase "I can't hear myself think" describes what occurs during masking. Many people with some hearing acuity loss find themselves tuning out when the noise level reaches a certain volume and density. It becomes too difficult for them to "hear" what they are "listening" to.

Another environmental factor that may impede hearing acuity results from attempting to focus on two or more conversations at once. This may cause a problem with the listener's *binaurality,* or ability, essentially, to listen with both ears. The inability to integrate the functioning of both ears may only be a problem in specific listening situations, but is a factor to be considered if a child appears confused in a multi-stimulus environment.

LISTENING. Once the ears have accomplished the task of receiving the sensory input of sound vibrations, it is up to the brain to transform these data into something intelligible and, potentially, useful to the individual. As in reading, during which little is achieved until the letter symbols on the page are translated into recognizable words and sentences, little is achieved by simply hearing sounds. The listener must begin processing this information by applying subconsciously and automatically the principles of auditory perception. These include auditory discrimination, blending, sequencing, and memory. These tasks must be performed before the listener even begins to apply the more cerebral operations of concentrating, focusing, and finally comprehending, even superficially, what the auditory organs have provided.

Proficient listening is dependent on an effective performance of each operation. If the listener is deficient in any one of these functions, less than optimal listening will be achieved.

Auditory Discrimination. Effective auditory discrimination is the ability to distinguish "significant sound 'bundles' " (Pearson and Fielding, 1982). Recognizing that *bit, bet, pet,* and *get* are all distinct phonological entities demonstrates accurate auditory discrimination. This skill is essential not only for listening comprehension but for any phonics-based program of reading or spelling instruction. Faulty auditory discrimination is also strongly related to mispronunciation and other speech difficulties, but it appears to be an acquired skill rather than a function of measured intelligence (Wepman, 1960). People with a good "ear" for language, such as actors who are proficient with dialects, mimics, or linguists who speak foreign languages with little or no accent, have a highly developed sense of auditory discrimination.

Children may be tested formally with the Wepman Auditory Discrimination Test (1973) or informally through a teacher-constructed measurement. In both cases the principle is the same. The student should be seated so that he or she can hear clearly but may not view either the words themselves or the lips of the person administering the test. Phonetically similar words are spoken in pairs and the child must state whether the words are the "same" or "different." Word pairs that test beginning sounds (*pig, big; hat, bat*), medial sounds (*bit, bet; pit, pet*), and final sounds (*buck, bug; muff, calf*) may be included. Heilman's handbook *Phonics in Proper Perspective* (1985) is an excellent resource for providing phonetic word lists.

Although auditory discrimination skills may be taught and drilled, formal instruction may not be necessary if teachers provide young children with a listening-rich environment. By exposing a child's ear to a variety of speaking styles, dialects, and even foreign languages, you develop a listening schema or mental framework that will help that child make the necessary auditory connections.

Auditory Analysis. The auditory analysis component of auditory perception encompasses various phonemic exercises, including intonation patterns, stress (intensity), and blending, all of which are recognized and incorporated continuously and unconsciously into the listening process.

A listener must be able to interpret rising and falling pitch to determine whether what is being said is a question, command, or simple statement. Such subtleties as irony, sarcasm, and very dry humor require sophisticated understanding of stress and intonation as well as a comprehension of the words and context. What many actors and comedians refer to as "timing," or the ability to carry off a joke, is largely based on their ability to use intonation and stress effectively. Listeners must be tuned into the nuances of pitch and stress in order to "get" the joke.

By placing emphasis on a word or part of a sentence, the speaker indicates what is being stressed in a sentence. For example

You're going to SELL the car?

is quite different from

YOU'RE going to sell the car?

In the first example the speaker may be thinking, "That car is such a piece of junk she should give it away," hence the stress on *SELL*. Alternatively, in the second example, the speaker's low opinion might be more about your ability as a salesperson.

Blending, or synthesis, involves the combining of individual letter sounds into meaningful word units. This is closely related to *juncture*, or the ability to determine where one word ends and another begins. When sounds are blended together, they must come out making sense in the context of what has been said. If they do not, then the sounds must be broken apart and analyzed before they are blended again to achieve comprehension.

For example:

"I scream at the movies."

may be misinterpreted as

"Ice cream at the movies."

This sort of listening miscue relates well to the sensation experienced in a reading miscue; the critical difference is that it is not always as easy to relisten as it is to reread when confusion occurs.

Auditory Sequencing and Memory. Closely related to blending and juncture, *auditory sequencing* is the operation of keeping sounds in their proper time sequence. An expanded form of blending, sequencing allows the listener to keep track of syntax by using the auditory memory essentially to put the perceived words on hold long enough to process them into comprehension. Auditory memory functions both instantaneously in the normal listening situation and in the long term to help us recall the sound of someone's voice, a complex piece of music, or a memorable or meaningful phrase that was heard or overheard. Comments such as "The song kept going through my mind" or "Her words came back to me again and again" are reminders of the power of auditory memory.

On a basic level, auditory sequencing and memory are the final links from listening to auding. Once the physical and technical components of the listening process are accomplished, the listener begins to understand the message and approaches the "cognitive leap" to auding.

Auding. Before taking this cognitive leap, the listener must first reach the intellectual ledge from which to jump. Again, this is accomplished systematically through a series of selections, comparisons, trials, and errors. As a teacher of language arts, you must be aware of the mental progression taking place in the minds of your students as they approach total listening comprehension. This awareness will help you to appreciate their puzzled looks and seemingly incessant questions. It will also help you to facilitate and anticipate their listening needs.

For our purposes, the comprehension process can be divided into three main areas (Figure 5–1):

1. Attention and code selection
2. Schema search and match
3. Comprehension

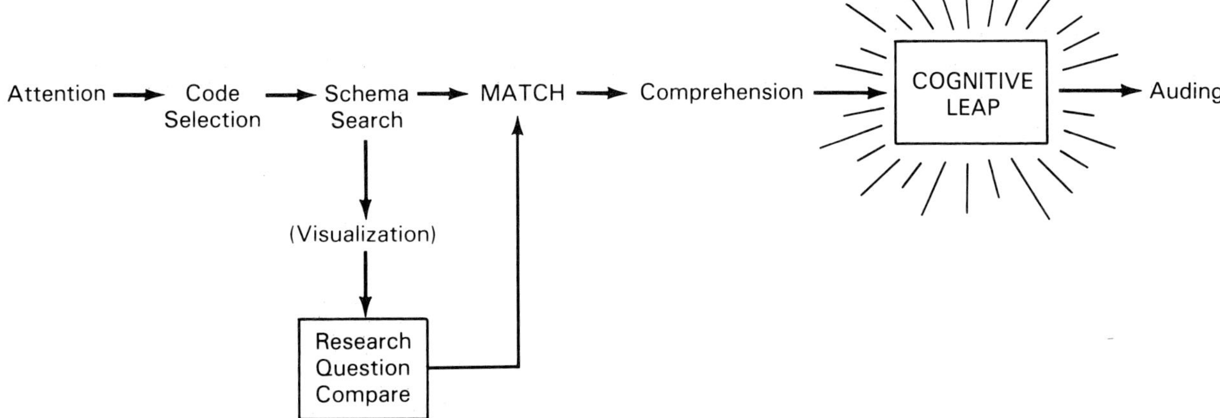

Figure 5–1. The comprehension process.

Attention and Code Selection. Attention makes the difference between hearing and listening. Attention is what brings the ears into "focus" so that sharp images may be picked out of the general buzz of auditory bombardment. Most teachers recognize all too well the glazed-over look of inattention that has often been referred to as being "tuned-out." To tune-in to what is being said requires a conscious commitment of attention and concentration. When a listener attends to a conversation or lecture, he or she begins the organizational process that produces comprehension.

Just as a proficient reader does not process every word, so a proficient listener selects those parts of the linguistic code that, upon analysis, yield the best return in terms of comprehension. According to Lundsteen (1979, p. 31), the listener makes selections not only against a background of noise but also from the stream of language. To phrase it linguistically, the user selects the most productive cues from surface structures, such as signals for the plural or the past tense. The language user can get to underlying structure and to language meaning, but avoid using every feature and relationship of every sound.

Code markers may include many of the elements discussed in the section on listening (intonation, stress, juncture, and so forth) as well as the body language of the speaker.

Schema Search and Match. Once focused on specific code units, the listener begins to decode the perceived sounds by attempting to match the particular configuration to sound configurations already in his experience. This auditory schema contains images and definitions of previously auded information. It is equivalent to a reader's internal lexicon. If the listener has previously heard and understood the code units, a match can be made and recognition and comprehension will occur.

Aiding in this search for understanding is the visualization mechanism. The phrase "I *see* what you mean" is not an accident of language. Words do paint pictures for us, and as we hear words spoken we instantly visualize what is being said. These images may indeed take the form of mental pictures, as when we listen to a competent storyteller draw us into a ghost story complete with cobwebs, rising mist, and supernatural apparitions. We may, however, visualize the words themselves as we search our auditory lexicon for meaning. Again, this phase of the listening process operates unconsciously and "as needed" to aid in comprehension of what is being heard.

If, however, the material is new or perhaps unremembered, visualization and schema searching may prove fruitless. The listener must then do some research to complete the process and arrive at comprehension. This research, depending on the listening situation, may include asking direct clarification questions of the speaker, requesting a rephrasing of the idea expressed, or simply asking the speaker to repeat the remark. Some situations—lectures, radio and television dialogue, song lyrics—cannot be easily researched. Unless there is an opportunity to record and replay these situations, a listener may just choose to quit attending until a word or phrase pulls the attention back to what is being said.

Quite often a schema match is impeded not because the listener is unfamiliar with what is being said, but because it is being phrased or pronounced in an unfamiliar manner. Speakers with an accent or pronounced dialect may be using known words that are not immediately recognizable. The inarticulate speech of young children and people afflicted with speech impediments also creates challenges for the listener. In these cases, a listener must compare both phonetic cues and contextual cues to his or her auditory schema until a match is achieved. Once the listener recognizes the pattern (if there is one) of unfamiliar pronunciation, it becomes easier to predict the meaning of what is being said. For example, a young child may say, "It nooks nike a yenow banoon." Once it is perceived that the child pronounces *n* for *l*, the code is broken and the gibberish clearly becomes "It looks like a yellow balloon."

There are, of course, instances when the speaker's message is so difficult or garbled that no amount of searching, researching, or comparing will produce a schema match. This results in listener frustration, tuning-out, and, during a lecture, lots of doodling.

Comprehension and the Cognitive Leap. Comprehension here refers to the literal understanding of the oral message. The sounds have been perceived, attended to, and matched to existing schema or to newly created schema, and the listener can now nod her head and say, "Yes, OK, I understand what has been said." At this level of comprehension, your students will "get by," they will "do nicely," but really they will not advance much intellectually. To achieve the desired state—total, complete understanding—indeed to achieve auding, they must go beyond OK. They must go to "A-ha!" The lightbulb must click on and their faces must light up with "thinking beyond listening" (Lundsteen, 1979). They must take that cognitive leap that takes them past comprehension to *meaning* in all its forms. When auding is achieved, the listener becomes aware of not only what has been said, but its relation on a personal level, a societal level, and a cosmic level. Comparisons can be made, and ramifications can be explored and discussed. Creative thinking can begin and intellectual gains can be made.

Types of Listening

Having explored the process of proficient listening from the simple to the sublime, we must emphasize that not every auditory situation requires deep thinking or cosmic leaping.

Different types of listening are really different degrees of involvement. Some activities call for much less involvement to be satisfying than do others that demand a higher degree of concentration.

1. Hearing sounds of words but not reacting to the ideas expressed: a mother knows that Daryl is speaking.
2. Intermittent listening—turning the speaker on and off: hearing one idea in a sermon but none of the rest of it.
3. Half listening—following the discussion only well enough to find an opportunity to express your own idea: listening to a conversation to find a place to describe the way you handled a student.
4. Listening passively with little observable response: the student knows the teacher is telling him once again how to walk in the hall.
5. Narrow listening in which the main significance or emphasis is lost as the listener selects details that are familiar or agreeable to him: a good Democrat listening to a candidate from another party.
6. Listening and forming associations with related items from one's own experiences: a first-grade student hears the beginning sound of *Sally, says,* and *said* and relates it to the letter *s.*
7. Listening to a report to discover main ideas and supporting details or follow directions: listening to the rules and descriptions of a new spelling game.
8. Listening critically: a listener notices the emotional appeal of words in a radio advertisement.
9. Appreciative and creative listening with genuine mental and emotional response: a child listens to the teacher read *Miracle on Maple Hill* and shares the excitement of sugar making.

These levels overlap, but they do describe listening with respect to situations that teachers know. In the classroom it is possible to guide student listening so that their auding may be selective, purposeful, accurate, critical, and creative, just as we guide growth in the skills of reading. A format for such instruction seems especially applicable today.

A. Social listening
   1. Listening courteously and attentively to conversation in social situations with a purpose (K–8).
   2. Understanding the roles of the speaker and listener in the communication process (K–8).

B. Secondary listening
  1. Listening to music that accompanies rhythms or folk dances (K–8).
  2. Enjoying music while participating in certain types of school activities such as painting, working with clay, sketching, and handwriting practice (K–8).

C. Aesthetic listening
  1. Listening to music, poetry, choral reading, or drama heard on radio or on recordings (K–8).
  2. Enjoying stories, poems, riddles, jingles, and plays as read or told by the teacher or pupils (K–8).

D. Critical listening
  1. Noting correct speech habits, word usage, and sentence elements of others (K–8).
  2. Listening to determine the reason why (1–8).
  3. Listening to understand meanings from context clues (1–8).
  4. Listening to distinguish between fact and fancy, relevance and irrelevance (1–8).
  5. Listening to draw inferences (1–8).
  6. Listening to make judgments (1–8).
  7. Listening to find new or additional information on a topic (2–8).
  8. Listening to find the answers to specific questions that require selectivity and concentration (4–8).
  9. Listening to interpret idioms anad unusual language (5–8).
  10. Listening objectively and appraisingly to determine authenticity or the presence of bias and inaccuracies (5–8).

E. Concentrative listening (a study-type listening)
  1. Listening to follow directions (K–8).
  2. Perceiving relationships such as class, place, quantity, time, sequence, and cause and effect (4–8).
  3. Listening for a definite purpose to elicit specific items of information (4–8).
  4. Attaining understanding through intent listening (4–8).
  5. Listening for sequence of ideas (4–8).
  6. Perceiving a speaker's or a group's main objective and organization of ideas (4–8).
  7. Taking notes of important facts (4–8).

F. Creative listening
  1. Associating meanings with all kinds of listening experiences (K–8).
  2. Constructing visual images while listening (K–8).
  3. Adapting imagery from imaginative thinking to create new results in writing, painting, and dramatizing (1–8).
  4. Listening to arrive at solutions for problems as well as checking and verifying the results of the problems solved (4–8).

Strategies for Teaching Good Listening Habits

Good listening habits involve not only thinking with the speaker but also anticipating the direction of his thoughts, objectively evaluating the verbal evidence offered in terms of the speaker's purpose (rather than arguing with it item by item as it is presented), and reviewing mentally some of the facts presented. Taking notes of ideas or phrases helps many people. There are others who find note taking a distraction. Some report that they find the ideas in their notes rather than in their heads. Brief summaries are probably better than detailed stenographic reports. This kind of critical listening must be done often and well. It has been shown by Giannangelo and Frazer (1975) that the necessary skills can be taught. Teachers bear the responsibilty to provide opportunities for this kind of learning.

Many bad habits develop in the listening area. Both children and adults have a way of avoiding difficult or unpleasant listening. Every parent knows the "Surely, he is not talking about me!" attitude of a child who is being corrected. Emotions interfere with listening to ideas: "Who is he to be saying that?" "They will never convince me that those ugly things are art" and "How would she know; she's never been a mother!" are emotional statements that reveal limited reception.

It is interesting to note the wide variation of responses to a distraction in a classroom. A lawnmower operating outside the window or music being played in the next room will command the complete attention of some and be ignored by others. Some individuals have a habit of seeking distraction even though they may be interested in the speaker or topic.

The expression of ego is as obvious in listening as it is in the constant use of *I* in speech. This is especially obvious in little children. A teacher or speaker may be telling about a trip to Europe or showing a cowboy lariat. A hand will pop up and a child will volunteer, "Tomorrow is my birthday" or "We have some baby chickens at our house." For some this is an innocent way to "say something, too." Usually it is an indication of a lack of interest in others. Adults will be listening or participating in a conversation about a topic, then suddenly one will say, "I think I'll have my hair done tomorrow" or "When do we eat?" or there may be a not too subtle attempt to impress, as in "When I was in Mexico," or "The President said to my cousin."

The responsibility of the listener should be discussed. There is the point of courtesy to a speaker that all children understand: "You listen to me and I will listen to you." Listening for meaning is just as important as reading for meaning. A listener may *disagree* but should not *misinterpret*. Causes of misinterpretation might be discussed with benefit to both speaker and listener.

The attitude of the teacher toward listening will influence students. Teaching is as much listening as telling. We listen to discover interests and needs. Those trained in nondirective guidance know the importance of the therapist's being able to listen. The psychologist listens a great deal as the patient talks. A good salesman listens to discover what customers want. The wise teacher listens to encourage the expression of children. At times a teacher listens because a student, or parent, needs an audience for a personal concern. The following suggestions will help in such situations:

1. Be sure to listen to your students. When someone is troubled or needs to talk, give him the time if at all possible. It will help clarify communication between you.
2. Encourage your students to listen to each other.
3. Always be attentive. Let tirades flow uninterrupted. Try to indicate that you want to understand.
4. Try to employ positive verbal reactions only—"Hm-m-m," "Oh," or "I see." Remain silent, nodding to show understanding. If the talker is unreasonable, restate what he said, putting it in the form of a question.
5. Never probe for additional facts. There is a difference between willingness to listen and curiosity. Your purpose in therapeutic listening is seldom to obtain information.
6. Be careful to avoid evaluating what has been said. Avoid moral judgments and the temptation to advise. The speaker is clarifying his problem through talking and then must define alternative solutions.
7. Encourage children to solve their own problems. The speakers are really talking things over with themselves as they talk with you.

Start instruction in listening by establishing standards for good listening habits. The discussion might be centered about situations in which listening is important: You are a waiter taking an order; you are to go to the principal's office with a message and return with his; you are to interview a famous person; you are to report on a news broadcast. These imaginative exercises could lead to an inventory of listening habits. A checklist or classroom wall chart like the following may be used:

1. Do I get ready to listen?
2. Do I give the speaker my attention?

3. Do I think with the speaker?
4. Can I select the main idea?
5. Can I recall topics in order?
6. Can I follow directions?
7. Can I retell what I hear?

Children learn from discussions of this nature that a good listener is polite, gets the facts, listens thoughtfully, listens for a reason, and makes intelligent use of what is heard.

What Is the Relationship Between Listening and Reading?

A review of the literature regarding the correlation between listening and reading (Jolly, 1980) indicates that because of the many shared skills in each process, instruction in one facilitates learning in the other. Research among fourth graders has indicated that specific training in listening skills resulted in improved reading comprehension scores (Hoffman, 1978; Lemons and Moore, 1982). How, then, do these two aspects of communication interrelate?

Both reading and listening require the learner to have a readiness for accomplishment. This includes mental maturity, vocabulary, ability to follow sequence of ideas, and an interest in language.

Listening in some respects is more difficult than reading. In the process of reading, a strange word may be the signal to stop, look at other words in the sentence or pictures on the page, or refer to the glossary. In listening, this is not possible. One must make a hasty guess as the speaker continues and rethink what the speaker has said while keeping up with the current ideas being spoken. Most college students know the experience expressed by a freshman when he commented, "I was with him until he mentioned the macrocephalic measurement; then he lost me." Children too have their frustration level in listening. The tuned-out look familiar to teachers can be a signal about either the interest level or the difficulty of what is being said.

The fact that we listen from six to ten times faster than a person can talk means that dedicated concentration must be practiced in some listening situations to avoid distractions. The printed page demands attention and can be read at a rate equal to that of our mental reactions. In listening this happens only if listeners discipline themselves to attend to what the speaker is saying. Interruptions of an oral explanation by a classroom visitor, outside noises, or any disruptive incident mean that the explanation must be repeated. Once listening is accepted as important, the learner must accept the responsibility of putting forth an active listening effort to learn. This activity should approach the effort to gain information from reading.

One element that makes listening more difficult than reading is that a person usually listens for the main idea rather than specific parts. In reading, one has a record of the specifics and usually remembers where they may be found. In listening, the speaker has designed the material to highlight a major idea that the audience is to remember. To do this a speaker uses facts, stories, and emotional appeals. These are recalled only if the listener relates them to the total effect of the talk. Political speeches and college lectures are good examples: a person may tell a friend that he heard a good speech or lecture, but when asked what was said may be able to recall only that it was "about brotherhood."

Related to this is the problem of listening to a discussion or conversation. Such speech is frequently disorganized, as the speakers explore various ideas or aspects of a topic. Strange to say, people seem to remember as much or more from such situations as from a well-organized lecture. Apparently the careful organization and fixed pattern lull some listeners into a comfortable enjoyment that is less involving than the disorganized rambling that permits or requires involvement with random changes of topic or subject matter.

In general, the purposes of reading and auding are both functional and appreciative. In functional reading and auding, students are concerned with finding facts, getting a general idea, following directions, or putting the material to work in some way. In appreciative reading and auding, students are ready to enjoy a selection for its own sake—a story for its humor or a poem for its expression. Students may also combine function and appreciation in reading or listening with a view to creating a dramatization.

In both reading and auding, the word is not usually the unit of comprehension, but it affects comprehension of the phrase, the sentence, and the paragraph. Students must hear certain key words clearly (*world* versus *whirled*) if they are to understand an oral passage, and they must see them clearly (*bond* versus *board*) if they are to read them exactly. But along with exact perception in both activities must go understanding

Table 5–1
Strategies for Becoming Effective Listeners

Listening Goal	*Reading Activity*
1. To discriminate and locate phonetic and structural elements of the spoken word.	Use selections with rhyming words.
2. To discover and to identify sounds, words, or ideas new to the listener.	Close eyes and identify sounds—man-made as well as natural. The tape recorder can be used. After listening, identify
3. To listen for details in order to interpret the main idea and to respond accurately.	the main idea with details radiating from it.
4. To listen to a selection for the purpose of answering a previously stated question.	
5. To listen for the main idea when stated in the topic or key sentence.	Have the key sentence occur in various positions.
6. To discriminate between spoken fact and opinion.	Listen to selections. Students write *Fact* or *Opinion*. Discussion and reading to verify should follow.
7. To distinguish between relevant and irrelevant details.	List relevant details in one column and irrelevant ones in another.
8. To listen to select the type of writing: narrative, descriptive, or expositive.	Use various sentences and paragraphs. Students select type.
9. To listen to music to determine mood.	After listening, select and discuss words that could be used to reflect the same mood.
10. To listen to poetry or prose to determine mood.	After listening, select and discuss words and phrases that were used to set mood.
11. To listen in order to visualize a scene.	After listening, draw the scene. Follow this by reading to verify the visual concept. Discuss.
12. To determine oral story sequence.	a. Ask for the sequence of events for a paragraph heard. b. Listen to a story and act out the story sequentially (possibly with puppets).
13. To list the stated facts used to obtain an inference.	Stated facts ____________ Inference ____________ ____________
14. To listen in order to understand space and time relationships.	
15. To associate descriptive ideas heard with more concrete objects and life situations.	Listen to descriptions of familiar people and determine the identities.
16. To draw conclusions or form opinions based on facts heard.	Use discussions on a topic followed by conclusions drawn. Group decides the validity of conclusions.
17. To recognize bias.	Use the tape recorder and reproductions of speeches and commercials. What indicates the bias? Are *all* facts given?

of word meaning. The grasp and interpretation of both oral and written paragraphs depend on understanding the meaning of individual words in their context and in varied relationships.

In both reading and auding, the unit of comprehension is either the phrase, the sentence, or the paragraph—rather than the single word. Comprehension is aided if the speaker or writer avoids common errors of pronounciation, spelling, and usage. Both reading and auding make use of signals in the form of written or oral punctuation.

In addition to an exact understanding of a sentence or passage, both reading and auding may involve critical or creative interpretation of the material. In both situations the receiver may critically question the reliability of the source, the relevance of the argument, or the emotive power of the language employed. In both cases the receiver may utilize his previous experiences to combine the materials into some fresh, original, and personal interpretation.

Reading and auding may take place in either individual or social situations. Critical, analytical activities often flourish best in the individual situation; creative and appreciative reactions, under the stimulus of the group situation. Analysis of the propaganda devices in a political speech is easier when the printed version of the speech is read in a quiet room than when a speaker delivers it in a crowded hall. Conversely, appreciation of the choral reading of a poem may be heightened by an enthusiastic group response.

In order to improve reading, each listening skill should be followed by its reading counterpart. As students advance, the material used for these activities should necessarily become more difficult in order to meet their growing needs. The listening-reading skills must be approached through direct and indirect instruction, with more emphasis on the direct than has been the practice in recent years.

Table 5–1 is a list of listening goals that aid in the development of all levels of listening. Reading activities for accomplishing these goals are also presented in an attempt to help you to develop lessons that provide the integration of listening and reading.

What Is Systematic Listening Instruction?

Organization and planning are the keys to a systematic approach to instruction in any subject. As in reading, math, social studies, physical education, art, or virtually any area of endeavor, a teacher must (1) diagnose student strengths and weaknesses, (2) teach to those needs, and (3) evaluate progress to determine the effectiveness of the measures taken.

Because listening is an integral part of every other activity included in the language arts curriculum, opportunities to teach listening skills abound. It is important to remember to teach listening skills systematically and not incidentally. When planning other lessons, incorporate listening activities into your plans. Additionally, set aside time that is only for listening. Assign listening projects as homework. Provide your students with the opportunity for becoming good listeners; the personal, social, academic, and creative benefits are enormous.

Diagnosing Listening Skills

There are both formal and informal instruments of measurement for diagnosing listening skills. Formal instruments include standardized, norm-referenced tests such as the Illinois Test of Psycholinguistic Ability (ITPA) and the Wepman Auditory Discrimination Test. These tests have been administered to a large representative population, and the results have been analyzed to determine the range and distribution of performance levels on the skills being tested. Percentile rankings are developed, and these can provide guidelines for prescriptive instruction. Standardized tests are widely used for testing reading skills. They may be quite useful for determining student needs based on areas of high and low performance. See Table 5–2 for a list of standardized listening comprehension tests.

Informal nonstandardized instruments for determining listening habits and skills can be made by the teacher and by the students. Surveys, checklists, and

Table 5–2
Diagnostic Tools for Listening Comprehension Group Tests—Standardized

Name	*Grade Level*	*Subtests*	*Cautions*
STEP (Sequential Test of Educational Progress)	4–college	Main idea Details and sequences Word meaning	Some reading involved; some items may be answered without listening completely
Cooperative Primary Test	1–3	Words, sentences, stories, poems, picture identification	
Durrell Listening Reading Series	1–9	Compares reading and listening abilities	Requires some reading on child's part
ITPA (Illinois Test of Psycholinguistic Ability)	Preschool–4	Auditory decoding, auditory—vocal association, auditory—vocal automatic, ability and sequencing	
Wepman Auditory Discrimination Test	K–4	Ability to discriminate changes in frequency, intensity, auditory pairs	
Brown-Carlsen Listening Comprehension Test	9–13 (college)	Immediate recall Following directions Recognition transition Word meaning Lecture comprehension	

Reprinted from S. Lundsteen, *Listening: Its Impact at All Levels on Reading and Other Language Arts*. Urbana, Ill.: Published 1979 by the ERIC Clearinghouse on Reading and Communication Skills and the National Council of Teachers of English. Reprinted by permission.

observation all fall into the category of informal assessments. Teachers may wish to make checklists for listening behavior and periodically assess students by observing, in a given time frame, which characteristics of good listening habits they employ, for example, following directions easily and correctly, responding to oral stimuli with proper body language, looking interested, asking appropriate questions, and making statements pertinent to the oral discussion. Students may wish to assess their own listening behavior by keeping listening diaries or evaluating listening experiences in survey or checklist form. (See Table 5–3 from Lundsteen, 1979, p. 91.) Teachers may also adapt informal reading inventories to test listening skills. These are taken from graded textbooks and can be used to determine a listening comprehension grade level. By asking questions regarding main idea, details, sequencing, and unaided recall, much can be learned about a student's listening proficiency.

Listening is pervasive. It is a part of almost everything we do; we even, at times, "listen" to ourselves think. Because of this pervasiveness, it would be quite easy to say that in teaching everything else in the language arts area, we also teach listening. This is a true statement up to a point. Much can be accomplished if we simply focus on the listening skills inherent in each subject area and incorporate specific listening skills and techniques in the teaching of these subjects. Even more will be achieved if the students are made aware of the importance of careful listening.

Table 5–3
Checklist of Listening Roadblocks

Hearing

1. I often have trouble hearing what people say. ( )
2. The speaker talked too softly. ( )
3. The speaker talked loudly enough, but not clearly. ( )
4. The room was too noisy: ( )
   The noise came from (a) people around me ( )
   (b) outside the building ( )
   (c) the hall ( )
   (d) other sources (explain) ( )

Listening

1. I didn't pay attention because I wasn't interested. ( )
2. I didn't pay attention because I was thinking about what I was going to say. ( )
3. The speaker or sounds began before I got settled. ( )
4. I was thinking about other things (explain). ( )
5. I missed some and could not figure out what was going on. ( )
6. I got wrapped up like a cocoon in my own argument and planning. ( )
7. I couldn't understand, so I quit listening. ( )
   a. I couldn't find anything I already knew about to match up with what was said. ( )
   b. I couldn't summarize in my own words. ( )
8. It was hard to keep up because I couldn't figure out what might come next. ( )
9. I listened like a sponge. I got so concerned with details I could not tell the main part from what was just supporting. ( )

Vocabulary

1. These words or sounds were new to me: (1) ________ (2) ________ (3) ________ (4) ________ (5) ________
2. I thought the word ______ meant ______.

Skills or things I think I do well in when I'm listening or am showing improvement in are:

Reprinted from Lundsteen, op. cit., 1979, p. 91. Reprinted by permission.

Preparing to Listen. Being in the mood to listen is crucial to learning. Causes of inattentiveness are as varied as individuals; however, Otto and Smith (1980) attribute "nonlistening" to four major causes: (1) poor student motivation, (2) excessive teacher talk, (3) physical distractions, and (4) lack of mental set for anticipating a speaker's message.

Perhaps the very first step toward better listening skills must be taken before the students enter the classroom. It is essential that the physical environment be as free from distractions as possible.

Proper ventilation and lighting, comfortable chairs, attractive materials, and low levels of noise "pollution" from outside sources are all important to a pleasant physical environment. Methods of improving the social and emotional environment are components of any beneficial language activity and will be discussed later in the chapter. The concrete physical environment can be altered to complement any activity if the class is fortunate enough to have lightweight chairs and desks. Modern furniture and a tolerant custodial staff enable a class to make frequent changes of seating arrangements. Horseshoe and semicircular seatings stimulate learning when visual and auditory perception is possible, as in any presentation to a group. Students enjoy creating new seating patterns and can be solicited for ideas and energy. These arrangements also accommodate variations in hearing acuity.

The use of listening posts and the tape recorder has provided substantial aid in teaching listening and speaking. Records, tape cassettes, and reels are valuable accessories; they provide stories, instructions for exercises, and commercials and reports to evaluate. Other materials children will enjoy include signs, decorations, displays, and, of course, books. Along with stimulating materials teachers must provide the freedom for boys and girls to use them and share their experiences.

> . . . the present educational set-up does the best it can to discourage the use of ears. The teacher, anxious to give the child a good start, repeats information and directions so many times that the child learns to expect such recapitulation. (DiSibio, 1982, p. 217)

The use of listening posts and the tape recorder has provided substantial aid in teaching listening and speaking. (Photo by Linda Lungren)

Constant repetition of instructions and talking *at* the students are forms of teacher talk that need to be minimized or eliminated. By making it clear from the first day of school that students are *expected* to listen, you will have an easier time *getting* them to listen. Gold (1981) suggests that by providing a specific purpose for listening (for example, "After I read the story to you, name everything that was the same color as the balloon"), you can minimize your teacher talk as well as motivate your students to listen.

Preparing your students for listening may take many creative forms. It is important that they be made aware of the power of accurate, purposeful listening. Here are some suggestions for creating a good mental set for listening:

1. Help your students create a vocabulary to use in describing sounds. For young children words like *squeak, buzz, hum, croak*—words that reproduce the sound (onomatopoeia)—are useful. For older students use words like *bellowing, timorous, resonant, clamorous, cacophony, grating,* and *hubbub*. Create a classroom "sound" vocabulary by playing tapes of various sounds and asking the students to compile a list of descriptive words. By being aware of the need to use words to describe sounds, students will become more conscious of the sounds they hear and will listen more closely.
2. State your intentions clearly before giving an oral assignment or test: "I will say the word once now and once when the test is over." "Listen carefully to these directions. I will say them only once."
3. At the beginning of the day ask each student to describe something he or she heard on the way to school.
4. To start a listening lesson or to begin the school day, play a record or tape of sounds or music to start the children thinking about listening.

In their review of research on listening comprehension, Pearson and Fielding (1982) have made the following suggestions for guidelines in teaching listening skills:

1. Teach the same skills for listening as you do for reading (main idea, supporting details, sequencing, drawing conclusions, differentiating fact from fantasy, poetry, and so on).
2. Elicit active verbal responses from the children during and after listening activities.
3. Expose your students to literature by reading classic stories to them or by playing records, tapes, or video cassettes.
4. Use writing and reading comprehension work to benefit listening skills.

5. Giving direct instructions helps the children become more aware of the importance of listening closely.

The examples in Unit 1, Inferring Word Meanings (Laird, 1981), illustrate the implementation of effective listening instruction.

Unit 1: Inferring Word Meanings

Instructions and Example

In this unit, you will hear selections that each contain an unfamiliar or a "nonsense" word. After you have listened carefully to the way the word is used in each selection, you will hear four words or phrases. Write the number of the word or phrase that best tells the meaning of the word or what it is like.

Here is an example to help you learn what to do. This is a selection about *ponderous* animals. Listen to it carefully.

> Mammoths were ponderous animals. Dinosaurs were ponderous, too. Because they were ponderous, these animals left deep footprints in the mud when they walked near water holes.

Write the number of the word or phrase that best tells what *ponderous* means.

1. plant-eating
2. prehistoric
3. very heavy
4. four-footed

Number 3 is the correct answer. Dinosaurs and mammoths were plant-eating, prehistoric, four-footed animals. But none of these answers tells why they would leave deep footprints. The phrase *very heavy* is a definition of the word *ponderous*.

Listen to the following selection about *ambrosia*.

> According to the Greek and Roman myths, the favorite food of the gods was ambrosia. They ate ambrosia at every meal, taking it with them on their travels. The gods liked to eat ambrosia because it was so sweet and delicious.

Write the number of the word that best tells what *ambrosia* is like.

1. vinegar
2. spinach
3. honey
4. turnip

Listen to the following selection about *pachyderms*.

Pachyderms are large, thick-skinned mammals. All pachyderms have hooves. Some pachyderms have tusks and big, floppy ears. Another type of pachyderm has a horn on its snout. Most pachyderms are found in the jungle, but some spend much of their time in river waters.

Write the number of the phrase that best tells what *pachyderms* are.

1. unicorns, crocodiles, or pigs
2. dogs, tortoises, or bulls
3. zebras, whales, or giraffes
4. elephants, hippopotamuses, or rhinoceroses*

Lessons of this type provide the student with instruction, examples, and practice exercises.

TEACHING SPECIFIC SKILLS. The following are some ideas for teaching various areas of listening comprehension.

Auditory Perception, Memory, and Sequencing.

1. Word games based on initial, medial, and final sounds are excellent for developing auditory discrimination skills. Read (or record) lists of words that are all similar in the desired sound. Every so often put in a word that does not belong there (examples—*p:* pat, pot, pin, bat, pat; *m:* mat, mom, mitt, nat; *at:* pen, pat, mat, gnat). Have the students raise their hand, write on paper, or call out the word that is out of place.
2. "I pack my grandmother's trunk" is a game that can be adapted to many auditory skills. Essentially it is a memory and sequence game, but by imposing other phonetic restrictions (all words must rhyme, must start with *t,* must end in *n,* etc.), any number of skills can be reinforced. Each child must offer a word (item) that goes in grandma's trunk but must first recite all the items that have already been "packed" by the preceding students.
3. Have children work in pairs with a tape recorder. One child records a series of word pairs (or a sentence) while the other listens. They replay the tape so the listener can hear the words again, and then the listener repeats what has been said. The two children listen again to both their voices and check to see whether the listener got it right. They then switch roles. This can be used for memory and sequencing by not allowing the listener to replay the recorded words before attempting to repeat them onto the tape.
4. Unscramble sentences. When using simple sentences for easy retention, mix up the syntax of the sentence. Students must then attempt to reshuffle the words to the correct order. For longer sentences use written material or recordings so they may be replayed.
5. Obtain or record your own tapes of sounds associated with various activities or times of day: breakfast sounds, walking to school sounds, traffic noises, restaurant sounds, playground or lunchroom noises, night sounds, etc. Play these for the children and have them identify the component sounds. For a lot of fun, turn on the recorder when the children first come into the room. They will enjoy identifying their own voices and those of their classmates.

* Laird, S. *Listening Comprehension Skills Kit,* Level B. Mass.: Curriculum Associates, 1981. © 1981, Curriculum Associates, Inc. Reproduced by permission.

For children with special problems in auditory perception, there are many commercial programs that may be available through resource personnel. The following materials may be useful for any child experiencing auditory perception difficulties.

Scholastic Listening Skills. Unit I: *Easy Ears.* Unit II: *Earpower* (H. Benham, ed.). New York: N.Y.: Scholastic Book Services, 1977.

Auditory Perceptual Enhancement Program, Volume 1–4. Tulsa, Okla: Modern Corporation, 1978.

DLM Auditory Perception Training Program. Niles, Ill: Developmental Learning Materials, 1980.

Listening to the World, by R. Goldman and M. E. Lynch. Circle Pines, Minn.: America Guidance Service, 1980.

Visualization and Schema Input

1. Play music and ask students to close their eyes and "see" what the music is about. Discuss their visual images and let them draw pictures or express their feelings with splashes of color. They may even wish to make marks on a page as they listen—smooth lines for soothing portions and slashes, dots, or zigzags to "describe" other parts of the music.
2. To educate their ears to other dialects and ways of speaking, play tapes for your students. Make this exercise literary by using portions of Shakespeare's plays, the tales of Uncle Remus, or recitations of ethnic poetry. Taped interviews and foreign actors or diplomats provide students the opportunity to hear English is spoken with a variety of accents. By "tuning in" on these deviations from standard English, your students will be more receptive and accepting of people who are struggling to master English.
3. On field trips, around the school and in the classroom, discuss the auditory elements of the environment. Make semantic maps of related information (see Figure 5–2).

Attention and Beyond. Just about any experience in life adds to a child's auditory schemata. What is most important, and perhaps most difficult, is to spark students' interest and gain their attention.

There is no more attentive listener than the student who asks a question that truly concerns him. These are probably the most "teachable moments" in any classroom. Choosing the question to ask a visitor or the principal or when planning material before a unit sets the stage for careful listening. Before oral reading, attention is assured if students are listening in order to answer a question. A good storywriter builds this interest or suspense into plots. Usually the reason readers get involved in a story is that they want to know how a problem will be solved.

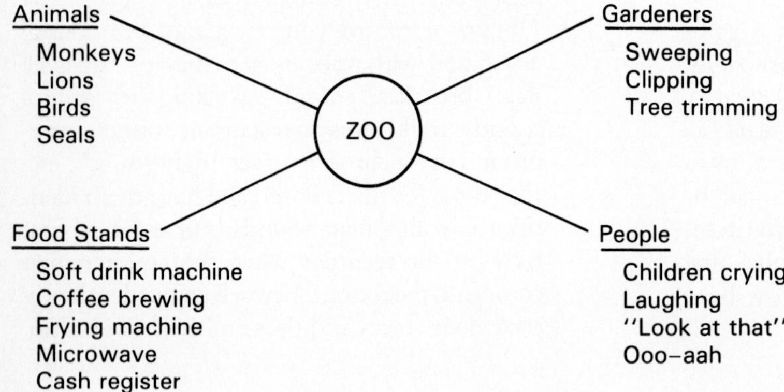

Figure 5–2. Semantic map: at the zoo.

In the classroom the language arts teacher wants to be sure that the listening experience will be worth the student's time and effort. The sharing period can be used to this purpose by asking students to think first of their audience and the way they want the audience to respond. This time may be considered valuable simply as a spontaneous period of free expression. At the beginning, that may be its purpose. But such items as "I have a new brother" or "Our cat had kittens" belong in the free conversational exchange of children rather than the crowded school curriculum. The following suggestions provide the same practice in language, but add a concern for the listeners:

1. Share the signs of the change of a season noted while going to and from school.
2. Share events that happened at home or play that were pleasant or humorous.
3. Share the most important event of a trip.
4. Share one toy by telling about it or demonstrating its use.
5. Share some good or kind act that a person has done.
6. Share the local or national news. Some classrooms have a television committee, a radio committee, and a picture committee. These students report events they have learned from those sources. In the intermediate grades, some teachers provide the clippings from which students select their reports. Others give a little quiz at the end of the week on the news reported. Sometimes better preparation will result if the listeners may ask one question about a report. Two standards should apply: the news must be told rather than being read orally, and it must not concern crime.
7. Share something an individual has made.
8. Share a riddle or joke (after first checking with the teacher).
9. Share a fact or interesting bit of knowledge about a bird, rock, stamp, coin, insect, star, airplane, seashell, object from a foreign land, book, or "believe-it-or-not" item.
10. Share a new word and its meaning or history. This might be a word in a foreign language if there are children from homes where a foreign language is spoken.

Material shared is better if children have to plan ahead a little. Students may sign on the chalkboard today for sharing tomorrow, or each row or cluster may have a day that is their sharing day. The teacher is responsible for the quality of material shared in literature. If students are to listen to material read, it should be material that offers true enrichment. Poetry appropriate to the students' interests that is read well will reveal the beauty of words.

Many of the suggestions for activities in Chapter 6. "Oral Communication," are also useful for reinforcing listening skills.

How Will a Listening Component Fit into the Language Arts Program?

As we have stressed throughout this chapter, listening skills are not automatic. They must be taught. Fortunately, they are somewhat semiautomatic. That is, by stressing auditory awareness in general and from the start, every exercise becomes multipurposed and multisensory. Direct instruction in listening needs only take up ten or fifteen minutes of your school day. Those few minutes may become the welcome break from more cerebral endeavors, and the benefits of good listening skills and habits will see your students through their academic life and on into the world.

Summary

The characteristics of an effective listener, and systematic instructional strategies for expanding effective listening habits were presented in this chapter. The relationship of listening to the other language arts, specific information regarding types of listening that one exhibits, listening assessment, and listening comprehension were also presented.

Suggested Classroom Projects and Questions for Discussion

Projects

1. Make a list of tapes and records available through your media center that provide an interesting variety of listening experiences (e.g., music, sounds, dialects).
2. Conduct a survey of basal readers used in your area to learn whether they provide specific lesson plans for listening exercises. If they do not, suggest ways various listening skills could be added to the material which is provided.
3. Evaluate your own ability as a listener in classroom or lecture situations. Use the same sort of inventory you have prepared for your students.
4. Evaluate yourself as a *speaker*. Base your evaluation on a listener's point of view. Do you organize your material? Do you give direct and specific instructions? Do you repeat yourself or use too much teacher talk?
5. Prepare a unit on auditory deficiencies and deafness to acquaint your students with the problems that hearing impaired individuals experience. Use tapes of the way various levels of hearing loss "sound," as well as the way speech sounds from individuals who have differing levels of hearing loss. Present videotapes of simultaneous signing (*A Child's Christmas in Wales* done by the Theater of the Deaf may be available in certain libraries) or ask a sign language interpreter to visit your class to demonstrate the skill of signing.
6. Collect stories and poems that are interesting to listen to from an auditory standpoint.
7. Explore listening skills as a factor of maturation and development. What are the effects of a deprived listening environment? Examine what the effects of having deaf parents are on a hearing infant.
8. Visit a local hospital or association for hearing impaired individuals to discover what is current in technology and training in all aspects of treatment for hearing loss.
9. Focus on professionals whose business it is to make people listen. What can you observe about the organization and speaking skills of newspersons, announcers, salespeople, and advertisements? Is there some particular aspect of those skills that makes you listen and keeps your attention?
10. Review the steps involved from hearing to auding. Attempt consciously to trace a listening experience from start to finish. Write a description of your impressions during this experiment.

Questions

1. A visual-minded individual is one who remembers best things that are seen. An auditory-minded person is one who remembers more of what is heard. Which of your memories are the more vivid—those you hear or see?
2. Do you know of any way of measuring individual differences in this respect? How might it be done by a classroom teacher?
3. Why is it often ineffective to correct the behavior of children by giving the class a lecture?
4. What listening experience had the greatest learning effect on you?
5. What sort of "management" system would you devise for keeping track of your listening curriculum and your students' progress?
6. What elements make up an effective listening environment, and how would you arrange your classroom and listening center(s) to achieve maximum benefits?
7. Is it possible to achieve a schoolwide awareness of listening skills? What programs could be implemented to facilitate this objective?
8. Explain what you might do with those inevitable few students who habitually do not listen or follow directions. What special provisions would you make to diagnose and teach to their needs?
9. If reading and listening are interrelated, can you adapt reading techniques into listening techniques? Which ones would you imagine to work best and why?
10. What are the advantages of using standardized group tests to evaluate listening comprehension? What are the disadvantages? When would informal measures be more effective?

Chapter 6

Oral Communication

(Photo by Linda Lungren)

OBJECTIVES

At the end of this chapter students will be able to:

1. discuss the significance of public and private language—on both personal and instructional levels.
2. develop an educational philosophy for the instruction of oral communication.
3. implement an effective speech program incorporating activities based on reading as well as those that are not reading-dependent.
4. assess personal speech qualities and understand the importance of excellent "teacher talk" and ways to achieve it.

What Language Skills Do Children Bring to School?

The topic of how to extend the language skills of students is a major area of study by educators. Theorists such as Lenneberg (1970) stress the innate aspects of language acquisition, whereas others such as Skinner (1972) emphasize behavioral reinforcement as a prime factor in language development. Still others such as Piaget (1962) focus on children's interactions within their environment as an essential factor in establishing concepts that will later be communicated through language. After reviewing, grouping, and labeling existing theories as "nativistic, behavioristic, and cognitive," Wanat states:

> Group differences have generally been ignored in research in language development. Thus, dialect differences, possible ethnic differences in capacities and strategies for processing information, differences in thinking style, and emotionally related factors are not adequately taken under consideration. None of the theories reviewed (Nativistic, Behavioristic, Cognitive) gives an adequate explanation of the way a child acquires his language. Each of the theories is wrong in that each unjustifiably claims to provide a complete explanation. Yet, each of these theories is valuable in that each provides part of the information we need to understand language (Wanat, 1971, p. 147).

What Is Public and Private Language?

Although there is a need for continued research involving larger sample populations with greater sociological and motivational controls, existing theories do offer much of what is needed in order to understand the language base of the communication process. A child may enter school with a "private" language as well as a "public" one (Patin, 1964). Because the private language is often better developed than the public language, some children may find reading a difficult task because most reading materials are written in public language, which linguists often call Standard English. All children must be encouraged to accept both their private and public languages through instruction about the phonological and grammatical variations that exist between them. With this growing knowledge, the child learns, respects, and applies the appropriate language in the appropriate setting.

Private language may be nothing more than the informal talk, shorthand language, or slang that native speakers use within the family or peer group. This is what sociolinguists call "styles" of speaking. A person's speaking style changes, depending on any number of variables including the social experience or environment, other participants in the conversation, and the speaker's age or level of maturation.

Among speakers of nonstandard English or bilingual individuals, there are many other influences on public and private language. Cultural traditions that specify times when it is acceptable to speak or to remain silent may cause misunderstandings about a child's willingness or ability to participate in classroom discussions. American Indian, Vietnamese, or Amish children who might chatter noisily on the playground with their peers have been taught to be silent in the presence of adults and to learn through watching and listening instead of speaking. Because adults often speak to them only for disciplinary reasons, these children would respond according to their training (that is, not speak) when called upon by the adult teacher (Philips, 1982; Kang Ning, 1981; Kiefer and DeStefano, 1985).

Children who speak in a nonstandard or dialectic English may be adhering to the correct underlying structure of their dialect, but this practice may be unacceptable for public or Standard English. Urban children who speak a form of Black English may leave off the final *t* so that *best* becomes *bes* and *test* becomes *tes*. Appalachian children may not differentiate the vowel sounds preceding *r* so that *far, for, fir,* and *fair* may all sound alike. As private language these speech forms have nothing inherently wrong with them. They must be recognized for what they are and accepted as private language—not as bad or wrong.

Extending the Public and Private Language Patterns of All Children. With the belief that language refinement and growth are highly dependent on teacher acceptance, you are encouraged to accept and extend the language presented by the child. Through your examples, you can provide further learning; for example, if your first grader says, "I busted it!" you can reply, "I see that you *broke* it. Delicate things *break* easily. *Broken* things are hard to repair, but let's try." You are beginning to help the child acquire public language skills while you are accepting his private language. If you can offer children such nonthreatening verbal interactions, they will continually *learn* language by *using* it.

This human need to refine one's language continually through using it is also expressed in interactions within the home. A child of four is probably silent nineteen minutes of his waking day. Given some direction, such oral practice has great potential for learning. Analysis of the relationship between the early reading experiences and patterns of parent-child relationships suggests that children who engage in two-way conversations at mealtime with parents who encourage them to talk can be distinguished from other children denied this experience. The child in a home where both parents are often absent because of work or social activities may get such experience by relating to another adult, such as a grandmother or babysitter.

It is certain that exposure to television does not have the same effect on a child. First, the child watching television does not get practice in speaking. There is limited interaction. Second, much that demands a child's attention on television is limited with respect to language. Many children's cartoons are based on sophisticated visual humor, and many of the words that are used mean little to a child. Third, television vocabulary is limited to the relatively few situations portrayed on this medium, such as the imagined life of the western cowboy, space adventurer, and police–gangster chases. However, it is quite possible that some television programs especially designed for children with an educational goal may influence their speech in a positive way.

As, perhaps, the only constant model of correct public language usage in a child's life, your role in the classroom is, clearly, to help the child arrive at an accepted public language without sacrificing his or her individual and cultural identity. As we have stated, this may be achieved continuously and informally through example and by specific usage exercises that will benefit all of the children in the class. Specific techniques for developing correct usage skills are provided throughout this chapter.

Special Speech Needs: How May the Teacher Help?

Although all children come to school with some sort of public and private language, many children are faced with the further challenge of overcoming a speech defect. About one of every ten children in the public schools has a speech defect. About half of these defects are relatively simple problems, such as substituting *wun* for *run* or saying *pay* for *play*. The remaining are more serious. These include hearing impairment, physical defects such as cleft palate and stuttering, and delayed speech resulting from psychological causes. The first group can be cared for by a classroom teacher; the second needs the help of a specialist. However, many of those receiving special training are in the regular classroom, and in all other respects their education is the responsibility of the regular teacher.

In all cases, early recognition and treatment of the defect help the child. Even if some of these defects cannot be corrected, children, like other handicapped individuals, can be shown how to adjust to their limitations. The teacher can aid in this recognition, but in so doing she must also recognize and be able to distinguish between those defects that can be corrected and those that cannot. It is as unprofessional to attempt to remove some of these speech defects without special training as it would be to treat serious illnesses without medical training.

Parents and regular teachers can assist the child in correcting simple articulation errors. Articulation errors of sound substitution, addition, and omission may be identified in a number of ways. Conversation, questions, counting, and naming the days of the week or objects in a room will reveal the existence of the error. Further identification of the habit can be made by test sentences or pictures of objects that contain the sound in different parts of words. Sometimes the child can say the sound in some words that he fails to articulate in others.

The first step toward correction is to help the child recognize the error and decide to change it. Once errors have been identified by the one making them, the emphasis is on listening. Discrimination consists of comparing and contrasting the correct and incorrect sounds both in isolation and in incorporation within regular speech. Without the ability to differentiate correct sound from incorrect sound, the student becomes discouraged and treatment becomes blind drill. Therapy should involve ear training to the extent that the learner hears himself. Hearing one's own error is the foundation for corrective habit formation.

Although some speech problems are beyond the treatment of the classroom teacher, students with such problems may be in your class, so it is important to understand some of these problems.

Cleft palate designates the pathological condition in which the roof of the mouth has failed to grow together before the child was born. Surgery can correct this problem, but sometimes the condition is neglected until after the child has developed speech, when correction requires relearning breath control. Ordinarily a classroom teacher is not trained to meet this problem, but she may have such a child in her class. The sounds made by these children are distorted, because they have no sounding board except the throat and nose chambers. During the long period of reeducation that follows a cleft palate operation these children need patient understanding by teachers, parents, and peers.

Malocclusion denotes a failure of the teeth to mesh, usually at the front of the mouth. During the intermediate grades this is a frequent condition of new teeth in the as yet undeveloped jaw. A large number of these problems adjust themselves with growth. It is frequent (and expensive) practice to correct malocclusion during the junior high school years.

Stuttering is the most misunderstood of all speech defects. In this situation the speech problem may be a symptom of a deeper psychological difficulty. Correction may not always be possible, since stuttering may be caused by pressure and tension at some critical moment in a child's life.

In the American culture stuttering is more frequent among boys than among girls, but in some cultures stuttering does not exist at all. At times when the child is facing considerable speech development, as at the age of three or in the first grade, ideas sometimes come faster than the sounds or words can be recalled and produced. Nearly every child "clutters" or says "ah-ah-ah" while seeking the word. Concern expressed by parents or teachers during this period seems to cause some to stutter (Van Riper, 1971).

We may forget the inner sensitivity of the child. A remark of concern, such as "I am afraid Susan is going to stutter," overheard at this time, may actually cause stuttering. Even an attempt by the parent to correct the speech by saying, "Stop and start again" may cause damage.

Because stuttering is misunderstood, parents of older children frequently think they are clinging to a childish habit that could be stopped. Stutterers can usually sing, speak, or read in a group, take part in a memorized play that involves them physically (such as sweeping with a broom), and talk while dancing without stuttering. Increased language facility that is the result of much writing and a growth in confidence and security usually helps a student who stutters.

The most important service a classroom teacher can perform for a stutterer is to help the child accept this defect without embarrassment. The student who can accept this speech pattern as one accepts being left-handed is a long way toward satisfactory educational and social adjustment. The following suggestions may be shared with the child's parents (Van Riper, 1973).

1. Do not provide words, finish a sentence, or act impatient when listening to a stuttering child.
2. Do see that the child is not subject to physical or emotional strain. Stuttering may be the weak and weary nervous system protecting itself from complete exhaustion.
3. Do praise the child's efforts and make him feel both worthy and loved.
4. Do not put the stuttering child in an exciting and highly competitive position. Overly ambitious parents or those who expect high behavior standards sometimes create ulcers for themselves at the same time that they make a stutterer of their child. Far too many stutterers are the sons of highly ambitious professional men.
5. Do not correct or reprimand the child for stuttering or call attention to it. He is already building up fears in meeting speech situations and is extremely conscious of his trouble. Anticipate some speech situations—such as telephoning, meeting strangers, answering questions—and provide confidence-building practice.
6. Help the child accept himself as a stutterer. "Sure I stutter sometimes, but I'm trying to get over it" is a healthy attitude. All of us on occasion do what the stutterer does more frequently.

And, finally, help the other children to accept the student as a *person* who stutters.

Self-Image

Whatever the "language luggage" your students bring with them to school, whether it be bilingualism, a nonstandard dialect, or a speech defect, as an effective teacher, you need to accept each student without prejudice or preconception. Children quickly and thoroughly sense rejection by their teacher. In the case of the bilingual child, the teacher must be quick to accept the child's language because it is the language of his home. Language and self-concept are so closely intertwined that a child can be made to feel foolish and worthless when his "accent," dialect, or manner of speech is ridiculed by his teacher or peers. Trust and confidence between the teacher and the child must precede linguistic corrections.

What Can We Hope to Achieve with Speech Instruction?

As teachers, parents, or simply as individuals living in a communication-crazed world, we sometimes wish that people would just BE QUIET! As Eliza Doolittle says in *My Fair Lady,*

> Words, words, words!
> I'm so *sick* of words!

In the chaos created by thirty first graders chattering away, it is quite easy to lose track of the incredible importance of the ability to speak. It only takes one severe case of laryngitis or one trip to a foreign country with a language you do not understand to realize how next to impossible it is to communicate meaningfully and effectively without speech. As human beings we have a need to interact with each other, and our most common and productive form of interaction is through oral communication. There is perhaps nothing quite so frustrating or potentially dangerous as the inability to understand or be understood. On a personal level as well as a social and political level, being able to say what you mean clearly and comprehensively is, arguably, our most important human skill.

It falls to the language arts teacher to provide the opportunities for young children to develop successful speaking skills. By providing these children with the tools to state their ideas, to ask and respond to questions in a clear and organized manner, you are preparing them for the challenges they will find throughout their educational, social, and ultimately, professional lives. People who feel confident expressing their ideas and emotions and who are capable of listening to the messages of others are going to be successful people. Success in these terms is not measured by intelligence scores or amounts of money. A scientist who cannot communicate will be much less successful as a person than a blue-collar worker who can.

Objectives of a Language Arts/Oral Communication Program

Oral communication skills need to be practiced, and recent studies have pointed out the fact that often these skills are neglected. Mead (1980) reports that children are experiencing relatively few opportunities to observe and use "practical" types of oral language. Similarly, Bennett (1984) found that in the presence of little or no real classroom oral language instruction, language arts programs should be restructured to encourage more genuine discussion. She further states that teacher education should begin to reflect the importance of oral communication.

In an effort to reaffirm a "focus, balance, and purpose," the National Council of Teachers of English (NCTE, 1983) has provided these guidelines for instruction in speaking:

> Students should learn
>
> to speak clearly and expressively about their ideas and concerns
>
> to adapt words and strategies according to varying situations and audiences, from one-to-one conversations to formal, large-group settings
>
> to participate productively and harmoniously in both small and large groups
>
> to present arguments in orderly and convincing ways
>
> to interpret and assess various kinds of communication, including intonation, pause, gesture, and body language that accompany speaking (p. 246)

In addition, we suggest instruction in the more specific areas of (1) asking for and delivering clear-cut information (directions, instructions, and so on), including knowledge of survival or emergency vocabulary; (2) demonstrating the ability to understand and use Standard English in appropriate situations; and (3) questioning information or opinions in a constructive way.

What Is the Relationship Between Speaking and Writing?

Both speaking and writing are considered output modes of communication, in contrast to listening and reading, the input modes. Speaking and writing both involve synthesizing information and readying it for delivery in a cogent form.

Speaking is, of course, the fundamental form of communication, starting in infancy with squalling protests, then gradually evolving to varying degrees of eloquence in adulthood. Writing follows when spoken thoughts are recorded on paper as in the language experience approach, or when unspoken but mentally "verbalized" words are written. Chafe (1982, 1985) delineates some of the major differences between speaking and writing, as well as some very useful similarities (see Table 6–1).

Table 6–1
Some Differences Between Speaking and Writing

Speaking	*Writing*
Accomplished "on the fly"	Accomplished in a slow, deliberate, thoughtful manner
Fragmented	Integrated
Usually a social experience—socially integrated	Usually a solitary experience—socially detached
The product (most often) reveals the process	The product conceals the process
Disappears instantly (discounting recording media)	Has the potential to last forever
Constantly changing	Static, codified, slow to change

Based on ideas presented in Chafe, W. L. (1985). Linguistic differences produced by differences between speaking and writing. In D. R. Olson, N. Torrance, and A. Hildyard (Eds.), *Literacy, Language and Learning*. Cambridge: Cambridge University Press. © 1985, Cambridge University Press. Printed by permission of Cambridge University Press.

The major similarities between speaking and writing result from what Chafe calls "idea units." Basically these units are designed to describe the pattern of spoken language wherein ideas are expressed in clauses of about seven words, lasting approximately two seconds. Theoretically these idea units develop because a speaker (*and* a listener) can only process so much information in a single "focus of concentration" (Chafe, 1985). These idea units carry over into writing in spite of the fact that writers have an unlimited amount of time and revision in which to express their ideas clearly and still hold the attention of the reader. Well-organized, "readable," material appears to be expressed in idea units that are delineated by punctuation. These marks serve the same purpose for writing as hesitations and changes of intonation do in speech. It appears that idea units carry over from speech writing for two basic reasons: (1) writing is historically secondary to speaking, and it is logical that the primary means of expression would serve as the foundation for the secondary form; (2) a reader who is used to comprehending spoken idea units will be more likely to understand writing in the same form.

The educational implications of these similarities between speaking and writing indicate the very interesting possibility that in teaching children to speak well, we may be enhancing their chances of writing well. Clearly, if writing in its simplest form is speech written down, the opportunities to improve oral communication become even more important.

How Can We Structure Oral Language Instruction?

As with listening, speaking is so much a part of our lives that we seldom remark on the need to define it or be instructed in it. It is only when we encounter a poor speaker—someone whose speech habits are distracting, disorganized, or disassociated from the context—that we recognize the need to speak well. Similarly, when we find ourselves at a loss for words in facing a group or engaging in a complex discussion, we realize that practice in oral communication is a valuable tool for personal and social fulfillment and satisfaction.

In the language arts curriculum, oral communication instruction should be constant. It is more natural for young children to be speaking than to be silent. Consequently, the teacher's challenge becomes, How can I channel all that talk into "oral communication"? This can be achieved by setting a standard for excellence in speech and by following it up with a program of instruction.

Setting the Standards for Oral Communication Environmental Factors. The physical environment conducive to excellence in speech is similar to the conditions discussed in Chapter 5, "Gaining Information Through Listening." Speakers feel comfortable when listeners are attentive. If the classroom is poorly arranged, causing the audience to squirm and dodge in trying to get a look at the speaker, the presenter may feel that the inattention is his fault and lose confidence. Every effort must be made to keep visual and auditory distraction at a minimum. As for any sort of learning experience, the physical surroundings should be as pleasant and comfortable as possible. If you are too warm or too cold, your students will be uncomfortable as well. These considerations may seem trivial. They are not. How well do you concentrate on a lecture, no matter how interesting, when your feet are cold?

"Atmospheric" Factors. We are, of course, not speaking barometrically here. The atmosphere of the classroom includes the social, emotional, and intellectual elements that exist in any social setting. If it is true that people and places give off "vibrations," you should strive to achieve a classroom humming with comfortable, accepting, "good" vibrations. As discussed earlier in the consideration of public and private language (page 103), children need to feel accepted and unthreatened. They need to feel that it is OK to ask questions and volunteer their experiences. We are not suggesting that the classroom dissolve into a chaos of chatter. Obviously children need to learn when it

is appropriate to ask questions or narrate their experiences, just as they need to learn when to be quiet and listen. The goal here is to create a classroom in which each child feels special and secure with the teacher and with the other children. The classroom should become a haven where cultural, social, and physical differences are understood and accepted.

Voice Qualities for the Classroom Teacher. Speech instruction in the elementary classroom begins with the voice of the teacher. The tone used, the manner of speaking, and the vocabulary employed all influence the quality of instruction.

The teacher's words carry meaning not only because she conceives and expresses her thoughts accurately, but also because her voice is properly attuned and controlled to convey this meaning. The tonal quality of your voice may make the difference between interested and inattentive children. Listening attentively to people whose voices you find attractive while consciously imitating some of their patterns of speech will also help. Barring a physical deformity in the throat or mouth, anyone can learn to speak distinctly and agreeably. Voice modulation means a "toning down," or tempering, of the voice to avoid nasal twang, harshness, stridency, shrillness, or shouting.

Relaxation is fundamental in all speech training. Not only the muscles used for speech but all other parts of the body as well should be free from tension in order to produce relaxed, clear voice tones and harmonious coordination of the many elements composing the speech mechanism. Relaxation may be achieved by reading a quiet story or a short poem or by looking at a restful scene or painting.

Flexibility and control of the lips are important in the projection of correct "labial" sounds. Proper placement of the tongue is essential to the production of well-rounded vowels and to the formation of distinct, clear consonants and other "velar" and "glottal" sounds.

The roof of the mouth or hard palate forms the top of a cavity that amplifies sound vibrations in addition to giving them a strong and more pleasing quality. Voice resonance can be cultivated by the way the oral cavity is used.

Intonation and emphasis give variety to the voice, which may fall emphatically at the end of an important idea or rise in suspense and wonderment. Parts of words, entire words, or complete phrase may be lowered or raised. What you, as the teacher-speech role model, say and the way you say it will set the standard for oral communication in your classroom. If you, personally, aim high, so will your students.

How May Correct Public Usage Habits Be Established?

Correct public usage is concerned with proper form. The agreement of verb and subject in number and tense, the form of the pronoun in various positions in the sentence, and the word order in sentences are some of the elements that present learning problems of proper form. The child who says "I done my work" is using the wrong verb form. Another who says "Him and me are friends" is using the wrong form of the pronoun. Children use these forms because they hear them at home, on television, and in the playground.

As stressed earlier, teachers should encourage children to enjoy their private language. The students know they will be accepted, no matter what they say or how they say it. Their language is a verbal expression of their thoughts and feelings. If we reject it, we reject the student. Furthermore, we reject by implication the family who has taught the child to speak and with whom there are strong emotional ties that are needed as the child develops as a human being.

Children's speech patterns are discovered and extended by encouraging them to talk. During the early school years the content of their "talk" will often be centered about themselves, their home, and their family. At first the teacher will accept the children's own word groupings, if they are in communication units, whether or not they are complete. But the teacher may also listen for and take note of patterns of substandard usage that can be brought to the children's attention later.

Important as it is to accept the child along with any immature patterns of usage, we cannot leave children here. As they develop to take their place in the ever-widening world, a corresponding development in their language patterns will be necessary. We can provide for this continuous sequential growth through carefully organized instruction.

At this point, individual deviations will be handled with respect for the child. Children are aided in expressing themselves by modeling their speech after a classroom dialect. The teacher may say something like "I understand what you mean, but in our classroom we say it this way" and then give the substitute form. The time and manner in which these substitute forms are given depend on the feeling of belonging that the child has in the classroom, a state to which the teacher will always be sensitive. In order to acquire this delicate balance, it is important to acquaint children with the need for both public and private language.

The teacher's attitude, too, plays a major role in achieving a standard classroom dialect. If the teacher is consistent in what is expected from the class and communicates this expectation firmly yet kindly, the pupils will respond with their best.

A peculiar problem of usage errors is that a child who has acceptable public speech in the primary grades may start making errors in later grades. Perhaps this is because students hear incorrect usage on television or in the playground or read it in a comic book. This can be a particular problem for the ESL student who presumes that everything a native speaker says must be correct. (See the discussion of bilingualism in Chapter 1.) Exercises in the textbook may help to counteract these external factors by reinforcing existing correct habits.

One other factor concerning textbook drill material should be noted. The sentence may require the child to select either *was* or *were*. If the problem is only one of selecting between the singular and plural, it will not serve the child who says, "You was." The drill or test should concern the error the learner makes.

To change a usage habit, three elements are necessary: the error should be identified, oral practice should be stressed until the established form sounds correct to the learner, and written practice should be given to maintain the desired habit and to test the learner. Oral exercises provide opportunities in listening to the correct form. The drill is for the listener as well as the speaker. "Game" situations provide such practice.

Children cannot learn to *improve* their language unless they first feel free to *use* language. Errors in the use of language, therefore, should be called to their attention only after they feel accepted by the group and sufficiently self-confident so that correction will not silence them. The spirit in which corrections are made is perhaps the most important single factor in the child's language development.

The following steps have proven effective in practice:

1. Discuss the need for both public and private language.
2. Listen to the children talk and note the type of patterns common to the group and to individuals.
3. Select the most common patterns of error for correction.
4. Choose a few errors at a time for concentrated effort.
5. Call attention to the correct use of words as well as to errors in usage.
6. Correct children at the time an error is made, but after they have finished what they have to say.
7. Follow a period of oral expression with a short drill period in which the child hears the correct form repeated several times.
8. Play games in which the correct form is used over and over again.

Methods for Correcting Usage Errors

Positive Reinforcement. Note how Shannon is complimented on correct word usage in first grade.

The children were saying, "I got" repeatedly. Shannon said, "I have."

Teacher: I am so glad to hear Shannon say, "I have."

This approval made the others eager to use "I have."

The children correct a common error in second grade:

Teacher: This morning I heard someone say, "The bird he was building a nest." Let's all think of something you have seen a bird do and see if we can leave out the *he*.
Child 1: The bird was feeding his babies.
Child 2: The bird was hopping on the ground.
Teacher: This morning I heard someone say, "This here book is mine." It would be acceptable public language to say, "This book is mine." Let's all take something out of our desks that belongs to us and tell about it.
Child 1: This pencil is mine.
Child 2: This chalk is yours.

The children begin to drop *ain't* when assisted to make proper substitutions.

Teacher: Lately I've been hearing some of you say, "I ain't got a pencil. I ain't going with you." Does anyone know a better way of saying it?
Child 1: I don't have a pencil.
Child 2: I'm not going with you.
Teacher: That's better.

Toy Phones. Pooley (1974) suggests that using toy telephones for conversation between two children is a helpful device to alert teachers to inappropriate usage such as "Me and my brother" or "I seen." Here, too, we detect baby talk that has been permitted in the home. Many five- and six-year-olds begin school unable to sound several of the consonants. A few examples are *fadder* for *father, Zimmy* for *Jimmy, yittle* for *little,* and *won* for *run*.

By listening and speaking to each other in the form of these "pretend" phone calls, children grow in the knowledge of a standard classroom dialect. The tape recorder is also a valuable instructional aid at this point as the children are able to hear their own voices and listen to the recording critically.

Pattern Practice Drills/Games. The best drills to teach English as a second language are known as pattern practice drills. The drills are presented along the following lines. Suppose the teacher wants to make automatic the use of *there are* and *there is*. The problem, of course, is that the students want to say, "There is two spoons on the table." We can set up a series of key frames thus:

There is one spoon on the table.
There are two spoons on the table.
There is a spoon on the table.
There are some spoons on the table.
There are several spoons on the table.

The teacher will say each one of these sentences and then ask for individual repetition. Then she can extend the exercise by giving a series of cues—word that will substitute in the patterns: *toast, dishes, bread, glasses, forks, two vases, several napkins, some food,* and so on. This can be varied further as follows:

Cue: How many spoons are there on the table?
Response: There are two spoons on the table.
Cue: Is there a spoon on the table?
Response: Yes, there is a spoon on the table.
Cue: There is . . .
Response: There is a spoon on the table. There is a dish on the table.
Cue: There are . . .
Response: There are forks on the table.

Or take another example: Our problem here is that the student says "them things." We can set up a series of frames as follows:

I don't like that thing.
I don't like those things.

That book's on the table.
Those books are on the table.

The student will repeat these and similar frames after the teacher, and then the teacher can proceed thus:

Cue: That man is my friend. (*men*)
Response: Those men are my friends.
Cue: That thing is on the table. (*things*)
Response: Those things are on the table.

Later a student may provide cues.

"Chain Practice." Chain practice can be played to substitute *he doesn't* for *he don't*. In this game each child asks a question, and the child in the next desk responds and then forms the question for the next, who then responds and forms a question for the next child, and so on. The teacher may ask the first question:

Teacher (to Eric): What doesn't Eric like to do?
Eric (to teacher): Eric doesn't like to mow the lawn.
Eric (to Denise): What doesn't Denise like to do?
Denise (to Eric): Denise doesn't like to wash the dishes.
Denise (to Maura): What doesn't Maura like to do?

Chain practice is more fun if it moves along quickly.

An imaginative pupil or the teacher may make a puppet for this activity by coloring a face on a lunch size bag with the mouth at the bottom of the sack so that the puppet can appear to be talking. Children may take turns talking for the puppet. The teacher will ask the puppet (the pupil) questions that will be answered using standard classroom dialect. Here the pupils will practice negative answers.

Teacher (to puppet): Ronnie, do you have any candy?
Ronnie (to teacher): No, I don't have any candy.
Teacher (to Ronnie): Ronnie, do you have any marbles in your pocket?
Ronnie (to teacher): No, I haven't any marbles in my pocket.

The responses to the teacher's questions are intended to replace "I haven't got no . . ." or "I ain't got no . . ." with the more desirable "No, I haven't any. . . ." Ronnie might develop as a special character who makes the errors the class is committing.

Word Substitution. The next language game is designed to substitute deviant words with acceptable ones (such as *isn't* for *ain't*). The teacher will list some words on the chalkboard. For example,

troposphere	atmosphere	forecast
scientific	ionosphere	thermometer
prediction	satellite	barometer
humidity		

These are scientific words that might be selected for a sixth-grade class that had become familiar with them in science. One student is chosen to begin. He thinks of one of the words on the list. Then he begins by saying, "What word am I thinking of?"

Classmate: Is it *humidity?*
Student: No, it isn't *humidity.*
Another Classmate: Is it *prediction?*
Student: No, it isn't *prediction.*

This game may be scaled down to almost any level by the use of more simple words.

What Speech Activities Are Presented in the Primary Grades? When organizing any formal program for speech instruction, it is important to access students' achievements and needs in oral communication. This is especially true in the primary grades, when some children come to school who have not yet mastered all the sounds of our language. As Poole (1934, p. 60) suggests most children can be expected to develop speech sounds in the manner illustrated in Table 6–2.

Table 6–2
Developing Speech Sounds

Age	*Consonants*
3½	*p, b, m, h, w* (lip sounds)
4½	*d, n* (tip-of-the-tongue sounds)
5–5½	*f, j, w, h, s, z*
6–6½	*v, th* (voiced), *sh, zh, l*
7–7½	*ch, r, th* (voiceless)
8	such blends as *pl, br, st, sk, str*

From I. Poole (1934). "The Genetic Development of the Articulation of Consonant Sounds." Doctoral dissertation, University of Michigan, p. 60.

The sounds most frequently defective are *s, a, sh, zh* (as in *pleasure*), *ch, j, th, l, r, wh,* and the *-ing* ending, which is shortened to *-en*. The way these and other sounds are voiced is discussed in Chapter 4.

Do not try to correct an *s* or *r* before easier sounds have been mastered. Instead, give much ear training on these sounds. Of course, there is no sense working on blends if the *l* and *r* have not been perfected.

Ear training is important if the children are to improve speech habits. Until they hear the difference between the way they are pronouncing a word or producing a voice sound and the way it should be pronounced or produced, they will not change their pattern of speech. Ear training to develop auditory discrimination for the sounds of speech is the first step in speech correction and improvement. For suggestions on some techniques to use for auditory discrimination see Chapter 5.

A picture test made by the teacher can check the child's ability to say the initial consonants. Frequently, an alphabet book or picture dictionary can provide the pictures needed. These are suggestions that might be used: *h, hat; m, man; wh, whistle; w, wagon; p, pig; b, ball; n, nail; y, yellow; t, table; d, day; k, kite; g, gun; ng, ring; f, fish; v, valentine; l, lamp; th, thumb; th, feather; sh, shoe; zh, tape measure; s, sun; z, zebra; r, rabbit; ch, chair; j, jar.*

A still more comprehensive test uses separate pictures for each sound in all three positions—initial, medial, and final. As the teacher points to the picture, the child names it, with the teacher recording all errors. Teachers may make this test themselves with pictures cut from magazines, or they may purchase any of the commercial tests that are available. Many authorities feel that at the kindergarten level, testing for errors in the initial position only is sufficient.

An individual test that is interesting for the child is a story using the rebus method of picture insertion. The tester reads the words, and the child "fills in" by giving the words for the pictures: for example, "Jimmy sat up in (picture of bed). He looked through the (window) at the bright (sun). It was time to get up. He put on his (coat) and (pants), his (socks) and (shoes). He put his magic (ring) on his (finger) and went downstairs." The story continues until all sounds have been tested.

Auditory discrimination is an essential skill in both reading and spelling. The following lessons indicate the way the sounds may be isolated in words (Smith, 1963):

Words Beginning with S—Paper Bag Game

Teacher: Today we are going to play a guessing game. In each of these paper bags is a toy or an article. The name of each thing starts with *s* as in sun. One person will be "It." He will peek into one of these bags and give you one clue about what he sees. He might say, "I see something we wear." Then we will take turns guessing what he saw. (These items can be in the paper bags.)

sock sailboat soap
salt (small package as served on airplanes)

Teacher: The game must be played by using complete sentences. When you guess, you say, "Is it ________?" putting in the name of what you want to guess. The person who is "It" must answer you by using the name of what you have guessed. After everyone has had one turn, if no one has guessed correctly, a second clue will be given.

Note: Stress the need for all questions and answers to be complete sentences using the forms: Is it a ________? No, it is not a ________! Depending upon the ability of your group, you may wish to add the following step in the lesson.

Teacher: Let's write the names of all the things we have guessed and any other words we have used that begin with *s* sounds. Tell me what to write on the chalkboard.

(The lesson that follows should be used soon after this one.)

Initial, Medial, and Final S Words—Paper Bag Game

Teacher: The game today uses words that have *s* sounds in the beginning, the middle, and the end. Your main clue is that there is an *s* sound somewhere in the word you are to guess. The things in the paper bags all have an *s* sound somewhere in their name.

(See the preceding lesson for detailed instructions for playing this game.) The items in the paper bags can be

basket	bus	sunglasses	nest
stone	purse	mouse	

Note: Stress the need for all questions and answers to be complete sentences using the forms: Is it a ________? No, it is not a ________. Write the words they have guessed and ask the class to tell whether the *s* is in the beginning, middle, or end of the word.

Auditory Discrimination Between S and Z

Teacher: When the letter *s* is in front of a word, sometimes it says *s* and sometimes it says *z*. *Scissors* is a word that has lots of *s*'s. See if you can tell which ones say *s* and which ones say *z*. Hold your throat as you say *scissors*. Yes, it begins with *s* and has a *z* sound in the middle and on the end."

Note: Put these words on the chalkboard in *mixed* order and ask the children to tell you whether they belong in the *s* column or *z* column.

S *column*	Z *column*
sister	rose
salt	houses (note that both *s*'s have the *z* sound in the plural of *house*)
seven	his
house	flowers
this	please
guess	does
school	ears
sleep	nose
just	these
said	present
across	

Speech Games. The following games are speech-centered and may be used with positive results in the primary grades:

1. I See Something You May See. A child makes three statements to describe something he sees. Children guess what it is by saying, "Do you see ________?"
2. Lip-Reading Game. Lip reading proceeds as follows:

   Teacher: I am going to say names of children in the class, but I am not going to use my voice. Watch for your name. Stand when your name is said on my lips.

3. CH Guessing Game. *Guess the answer.* Example: two sides of the face (*cheeks*). I write on the board with (*chalk*).
4. I Have Something in My Sack. In a large

box put small paper bags, in each of which is a small toy. The names of the toys may contain specific sounds for improvement. A child chooses a sack from the box, peeks in, and discovers his toy. He then describes the toy without naming it. The child who guesses correctly then chooses a sack from the box and the game continues.

5. Telephone Games. One child chooses from a list of toys and telephones the order to the toy store. The child then goes to the storekeeper and asks whether the package is ready. Storekeeper answers, "What is your name?" "My name is ________." "Yes, your package is ready."
6. Fishing Game. Select pictures representing words that contain sounds on which you have been working. Put paper clips on each picture, and then put pictures in a pail or box. Attach a magnet to a string hanging from a pole. After lifting the picture out of the pail, the child tries to say the name of the picture. If he does, he keeps the picture; if he does not, he must put the picture back (after having practiced it a little) and try again.
7. Sound Ladder or Word Ladder. Draw an outline ladder on paper on the blackboard. Place syllables or words you are practicing on each rung of the ladder. The child begins at the bottom and climbs ladder by pronouncing each of the words or syllables correctly. The purpose of the game is to climb to the top and back down again without "falling off." A child who misses, must start at the bottom again.
8. Animal Talk. The sounds *quack-quack, moo-moo, baa-baa, oink-oink,* and *peep-peep* are good for lip movement. Pictures of animals may be shown and the children imitate those animals. A story may be told about a farmer; when an animal is mentioned the children make the proper sounds.
9. Noise Cards. Make picture cards that suggest sound effects. The pictures are face down in a stack. A child takes the top card. Questions and answers should be in sentences.

   Child: My picture says ________. What do I have?
   Answer: Do you have ________?
   Child: Yes, I have a ________. or No, I don't have a ________.

10. Sound Boxes. Collect and place into boxes small objects starting with easily confused sounds: for example, *s–z, th–s, th–f, w–r.* Review the contents of the boxes periodically, letting children use names of objects in sentences.
11. I See Something. Use the sound boxes mentioned previously. Teachers says, "I see something in this box that starts with ________." A child chooses the object and asks, "Is it a ________?"
12. Balloons. Make colored paper balloons about six inches in diameter with a string fastened to each one.

First Child: I am the balloon man. Balloons! Balloons for sale! Who will buy my balloons?
Second Child: I will buy a balloon.
First Child: What color would you like?
Second Child: I would like a ________balloon.

Continue the game until all balloons have been chosen. After all balloons have been chosen, ask for them to be returned by colors, using only the lips to form the words without speaking. Do not exaggerate lip movements when forming the words.

WHAT INSTRUCTIONAL ACTIVITIES ARE APPROPRIATE FOR ALL GRADES? Another very basic oral composition activity that very young children enjoy is to be asked to provide *descriptions* of specific people, places, and things. Although a sixth grader might feel ridiculous participating in something called "Show and Tell," and a kindergartner is usually not ready for oral reading demonstrations, most speech activities are appropriate to most grades—with obvious modifications.

Starting with the most basic forms of oral communication and moving to the more imaginative and elaborate, use the following suggestions as the substantive basis for an oral language arts program.

Conversation. Conversing with another person is, at the same time, oral communication in its most elementary and most sophisticated form. Children talk to each other easily and naturally all the time, whereas many adults find conversation an "art" that they have difficulty mastering. Your job as a language "arts" teacher is to help your students gain this mastery over the art of conversation by providing them with guidelines and practice in conversing. These skills will include not only being able to organize thoughts on the spot and deliver their message clearly, but also learning to listen, ask appropriate questions, and draw out the other person—in other words, learning to keep a conversation going. The skills needed to lead a discussion on growing wheat on Mars or sharing the time your pet turtle Big Daddy lost himself under your bed are essentially the skills of conversation. These skills can all be taught, and they are all based on developing the awareness that it is OK to share ideas by talking about them. Some children do not get that opportunity at home. They *must* get it in school.

Language Experience or Whole Language Approach. One method that develops all areas of the language arts curriculum and is derived from conversation is the whole language or *language experience approach* (LEA). One view of the language experience approach is that the teacher guides students to realize that written material is "talk written down." Because some of the important aspects of oral presentation (such as gestures, facial expression, voice inflection and control, and rate of speech) are seldom recorded as "talk written down," this view is inaccurate. It is, however, desirable to help children realize the connections among listening, oral expression, writing, and reading.

Although this method integrates activities in all four areas of language arts skills, it does not include a heavy reliance on published materials. Instead, activities are meant to grow out of children's group or individual experiences. Recess games, art activities, celebrations of holidays, and field trips are the kinds of activity that stimulate interest and language growth. To coordinate the visual, oral, auditory, and kinesthetic impact of the experience, children need freedom to discuss feelings in their own words. These impressions can be recorded and then written where the class can see what they have produced. Large chart paper makes a more permanent record than a chalkboard. Individual reports can also be written or typed so that each child has a tangible representation of his or her own reactions. Both these writing activities lead to improvement of reading and enlargement of sight vocabulary. With the reports as texts, phonics and word attack skills can be learned without the difficulties involved in isolated units of work. The great strength of the language experience approach is its integration of all language activities. The following six procedures will enable you to implement a successful language experience program.

1. Find a subject of interest to the students.
2. Invite them to think of what they wish to say about the subject.
3. Record, on the board or on chart paper, exactly what the children say.
4. Read the results individually and as a group.
5. Ask students to note unknown words for study.
6. Follow-up activities may include use of sentence strips, illustrations, expanded discussion of the topic or related topics, dramatization of the language experience story, or making a "book" or scrapbook with a variety of stories and illustrations.

Discussions. Classroom discussions are, essentially, structured extensions of informal conversations. Most of the rules related to successful discussions deal with the ability to keep the discussion on track, involve everyone, and express differing opinions on a subject without becoming overly emotional or argumentative. These rules are usually enforced by a discussion leader, whether formally chosen or naturally evolved from the group. Both formal and informal group discussions are important for developing speaking and listening skills. As an evaluative tool, discussions provide information on not only the speaking ability of a child, but his leadership traits, attention span, social maturity, thought processes, organizational skills, and listening comprehension. Varying the type of discussion used in your classroom will help your students soon become adept at making themselves heard in an articulate and useful way. Here are some suggestions for types of discussions to incorporate into your program.

1. *Informal Discussions*

Common interest: Create opportunities for your students to meet in small unstructured groups to talk about topics of interest to them. You may wish to list ideas for discussion on the board and let students form their own groups. Students may spontaneously come up with ideas they wish to discuss with peers. Informal groups like these help children experience starting and structuring a discussion. Decisions like choosing someone to lead, summarize, take notes, make a presentation to the whole class, and so on, are part of the process of informal discussions.

Problem solving: Structured in the same way as the interest group, problem-solving groups are slightly more directed or goal-oriented. In addition to the skills for interest groups, these groups must evaluate and interpret more to reach a consensus on the viability of suggested problem solutions.

Roundtable discussions: This format involves either of the preceding discussions when a formal leader is chosen by the teacher or by the group. Again, it is a small group discussion without an audience.

2. *Panel Discussions*

The participants in a panel discussion will have researched their topic and will be directed by a formal leader in front of an audience. After ideas have been presented and explored, the panel presents the discussion to the audience. This is an excellent introduction to oral presentations because the students on the panel are in front of the class, but the "safety in numbers" mentality is at work. The leader's job is to field questions and direct them to members of the panel. This method is a useful way to summarize a unit of study or to explore many aspects of a single subject, for example, in a social studies unit on Mexico, various panels can be in charge of such aspects as geography, culture, economy, history, and politics.

3. *Debate*

Perhaps the most formal and structured method of discussion or debate depends on excellent research, organization, and speaking presence of the debaters. By allowing the strict debate format to include questions from the audience, the entire class can be involved in the debate experience.

As the major facilitator in organizing any kind of discussion, the classroom teacher should be aware of two major responsibilities:

1. To stimulate creative thinking by using questioning techniques appropriate to generating discussion (moving from detailed, concrete facts to abstract thinking).
2. To provide an optimal environment for engendering effective discussion skills through efficient grouping strategies.

Begin with asking factual or data-gathering questions to provide the information on which to build further discussion. Then proceed to process the data by asking questions related to relationships among the data. The final step involves abstracting the material discussed into broader knowledge that relates to other situations and information. Questioning is an art unto itself, and there is an entire body of research relating to it. Lapp and Flood (1986) provide a comprehensive discussion of questioning.

It is obvious to any classroom teacher that certain

group dynamics operate with any given group of children. The leaders will make themselves known, and the quiet ones will make themselves invisible. By varying the composition and sizes of the groups, you can encourage appropriate interaction whereby all children learn to handle all aspects of discussion mechanics.

Oral Reports. The "dreaded" oral report has been the bane of many a student's educational career. The horror of facing our peers, one against the multitude, is an experience many of us, at all ages, have been tortured into. However, with practice and the proper preparation and environment, oral reporting can become just one more feature of a normal working (educational) day. Beginning with "Show and Tell" in kindergarten right through to arguing your proposal on the Senate floor, oral reporting is a cornerstone of oral communication. Provide your students with many opportunities for all kinds of reports in a variety of guises. They will love you for it (later).

Sharing/Show and Tell. Generally relegated to the primary grades, sharing time can be handled in many different ways to suit all ages of children and many oral language skills. Research has shown that quite often teachers do more of the talking during this time than the students by teachers leading the discussion, asking the questions, responding to the topics, and evaluating the student's presentation (Barnes, 1976; Mehan, 1979; Michaels, 1981; Wilcox, 1982; New, 1982). In the primary grades, initial guidance is of course necessary; however, frequently students begin to conform to what the teacher explicitly or implicitly considers "good" sharing.

Michaels and Foster (1985) provide a model for student-led sharing time that can be adapted for all grades. This method is basically a small discussion group with a leader who enforces rules (with help when necessary from the ever-vigilant teacher). The rules govern behavior only. The children may select their own topics, the way they wish to present their sharing topic, and the time they will take. These selections are then evaluated by the other students in the group. This means of sharing helps develop various styles of sharing ("lecture demonstration" or "performed narrative") as well as an awareness of the mechanics and dynamics of public speaking.

Other suggestions for oral reporting include the following: news time; interviewing and surveying; demonstrations and directions; and selling, describing, and persuading.

News Times. Ask individual students to become experts on a person of their choice, such as the president, an astronaut, a sports figure, a music group, the governor, or the mayor. When appropriate, the class is given a briefing about the activities of the person.

Have individuals or small groups follow a single problem or activity and keep a bulletin board or notebook for periodic reporting of the collected data. Suitable topics might include air pollution, effects of DDT on animal life, political changes in other countries, Africa (or a single country), nutrition health news, the new school building, the new bridge, or the strike.

When a student reports a news item, he or she might first locate the place on a map, write on the board two (or more) words that may be new to the class, and ask a question at the end, or give the teacher a question for inclusion in a listening test at the end of the week. Such procedures help children prepare their reports with the listeners in mind.

All news reporting may be centered on a large topic until the students become expert; such topics may include an election, a war, our national policy, use of leisure time, animals in the news, humor in the news, human interest stories, and characters in comic strips. Alternate groups should use news of the class and home, which can be dictated and written as *Our Day* or *Our Week* for future reference. This activity should occur at the end of the period.

Editorials also have a place in news time. In turn, each one who wishes might talk on such topics as

How I think TV could be improved.
Why I think ten-year-old students should be in bed by 10 o'clock.
Our school lunch program needs to be changed.

Safety hazards in our school.
Our school needs ________.
My parents don't understand me.
Ugly spots in our neighborhood that can be changed.
There should be a special period for ________.
Let's write to the mayor (governor) about ________.

Interviewing and Surveying. Planned interviews also provide exceptional opportunities for oral communication practice. The interview subjects may range from family and friends to important figures in the community. The student will need help setting up the questions, which should be written ahead of time.

Students are often asked, "What did you do at school today?" The teacher might introduce interviewing with such a question (which would also prepare the children to promote good public relations at home). Preference surveys are a common commercial practice. A committee might make a preference survey of the class with respect to favorite toothpaste, soap, cold drink, music, or television program.

This activity may be extended to planning interviews with the principal, the superintendent of schools, the school secretary, the janitor, the oldest person in a child's family or neighborhood, or a neighbor with a hobby (tropical fish, cooking, collecting). Interviewing others in the class in order to write a short biography increases the interest in reading biographies and in the author's techniques.

Surveys provide an equally interesting extension of the interview. Each child might interview one adult on a problem and pool the results. Such questions as the following might be used:

What do you think is the greatest problem our city must solve?
If you were my age, what business would you prepare for?
What gives you the most enjoyment?

Some surveys can be made without interviews, such as "How many cars stop between 8 and 8:30 A.M. for the traffic patrol?" "What is the most popular make of car in the school parking lot?"

To give meaning to the occasion, the interview and survey may be used during such special weeks as Education Week, Book Week, Safety Week, or on such days as Poetry Day, Veterans' Day, and Arbor Day. On Arbor Day a nursery might be visited to learn which trees grow well in the area, or a survey of different varieties of trees in one block might be made.

Demonstrations and Directions. Students who have traveled can demonstrate a skill they learned (instead of "What I did on my vacation"). This might involve the use of chopsticks, Japanese paper folding, hobby or craft projects, magic tricks, slides, post cards, photographic talks, care of plants or pets, or experiences earning money (newsboys and babysitters have adventures and problems).

Teach the class a game to play on a rainy day or at a picnic, or imagine you were telling an Eskimo about baseball, football, tennis, horseshoes, and so on.

Play *How do I get there?* One child asks how to get to a place in the community, school, or state. Volunteers who answer may be given one to five points for their accuracy, simplicity, and brevity.

Talks on *How does it work?* stimulate a great deal of research either in books or through field trips. A vocational slant can be given by interviewing neighbors and parents on what they do at the ________(bakery, movie theater, clinic, service station, supermarket, and so on).

Selling, Describing, Persuading. Your Scout troop is selling cookies (peanuts, tickets, and so on). What should you say as you go to potential customers?

Take any object in the room, including clothing, and make a commercial for it like one you might hear on the radio.

Describe *The car (bicycle) I want, The dress I need, The best meal I remember, My grandparents,* or *My old school.*

You need a quarter, a larger allowance, a new pair

of shoes, and so on; what would you say to your parents?

Creative-Imaginative Situations. Many suggestions for creative writing are impressively effective in increasing the oral vocabularies of some students.

Show any three objects and ask about ways they may be related. Examples of such objects might be a pen, paper, and a book; a book, a lamp, and a toy; pictures of a house, a dog, and an airplane. Let the children think of the most unrelated objects possible and show ways they may be associated through imagination. A salt shaker, an old tire, and a worn hat might be a challenge. A student teacher brought a bag to school with three strange items in it. She explained, "I found these in the old house I bought. What do you suppose the people who lived there were like?"

To make children aware of the ordinary, it might be good for some classes to start the day at least once each week with a creativity exercise. Such an exercise might proceed from the following questions:

1. What would happen if you woke up and the ground were covered with red snow?
2. What would happen if we could talk with insects?
3. What would happen if you had an experience like Rip Van Winkle's and today were a day twenty years from now?

Role-playing experiences are exceptional opportunities for language growth. The child must project his personality into that of another. This may require changes in dialect, age, sex, class, or race.

A friend borrowed a book from you. When he returns it, you see that someone has spilled ink on it. What do you say? Why?

Newspaper accounts can be made into role situations by asking, "If you had been ________, what would you have done?"

Telephoning. This instrument which is so much a part of our lives lends itself to many imaginative oral language situations. Ideas for using the telephone as a language arts tool include the following:

1. Create one-sided conversations—by asking the class to attempt to fill in what has been said on the other end of the phone.
2. In many communities the telephone company will arrange a conference interview for a class. It may be with a local author, an official, or another classroom, sometimes in a distant state. The entire class can listen while individuals participate. All aspects of telephone courtesy and use can become a part of the preparations of such a call.
3. Some schools select a student to help in the principal's office at noon hour. A specific task is to answer the telephone and take messages.
4. As a science activity, two fourth-grade boys in Poway, California, installed a telephone between their classrooms. As an independent reading activity, students read aloud to each other on the telephone during a scheduled period. Find out whether a similar project can be accomplished at your school.
5. Practice giving directions over the "phone" (place students with their backs to each other so no hand gestures can be seen). Try directions to a destination or on the way to do something.

Wordless Pictures. By showing your students well-chosen pictures, you should get your "thousand words'" worth. Using pictures in a series and asking students to describe what is happening or to explain the background they imagine for interesting-looking people in a picture is an excellent stimulus to oral language. Round-robin games based on pictures can create amusing and unusual stories. One student begins the story with one sentence, and as it continues around the circle each student, in turn, adds another sentence based on the preceding one.

What Is the Place of Creative Dramatics in the Classroom?

Drama in the classroom can be as simple or as formal as the teacher cares to make it. Many teachers, unfortunately, think of creative dramatics only in terms of full-blown productions complete with costumes and scenery. Although this sort of total commitment and challenge are admirable and can be extremely rewarding for everyone, children can benefit from and enjoy dramatic experiences on a much less complex level. It is useful to divide creative dramatic exercises into those that require oral reading skills and those that do not.

Reading-Independent Activities

Role Playing. Creative dramatics starts with the simple, natural play of the preschool or kindergarten. Here the children play house in the roles of father, mother, child, and the lady next door. In these roles the children try out the vocabulary they hear spoken in the situations of the adult world around them. There is no better way to teach children the social amenities of greeting and farewell. Teacher suggestions as to what should be said are usually welcomed and frequently sought. Some of the more imaginative children will provide patterns that others will imitate.

Students will observe the storekeeper, bus driver, and waiter with new interest after playing any of these roles in the classroom. Although the teacher is seldom imitated in the classroom, playing school is a favorite home activity. Parents frequently know many of the teacher's mannerisms and practices through such play. However, most students seem to invest the role of teacher with a crossness and severity that is more a part of childhood's folklore than actuality.

A few items to use as props help children give realism to a role. An apron establishes a grandmother, just as a cane identifies a grandfather. A hat makes a boy a man, and nothing gives a girl more maturity than a long skirt.

Creative dramatics in the school is not concerned with making children into actors or with producing story plays for a guest audience. In some situations the presence of an audience may make the children self-conscious in their roles as actors rather than assist the process of creating the play. The stage may be the front of the classroom, but the whole room may be involved in order to indicate a change of scene. Aisles are used as roads, scenery is drawn on the chalkboard, and tables become bridges, mountaintops, or castle towers.

Preschoolers engage in role playing in the form of make-believe or "Let's pretend" from the moment they make cars go "vroom" and tuck their "baby" into bed. Even when their imaginary worlds are populated with monsters or dragons, the children invest their creations with observed human behavior, hence, the mommy monster or the friendly dragon.

In the primary grades the attitude is one of creative play. "Let's play that story," the teacher will suggest. "Who wants to be the mother bear?" Some children are quite content to be a tree in the forest, and others will need suggestions as to what to say, but the values of released imagination, language practice, and dramatic interest are always there.

In the intermediate grades, children imagine that they are the Pilgrims or pioneers. Such dramatics frequently become organized to the extent that the main ideas are outlined, and children experiment with different scenes, select the ones that seem most effective, and actually write a script that is later presented as a formal production.

Role playing is a nonthreatening, simple way to introduce children to classroom dramatics. By demonstrating in front of their classmates short scenarios they would normally play anyway, students can become aware that drama is just one more creative activity—nothing awesome or intimidating.

From Pantomime to Group Dramatics. It may help some students to start with simple pantomime, wherein situations or ideas are conveyed without the help of speech. Simple situations such as pretending to walk through deep snow or falling leaves; pretending to eat ice cream, a pickle, or cotton candy; pretending to toss a baseball, a chunk of ice, a hot potato, or a pillow are useful for introducing the concept of pantomime. Another pantomime exercise called "reflections" involves two students who face each other. One acts as a mirror reflection of the other, who makes movements or facial expressions that the "mirror" must reflect. Developing body awareness, or kinesthesia, is important not only in dramatic experiences but in general life experiences. Proper posture, carriage, and grace of movement are all desirable qualities that stem from this "muscle sense."

Although pantomime may be used, in a sense, as a warm-up to other dramatic forms, it is in its own right an accomplished theatrical art form. Anyone who has had the pleasure of seeing Marcelle Marceau or any other truly great mime perform knows what a tremendous thrill it is to experience this form of drama.

From such pantomimes, move to sketches involving one-way dialogue. For example, you might get a telephone call inviting you to a party, or telling you that your parents were in an accident, or informing you that you won a contest, or announcing that your team lost.

Situations involving two or more students may be suggested by the teacher. For example:

1. Your friend has asked you to go to the movie; your mother has said you must stay home. She is nearby.
2. A shy schoolmate has just returned from being ill and absent from school, and you want him to feel at home at school again.
3. You are studying for a test, and a schoolmate asks for your help.
4. A classmate has just had a religious holiday. You want to know about it.
5. Your mother wants you to go to camp, but you want to stay home.
6. You have borrowed a camera and broken it. Return it to the owner.
7. Your class is going to elect a president. You want a friend to run, but he is reluctant.

Ordinarily the group decides who will take the various roles in a play. After discussing what a character should be like, it is wise to have different individuals try out for the part. The king should walk with lordly mien, speak deliberately and loudly because of his vast authority, and perhaps flourish a wooden sword. After such a character is established in the minds of the children, let them take turns feeling like a king or whatever character is being developed. At the beginning, most teachers cast parts by type. This means using the child whose personality most nearly fits the part. But after children have had some experience with dramatics there will be opportunity to use the story to help a child with a social or personality problem. All the parts, however, should not be assigned on a "problem" basis because children will then lose interest. One case of "play therapy" at a time is enough for most teachers to handle.

Sociodrama. Sociodrama is closely related to group dramatics as an aid to personality adjustment. Its main purpose is to assist children in being aware of the feelings and problems of others. "How does it feel to be the only child in a room not asked to a party? Let's act it out in a story." The situation may be centered on any problem: the child who acts as a bully and mistreats little children, the child who does not speak English, the lonely lady who complains about the noise children make.

Although sociodrama may be strictly a nonreading, role-playing situation, children sometimes write stories that lend themselves to sociodramatic role playing.

Puppets. Puppets are used as a vehicle for dramatic work in all grades. Some shy children find it easier to project their language through a puppet actor. Certain dramatic effects can be achieved with puppets that make the productions much more satisfying. Animal actors, folklore characters, magic changes, and exotic areas (such as the bottom of the sea) are much easier to manage with puppets than with human actors. Somehow the simple plays written by children seem more spirited when given with puppets.

Puppets are used as a vehicle for dramatic work in all grades. Somehow the simple plays written by children seem more spirited when given with puppets. (Photo by Linda Lungren)

Puppets should be kept simple. Finger puppets, figures on a stick, sacks on the fist, and even the toy hand puppets that can be purchased are better than elaborate string marionettes. Marionette making is an art rather than a language project. The time taken to make and manipulate these figures does not stimulate enough language activity to warrant the effort. See Figure 6–1 for ideas for making effective, simple puppets.

It is not enough simply to make the puppets. They must be given a chance to perform! Informal, nonscripted use of puppets may include telling fairy tales that children are very familiar with; bringing to life LEA stories created by the class, or role-playing situations wherein a puppet expresses feelings that students may have trouble articulating on a more personal level. More formal puppet productions may be accomplished when children can read and/or memorize scripts. Simple sets, a minimum number of characters, clear dialogue, and lots of action are all elements of effective puppetry. Well-known tales like "Jack and the Beanstalk," "Hansel and Gretel," and "Three Billy Goats Gruff" work out very well, as do some of the tales of Beatrix Potter, such as *Peter Rabbit* or *Jemima Puddleduck*. Nursery rhymes and poems can also be adapted to puppet presentations. Older children may wish to dramatize excerpts from longer works such as historical novels based on famous people—Florence Nightingale, George Washington, Paul Revere, and others. Melodrama is an excellent source of puppetry, with its villian, hero, and lady in distress. This format can be scrambled to suit liberated tastes by making the heroine save a "gentleman in distress." Children who speak a foreign language may wish to follow up an English presentation with one in their native or acquired language. The possibilities are endless—let your students' imaginations create the drama and let the puppets bring it to life.

Reading-Dependent Activities. Although drama that does not depend on reading accomplishes many beneficial objectives, reading-dependent activities have the obvious added advantage of reinforcing and improving a diversity of reading skills, both silent and oral.

How May Oral Reading Skills Be Improved? A good oral reader is eager to share with his listeners something that seems important. It may be new information, an experience, a vivid description, an interesting character, a bit of humor, or a poetic phrase. Without a motive of this kind, oral reading is impersonal and lifeless. The reader should know his audience's interests

Sock puppet:

Put your hand inside the sock and manipulate your fingers to create a face and mouth. Embellish with buttons, felt, pipe cleaner, etc.

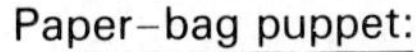

Paper–bag puppet:

Draw or paste a face on the flat bottom of the bag. The fold becomes a mouth. Arms, hats, clothes, etc., can be drawn or pasted on. Insert hand to manipulate by opening and closing "mouth."

Stick puppet:

Draw a picture of the puppet character on stiff paper. Cut it out and glue, tape or paste it to a stick (popsicle, tongue depressor, straw, dowel).

Variation:

Use a styrofoam ball, cloth and stick. Drape cloth over stick and put into styrofoam.

Tube puppet:

Using a cardboard cylinder (paper towel or toilet roll) apply features and/or clothes by using paint or by pasting on colored paper, yarn, fabric, glitter, etc. A stick can be glued inside, or fingers inserted in tube to manipulate the puppet.

Figure 6–1. Constructing simple puppets.

and needs and interpret the material accordingly. To read aloud well, the reader must have mastered the skills of perception so that he recognizes words quickly and accurately. Equally important is the ability to group words together in thought units and to read smoothly. To help listeners grasp the author's meaning, the reader uses various devices. The reader highlights new ideas through the use of emphasis, makes clear the transition from one idea to another, indicates by proper phrasing the units of thought within a sentence, relates the ideas of a series by keeping his voice up until the end is reached, and indicates climax by force and vigor of expression.

Most teachers will ask, "Does such reading really take place in the elementary school?" They are thinking of the slow, halting oral reading of the reading circle. Day by day, teachers have urged children to read as if they were talking, to read to find the answer to a question, or to read the part of a story they liked best. But seldom has such reading produced anything like that just described. It was usually considered good if the child knew all the words. Nor was anyone in the listening group charmed by what was read. After all, they had read the same material.

Unfortunately, most oral reading in a classroom has been for the single purpose of evaluation. In addition, there has been an emphasis on speed as an indication of growth. Children have sat before machines to increase eye movement, have taken timed tests, have been taught to skim, and have received vast amounts of materials to read for information. Little wonder, then, that few read well orally.

The skills of oral reading are most naturally developed in the reading of plays. The reading of plays adds many values to reading: it enlists the delight in dramatization that appears in the everyday make-believe of all children; it enriches imagery in the reading of fiction; it provides disciplines not found in other types of reading; and it enhances comprehension, vocabulary development, phrase reading, expression, and general speech skills.

Children with varying reading abilities may be cast in a play. Undiscovered personality qualities are often brought out in play reading. When a child is someone else while reading a play, new and delightful aspects of his personality are revealed. Plays are good for reducing shyness in timid children and for revealing sympathetic qualities in aggressive ones. Plays allow discussion of personal qualities, manners, habits, and ethical choices without self-consciousness in the pupils or moralizing by the teacher. The children can talk objectively about the actions of the characters, knowing that the roles they have played are only make-believe.

Play reading requires discipline not encountered in other reading. Alertness to timing of speeches, speaking on cue, keeping one's place on the page, reading words and phrases correctly, expressing oneself well—these and other factors are recognized by the child as important in the success of the play.

The motivating power of the true audience situation is always found in play reading. Comprehension is assured; the child cannot interpret his lines unless he understands them. Phrase reading is improved by play reading. The child who is inclined to read a word at a time or to ignore commas and periods in oral reading will strive for complete phrases and attend to punctuation when he interprets his role. Improvement of expression through emphasis, pause, and interpretation of mood and feeling is the main outcome of play reading. Basal readers often contain plays designed to achieve these goals.

Another effective way of practicing oral reading in many schools is asking children in the intermediate grades to prepare a library book to read to a small group in the kindergarten or first grade. One fourth-grade class motivates itself by keeping a record of "Books I Have Read to Others."

Some selections in great literature especially lend themselves to oral reading. The whitewashing of the fence in *The Adventures of Tom Sawyer* is written as if it were a play. Some of the scenes in *Freddie the Pig* by Walter R. Brooks consist almost exclusively of conversation that makes delightful oral reading.

For the lower grades, parts of *Winnie the Pooh* by A. A. Milne may be presented as a Reader's Theater. *Charlotte's Web* can be an excellent assembly or PTA program, with a narrator and four readers sometimes reading dialogue and at other times reading exposition.

Formal Play Making. Formal dramatics, involving the memorization of a well-written play, has many values for children able to participate in it. The discipline of memorization, the work on characterization, the team spirit developed in presenting the material, and the gratifying applause of a truly appreciative audience are valuable experiences. The beginning teacher is often tempted to start with a play that is too difficult. Professional children's theaters with well-equipped stages and trained staffs can produce elaborate plays with such apparent ease that a teacher is tempted to try the same in the classroom. Do not do it unless you are willing to spend *hours* rehearsing after school, devote weekends to painting scenery and making costumes, and act as a military policeman during the rehearsal and performance. Perhaps in a summer school or with an especially talented group you can realize your ambitions. In the meantime, be content with less professional material. By all means avoid plays that require large casts or run more than an hour.

Plays such as *Why the Chimes Ring, Strawberry Red, King of Nomania, Knights of the Silver Shield, Elmer,* and *Cabbages* are favorites for the junior high school age group. The little plays published in the magazines *Teacher, Instructor,* and *Plays* are widely used in the lower grades and are relatively simple to prepare. (See Appendix A at the end of this section for further suggestions.) Most children will learn their parts in six or eight readings. By the time of the production almost all of them will know all the lines. Involve parents in making costumes, and on the day of the show ask

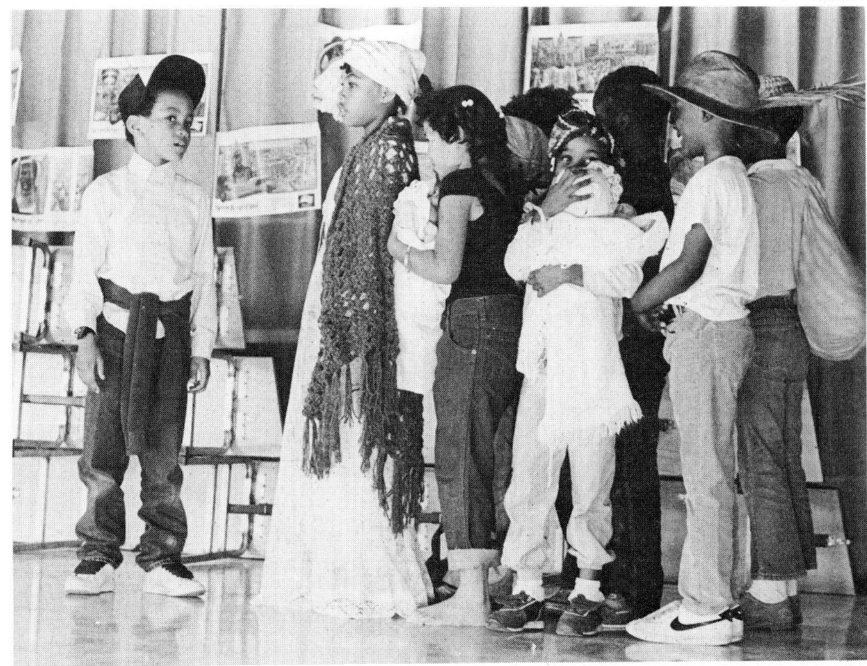

The discipline of memorization, the work on characterization, the team spirit developed in presenting the material, and the gratifying applause of a truly appreciate audience are valuable experiences in formal dramatics. (Photo by Linda Lungren)

at least one adult to supervise children backstage who are not performing. If makeup is used, keep it simple. A little rouge on the cheeks, a dab of lipstick, and a stroke or two with the grease pencil will transform most child actors sufficiently. No matter how well it is put on, a beard never looks right on a child. Crepe hair applied with spirit gum, available at all theatrical supply stores, is about as satisfactory a method of "aging" as any.

Most scenery problems can be solved by using sets of folding screens on which the outline of a forest, window, or fireplace has been drawn in colored chalk or water colors. Children's imaginations are so vivid that anything more than this is lost effort. Various sound effects are available on records, or they can be put on a tape and amplified at the proper time.

Children are usually excited after a performance. If possible, plan to have a postperformance period with refreshments and general relaxation while costumes are put away and other details attended to. Children are seldom ready for a scheduled class after a play, and the wise teacher will recognize this fact in making plans. Avoid showing concern over forgotten lines or things that did not go just right, but instead find much to praise.

Radio and Television Production. Radio and television scripts offer excellent possibilities at the elementary level for group composition and speech. The definite pattern in which action and dialogue must be cast gives pupils needed support as they plan scenes the cameras should focus on or sounds the microphone can hear. In a television script, the scenes for the cameras ("video") are placed on the left-hand side of the page; the words spoken, music, and sound effects ("audio") are placed on the right, opposite the scenes they will accompany.

The use of the videocassette has made film production a fairly uncomplicated reality for most classrooms. As the cameras become more compact and easier to handle, television show and film production for the classroom becomes less of a "production."

Children should be told to speak in a clear and natural voice without "rushing" their lines, yet moving along as though they were talking normally to other students. They should not try to imitate or exaggerate. This does not mean, however, that they should not strive to get some feeling into their voices.

Lettering on posters should be large and simple, not less than two inches in height. Remember that lowercase lettering is more legible than capitals. Do not use fancy lettering. Try to use dark letters when possible.

Prints or photographs can show specific objects, scenery, or people. They should be mounted on an eleven-by-fourteen-inch board, preferably horizontally.

Because the videotaping process is uncomplicated and inexpensive, it will be interesting for your students to tape rehearsals as well. These can be reviewed for evaluation and improvements can be made.

If you have access to a community television or radio station, perhaps a tour or guest speakers may be arranged.

Choral Reading or Speaking. For more immediate dramatic results, choral reading or speaking gives children the sense of producing a completed performance without the complicated process of actually "making" a play. Choral reading is the dramatic oral interpretation of a poem or story by groups of children speaking at once. Voices can be combined in many ways, to many ends. Children learn the importance of clear pronunciation, rhythm, inflection, pitch, emphasis, and interpretation. By recording their choral efforts, students will hear for themselves what is effective and what is not. Selections can be lighthearted or serious. Again, for younger children nursery rhymes work well, as do song lyrics. For older children, experiment with classic poems (*"The Raven"* by E. A. Poe, *"A Ballad of John Silver"* by John Masefield, *"O Captain! My Captain!"* by Walt Whitman) and with modern ones like those by Shel Silverstein and Langston Hughes.

One of the main interests in choral reading or speaking is in trying various arrangements or groupings. Table 6–3 depicts some examples of these possibilities.

Table 6–3
Examples of Choral Groupings

Refrain	Leader followed by group speaking the refrain	Leader: verse Group: refrain Leader: verse Group: refrain
Line-a-child or group	Each child (or group of two or more) reads one line followed by the next child and the next	Group A Group B Group C Group D Group E
Dialogue	Heavy voices are grouped together, opposed by light voices in another group. Groups alternate speaking the lines in question and answer or contrast form	Group A Group B A B A B
Cumulative or crescendo	Starts with a single group and picks up groups as the selection continues—to finish with unison speaking	Group A A & B A, B, and C A, B, C, and D A, B, C, D, and E

Reader's Theater. The success of the Reader's Theater technique depends on the readers' ability to create images for the audience. This is accomplished through excellent interpretation, timing, and staging of the piece. Staging in a Reader's Theater production is not the props, scenery, or action. Rather it is the manner in which parts are created for individual readers and are integrated throughout the entire reading. The readers must have a complete understanding of the reading material in order to convey the drama to the audience. There are no props and minimal, if any, movement. A Reader's Theater stage may consist only of stools or chairs and, often, music stands for holding the scripts.

To a large extent, the process of Reader's Theater is as important as the product. From an educational point of view there is nothing quite like Reader's Theater to stimulate enthusiasm for words and the music and intensity of language. Because the success or failure of the whole production pivots on the way words are read, students concentrate on meaning and on conveying that meaning orally. There are no visual signposts—props or gestures—that will save the meaning if the words fail them.

Just about anything, from Shakespeare to Paul Bunyan, can be adapted for Reader's Theater. Let the students flex their creative muscles in preparing the scripts. They should be encouraged to choose stories or poems with lots of dialogue or narrative that can be adapted to dialogue. Stories with suspenseful, intriguing plots that involve the characters with each other dramatically and then have a definite, snappy ending are excellent Reader's Theater material. Students should prepare an introduction including the title, author, and a brief introduction of the characters or pertinent background material. The parts should be assigned, and after each child has studied the whole script and understood it completely, the players (or readers) can discuss their interpretation and devise a cohesive production. Rehearsals are important for confidence and timing. The whole production can be achieved in several class periods, or, if the script is a prepared one, a single class period will produce wonderful results. Reader's Theater is a terrific confidence builder and is the perfect tool to reinforce every skill in the language arts curriculum.

How Is Courtesy Taught in the Language Arts Program?

A part of the awkwardness of children in a social situation arises from not knowing the proper thing to say. Greetings, introductions, apologies, interruptions, and expressions of appreciation involve established patterns of language. At first these may be taught as examples to be imitated. "Say bye-bye," a mother urges the infant. Or the parent will, by asking the child, "What do we say when someone gives us something?" eventually elicit a "Thank you" response.

Courtesy instruction will seem a little silly to children unless it is presented in terms of situations. These situations should reveal the need for some type of social convention. At the time when the school is having an open house or a parents' evening, present the problem of the right way to introduce a parent to a teacher, a parent to a classmate, or one child's parents to other parents.

In a social studies class there will be times when opposing opinions must be expressed. How do we express disagreement without offending people or starting an argument? And if we should offend a person, how can we express our apologies? It will interest children to learn the ways these problems have been solved in other lands. Many of our concepts of courtesy reflect our democratic belief that everyone has certain rights and freedoms. We do not avoid direct contests in athletics even though we know someone will lose, whereas in some other cultures direct contests are avoided, and ideas are generally expressed indirectly.

There is no better place to discuss table manners than in a health class. Start with problems like this: "Do you like to sit at a table where someone is messy with food? Talks with his mouth full? Shouts and plays at the table?" Lessons about the use of knife and fork, setting the table, refusing food you dislike, discussing certain topics at the table, and even ordering food at a restaurant all involve language skills in this area.

Basic to all courtesy are two concepts, respect and kindness. Respect is shown to our parents and to older people, to our country and its flag, to those who serve us, and to our friends and neighbors. Kindness covers a broad area of human virtue and includes goodwill, compassion, generosity, and love for one's fellow man. Rudeness is the opposite of kindness in that it makes another person suffer. Even following the rules of etiquette can be unkind if it causes others to be embarrassed. The story of Queen Victoria's blowing on her soup to cover up a guest's bad manners can be told as a true act of courtesy.

Both respect and kindness are implied when we speak of consideration of others. A discussion on this topic should also include acceptance of cultural differences. This must go much deeper than the language aspect, but knowing the language is a way of establishing the behavior desired as well as the inner sensitivity that is true courtesy.

Again the importance of example must not be forgotten. The teacher's everyday manners will provide many object lessons in this area. It might be well for the children to know more about the teacher's prerogatives and responsibilities.

Summary

The development of oral language and instructional practices that foster public and private language expansion for *all* children received primary attention in this chapter. Instructional activities were grouped for presentation according to type and grade level. The role of creative dramatics as a base for whole language learning was also extensively presented.

Suggested Classroom Projects and Questions for Discussion

Projects

1. Observe a classroom. Note the different tones of voice the teacher uses as she explains material to the total class, talks with an individual child, or gains attention of a group.
2. Access your own voice qualities according to the criteria presented in this chapter. Develop a rating scale for effective teaching voices. Use it for yourself and any volunteers you may find. Do you have a speech habit that you would not wish your students to imitate? If so, how would you correct it?
3. The term *bicultural* is used with respect to some programs. Contrast the concept of biculturalism with uniculturalism. Do you see any reason for seeking a one-culture population? Explain your findings.
4. Describe how you would adapt such programs as *60 Minutes* for the classroom.
5. You work in a school where assembly programs and PTA programs are assigned to teachers a year in advance. As a result, the teachers stage elaborate productions and compete with each other. This year you have drawn the Thanksgiving assembly. What will you do?
6. Design some games to play at home for a child who has not mastered the major speech sounds.
7. In order to encourage participation and expression, teachers sometimes permit or encourage children to participate in activities of questionable taste. Should a second-grade girl dance a hula and sing *Lovely Hula Hands?* The love songs that constitute the popular music of the day have their place, but should one be sung by primary school children simply because their childish innocence adds cuteness? Sometimes boys appear on TV singing in the manner of popular singers whose facial and bodily expressions accentuate the sexual suggestions of the lyrics. Are there aspects of taste and propriety that students might discuss with respect to such programs? Create a script about ways you might approach the subject of taste and propriety with a student who wishes to perform an unsuitable selection in a school program.
8. Design a speech activity that would reinforce Chafe's "idea unit" theory. Discuss ways that this activity would theoretically (or actually) help in student writing efforts.
9. Attempt a Reader's Theater project of your own by selecting the material, revising it into a script, recruiting readers (students or peers), and rehearsing, and presenting the production. You may wish to videotape the performance for taping practice as well as for evaluation.
10. Develop your own resource center for creative dramatics by collecting selections appropriate for puppetry, choral reading, Reader's Theater, radio or TV drama, or formal dramatics. Keep in mind the length of the selection and its appropriateness as to interest and grade level.

Questions

1. How can correct public usage be stressed without establishing the discourteous habit of correcting each other? Should children ever politely correct adults or other children?
2. A city child may have a cultural background quite different from those presented in reading textbooks. The same would be true of a rural child with a Mexican or Indian heritage. What should be the content of their early reading material?
3. Why have many adults studied a foreign language for the purpose of reading it rather than speaking it?
4. Would it be wise to have foreign-language–speaking children learn to read their language prior to reading English? What is their learning goal?
5. You have a class with many emotionally disturbed children. These children come from broken homes, attend clinics, and so on. Should you attempt creative dramatics?
6. Current textbooks for language instruction contain a great deal about the linguistic history and structure of English. Is this content more appropriate to social science than a language text? How much help does the teacher find in current textbooks with respect to oral composition?
7. Should a child be expected to read a word containing a sound that is not present in his speech?
8. Do you feel that every child in a classroom should have a part in a program presented for an audience?
9. Can you tell from a person's voice whether he is tired or emotionally upset? What are the signals?
10. How might singing games help in the development of a child's speech?

Chapter 7

Learning to Read/Reading to Learn

(Photo by Linda Lungren)

OBJECTIVES

At the end of this chapter students should be able to:

1. understand the important role of the teacher in teaching reading.
2. understand that reading is comprehending.
3. analyze the significance of "being ready" to read.
4. understand teaching phonics as part of a reading/language arts program.
5. examine techniques for teaching reading throughout the curriculum.
6. perceive the importance of assessment as a dimension of instruction.

Early last summer I was invited to spend a day sailing aboard a twenty-two-foot sailboat that belongs to a friend. Since I had had little prior experience with sailing, I decided to prepare myself by reading a basic sailing manual.

To gain the information I needed I went to the library and secured an introductory sailing manual. I settled in to read. About ten minutes into the experience, I was losing my confidence. I could not read the book.

You are probably thinking that this is impossible—a well-schooled university professor not able to read a sailing manual.

Let me explain. One of the initial passages read like this:

> Bend to boom and attach outhaul. Secure tack to gooseneck and attach main halyard. Hoist mainsail while making sure battens are in their pockets. Sail will not go to masthead if vang, mainsheet or outhaul are not loose.

I could say all of the words. I could even say them with expression; but, since I had no experience with boats, I could not read them because *reading* means *comprehending*. I was unable to comprehend because I did not have the necessary experience to add meaning to the words as they appeared in this context.

This did not mean that I was not smart, or that I could not read some things very well. It also did not mean that I could not learn to read the manual. It only meant that right at that time I did not have the necessary experience that would allow me to unlock the information in the printed word.

Sometimes this happens to children in school. They are unable to read a specific text because of a lack of reading skills or lack of necessary experience that is needed in order to understand the topic. Unfortunately, students are often incorrectly labeled as dull or retarded because of this inability. In most instances, good teaching could have unlocked the barrier for them.

I realized that in order to understand the passage I needed to learn the parts of the sailboat. I decided to teach myself, just as I would teach a child who could name the words but could not comprehend them. Such a child would not need help with phonics or structural analysis because he or she would have no difficulty sounding out or saying the words. The difficulty was with understanding. The child, like me, would need help with understanding the words in this context.

Therefore, I secured a model (Fig. 7–1) from a friend and set about gaining an understanding of the parts of a sailboat since this was the information I had to understand in order to be able to read the manual.

As teachers we have to provide students with the background information needed for reading and we must also help them learn to obtain such information for themselves when we are no longer beside them. The information that they need will be *topical* or *process*. *Topical* information is that which is related to the content of a passage. *Process* information is that which the reader employs to decode the print (for example, phonics or structural analysis).

In an attempt to accomplish the goal of helping each student to become an independent reader/learner, we are continuously in search of effective teaching methods.

The Teacher: The Most Important Variable in Teaching Students to Read

Throughout the history of American reading education, millions of dollars have been spent on research attempting to determine the best methods and materials for the teaching of reading. Important differences among programs with different emphases have been found, but none of these differences is as significant as the finding that different teachers using the same materials and methods produce a greater range of results than any range found for the different programs. Some teachers, because of unique abilities to under-

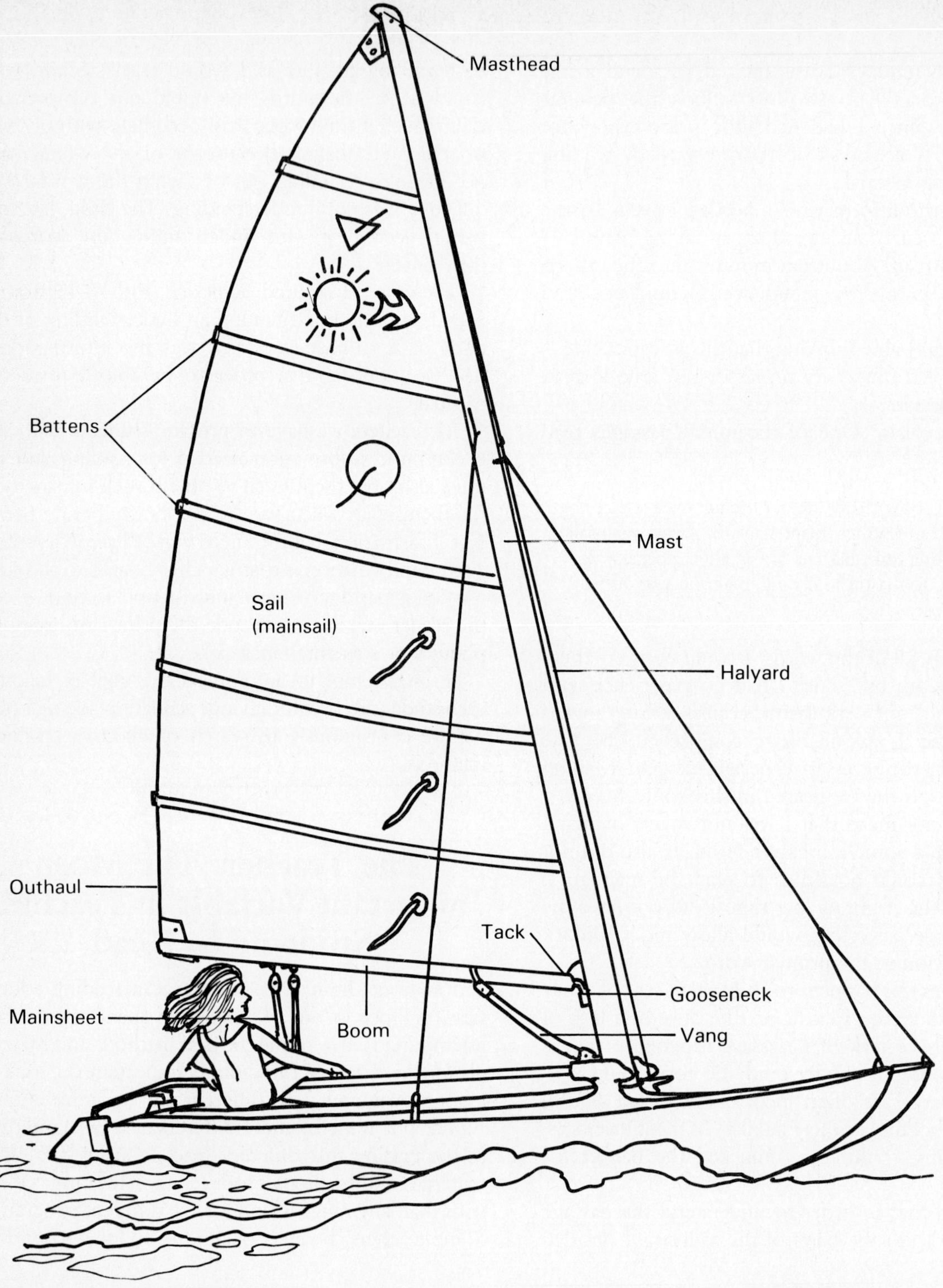

Figure 7–1. Sailboat design.

stand the needs of a learner and to make the available materials relevant, are successful in developing reading abilities regardless of method.

This does not mean that reading methods and materials are unimportant. It does mean that a competent teacher, using materials in which she has confidence, is essential to a successful program in reading instruction. If the teacher knows *why* she is using a certain book with a child or *why* she is helping a child master a specific reading skill, she is operating at a professional level that assures positive results.

Reading is a process of comprehending written discourse that involves decoding and encoding. One aspect of decoding is to relate the printed word to oral language meaning, which includes changing what is seen in print into meaningful sound. Consistent sound clues in the English language may be represented by total words, word groups, or bound morphemes such as *-ing*. Children learning to speak a language usually associate sounds with meanings; that is, they hear sounds as words or sentence parts. A child's first association between writing and reading is usually based on meaning. The child of three or four can select his favorite record or book through visual clues; there is also visual recognition of the names of stores, the names of streets, and the names of some of the products advertised in commercials on television.

There are ideographs in our language as well. The $ sign contains no clues to its sound, but you know its meaning. All our numbers are ideographic. The symbols 9, 10, and 11 for example contain no sound clues but represent only meanings.

Few books read by adults are printed "talk." Certainly, the authors of this textbook have never talked in the manner in which it is written. When teachers work with comprehension and understanding as reading skills, they have a controlled situation that permits them to prepare the oral language and the background experiences of the reader that are essential to interpret the thought presented by the writer. It does not matter whether these are called reading-thinking skills, as they are listed in many courses of study since 1900, or creative or critical reading skills, as they are in more recent publications.

A part of our problem in the language arts is that the term *reading* has many meanings. Some of these are related to purpose, such as *oral* reading, through which a writer's ideas are projected through speech; reading that describes an *area* in the curriculum; reading that means *action* and may refer to anything from a child's telling what was seen in a picture to a judge's interpretation of a point of law. Children may read a word by changing it to sounds that they recognize in their language, or they may change it to sounds and discover that it is still meaningless. Another child may understand a word's meaning without being able to pronounce it. In terms of response, a word means different things. Sometimes the response is careful and profound thought; at other times it is an imaginative fantasy. There may be great emotional feeling in the response or only casual notice.

Eventually all aspects of reading are mastered by most students. But to the beginner the problem is one of looking at words in their printed or written form and discovering the meaning intended by the one who wrote them. Reading is the method by which we communicate to ourselves—and sometimes to others—the meaning contained in printed symbols.

Reading may be thought of as looking *through* words to the fields of thought *behind* them. The degree of relationship between the meaning of the writer and the interpretation of the reader determines the accuracy of the reading. The meaning does not reside totally on the printed page, but also in the mind of the reader. Thus, meanings will differ, because each reader possesses different experiences in terms of which one interprets the words. Reading is an interactive process between a reader and a text.

To the beginner each word represents a puzzle to be solved. A word like *mother* or *baby* presents little or no difficulty because the meaning is definite, the word is familiar, and the feelings associated with the word are usually pleasant. A word like *fruit,* however, which can mean *apples, bananas, oranges, grapes, lemons,* or *peaches,* is a different problem. A word like *here,* which may mean at *school, by the teacher, where I stand, on the desk,* or almost anyplace, is a puzzle indeed. Then there are words like *at,* which even the teacher cannot define without talking a long time. Some printed words are interesting visually, such as *look,* which has a pair of eyeglasses in the middle, and *oh,* the first letter of which is the shape of the mouth when you say it. Each new word that is recognized and remembered represents a satisfying experience when one is learning to read.

From the teacher's point of view the process is one of language expansion, rehearsal, encouragement, reteaching, searching for material, making special material, being pleased by the success of some, and being concerned about the needs of others. Teachers do not expect beginners to identify words that are strange in meaning or new to their oral language since in the early grades students are learning to read and in the later grades they read to learn. Early instructional efforts are directed toward the establishment of word analysis skills that will help children change the printed words to their proper sounds and meanings that are already part of their oral vocabulary. The focus of the teaching effort is on the individual child. Reading is not taught to a child, but rather a child is taught to read.

Reading Is Comprehending

A child who is learning to read probably remembers each word through the same kind of association process that an adult uses in recalling the identity of people. Such factors as age, hair color, size, profession, place of meeting, and topic of conversation serve as memory aids. If we are seeking to recall a person's name, we use these factors as clues. In much the same ways, children learn to look for certain clues that will help them to understand the message of the printed word. Five types of reading clues are taught as a part of a child's word skills:

1. *Phonetic clues.* None of the reading programs widely used today neglects the importance of this knowledge. Phonetic clues should probably be called linguistic clues because both individual sound and the language flow of words, sentences, and story are involved.
2. *Word-form clues.* These are sometimes called configuration clues. They are the forms of the word that give it some identity. *Christmas* and *grandmother* are relatively easy words because of their meaning and length. *Elephant,* with its silhouette or shadow of tall and long letters, may be recognized because of its form. For some words these configuration clues render little assistance. Words like *such, said,* and *word* have similar silhouettes or, as some teachers say, have like shadows.
3. *Structural clues.* These are noticed in common endings such as *-ing, -ed,* and *-tion.* Compound words also contain structural clues since children are required to recognize that in "cupboard" and "raincoat", two words have been combined.
4. *Sight word clues.* These are clues that must be memorized through repetition. Words with tangible meanings, such as *of;* those with difficult phonetic combinations, such as *one;* and some proper names are examples of sight words. Children with keen visual memories will usually learn almost all primary words by sight. Certain words need many repetitions before they are mastered. Words like *here, there, who, what,* and *where* are especially difficult. Others will be remembered after only a few repetitions. Dictionary skills are sometimes referred to as reading clues. Certainly for older students the dictionary is a way of determining the meaning of a word.
5. *Context analysis clues.* These are found in the pictures in a book, in the meaning of known words in the sentence, or in the oral discussion of the class. It is always wise to discuss the pictures in a story first, or the children will move their eyes away from the new word to

look at the picture for help. If the oral discussion has set the story in Africa, the child may use that clue to understand a new word when he or she comes to it.

When teaching a child to read, these clues should not be taught through isolated activities. They should be taught in an integrated process through the child's language experiences. Through the experiences of the reader word forms and phonics are combined.

These word analysis processes enable the reader to examine a printed word and determine its language sound and meaning. The reader is then able to organize, interpret, and interact with what the writer has said. This interaction is a process of comprehending or understanding the main idea expressed, noticing details that add meaning, determining whether the idea is true, and noting the personal responses or appreciation.

The understanding of meaning is closely related to purpose or incentive for reading. We can insure meaningful reading experiences by engaging children in activities similar to the following.

Read to find out what discovery the character made, what the character did, or what happened to a particular character, or to answer the questions the group had about Indian life or space flight. (Reading for details or facts.)

Read to find out why it was a good title, what the problem is in the story, or what the character learned, and to summarize what the character did to achieve his purpose. (Reading for specific information.)

Read to find out what happened in each of the parts of the story, what happened first, second, and third—each step taken to solve a problem, scenes and events for dramatization. (Reading for sequence or organization.)

Read to find out why the characters feel the way they do, what the author is trying to show us, why the characters changed, what qualities the characters had that helped them succeed or caused them to fail. (Reading for inference.)

Read to find what was unusual about a character, what was funny in the story, or whether the story was true. (Reading to classify.)

Read to find out how the character changed, how his life is different from the life we know, how two stories are alike, and how the character is like the reader. (Reading to compare or contrast.)

Read to find out whether the character was successful or lived by certain standards, or whether you would like to do what the character did or work the way he did in the story. (Reading to evaluate.)

The reading process involves a number of specific processes, such as the use of word analysis techniques. While it may seem at times that the mastery of a particular process is the focus of instruction, it must never be the end purpose of a reading program. Our goal as teachers must be to help children attain a level of reading proficiency that will enable them to acquire, organize, and share ideas.

Comprehension of written material requires many kinds of processing. The activities of a proficient reader include operations performed both on the text that is being read and on the knowledge of the world. Flood and Lapp (1977) have demonstrated that readers must process by inference before they can extract meaning from the text. Inference unites the text with the world through the reader's knowledge. For example, a successful reader performs the operations as shown in Table 7–1 to extract the meaning of a sentence.

These operations occur almost simultaneously if the reader is an active participant in the process of reading. If the reader is passive, none of the critical operations can occur and no comprehension will result. Long ago, Thorndike stressed the importance of recognizing reading as an active participation task:

> Understanding a paragraph is like solving a problem in mathematics. It consists in selecting the right

Table 7–1
Reader—Text Interaction

The text says: The duck is ready to eat.

Operation 1: The reader must resolve the ambiguity of this sentence.

Operation 2: The reader must apply his world knowledge (experience).
- a. The reader generates the possibilities of the meaning of the sentence.
  - i. The duck is ready to eat corn, his supper, a worm . . .

    or
  - ii. Andy is finished cooking and the duck is ready to be eaten.
- b. The reader waits for more contextual information from the passage; that is, he reads farther.

The text says: The duck is ready to eat. He always squawks to announce to the farmer that he is hungry.

Operation 3: The reader extracts the implicit meaning of the first sentence (i.e., the duck is ready to eat something).

elements of the situation and putting them together in the right relations, and also with the right amount of weight or influence or force for each. The mind is assailed as it were by every word in the paragraph. It must select, repress, soften, emphasize, correlate and organize, all under the influence of the right mental set of purpose or demand (Thorndike, 1917, p. 329).

How Has the Readiness Concept Influenced Instructional Practice in Reading?

In the development of each child there is a time when the individual language facility, experience, or social development indicates that the child is ready for a particular aspect of reading instruction.

As children mature, the responsibility with respect to readiness for meaningful reading is shared with them by the teacher. In all areas of the curriculum the teacher accepts responsibility for these tasks:

Helping students construct the concepts that are needed to understand what is read.

Expressing the assignment in questions that are stated and organized cooperatively by the teacher and the pupils. Such cooperative activity defines the assignment, sets purposes that motivate the reading, and provides opportunities for the pupil to evaluate and organize ideas read.

Providing for individual differences in reading by supplying a variety of books that can be read by children with various reading abilities.

Setting purposes for the discussion and additional activities that give the pupil opportunities to evaluate, organize, and plan for the retention of ideas gained through reading.

Giving attention to each pupil's deficiencies in the reading-thinking jobs. The point of breakdown in locating information, arranging ideas, and so on, must be diagnosed for each student.

In classroom practice the readiness concept has led to some specific ways to handle individual differences. These include (1) dividing the class into groups of children with similar needs, (2) creating reading material that will interest older children yet will not be too difficult in terms of word-attack skills, (3) planning so that children will learn from each other, (4) providing special rooms for those who need additional instruction, (5) individualizing all reading instruction in a single classroom, (6) organizing the curriculum as a nongraded primary school, and (7) planning summer school programs that are both remedial and enriching.

What Is the Place of Phonics in the Language Arts Program?

As suggested earlier in this chapter, *phonics* and *phonetics* are terms that are often confused. *Phonetics* is the science of speech sounds in actual use. *Phonics* is the application of phonetics in the teaching of reading and spelling. The phonetic symbol in speech for the *s* sound would be the same in all these words: *bus, kiss, scene, face, psalm, listen, schism, six, answer, city*. Yet in the use of phonics a child must remember that the sound is made by various letter combinations. The sound element is called a *phoneme*. In the words listed here, the sound /s/ is a phoneme.

One point must be understood from the beginning of any discussion of phonics. Communication involves an exchange of meaning. It is quite possible for a child to learn to sound out the letters of a word like *d-a-w-k-i-n,* but unless the sounder then associates the word with its meaning (stupid), it is not reading. In such a case all that has been done is to write a design with letters of the alphabet. Although phonic skills can be used in such meaningless ways, it does not follow that they are valueless skills. Indeed, the ability to use the sounds of our language as it is written, combined with a demand for meaning, is basic to both reading and spelling. However, because ours is not a strictly phonetic language, it is inappropriate to rely solely on phonics as a reading program.

In reading, children use phonics to perform these major reading tasks:

1. To identify the initial sound of a word.
2. To divide a word into syllables in pronunciation.
3. To check a guess when a strange word is identified from context.
4. To identify prefixes and common endings.
5. To identify the word root.

The phonics problem in reading is that of changing printed letters to sound and then giving meaning to the combination of sounds that makes a word. Without a meaning clue this process is difficult; if the word is completely unknown to the child, it is almost impossible. Relatively simple words like *adage* and *adobe, table* and *tablet,* or *tamable* and *tamale* require distinctions of pronunciation that are not easily discoverable by phonetic analyses.

On the market today are programs that teach sounds independently and then apply them to words. Some start with vowels, others with consonants, and still others with consonant-vowel combinations, such as *fe, fi, fo, fu*. When this material is well taught, children memorize many of the sounds and alphabet letter associations of our language.

In application of the sounds, this material usually ignores the many nonphonetic words common in our language, such as *was, been, have, come,* and *you,* and does use those that can be built phonetically, such as *gun, sun, fin, mold, ill, dill,* and *kill,* which are not very useful in the reading material of the primary grades.

A more serious problem is that the skills learned do not apply to the analysis of longer words. The ability to sound *pat* simply does not apply to *patriot, pathetic,* and *patience*.

In the classroom one observes wrong teaching practices concerning phonics. Some teachers confuse visual similarity with sound similarity. Words like *grow, snow, low,* and *grown* are included with exercises on the *ow* sounds in *owl, cow,* and *clown*.

Finding little words in big words gives a sound clue less than half the time, yet teachers persist in telling children to look for the little word. There is no sound like *an* in *thanks, fat* in *father, is* in *island, of* in *often,* or *all* in *shall*. Finding the little word may give a false sound value, such as *bat* in *bathe, am* in *blame, doze* in *dozen,* and *row* in *trowel,* or prevent proper syllable identification, as in *am* in *among, even* in *eleven,* and *beg* in *began*. Finding the base or root word is quite another matter. Finding *father* in *fatherly* or *forget* in *unforgettable* is quite different from attempting to find *fat* in *father* or *table* in *unforgettable*. Take any page of material and note the little words in the big ones. In the previous sentence a child might find *an* (any), *age* (page), *at, ate, mat* (material), *an* (and), *no, not* (note), *he* (the), *it, lit* (little), *or* (words), *on* (ones). In none of these is the meaning of the small word a clue to the meaning of the large word. If a child considers *no* as a meaning, the meaning of the little words read into the larger word could create confusion or establish a habit of not seeking meaning.

An observation of a first- or second-grade class will reveal that the teachers do a great deal of prompting with phonetic clues. Suppose the child is trying to read the word *mumps*. After he has determined the initial sound, the teacher will say, "It rhymes with *jumps*." With that degree of help the child says the word. It should be noted that the student alone would never have been able to provide the clue "It rhymes with *jumps*." If the child could do that, he or she could have read the word. We do not know whether such figuring out with teacher clues really helps the child remember the word. Some evidence indicates that the beginning sound and meaning are all some children need. If they cannot identify the word, it should be told to them and be taught as a sight word along with some nonphonetic words, such as *laugh, each,* and most proper names or place names.

Basal reading series differ considerably in their use of phonic material. Some use any device that will work with specific new words as they are introduced. One new word will be remembered by the shape, another by the fact that it starts with the *m* sound, still another because it rhymes with a known word. Other programs attempt to teach patterns of attack that the child should use with each new word.

At present the following sequences of learning are commonly followed:

Sequence # 1

1. Listening to and understanding oral language.
2. Recognizing names that begin alike.
3. Recognizing the beginning sound of a word.
4. Recognizing letters and word differences.
5. Matching letter and word forms.
6. Expressing speech sounds and using language.

Sequence # 2

1. Hearing and recognizing in the context of words the following single consonants in the initial position: *b, c* (hard sound only), *d, f, g* (hard sound only), *h, j, l, m, n, p, r, s, t,* and *w*. Omit *k, v, x, y,* and *z*.
2. Hearing and recognizing in the context of words the speech consonants *ch, sh, th,* and *wh;* the consonant blends such as *sk, sm, sn, sp, st, sw, tw, br, bl, gl, pl, fr,* and *tr* in initial positions. Any one of the initial sound items may be introduced as soon as the pupil knows two or more words that begin with that item.

Sequence # 3

1. Introducing, in the context of a word, *v* and *y* in addition to reviewing the initial consonants presented in first grade, and later presenting *g* and *k*.
2. Continued teaching of blends *gr, fr, cr, dr, bl, cl, gl, sw, tw, scr,* and *thr,* in the context of a word.
3. Emphasizing the short vowel sounds.
4. Introducing the long vowels (the terms *vowel, long,* and *short* are used).
5. Teaching the speech consonants in final position.
6. Introducing the vowel blends *ow, ou, oi, oy, ew, au, aw,* and *oo*.
7. Teaching the double vowels *ai, ea, oa, ee, ie, ay,* and *oe*.

Sequence # 4

1. Maintaining single consonants and consonant blends.
2. Teaching the silent letters in *kn, gh,* and *wr*.

3. Teaching the variant consonant sounds *c, g, s, z, ed,* and *t.*
4. Continuing work on double vowels.
5. Teaching the influence of final *e.*
6. Teaching the vowels followed by *r.*
7. Teaching the prefixes *a-, be-,* and *un-.*
8. Teaching the suffixes *-y, -ly, -er, -est, -less, -ful,* and *en.*
9. Teaching the division of words into syllables.
10. Teaching alphabetization.
11. Teaching the three-letter blends: *str, thr.*
12. Teaching contractions: *can't, don't.*

Sequence # 5

1. Maintaining all previously taught skills and addition of appropriate difficulties.
2. Teaching the prefixes *dis-, ex-, in-, out-, re-, trans-,* and *un-.*
3. Teaching the suffixes *-eenth, -ese, -ical, -ion, -ous, -ship, -sun,* and *-ty.*
4. Teaching the placement of accent on words divided into syllables.
5. Teaching the use of key words for pronunciation in dictionary.
6. Teaching the use of diacritical marks.

How Are the Consonant Sounds Taught?

To use a consonant sound in reading, the children must do two things. First they must identify the sound of the letter in a word, and then they must use that sound in combination with the other letters to identify a word.

In order to identify the sound of *b* in a word, this type of exercise or a combination of exercises may be used. There are others used in workbooks and suggested in teachers' manuals.

1. The teacher says, "Listen to find in what way these words are alike: *ball, bell, bent, bill, book.* Yes, they sound alike at the beginning."
2. "Now look at these words while I say them: *ball, box, beg.* In what two ways are they alike? Yes, they sound alike at the beginning and start with the same letter. The letter is *b.*"
3. "I am thinking of a girl in class whose name begins with *b.* Who is she?"
4. "Here are some pictures. Which ones start with the letter *b? Ball, bed, bat, bus.*"
5. "Listen while I say a sentence. Name the words that start with *b.* 'The big ball is baby's. Bobby will buy a book.' "
6. "Color each picture that begins with the letter *b.*"

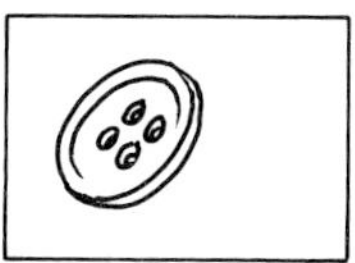
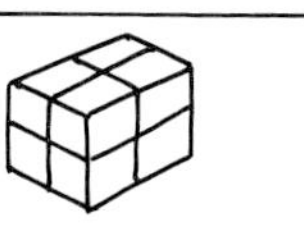
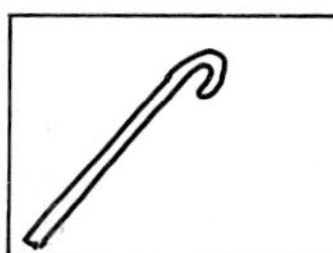

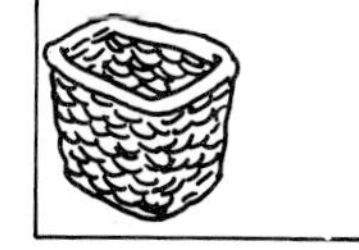

7. "I am thinking of something that is good to eat that starts with *b.* Can you name it?"
8. "Say 'Little Boy Blue' and 'Baa Baa Black Sheep.' When you hear a *b,* hold up a finger."
9. Mark *b* on four letter cards. Do the same for some of the other letters. Put them all together. Show the letter *b* and ask the children to find others like it. Or, ask the children to place all letters that are like it in a row.
10. The teacher says, "I am thinking of a *b* word that rhymes with each of the following words: *fall, cone, maybe, cat.*"

Once the sound is identified in words and associated with the letter, then the task is to substitute the sound into a word in a way that helps identify the word. This type of substitution exercise is widely used. The teacher reviews the sound. "You know these words on the board: *ball* and *big*. I have put a line under the new word in the sentence: 'The apples are in the box.' With what letter does box start? Yes, it is a b. What sound does the b in box have? What is the sentence talking about? What other words that start with the letter b do you know that will make sense in this sentence?"

Sometimes the substitution must be made in other parts of the word. "What letter does the new word start with in this sentence? 'Daddy has a new *job*.' Yes, it is a *j*. What word do you know that would make sense? No, it is not *jet*. Look at the last letter in the new word. What sound does it have? Does *jet* have the sound of *b* at the end? Can you think of a word that would make sense that starts the way *jet* does but has a *b* sound at the end? Yes, the word is job."

Or the sentence may be *Mary has a red ribbon.* "No, the word is not *raincoat*. What letters are in the middle of the word? What words do you know that start with an *r*? Use that sound and the other words to read the new word."

Special practice in substitution should be used with exercises like this: "You know these words: *ball, big*. You also know these words: *get, look*. What new word do we make when we take away the *g* in *get* and put a *b* in its place? What new word do we make when we take away the *l* in *look* and put a *b* in its place?

In order to construct this type of exercise follow these steps: Start with words that contain the letter on which the students are to practice. In the preceding example, start with *book* and *bet*. Then change them to words such as *look, took, cook,* and *get, jet, let*. Select the one that is best known by the children. These words can be used in substitution exercises for the letters indicated:

c not, ball, now, look
f ball, box, can
l dog, tip, not
n cap, hot
p will, not, get, can, big
w bent, hill, lake
s get, funny, no, Jack

Another form of substitution exercise asks the student to choose between two words in a sentence. Write the word *live* on the board. Ask the class, "Who can read this word? Tell me what happens to the word *live* when the first letter is changed?" Write *give* under *live*. Have the new word pronounced. Then ask the children to select the proper word in these sentences:

John and Paul (give / live) on High Street.

John will (give / live) Paul a cake.

"Can you tell these new words that are made from words you know?" Write the words *dog, get, night,* and *cake* on the board. Substitute *l* for the first letter in each of these words. Follow this by asking the children to select the proper word in a sentence using these words.

Consonant blends present some difficulties. The major error to avoid is that of adding an extra vowel sound at the end of the blend. *Clear* becomes cul-ear, blue becomes *bul-oo, scream* becomes *sker-eam,* and *stream* becomes *struh-eam* or *stur-eam*.

In some words a *trigraph,* or three consonants blended together, can be sounded before the vowel is sounded, as in *scratch, stream, splash, sprint,* and *scream*. At the end of words there are many possible combinations of two or more consonants that form blends in words such as *bulb, self, held, hard, earth,* and *spark*.

To develop skill in attacking new words through the visual and auditory recognition of consonant blends, proceed as follows:

1. Write *bring* and *bread* on the chalkboard. Have the children pronounce the words and the let-

ters *br* underlined in each word. Say: "Listen as I say *bring, bread* again. Do the letters *br* have one sound or two?" Call attention to the sound of *b* in *ball* and *r* in *ride*. "Let me hear both sounds when you say *bread, bring*." Ask several children in turn to repeat the words. "Listen as I read some sentences to hear other words that begin with the same two sounds as *bring*." Read the following sentences, pausing after each for a child to repeat the *br* words.

Throw the *broken branch* in the *brook*.
The *bridge* over the *brook* is not *broad*.

Write the following sentences on the chalkboard and have them read silently and orally. Help the group to identify *brook* by comparison with *bring* and *book*.

Bring this *book* to the *brook*.
Go down to the store and get some *brown bread*.

2. Use the method described in the preceding activity to develop recognition of the consonant blend *tr*. Use the known words *train, tree, truck* and the following sentences on the chalkboard:

   Will you *try* to make my *train* go?
   Joe can do a *trick* with his *truck*.

3. Provide each child with a pair of cards one by four inches on which you have written *br* or *tr*. Ask the children to listen as you pronounce the following word groups and to hold up the card that has the two letters with which all the words begin.

   tr: traffic, trick, traveler, trip, tractor
   br: break, brothers, breakfast, brook

Drill on consonants and blending can also be accomplished through a "word wheel." Two circles are cut from heavy paper or oak tag. One is larger than the other. The upper circle has a consonant or consonant blend aligned with a slot that exposes the remainder of the word on the other disk. As the top disk is revolved, the words are formed for the pupil to call.

Picture dictionaries or student-made charts are helpful tools. Students may gather pictures, take them to school, and paste them on the page in the dictionary where the appropriate beginning consonant sound is identified or on the chart labeled with that consonant. This should be a group activity because children usually tire of making individual sound dictionaries.

An initial consonant game based on "word families" provides a check on a student's understanding. The student has a card on which an entire word is written or printed. Used with this card are a number of single-consonant cards that may be placed one at a time on the initial consonant to make another word. For example, if one uses the word card with the word *man* on it, the consonants *p, r, t, f, b, c,* and *v* may be written on the smaller cards. By superimposing each small card on the first letter of *man,* the child may form the words *pan, ran, tan, fan, ban, can,* and *van*. When not in use, the small cards may be clipped to the large one.

Exercises in which the student writes an initial consonant to complete a word and then says the word give him the opportunity for *seeing, saying, hearing,* and *doing* activities. These are effective in all phonics work and are particularly good in corrective work. Such an exercise appears here:

Directions: Write the initial consonants indicated in each of these words. Then say the words.

m	c	b
__ad	__at	__all
__other	__ome	__ig
__ud	__old	__oy
__ay	__up	__ack
__eat	__ar	__ox
__op	__all	__ell
__ill	__ap	__ut
__itt	__an	__ook

In studying individual consonant sounds, there are many word-card devices that can be used. A card is made so that the initial consonant shows only when the card is folded. When the card is unfolded, a key picture replaces the initial consonant. For example, with the word *cat,* when the card is not folded, the student sees the key picture of a cat and the element *at;* when it is folded, the *c* appears, making the word *cat.*

One of the card devices resembles the first one mentioned for use with initial single consonants. It differs only in that there is a consonant blend that may be superimposed on the initial letter of a *known* word to make a *new* word. For example, the known word may be *black.* On separate cards, the consonant teams *tr, st,* and *cr* are printed. By manipulating these cards, the child can make *track, stack,* and *crack.*

Children may easily make their own individual consonant key cards by using heavy folded paper. One side of the card contains the consonant. When the card is opened, the picture and key word appear. These cards serve as excellent aids when children are still learning the initial consonant sounds and need frequent help with them. On the back of the folded card a simple sentence is written to help the child to see the word in context.

A knowledge of the consonant sounds is one of the most helpful ways phonics can be used in reading. Teachers frequently ask the children to ignore the vowels but to use only the consonants in sounding a word. A sentence in which all vowel letters have been omitted can be read by most children. For example:

> Th__ m__ther w__s s__ h__pp__ t__ f__nd h__r ch__ld wh__ h__d b__n l__st th__t sh__ cr__d.

How Are Vowel Sounds Taught?

The first step in use of vowels is the ability to recognize *a, e, i, o,* and *u* as letters that represent vowel sounds. As recognition is being mastered, the child should also understand that when these letters make the same sound as their names we call them long vowels and put a straight line over them. The letters *a* and *I* are little words that children know. The *e* in *be* and *o* in *no* are long because we hear the letter names in them. The long *ū* as in *use* and *Utah* is quite rare in the basal reading vocabulary.

The short *e* is one of the most difficult phonetic elements a child is asked to master. Here is one way of presenting it:

(Print *men, bed, get, let, red,* and *neck* on the board). "Let's took at these words and say them together." (Point to *men.*) "What is the vowel in this word?" (*e*). "Do you hear the long *e* sound or the short *e* sound in *men?*" (The short *e* sound. Continue in the same way with the remaining five words.) "What did you notice about the *e* in each of these six words?" (Each *e* has the short sound.) "When *e* is the only vowel in a word and it is followed by one or more letters, the *e* usually has the short sound. . . ." Let's use what we have learned about the short *e* sound to help us read some words that we may not know." (Print the following short sentences on the board.)

> Ben had a pet dog named Shep.
> Shep sat up to beg for his bones.
> Ben put a bell in Shep's pen.
> Shep could make Ben hear the bell when he wanted to be fed.

Then say: "In the sentences on the board, some words are underlined. Read the sentences to yourself. Use what you know about the short sound of *e* to help you decide what the underlined words are. Be sure the word you decide on makes sense in the sentence. Will you read the first sentence aloud?" Ask two or more pupils to read each sentence aloud. Then have one or two pupils read all four sentences aloud.

Ea presents a special problem because it may be either long or short. Print the words *ready* and *head* and say them together. What two vowels are used together in these words?" (*ea*) "Do you hear the long *e* sound or the short *e* sound in these words?" (The short *e* sound. Print *clean, dream,* and *deal* on the board. Point to *clean.*) "What is this word?" (*clean*) "Do you hear the short *e* sound or the long *e* sound in *clean?*" (The long *e* sound. Treat *dream* and *deal* in the same way as *clean* was treated.) "The vowels *ea* usually stand for the long *e* sound. When you see the vowels *ea* in a word you don't know, try the long *e* sound first for those vowels. If that doesn't give a word you know, try the short *e* sound. Let's see whether we can use what we know about the sounds of the vowels *ea* to help us read some words that we may not know." (Print the following sentences on the board.)

> Ann went to one store for some beans, some bread, and some meat.
> She went to another store for some white thread.

Then say: "Read the sentences on the board to yourself. Use what you have learned about the sounds that the vowels *ea* can stand for to help you decide what the underlined words are." Then say to a pupil, "Will you read the first sentence aloud?" (Ask two or three pupils to read each sentence aloud.)

With upper-grade students the first step is to discover the nature and extent of the child's knowledge of vowels. Write four or more familiar words on the board and ask the students to identify a vowel sound that may appear in only one or two of them. For example, write on the board the words *cake, man, ran,* and *made.* Ask the children to say the words to themselves. Then ask in which words they hear the short form of the sound *a.* This activity may be repeated for all of the vowels.

How Are Reading Skills Taught at the Primary Level?

The first step in word recognition is to help the children realize that the printed letters represent language. This first step becomes a reality by beginning each lesson with conversation about the theme/topic to be read. In preprimers the story is told through the pictures. The children discuss what is happening, and at first the teacher reads what the book characters are saying. As the story progresses and one of the characters is calling to his mother (or dog or baby) the teacher asks, "What would you say if you were the boy in the story?" Eventually a child will say, "Come here, Mother." "That is exactly what the story says," explains the teacher. "Now you read the words that tell us what the boy says."

The first step in word recognition is to help the child realize that the printed letters represent language. (Photo by Linda Lungren)

The clue used here is the context or meaning clue. Through repetition of the words, the child eventually remembers what the word says whenever he sees it. Some words cannot be developed from the meaning alone. Such words as *said, at, was, am, is,* and *blue* must be learned through planned repetition.

The beginner seldom depends on sound clues alone to recognize a word but uses the sound represented by a letter in combination with meaning or word form. As soon as the child knows by sight two or more words that start the same way, he has a clue to the sound of all words beginning with that letter. Some letter-sound associations seem to be used by most children. The consonants *m, s, b, t, n,* and *j* appear to be quite easy as sound clues.

Primary sight vocabulary is based on words that the children use frequently and that have meaning in their oral language. Familiar objects in the room can be labeled. Words to be presented emerge from the discussion and are written on the board or on the chart. "This is what Juan said," the teacher comments as she writes, " 'Come, Anita, come here.' Who will read these words for us?" Then the word will be used in other situations until it is repeated many times and the children recognize it without prompting. Small cards with words printed on them are used. The children place the words on the proper article in a picture. Or the words are distributed and in turn each child puts a label on the proper article in the room. A box of variety-store items may provide the models. Names of the articles are pasted on a large cardboard designed to lie flat on the table. The children in turn place their article on the correct word. Color names are learned by matching two cards—one with only the name, the other with the name and color. The children in turn place their article on the correct word.

Word-form clues are indicated in a number of ways. Tell the children to notice the form of a word, its general length, shape, size, and configuration, without reference to individual letters. This is always done with a left-to-right motion of the hand under the word. After a short sentence, phrase, or word is read to the children, the word or words are displayed. The children are then asked to choose the one of several pictures that illustrates what the word says. After a word is shown to the children, it is taken away. Children then close their eyes and try to "see" the word. Check by showing two words and ask the children to select the one they saw first. During this period words of unlike appearance are used, such as *name, bed, funny*. Attempting to distinguish between words that look alike—*this* and *that* or *funny* and *bunny*—will only cause confusion at this time.

Students may be helped to understand the structure of words by analyzing word endings such as: *–s*, *–ing*, and *–ed*. Emphasis is placed on the part of the word that helps a child to remember which is the base or root word. Too great an emphasis on these endings will cause children to start looking at the wrong end of the word. The left-to-right habit of observing words can be stressed by presenting some words for drill in this fashion:

help + *s* = helps
or
help + *ed* = helped

or by direct contrast:

help	help
helps	helped

Phonetic analysis at this time is directed toward auditory discrimination. Speech jingles that repeat sounds should be used. If two or more words start with the same sound, that feature should be noted. Names that start the way words do provide a personal association with a sound. The emphasis is still on hearing parts of words, hearing the beginning of a word, or hearing the ending of a word. Names of letters are still being learned by some children during this period.

In preprimers the story is told with the pictures, and the reading usually involves the words the characters in the book say. Some stories are more easily reviewed if the pages are mounted in sequence like a cartoon strip. Ask the children to tell the story, then to read what the story people are saying. Many series have the first preprimer in the form of a big book. This can be used for group instruction without the physical handling of the reading material during the initial introduction periods. When the child does get his own book, it is a tremendous psychological experience for him to be able to read the first story independently.

The preprimer level will be completed by many children during the first half of the year. Some children will remain at this level throughout the first grade; a few need to start at the preprimer level in the second grade.

Most children arrive at primer level after reading the preprimers of the basic series. Children are ready to read a primer story when their interest has been aroused, their previous experiences have been keyed in with the story, and their speaking vocabularies have become adequate to deal with the concepts. Guided discussion and sharing of experiences pertinent to the story to be read give the children experience in talking and listening and develop readiness. A motivating question before silent reading helps children to read for meaning. Good reading and study habits are developed during the silent reading of the story. The children learn to identify their own problems of word recognition and comprehension and to ask for help when needed. In the beginning, a lesson may consist of only one page of a story. As reading skills are developed, the children can manage larger units.

Discussion after silent reading helps the children to clear up comprehension problems. They can enjoy the humor of the story together and discuss relationships of characters. The teacher is able to check comprehension further by asking questions.

Rereading may be done after the silent reading of each page or after the reading of the entire story. The motivation of rereading should be to find the answer to a question, to find out the emotions the characters felt, to enjoy the story, or to find the most interesting parts.

With respect to phonics, the children and teacher start to build a chart of "key" words to use in working out new words. This chart is built slowly, adding words as they are met in reading.

The following single-consonant chart is typical. Words used on the chart should be words in the reading series being used. One series would use *work* instead of *wagon;* another, *look* instead of *little.*

B b	baby	*N n*	none
C c	candy	*P p*	pet
D d	day	*Q q*	quack
F f	father	*R r*	run
G g	go	*S s*	something
H h	house	*T t*	toy
J j	jump	*V v*	valentine
K k	kite	*W w*	wagon
L l	little	*X x*	x-ray
M m	money	*Y y*	yes

Children will usually encounter *x* at the end of a word, as in *box.*

From the very beginning, children should be taught to skip over a word and then think it out from context, because they must necessarily do a great deal of this in later independent reading. After the students become familiar with the sounds of initial consonants, they should be taught to check their guessed word with the beginning sound of its printed form.

First-Reader Experiences

At the first-reader level the children show more independence in reading. They are able to read and grasp the meaning of longer and more involved stories, to use context clues, to predict outcomes and draw conclusions in stories, and to feel success and joy because they have a substantial reading vocabulary. Many children need review at this level during the beginning of their second year in school, while others will have completely mastered this material by the end of the first year.

Through auditory and visual discrimination activities children begin to recognize initial consonant blends such as *bl—black, fr—friend, sp—spell,* as well as *dr, gr, pl, st, tr.*

Children at the first-reader level begin to learn the following final consonant sounds:

d	red	*g*	pig	*k*	book
l	wheel	*m*	him	*n*	hen
p	up	*s*	us	*t*	bat

Picture dictionaries made by the children will reinforce most of the consonant sounds as well as establish a dictionary concept. It also helps them to visualize their language in print. Such an activity might be an early homework assignment. Use a notebook or single sheets that may later be assembled. At the top of each quarter-space the child may paste a picture of some familiar object. Each object picture must start with a different sound. They may then cut words starting with those sounds from old magazines and paste them in the correct column.

Second-Reader Experiences

Most children at second-grade level are beginning to develop independence in word recognition, realization of the many happy experiences that they get from books, and an understanding that reading can help them to solve problems and to satisfy their curiosity. Creative reading and creative problem solving may be encouraged through selection of stimulating materials, sensitive questioning, and a nurturing environment.

The first two weeks of the second school year should be spent in reviewing the subject matter of the first grade. At the end of this period the teacher will have discovered children who are not yet able to make use of these skills in attacking unknown words. Such children may be grouped together and given instruction suited to their needs.

The remainder of the class can begin their work with the short and long sounds of the vowels. The ability to make intelligent use of the long and short sounds of vowels in attacking unknown words has been acquired with difficulty by the average and below-average child. Therefore, these sounds should be developed with particular care.

The order of development of the word elements and phonograms depends on the difficulties the children encounter in their reading.

Third-Reader Experiences

When children come to the third-reader level, they have already met many words of more than one syllable, some of which they have learned as sight words. They have had experiences in listening to spoken words to identify the number of parts in each. At the third-reader level, the children have gained much skill in attacking words independently. They should use and apply these skills in all school work. Periodic checks must be made to be sure previous learning has not been forgotten.

How Is Reading Instruction Directed in the Intermediate Grades?

Teachers seek to achieve the following purposes in the reading program of the intermediate grades:

1. *Continue* development of word-recognition skills started in the primary grades. There will be many children at this level who are operating at second- and third-grade levels of reading. Others may follow a delayed pattern of achievement in reading. For a number of reasons, about one child in ten does not read comfortably until late in the tenth or eleventh year of age. A part of this is lack of purpose. Apparently the reading materials of previous years did not appear worth the effort to read them. But now that students need to read directions as part of a hobby, or as they are exploring vocational interests, reading assumes a new importance.
2. *Develop* discrimination with respect to reading material. This involves elements of critical judgment, appreciation of literary quality in writing, and ability to select material needed to solve a problem from material less important.
3. *Teach* the reading skills needed in association with the school program. Intermediate students need to practice increasing reading speed, skimming, using the index or other aids to locate material, and interpreting new concepts, terms, and representation of ideas such as graphs. The dictionary is studied in detail.
4. *Help* the student to *integrate* all of the language art skills so that they reinforce each other. The close association of these skills may be noted in many of the activities presented throughout this textbook.

In the classroom the teacher uses sets of basal readers, library books, weekly and monthly magazines, and daily newspapers to teach reading. At the beginning of the year it is wise to use a reader at least one grade below the level of the students as a review reader. This gives the teacher a chance to get to know the students without discouraging those below grade level. It is normal that from one-fourth to one-third of an average fifth-grade classroom will be able to read only third- or fourth-grade material. Social studies books and some science books will be difficult for many to read until concepts are established through life experience that provides meaning and language experience.

Intermediate-grade teachers soon learn that many of the study strategies, such as drawing conclusions, reading for detail, determining the main idea, and locating information, must be reinforced and transferred to materials other than the reading textbook. Intermediate readers are a source for developing some of these strategies, but the initial attempts may be made in the area of literature.

Because a great range of ability exists in any intermediate-level class, lesson planning usually involves groups with similar needs. The following procedures in a reading lesson are suggested to help you ensure that your students will comprehend the material they read and will also become independent readers.

Procedures That Ensure Comprehension

1. Background knowledge: Pictures, questions, and experiences of the students or the teacher are used to arouse interest and build the necessary background information needed for understanding what is about to be read. At this time teachers anticipate and present some of the language and vocabulary needed to read the story.
2. Vocabulary expansion: Seldom is it necessary to present all of the new words, because the students need to practice the information in the context of what they already know about the word or concept. Lapp and Flood (1986) suggest that effective vocabulary instruction involves the following:
   a. Presenting the unknown word with the selected synonym or definition. Example: The word is *silence*. *Silence* means no noise. Ask your students to tell you what the word means. When they have answered, "*Silence* means no noise," reinforce the example by saying, "Yes, *silence* means no noise."
   b. Presenting the target word in expanded context that is designed to clarify semantic and syntactic meaning. Example: Linda and Carla sat in the library reading their books. They didn't talk or get up from their chairs. They read in silence.
   c. Presenting examples and nonexamples that have minimal difference. Example: Norman walked down the forest path. He listened to the water rush by in the stream. He heard his dog bark at a squirrel. After presenting this example, ask the students, "Was there silence in the forest? How do you know?" Example: Norman continued down the forest path to a clearing. He could hear nothing, not even birds' chirping. Ask, "Was there silence in the forest? How do you know?"
   d. Presenting expansion activities and emphasizing word synonyms, categories, similarities, and differences. It is through these activities that vocabulary is developed.
3. Clear expectations: Students need to understand what is expected of them. They, like us, obtain the goal more successfully if we have a clear understanding of the goal. Remember that there are *many* ways to complete *one* goal. *Praise* and *encourage* individuality.
4. Direct input: The activities with the group must be viewed as developmental and sequential. These may start by the teacher checking previously assigned work. This work may remain with the student for further practice or be collected for checking. The passage may be read

orally or silently, depending on the teacher's purpose. The passage that has been read is then discussed. This discussion will involve questions concerning the main idea, evaluating characters and conduct, drawing conclusions, predicting events and behaviors, enjoying humor or literary style, making judgments, and evaluating and applying new information. Oral reading is also often a part of this period as students clarify points, read dialogue for expression, choose parts, or check understanding. Interest and purpose in the next lesson are established. Some of the new words may be analyzed or checked for meaning. Nearly every lesson provides some opportunity to strengthen language, thinking, and research skills.

5. Self-monitoring: Diagnostic teaching depends on continuous evaluation by both the teacher and learner. The usual methods used are informal tests, oral questioning, and student reports. In addition, the student should be learning to evaluate his own achievement. When an error of understanding is made, he must analyze why he misunderstood. Did he skip an important word? Did he use the wrong meaning of a word? All errors are simply learning opportunities when handled in this way. At no time should a student be concerned about being better than another reader. He may recognize differences in performance, as he would in any other activity, but such comparison is not the basis for diagnostic teaching.

   Conclusions from evaluation by a learner may be similar to the following: "This book is too difficult. I need to know more about finding root words. I need to know how to locate words in the dictionary. I need to learn how to locate places on a map." The illustrations will provide meaning clues.

   Self-determined "next steps" by teacher and student provide the motivation for continuous growth in reading skills. A positive approach would be to keep a record such as "Today I learned ________." Another way to do this is to keep records at times of only the things that were done right until the recognition of what is needed loses any negative feeling in much the same manner an athlete uses when he says, "I need to practice ________," or a businessman says, "I need to improve ________."

   In order to free the teacher's time to meet individual and group needs, purposeful work must be found for those at their desks. Some able students like to prepare challenging materials for others to read. These may be a series of questions concerning an article from a magazine or newspaper. If mounted in a manila folder, the article on one side and questions on the other, they may be used many times or sent to another room. The circulars children receive when they write to firms or communities are also interesting reading experiences when prepared in this fashion. There are well-planned workbooks for all the intermediate grades. Although few classes would use one of these for all students, small sets of this material will save hours of teacher time as he/she helps students who have been absent, who need special help, or who may need more advanced material.

6. Practice and transfer: Students need to practice these newly acquired reading processes by applying them to new activities and materials. Any related work in the form of workbooks, chalkboard work, or follow-up assignment must be presented and explained clearly if we expect students to achieve work success. The following activities have been found to be of value in providing practice and transfer.

Practice and Transfer Activities

1. Reread the first paragraph of the story. Answer the following questions:
   a. *Who* are the characters introduced?
   b. *Where* does the beginning of the story take place?

c. *When* does the beginning of the story take place?
d. *What* problem is being introduced?

2. Make a list of the leading characters in the story and skim the story to find descriptive phrases of each.

Appearance	Characteristics
Action	Expressions
Feelings	Attitudes

3. Write a description, in your own words, of each character.
4. Choose your favorite character. Pretend you meet this person. Write a conversation you might like to have with him.
5. Choose two characters in the story. Write a conversation between them.
6. Choose one location mentioned in the story. Make a list of all words and phrases used in the text to describe this location.
7. Write a description of this place in your own words.
8. Read the ending of your story. Make a picture as you see the scene.
9. Choose a title for the picture. Write a short paragraph to go with the picture.
10. Reread the story. List the scenes presented. Make characters for each scene that can be used in a display.
11. Practice the story, using the pictures to illustrate the points of emphasis.
12. Work with a committee to choose one scene from the story that can be told in pantomime. Plan for one pupil to read from the text while others pantomime what happens.
13. Choose one character from today's story and one from another story you have read. Plan a meeting of these two characters. Decide what they will be doing at this meeting. Paint a picture of this scene. Choose an appropriate title. Write conversation.
14. Choose an experience one of the characters had in the story. Write about a similar experience you have had.
15. Choose a situation described in the story. Write a myth or a "whopper" about this situation.
16. Write a personal, newsy letter to one of the characters in the story, telling about your activities and inquiring about something the character has been doing.
17. Write a personal letter from one character to another. Write an answer to the letter from the other character.
18. Make up a limerick about a person, place, or thing mentioned in the story.
19. Make a sequence chart of incidents that happened.
20. You may want to make illustrations to go with the chart.
21. Choose a scene in the story. Make stick puppets to go with this scene and plan to put on a show for the class.
22. Write an advertisement for the lost and found column of the daily paper.
23. Write riddles using characters, places, or objects from your story.
24. Skim the story and choose one or two sentences as titles that you consider appropriate.
25. Look for figures of speech in the story. Explain their meaning.
26. Choose single words that describe each character.
27. In a column to the side of these lists, write words that are opposite in meaning. For example: *happy, sad; laugh, cry.*
28. List all of the words on a certain page that express actions or things a character did.
29. Tell briefly why you think each character acted as he did in the story.
30. Use the table of contents in the reader to find another story similar to this one and tell why you chose that particular one.

31. Read in some resource book in the room more information about something mentioned in the story.
32. List all of the words which have unfamiliar meanings. Find them in the dictionary or glossary if the book has one. Choose the meaning that you think best applies to the use made of the word in the story.
33. Write statements from the story; ask others in the class to decide whether they are true or false. Be sure you know the correct answer.
34. Write sentences for others in the class to complete.
35. Find passages in the story that make you feel sad, happy, drowsy, or excited.
36. Find parts of the story that you consider humorous.
37. Write a fable, legend, or fairy tale about some incident or character in the story.
38. Look back through the book. List the stories you have read under the following headings: fanciful tale, biography, true story, realistic.
39. Find words that begin with *dis-*, *en-*, *in-*, *un-*, and *re-*.
40. Find words that end with *-ion*, *-ist*, *-ment*, *-ant*, *-er*, *-ance*, *-ish*, *-able*, *-ful*, *-less*. Note the influence of these elements on meaning.
41. Select an advertisement or news story and note the words that have emotional appeal.
42. Take a circular of a city or park and make a series of questions that a visitor might ask that are answered in this circular.
43. Clip a week's TV schedule from the Sunday paper. Make a series of questions that might be answered by reading this schedule.
44. Read an advertisement of something you would like to buy—a bicycle, toy, car. What questions are *not* answered in the material?
45. Summarize the story and try to show the information in the form of a cartoon, news story, poem, or any other format you wish to try.

What Is the Role of Assessment in the Reading Program?

Assessment of learning must be a continuous process in your classroom because you must be ever aware of the learning growth of your students.

Most reading programs will provide you with a variety of measures that will help you assess student growth in many of the areas emphasized in the program. You may wish to do further evaluation since gaining a clear understanding of student growth is essential for making decisions related to instruction. Correct use of assessment helps the teacher in planning for both group and individualized instruction. The process of diagnosing the strengths and needs of your students forms your instructional base. It is imperative in the area of testing never to rely on a single measurement to provide the necessary diagnostic information. Test results should serve as a reference point from which to provide instruction, never as an end in themselves.

Formal Assessment

Many publishing companies provide standardized tests that may be used to assess student reading abilities.

Standardized tests are ones in which the criteria or skills being tested have been tried out or normed on a large sample population.

Two of the most commonly used standardized group tests are:

1. California Achievement Test: Reading, California Test Bureau/McGraw-Hill Book Co., 1221 Avenue of the Americas, New York, New York 10022.
2. Metropolitan Achievement Tests: Reading, The Psychological Corporation, 757 Third Avenue, New York, New York 10017.

Informal Measures

In addition to formal standardized tests you will find that informal assessments provide you with valuable information. Informal measures differ from standardized measures because they do not involve the formalized procedures for constructing, administering, and scoring. Informal measures that will be useful to you are *basal reading program tests, informal reading inventories,* and the *cloze readability technique.*

INFORMAL READING INVENTORIES (IRIS). Informal reading inventories are used to gain an estimate of a student's *independent, instructional,* and *frustrational* reading levels. When a student is reading successfully without help, the independent level has been attained. When the teacher's help is needed, the reader is reading at the *instructional* level. When the material is too difficult to understand even with assistance, the reader is at the *frustrational* level.

More detailed information regarding the construction of an IRI may be found by reading:

Burns, P. C. and Roe, B. D. (1985). *Informal reading inventory (preprimer to twelfth grade),* 2nd ed. Boston: Houghton Mifflin Co.

Ekwall, E. E. (1986). *Ekwall reading inventory,* 2nd ed. Boston: Allyn & Bacon, Inc.

Johnson, M. S. and Kress, R. A. (1965). *Informal Reading Inventories.* Newark, Del.: International Reading Association.

Silveroli, N. J. (1986). *Classroom Reading Inventory,* 5th ed. Dubuque, Iowa: Wm. C. Brown Company Publishers.

CLOZE TECHNIQUE. Another informal measure that will help you is the *cloze technique,* which is based on the student's ability to comprehend a given text. To use the cloze technique:

1. Select a passage of approximately 250 words.
2. Delete every fifth word.
3. Substitute a horizontal line for each word deleted.
4. Ask students to read and insert missing words.
5. Responses are correct even if misspelled.
6. Each correct closure is worth two points.
7. Score as follows:

   58–100 points (independent reading level)
   44–57 points (instructional reading level)
   Below 43 points (frustrational reading level)

If the text is at the instructional level, it may be used to develop lessons in class. A text at the frustrational level is too difficult, and one at the independent level may be read without assistance. The following informal inventory may aid in this assessment:

De Santi, R. J., Casbergue, R. M., and Sullivan, V. G. (1986). *The De Santi cloze reading inventory.* Boston: Allyn & Bacon, Inc.

Summary

Reading as a process of comprehending written information was thoroughly examined in this chapter. Methods of teaching reading to all children at all grade levels were examined. Specific strategies for assessment and the development of comprehension through whole-language experiences were presented.

Suggested Classroom Projects and Questions for Discussion

Projects

1. Observe a first-grade teacher at work. Note the similarities between what the teacher does and what was described in this chapter.
2. Defend or criticize this statement: "The teacher should spend as much time finding the right reading material for students as instructing them in reading."
3. Design a plan for involving parents in the creation of instructionally related reading materials.
4. Examine some of the study skills such as reading for details, drawing conclusions, and determining the main idea in association with the content subjects. Find examples of reading details in a mathematics problem, in a science experiment, and in a geography book. Would it be possible for a student to use the skill in one area and not in another? Discuss the factors that are operating to make these situations similar or different.
5. Although some students will have mastered much of the reading process early in their school careers, we

know that it is quite normal for others of equal mental ability to reach the fourth grade before this happens. Write a statement explaining this to parents. Describe ways to give each student praise and recognition in a nonreading activity.

6. Design a cloze passage to determine the reading level of sixth-grade students in a social studies class.
7. Survey the teacher materials of several widely used basal reading series and analyze the instructional strategies for teaching vocabulary.
8. Survey the teacher manuals of several widely used elementary social studies, science, or math texts to determine the instructional strategies for teaching vocabulary.
9. Visit the library and review students' magazines to determine ways they may be used as supplemental instructional materials.
10. Visit a local store that sells student games. Preview some games to determine whether they can be used as supplemental instructional materials. Design a chart that lists the name of the game and the skill area it could extend.

Questions

1. What sight words might a student learn from watching television? Should such words be used in beginning reading instruction?
2. In what sense would the term *reading* be synonymous with *thinking*? Are there thinking skills that should be taught? In what way is thinking influenced by reading? Is the detection of propaganda a reading or a thinking skill? Is the response to poetry a reading or a thinking activity? Is it a learned response?
3. Do you agree that vocabulary is best developed in situations that require its use, or would you plan lessons involving lists of new words for lessons similar to spelling lessons for vocabulary development?
4. Would you defend the use of special skill textbooks in addition to the readers being used?
5. Do you think that primary students should make greater progress in reading than we now expect? How might this be done? What factors other than reading skill should be considered in instruction?
6. Should phonics instruction start with the vowels?
7. When should students be permitted to read library books in the classroom?
8. Should a student in the sixth grade who reads as well as an adult be expected to participate in the reading class?
9. Why do you feel a teacher is justified, at the beginning of the year, in asking the better readers to do a great deal of oral reading in the social studies and science classes?
10. Why are some students more likely to enjoy reading circulars they have received in the mail, or a scout manual, or an item in *Popular Science* than a story in a basal reader?

Chapter 8

Exploring the World Through Literature

(Photo by Linda Lungren)

OBJECTIVES

After reading this chapter the student should be able to:

1. understand the purpose of teaching literature in the elementary school.
2. understand major issues in children's literature.
3. understand ways to select and present literature for all children.
4. understand the importance of observing children's response to literature and be able to select appropriate ways of extending the literature.
5. understand methods for selecting and presenting poetry to children.

What Is the Purpose of Teaching Literature in the Elementary School?

Ultimately the goal of the literature program is to develop in all children a love of reading and an appreciation for a wide variety of literature. Through literature, children can vicariously experience places and people they may never have the opportunity to experience first hand. It is also through literature that children can enrich their lives by expanding their knowledge of concepts and ideas, and by viewing a familiar situation from a new perspective. These experiences with literature will help children cultivate and extend their powers of imagination.

Teachers hope that their efforts in literature instruction will enable children to develop insights into human behavior that will lead to a better understanding of self and others. Each person needs to feel that he or she belongs, has a contribution to make, and is respected by others. Stories promote these feelings in many ways. It is comforting to know, for example, that others feel the same way about a situation as you do.

All children have a right to their literary culture, and experience with this literature is an important aspect of reading skill. One textbook cannot give all that is needed, but the heritage of folk literature should be a discovery of young readers. Many selections in contemporary reading programs are designed to lead to wider personal reading. The classic plots and themes found in such tales as *Cinderella, Puss-in-Boots,* and *Snow White* are a part of the literary background needed to understand the many stories based on overcoming evil with wit or innocence, gaining success in spite of great odds, and changing the ugly into the beautiful.

Certainly the child learning to read needs to know that reading can be a pleasure, whether in the form of listening to material well read or participating in silent or oral group reading. Children should also know the pleasure of personal writing, which can be stimulated by literature.

Salient Issues and Children's Literature

A child's concept of self and of the world can be influenced by children's literature. The issues of sex and racial stereotyping, stereotyping of the elderly, empathy, and death are among those of concern to both authors and teachers.

Sex Stereotyping

The issue of sex stereotyping in children's literature has received considerable attention in recent years. In general, books stereotyping the roles of males and females portray boys as more competent than girls in physical tasks and in creativity. Girls are portrayed as lacking the freedom to inquire, explore, and achieve.

The ubiquitous and pervasive nature of sex stereotyping was illustrated by Jennings (1975) at the preschool level. Her study revealed that, in general, girls found the male role much more acceptable than the boys found the female role. The portrayal of women in occupational roles has been examined at the preschool level (Murphy, 1975) and in comparison with the literature of the 1930s (Hillman, 1976). Hillman found little change in the range of occupational roles of women in children's literature despite the recent political, social, and economic changes.

However, a study by Collins et al. (1984) indicates that, in recent years there has been a move toward greater sexual equality in children's literature. As a follow-up to Weitzman et al. (1972), who studied male-female role portrayals, Collins et al. analyzed sixteen Caldecott Award–winning picture books and runners-up from 1979 to 1982. The books were assessed in terms of the ratio of males to females presented in the titles and illustrations, and as the central character, as well as the role functions of males and females, and the major theme. Collins found that the male-female ratio differences had decreased significantly in comparison to those found by the Weitzman study. In addition, when females were in the central role in the story, they had nontraditional characteristics. However, when females were not in the central role, they were portrayed in the traditional female stereotypes.

Awareness of the existence of sex stereotyping is a beginning. The teacher and school librarian should make available books portraying women in roles traditionally considered to be men's roles. Appendix A includes some books that may be helpful for this goal.

Not only is there a need for reorientation in depicting women's role behaviors, but men should more frequently be portrayed in tender, caring, and empathic situations. The goal is to provide children with positive role models, regardless of sex, to allow for self-expression and enhancement.

In addition to an awareness of sex stereotyping in children's literature, teachers need to be conscious of the existence of sex differences in the perception of the act of reading. A study by Kelly (1983) indicates that the content of the reading material influences whether children perceive reading as a masculine or a feminine activity. Kelly found that reading in general is perceived by both boys and girls to be a feminine activity. However, boys and girls in the study viewed reading the funny papers, a TV guide, and a science book as masculine activities. Reading a poetry book and a dictionary were viewed as feminine activities; reading a mystery book was perceived to be equally masculine and feminine.

This perception that reading is a feminine activity may account in part for the achievement differences in reading between boys and girls in our society. By providing male readers with the types of materials that are perceived as highly masculine, teachers can encourage boys to perceive reading as an appropriate activity for males, and their interests and achievements in reading may increase.

Racial Stereotyping

Children's literature may be a source in shaping a child's concept of race as well as sexual identity. Some children's books promote negative attitudes toward blacks by portraying them in stereotypic roles (Adams, 1981; Reid, 1983; Sims, 1982). To counteract such possible bias, Sims (1982) compiled a list of books that depict blacks in a positive way and that reflect the social and cultural traditions that are a part of being black and American. Appendix A contains Sims's list.

In an analysis of the depiction of South Africa in forty children's books, Randolph-Robinson (1984) found numerous examples of incorrect definitions and incorrect terminology used to refer to the people and the culture of Africa. Schon (1984) found similar examples of misconceptions about the Mexican people and their culture in children's books about Mexico, Mexicans, and Mexican-Americans. Inaccurate information presented in books read to or by children can result in the formation of stereotypic images and unfounded attitudes toward other people.

In selecting interracial books for inclusion in the class library, the teacher should determine that they present accurate information and that they portray all races as composed of individuals with positive traits and personalities in a variety of social positions. Such books should have appeal for all children.

Stereotypes of the Elderly

Children's literature that stereotypes the elderly can create myths that may become a part of the child's concept of old people and of the aging process. However, children's literature that presents elderly people realistically and in a perceptive and sensitive manner can help children develop a positive and realistic attitude toward the elderly as individual people and as a part of our society.

Studies (Fillmer, 1984; Rich et al., 1983) indicate that young children do stereotype elderly adults. Rich et al. (1983) state that many young children view the elderly as passive and unproductive, tired, helpless, and ready to die.

In an analysis of the portrayal of old people in four basal reading series, Serra and Lamb (1984) found that they were underrepresented as compared to their number in the United States. Only 6.8 percent of the stories discussed or included older characters. However, all but two of the stories analyzed portrayed the elderly in a positive and realistic manner.

Although underrepresented in stories in basal readers, the elderly are presented with positive images in many children's books. Mavrogenes (1982) has compiled an extensive list of books that deal with old age and death in a sensitive way. That list is included in Appendix A.

Empathy

The development of the characteristics that contribute to one's humanity is a gradual process with roots in early childhood. Children's literature may be instrumental in the growth of such qualities as empathy. Wolf (1975) proposes four stages in the development of empathy during the preschool years: (1) trust in the constancy of the object world, (2) trust in the constancy of the human world, (3) experience of emotional pain when faced by problems lacking ready solutions, and (4) desire and quest for resolution of complex emotional dilemmas. Wolf recommends the following books, which correspond to these developmental stages: (1) *Goonight Moon* by Margaret Wise Brown, (2) *Little Bear* by Else Holmehind Minarik, (3) *Sam* by Ann Herbert Scott, and (4) *Crow Boy* by Taro Yashima.

Robinson (1985) recommends bibliotherapy discussions to enable upper elementary children to develop problem-solving skills and to gain insight into coping with stressful situations that may arise in their own lives. Appendix A includes books appropriate to use for such discussions.

Children also need to develop empathy for their handicapped peers. A study by Salind and Moe (1983) indicates that the attitudes of nonhandicapped peers can be changed by exposure to books depicting disabled people in a positive way coupled with instructional activities highlighting the critical information to be learned about such individuals. Doherty-Hale (1984) recommends a list of books for developing an understanding attitude toward the learning disabled (Appendix A).

Death

The concept of death has largely been avoided in children's literature until recent years. Some researchers (Swenson, 1972; Sadker, 1976; Brennan, 1983; Speece and Brent, 1984) recognize that young children do have perceptions about death, although such notions may not coincide with reality.

Ordal (1983) suggests selecting those books that deal with death in a positive way by:

1. using direct and concrete words and avoiding euphemisms.
2. involving the main characters in the funeral and at the cemetery.
3. showing respect for and acceptance of feelings.
4. understanding the child's grieving process, and/or
5. ending on a hopeful note with the main characters getting on with life (p. 249).

Selections that may contribute to a child's awareness and acceptance of death and the attendant realization of the value and wonder of life are provided by Sadker (1976). Books designated for preschool and primary grades include *The Tenth Good Thing About Barney* by Judith Viorst, *Growing Time* by Sandol S. Warburg, *The Dead Bird* by Margaret Wise Brown, and *Annie and the Old One* by Miska Miles.

Death is treated in the following books for older

children: *A Taste of Blackberries* by Doris Buchanan Smith, *By the Highway Home* by Mary Stolz, *The High Pasture* by Ruth Harnden, *The Magic Moth* by Virginia Lee, and *Death Be Not Proud* by John Gunther. Two other outstanding books that deal with the process of death are the children's favorites *Charlotte's Web* by E. B. White and *Little Women* by Louisa May Alcott.

Concept Development and Children's Literature

Toothaker (1976)* suggests books illustrating the extent to which children's literature may satisfy a child's curiosity about himself and his world:

Curiosities of Children That Literature Can Satisfy

1. Curiosity about themselves.
   a. *Where Do Babies Come From*—Sheffield
   b. *The Human Body*—Lewis and Rubenstein
   c. *What Makes Me Feel This Way?*—LeShan
2. Curiosity about the natural world.
   a. *Let Me Take You on a Trail*—Hawkinson
   b. *Come Along!*—Caudill
   c. *The House That Nature Built*—Kalina
   d. *What's Under a Rock?*—Gannon
3. Curiosity about people and places.
   a. *Natural Wonders of the World*—Stocks
   b. *The Seven Seas*—Clemons
   c. *Me and Willie and Pa*—Manjo
   d. *Bloomers and Ballots: Elizabeth Cady Stanton and Women's Rights*—Clarte
   e. *Rosa Parks*—Greenfield
4. Curiosity about machines and how they work.
   a. *Making Tools*—Zim and Kelly
   b. *Hoists, Cranes and Derricks*—Zim and Kelly
   c. *What Makes a Computer Work?*—Halacy
   d. *Hold Everything*—Sam and Beryl Epstein
   e. *How Automobiles Are Made*—Cooke
5. Curiosity about facts and proofs of facts.
   a. *Guinness Book of World Records*
   b. *Statistics*—Srivastava
   c. *Science Experiences: Observation*—Bendicks
   d. *The Chemistry of a Lemon*—Stone
6. Curiosity about the ideals by which men live.
   a. *The First Book of Ethics*—Black
   b. *Religions*—Haskins
   c. *The Quakers: The Religious Society of Friends*—Elgin
7. Curiosity about the social world.
   a. *Families Live Together*—Meek and Bagwell
   b. *Behind the Magic Line*—Erwin
   c. *Somebody Go and Bang a Drum*—Caudill

* From Toothaker, R. E. (1976). Curiosities of children that literature can satisfy. *Childhood Education 52, 5,* 262–267. Reprinted by permission of R. E. Toothaker and the Association for Childhood Education International, 11141 Georgia Avenue, Suite 200, Wheaton, Mo. Copyright © 1976 by the Association.

Literary Analysis for the Young Child

The literary emphasis for the young child should be on verse, fable, and folklore. When children have developed the ability to identify these types of literature, they will have acquired initial literary skills. Eventually they will note the different ways stories start and end, the way that some characters seem real and others remain as flat as the paper in the book, and the way that writers, by the use of words, can make the reader feel happy or sad. All of this in time becomes an awareness of writing style. When a child discovers that a single writer writes a kind of story with which the child can identify, the reader has made a basic literary discovery.

Teachers who wish to extend emphasis on literature should limit their efforts to the following types of analyses:

1. *Character:* What are the clues to characters suggested in the writing? From what is said or done, what inference can be drawn about the

individual? Why does the character act the way he does? What are his values? Did anyone change in the story? Why?

2. *Setting:* Can you see where the story is happening? How do those in the story act because of the setting? Is there a basic struggle between the people in the story and the nature of the place where they live?
3. *Mood–feeling–tone:* What words are used to tell you the way the writer feels? What is the tone of voice of the storyteller? Is it serious? Humorous? Is this a true experience?
4. *Story pattern:* What story would you tell if you had only the first paragraph to guide you? Can you tell what happened by reading only the last paragraph? Is there a theme or lesson that the writer is illustrating? Who is telling the story? What difference does it make?

The teacher's goal is to enhance what is read; for example, discovering the subtle bits of humor and character that might be lost as the reader becomes involved in the plot.

Children's appetite for more reading can be stimulated by individualizing the selections along the following guidelines:

1. Guiding children to reading that will broaden and deepen their experiences.
2. Fitting a library book to the child, not the child to the book.
3. Bringing masterpieces of children's literature from the past and those of the present into proper perspective.
4. Challenging, but not pushing, the child.
5. Waiting with wisdom and patience for the child's own pattern of reading growth to unfold.

The following procedures can be used to encourage wide reading:

1. *Storytelling and oral reading* carefully selected from various types of literature that children might otherwise miss. Certain books or passages from books for increased appreciation of skillful use of language, vivid characterization, or dramatic incident are savored best when they are shared.
2. *Book talks,* including introductions to authors, illustrators, background material, stories behind stories, and sampling of passages to broaden reading interests and add zest to reading.
3. *Roundtable discussions* to provoke and help children discover for themselves the deeper meanings and values that transcend the plot in good books. This does not mean overanalysis, which would destroy the pleasure of a good story for children, but it does mean a voluntary sharing of the fresh, individualized interpretation of the universal truths of a good story as children see them in relation to their own experience.
4. *Literature* presented in such a way as to vitalize and enrich all areas of study and school experience so that children will come to recognize reading for pleasure and self-enlightenment as a natural part of living. Teachers should not feel that every literary experience must be followed by a related activity. However, frequently the interest of the children and the nature of the literature enjoyed guide individuals or groups quite naturally into creative writing, art experiences, creative drama, quizzes about authors or stories, or other interpretive activities.

Children need the opportunity to follow their interests and read for their own enjoyment. Personal reading within the curriculum can provide this opportunity. Such reading can be motivated through the use of records, visits to the library, and book talks. Although many teachers feel that these activities are adequate, others feel that children need guidance to find the books that have lasting merit. Few children will read more than four hundred books of children's fiction in their lifetime. It is important that some of these provide true literary experiences.

Observing Responses to Literature

Children's response to reading material is an important part of the literature curriculum. By being consciously aware of children's responses, teachers will be more effective in selecting appropriate books and in planning activities to encourage and nurture these responses.

Response is an ongoing interaction between the student and the text (Purves, 1973). The student may make the response explicit immediately, either verbally or nonverbally; he may delay making it; or he may respond implicitly, in an unobservable manner. It is the responsibility of the teacher to acknowledge the responses made by children and to provide opportunities that will elicit and nurture further response.

The teacher should organize reader response into descriptive categories in order to make objective evaluations of the effectiveness of eliciting response within the literature program. Purves and Monson (1984, p. 143)* suggest the following categories:

Descriptive: Retelling the story, naming the characters, listing the media used in illustration.

Analytic: Pointing to the uses of language, structure, point of view, in the work.

Classificatory: Placing the work in its literary historical context.

Personal: Describing the reader's reactions to the work and the emotion and memories that have been evoked.

Interpretive: Making inferences about the work and its parts, relating the work to some way of viewing phenomena (for example, psychology).

Evaluative: Judging the work's merit on personal, formal, or moral criteria.

* From Purves, A. C. and Monson, D. L. (1984). *Experiencing Children's Literature*. Glenview, Ill.: Scott, Foresman and Company. Copyright © 1984 Scott, Foresman and Company. Reprinted with permission.

The major goal of the literature program with regard to response is to increase the student's ability to respond within a range of categories.

Factors Influencing Response. In order to achieve the goal of affecting children's reactions to books, the teacher must be aware of the factors influencing response. These factors can be categorized as characteristics of the text, the reader, and the educational environment. Characteristics of the text include genre (Studier, 1978; Golden, 1978), degree of text ambiguity (Petrosky, 1976), difficulty of the text (Purves, 1979), and illustrations (Barto, 1980). In a study by Wagner (1985), children verbalized more during the reading of a picture book with an expository text than during the reading of one with a narrative text. The children asked more questions and made more comments during the reading of the (expository) text that did not fit into their schema for story. This also suggests that the child's background knowledge, including knowledge of story schema, influences response. Another reader characteristic influencing response is the child's developmental stage (Applebee, 1978; Cullinan et al., 1983; Hickman, 1980, 1983). An influential characteristic of the educational environment is the teacher. Questions and comments made by the teacher significantly influence the range of response (Lucking, 1976; Bunbury, 1980; Hickman, 1983). In order to elicit a wide range of response, teachers should be cognizant of the types of questions that elicit various tyes of response.

Extending Activities. When encouraging response, teachers must plan activities that extend the text in a manner that is appropriate for both the text and the reader. Some activities that can be used are reading aloud, storytelling, discussions, creative dramatics, reader's theater, choral speaking, puppetry, and types of written response.

Teachers of children's literature need to be familiar with many selections. Keeping a card file of books read is recommended for easy reference. Each card should contain information about the book and suggestions for activities to encourage response. *Response Guides for Teaching Children's Books* by Somers and Worthington (1979)* is an excellent source of response activities for several children's books. Their format includes

Title, author, publisher
Summary—of plot and themes
Appraisal—strengths, background information
Reading considerations—vocabulary, reading and concept levels
Initiating activities—to provde a set for the story
Discussion questions—to prompt responses
Art and media—extending activities
Creative dramatics—extending activities
Instructional resources—other appropriate materials

Recording the book's call number and the library in which it is located is also helpful.

Promotion of Group Discussion and Appreciation of Literary Works

Children may acquire an appreciation of literature by *in-depth* discussions of prudently selected works. In addition to generating enthusiasm about a given story through personal experiences, a teacher's careful guidance may bring about observation and inference concerning plot, characterization, mood, and setting.

The following examples of lessons on children's literature illustrate ways that children may derive interpretations and definitions of literary attributes through thoughtful questioning.

> *The Good Master* by Kate Seredy was used in an intermediate class. Setting was ascertained by having a child locate Budapest and the Hungarian Plains on the map. Discussion ensued concerning the time (prior to World War I) during which the story takes place.
>
> The following questions were raised in order to bring about the realization of the plot: "At the beginning of the story, what particular feelings did the family have about Kate's actions? What caused her to become more gentle in her way? What was the feeling at the end of the story?" Such questions exemplify the interrelation of story attributes. Through answering such questions a child derives not only the theme but also the delineations of the characters and their moods and feelings, which in turn convey the tone of the story.
>
> Direct questioning was instrumental in evoking plot definitions of the following works. The plot of *Wheel on the School* was brought out by this question: How do Lina and the people of the Dutch fishing village get the storks back? In discussing *My Side of the Mountain* by Jean George, the children saw that Sam had dozens of problems to solve in living off the land for a year. In reading *Hans Brinker* by Mary Mapes Dudge, the teacher helped the children identify the main plot by asking, "Why does everyone try so very persistently to restore Raff Brinker's memory?"
>
> As suggested, investigation of characterization and mood contributes to the manifestation of the plot. In reading *And Now Miguel* by Joseph Krumgold, the children followed Miguel's experiences as he grows up to be a man in his father's family. The plot of *Mary Poppins* by P. L. Travers is revealed through the following discourse: "Mary Poppins was a magical character, vain and stern. Would you like Mary to sit beside you? Why?" To direct their thinking about the plot of *Johnny Tremain* by Esther Forbes, the teacher asked the children how the story would be different if Johnny lived today. In discussing *Henry Huggins* by Beverly Cleary, the teacher asked, "Have you experienced some of the frustrations Henry had? How did Henry meet his problems?" In an activity to develop plot for *The Secret Garden* by Frances Burnett, the teacher suggested that the children portray Mary's bad temper by role playing. Similarly, children may gain understanding of the feelings of the Cratchit family in Dickens's *A Christmas Carol* by reading expressively the episode of Christmas dinner at the Cratchits'.

The following are further examples of developing insights as to the nature of setting, mood, and theme:

* From Somers, A. B. and Worthington, J. E. (1979). *Response Guides for Teaching Children's Books,* Urbana, Ill.: National Council of Teachers of English. Reprinted by permission of the National Council of Teachers of English.

The setting of *Blue Willow* by Doris Gates was represented in a mural composed by the class. Attention to illustrations and the author's name suggested the Japanese setting for *Crow Boy* by Taro Yashima. Pictures and slides were used to show the environment for the story *Wheel on the School* by Meindert DeJong. A recording and filmstrip provided setting and mood for the story *The Sorcerer's Apprentice* by H. H. Ewers, translated by Ludwig Lewisohn. In the story of *The Silver Llama* by Alida S. Malkus, pictures of Peru were helpful. A sense of time and place setting was developed for *The Tree of Freedom* by Rebecca Caudill by making a table map of clay showing the mountain and the passes in Kentucky at the beginning of the westward movement.

Children may particularly enjoy stories in familiar settings. For example, children from Wisconsin would recognize scenes from *Caddie Woodlawn* by Carol Brink as similar to their own environs. In *King of the Wind* by Marguerite Henry, the teacher explained that Henry lives in Virginia and asked the children why they thought the author could write so vividly about horses. In *Paddle to the Sea* by Holling C. Holling, the children quickly discerned how the illustrations show the beauty of the Great Lakes, the St. Lawrence, and the Atlantic.

The teacher developed sensitivity to mood in the following stories by asking appropriate questions: How is a mood of suspense created in *Matchlock Gun* by Walter Edmonds? In *Call It Courage* by Armstrong Sperry, the children felt the excitement of being marooned on a desert island and sighed with relief at the outcome of the story. They admired the courage of Mafatu. They were asked these questions: What makes this story exciting? What other feelings do you have as you read the story? In *The Story of Doctor Dolittle* by Hugh Lofting, although the animals are continually in trouble and are fearful, the story is very humorous. The children were asked: Why is this story so funny? Do you like this kind of humor?

An awareness of theme was developed by discussion of the main idea in a story. In *Beatinest Boy* by Jesse Stuart, the teacher asked, "What is the relationship of the boy and his grandmother?" After reading *Apple and the Arrow* by Mary Buff and Conrad Buff, the children were asked how the Swiss people won their struggle for freedom against the Austrian tyrant, Gessler. Before reading *Door in the Wall* by Marguerite De Angeli, the children saw a filmstrip showing the fortification of a castle so that they would be better able to visualize the difficulties of the small invalid boy who was able to save a castle.

It is hoped that the foregoing discussion will provide a useful resource for you as you attempt to involve your students in the quest for meaning in literature and in the appreciation of the value of studying literature.

Preparation for Discussion. In preparation for leading an in-depth discussion with your class, you must first acquire a thorough knowledge of the book's content. In addition, you should plan a direction for the discussion that is appropriate for the book and the students. Huck (1979) suggests using a webbing or organizational technique to explore all the possibilities for discussion and to help the teacher decide on those most appropriate. The categories Huck used for webbing or grouping activities are art interpretation, drama, values clarification, personal response, development of characterization, development of literary awareness, and related literature. Although no discussion would include all areas, an initial comprehensive diagramming can enable the teacher to select the most appropriate area.

Sources of Children's Literature

The field of children's literature is rapidly expanding. Thousands of new titles are published each year for children and youths in the United States. Although many of these books are of only temporary importance, some have real worth. Teachers and parents do not have the time to read and evaluate all the new literature. Fortunately, there are many excellent reference books from which teachers can seek this information.

When preparing to teach children's literature, read at all grade levels in order to find out what type of material is available. Later, concentrate on the grade levels that most concern you.

One source of information concerning children's literature is the *Children's Catalog* published by the H. W. Wilson Company, New York. This is primarily a reference work for use in libraries. In it are listed recently published books considered of highest merit as well as works of the past of enduring value. If you are establishing a library for the first time, you will find in it a special list recommended for initial purchase as a nucleus for future growth. The *Children's Catalog* is expensive, and therefore should be made available by the school district with library funds.

A promising guide to children's literature is *Children's Literature Review,* Volume 1 (Block and Riley, 1976) and Volume 2 (Riley, 1976). A resource that is published semiannually, the *Children's Literature Review,* provides critical reviews of selected works, submitted by well-known children's authors and book reviewers. A biographical sketch of each author is given along with the plots of the works represented.

Children's Choices: Teaching with Books Children Like (Nancy Roser and Margaret Frith, eds., 1983) is a unique source for selecting books preferred by children. In addition to this comprehensive listing, annual lists are published in the October issue of *The Reading Teacher.*

Other sources of children's literature that may be consulted are *The Bowker Annual* (published yearly), *Children's Books in Print, Subject Guide to Children's Books in Print, Index to Children's Poetry, Negro Heritage Reader for Young People, Index to Black Poetry, Adventuring with Books,* and *Bibliography of Nonsexist Supplementary Books (K–12).*

In order to recognize merit and to direct the attention of the public to children's literature, a number of awards are made each year. The John Newbery Medal is awarded to the book considered to be the most distinguished contribution to American literature for children. Table 8–1 is a list of the most recent Newbery Medal winners.

The Caldecott Medal honors the best-illustrated book for children. Recent winners of the Newbery and Caldecott Medals are listed in Table 8–2.

There are other awards that call attention to books of merit. These include the *Laura Ingalls Wilder Award* and *The Regina Medal.* In Canada there are two Book of the Year for Children medals. The *Hans Christian Andersen Award* is an international children's book award. In England, the *Carnegie Medal* and *Kate Greenaway Medal* correspond to the *Newbery* and *Caldecott* awards in the United States. There are awards

Table 8–1
Newbery Medal Awards

Title	*Author*	*Date and Publisher*
M. C. Higgins the Great	Virginia Hamilton	1975; Macmillan
The Grey King	S. Cooper	1976; M. S. McElderry/Atheneum
Roll of Thunder, Hear My Cry	M. D. Taylor	1977; Dial
Bridge to Terabithia	Katherine Paterson	1978; Crowell
The Westing Game	Ellen Raskin	1979; Dutton
A Gathering of Days: A New England Girl's Journal, 1830–32	Joan W. Blos	1980; C. Scribner's Sons
Jacob Have I Loved	Katherine Paterson	1981; Crowell
A Visit to William Blake's Inn: Poems for Innocent and Experienced Travelers	Nancy Willard	1982; Harcourt Brace Jovanovich
Dicey's Song	Cynthia Voigt	1983; Atheneum
Dear Mr. Henshaw	Beverly Cleary	1984; Morrow
The Hero and the Crown	Robin McKinley	1985; Greenwillow
Sarah Plain and Tall	Patricia MacLachlan	1986; Harper and Row

Table 8–2
Caldecott Medal Awards

Title	*Author*	*Date and Publisher*
Arrow to the Sun	Gerald McDermott	1975; Viking
Why Mosquitoes Buzz in People's Ears: A West African Tale	Retold by V. Aardema	1976; Dial
Ashanti to Zulu: African Traditions	Margaret Musgrove	1977; Dial
Noah's Ark	Peter Spier	1978; Doubleday
The Girl Who Loved Wild Horses	Paul Goble	1979; Bradbury
Ox-cart Man	Donald Hall	1980; Viking
Fables	Arnold Lobel	1981; Harper and Row
Jumanji	Chris Van Allsburg	1982; Houghton Mifflin
Shadow	Blaise Cendrars	1983; Scribner's Sons
The Glorious Flight: Across the Channel with Louis Bleriot, July 25, 1909	Alice Provensen	1984; Viking
Saint George and the Dragon	Margaret Hodges	1985; Little, Brown & Co.
The Polar Express	Chris Van Allsburg	1986; Houghton Mifflin

given in France, Germany, Norway, Sweden, and Switzerland for outstanding children's books published each year in these countries.

The book reviews that appear in *The Horn Book, Childhood Education, Elementary English, The New York Times, The Christian Science Monitor,* and *Kirkus Reviews* provide other sources of aid in selecting books for children.

The Children's Book Council, 175 Fifth Avenue, New York, New York, 10011, promotes the nationwide Book Week. Posters, book jackets, wall charts, and other materials are available for school use at very low cost.

With all this emphasis on newness it must not be forgotten that we share a great cultural heritage from the past. There are constant references in our language that assume that we know the meaning of such expressions as "my man Friday," "the golden touch," "the patience of Job," and "whitewashing the fence." A good source offering new ideas for teaching literature classics is *Literature—News That Stays News* (Urbana, Ill.: National Council of Teachers of English, 1984).

Anthologies of children's literature contain collections of old and new verse, fairy tales and folktales, short selections from modern writers, notes on authors and illustrators of children's books, and excellent suggestions for their classroom use. In time most elementary teachers will want to purchase one of these anthologies to keep on their desks as a constant source of classroom material. A book of this nature is as basic to good instruction as chalkboard and chalk, but some districts hesitate to spend funds for individual teacher references. In that case, the teacher has no choice but to purchase the book as a basic tool of the profession and use the expense as a tax deduction.

The *Anthology of Children's Literature* by Edna Johnson, Evelyn R. Sickels, and Frances Clark Sayers, published by Houghton Mifflin Company, and *Story and Verse for Children* by Miriam Blanton Huber, published by Macmillan Publishing Company, Inc., are outstanding single-volume collections. May Hill Arbuthnot has written several books: *Time for True Tales, Time for Fairy Tales, Time for Poetry,* and *Children and Books,* all published by Scott, Foresman and Company.

A number of special bibliographies have been issued to help teachers locate material appropriate to the needs of children. Some of them are periodically brought up to date. The following are helpful: *Reading Ladders for Human Relations,* edited by Eileen Tway (Urbana, Ill.: National Council of Teachers of English, 1981); *Behavior Patterns in Children's Books* by Clara J. Kircher (Washington, D.C.: Catholic University Press); *About*

100 Books, A Gateway to Better Group Understanding by Ann G. Wolfe (New York: The American Jewish Committee Institute of Human Relations).

In the area of children's literature we are endowed with great riches. Our problem is to share them with wisdom.

How Can Teachers Involve Parents in the Literature Program?

Our objectives in the teaching of literature will never be realized if our efforts are limited to what can be accomplished in the school day. Appreciation of literature as personal enrichment takes time. The rhythm of the school day, with its schedules and demands, is not right for some literature. It is when the reader is alone, unscheduled and undisturbed, that a story can truly come alive. But children complain that they do not have time to read at home. There is so much time needed for music lessons, homework, chores—and television. Once the "rhythm of the night" was the inspiration of storytelling. Parents shared the stories of their youth, and children discovered the world of imaginative writers. Today the rhythm of the night has come to mean the sound of ricocheting bullets on television, the wearisome exhortations of announcers, and the tasteless prolixity of commercials. Somehow we must work with parents to find time for children to read. Our first task is to show them the values of literature in contrast to the thirty-minute exercises in violence or inanity of TV drama. Annis Duff's book *Bequest of Wings* tells of the joys shared by a family as modern books were used in the home. If a teacher cannot get parents to read this book, it might be wise to discuss it with them at a parent-teacher meeting or conference.

Most parents will respond to the teacher's appeal for their help in providing good books for their children. Explain to them why we need so many children's books and the difficulty of securing the right ones. Suggest that at Christmas or Hanukkah or on a birthday they buy a book for their child that might be shared with the class. A group of parents and teachers might suggest a list of books to be purchased or the criteria to be followed when buying books for children.

Ownership of a book means a great deal to a child. When members of a sixth-grade class were asked to list their three favorite books, the final list did not correspond to any bibliography of children's books, but one element was noted: If a child owned a book, it was listed as a favorite.

Another way of making parents aware of the material available for children is a planned summer reading program. As summer approaches, a fifth-grade class might ask the sixth grade to suggest books that it would enjoy. The fifth-graders should also note the books their class has enjoyed but some members have not had time to read. From these two sources each child might select six or eight books that he or she plans to read during the summer. A simple folder or notebook can be made and used for an early report at the beginning of the next school year.

Parents are sometimes concerned about the expense of children's books. It does seem like an extravagance to pay six dollars for a picture book that only takes twenty minutes to read. Nancy Larrick, in *A Parent's Guide to Children's Reading,* makes an important point by comparing the costs of good books and toys and then pointing out that long after the toys are broken or discarded the books are still available for rereading. This is one criterion to use in buying a book: Will it be worth rereading? If not, do not buy it. There are other sources for books of only temporary interest.

There are good, inexpensive books available. *Scholastic Magazine* publishes a series of paperback books for children. These are reprints of the finest modern books available. The E. M. Hale Company of Eau Clair, Wisconsin, also publishes reprints of outstanding children's books. Some of the grocery-store and supermarket books are also good. A committee of the PTA might evaluate some of these and suggest a few for purchase.

"'Tis a strange sort of poverty to be finding in a

rich country". These are the words spoken by an immigrant lad in Ruth Sawyer's *The Enchanted Schoolhouse.* Though these words refer to the inadequate and dilapidated school facilities to be found in a wealthy and thriving city in America, they can well apply to all of America today—a land wealthy with a multitude of fine books that children and parents have not discovered.

How Is Poetry Presented in the Modern Curriculum?

Our culture is rich in poetic tradition. Many communities have a Longfellow School or one named for Lowell, Whitman, Field, or Stevenson. The respect for poetry was reflected in the curriculum of the recent past, which frequently specified selections that were to be studied and memorized in each grade. Some schools had as many as a hundred "pieces" to be mastered in the seventh and eight grades.

This requirement was intended to ensure that each student would know this aspect of our culture heritage. Although it was recognized that some of this material was beyond the understanding of the students, and that memorization added a burdensome routine, teachers sincerely felt that eventually this material would enrich lives. Many adults today get great satisfaction in reciting *About Ben Adhem* or *Snowbound.* Some will say, "This poem did not mean much to me when I was in school, but each year I seem to enjoy it more." On the other hand, some who were taught this way learned to detest poetry and still think of it as a disciplinary activity.

In the curriculum of the past, poetry was frequently associated with programs. One learned a piece to recite on Friday afternoon or at a parents' meeting. Grandparents especially were delighted with this accomplishment and usually rewarded the speaker with a gift. Contests were held in which all the participants recited *The Highwayman.* Audiences would spend an afternoon listening to ten or more elocutionists repeat the same selection.

Good poetry is sometimes found in popular magazines and daily papers. Although many of these poems are of transient value, some very good material undoubtedly goes unrecognized in the great mass of published verse. Some of the more talented poets of our day may turn to song writing or prose because of the greater financial returns involved. Just as such poems as *Trees* and *America, the Beautiful* have been made into fine songs, the lyrics of many popular songs have merit as verse.

In a modern classroom, poetry serves many purposes and needs. It is used to enrich all curriculum areas. Modern anthologies contain a great deal of verse appropriate to the age and reading level of the student for whom they are intended, although this places a severe limitation on the choice of material. Mary Hill Arbuthnot has a useful collection in *Time for Poetry* that the teacher reads to students rather than requiring them to read it aloud themselves.

Most teachers today start with the students with whom they work rather than with a collection of poetry that they feel must be mastered. They recognize the truth of Carl Sandburg's statement:

> Poetry for any given individual depends on the individual and what his personality requires as poetry. Beauty depends on personal taste. What is beauty for one person is not for another. What is poetry for one person may be balderdash or hogwash for another. (Sandburg, 1930, p. 20)

The teacher seeks to present material that will meet the immediate appreciation level of students as well as build sensitivity for growth in appreciation. Many teachers keep a file of poetry and draw from it when appropriate throughout the school day. As the seasons change, verses are used to express the students' feelings or to call attention to the flight of birds or the budding of our pussywillow. Holidays are made special days through poems that may be used as the theme of a bulletin board display. In social studies, the life of the Indian becomes more accessible as the group recites a Navajo prayer or chant. On the playground, the ideals of fair play and good sportsmanship are remembered because a verse suggests meaningful behavior. Throughout each day and year the student grows in perception and understanding through the planned use of poetry. One learns to listen to words for both meaning and sound. One finds that some words create an atmosphere that is sad or frightening, whereas others have a warm or relaxing effect.

To accomplish this, the teacher starts with herself. Teachers who experience most difficulty at the beginning are those who have a love for great poetry yet are unwilling to discover the appreciation level of the students with whom they work. Walt Whitman's *When Lilacs Last in the Dooryard Bloom'd* will probably not be accepted by a student who delights in *Little Orphan Annie* by James Whitcomb Riley. The most important consideration in selection of material is to avoid any value judgment as to what students *should* like. Stated positively, the most important consideration is to discover what they *do* like.

Start by reciting a poem to your students. Avoid any discussion of word meanings. Students do not need to understand every word in order to enjoy a poem. After you have recited it, a student may ask what a certain word means. If this occurs, by all means explain the word in a sentence or two. Then repeat the poem a second time. Select for recitation a few of the very best students' poems.

Reading poetry to your students requires preparation. Begin by reading the verse aloud to yourself, noting the punctuation, the mood of the poem, and any unusual expression or words. Before reading aloud, a few remarks may help the students orient themselves. Introduce *Little Orphan Annie* in this manner: "Here is a poem your parents liked, and I think you will like it, too. There are a few words like *hearth* and *rafter* that you may not know; they mean. . . ." Then, you might ask a few questions after the first reading. Appropriate ones would be, "Why do you suppose the author repeats the words *If you don't watch out*? Notice how they are written in the poem to show how they might be read." After the students have been shown the printed poem, another question would be, "How do you feel when you hear the words *the lamp wick sputters and the wind goes whooo*? What was the writer trying to do?" If the students wish, you might read the poem a second time, then place it on the reading table for those who wish to read it themselves.

Some students will bring poems they have found and offer to read them to the class. Others will respond to the invitation to bring poems for the teacher to read. Reading poetry aloud is difficult, and many students do not do it well. As a result it may be a deadly listening experience. We want to develop good listening habits, but there are better ways of doing it than by forcing attention to poorly read poetry.

The poems found in students' readers are much more fun to read if they have first been heard with pleasure. These selections are the basis for instruction concerning the oral reading of poetry, but that instruction should follow an appreciative listening. Good oral reading is largely imitative, and the example followed should be a worthy one. It is the poet who has to speak through the oral reader. It is not the reader speaking poetry.

Sometimes a poem is presented by being read well by the teacher or pupil, then read in unison by the class. At other times a carefully prepared lesson plan helps students identify with the purposes of the poet and the beauty of language used.

Sample Lesson Plan

The following sample lesson plan is intended to be a guide or outline to be expanded on or altered to meet the demands of the individual teaching situation:

Grade 4: Sample Lesson Plan for Teaching Margaret Widdemer's "The Secret Cavern"

Goals

1. To introduce the poetry of introspection.
2. To point out how the speaker's character is revealed through the imaginative experience of the poem.
3. To lead the student to reason about himself, his desires, his imaginative experiences, his actions.
4. To indicate to the student the close affinity that usually exists among his natural desires (his likes and dislikes), his imagined experiences, and his actions.

Presentation

1. Introduction: Life would be quite dreary if we didn't have any friends, wouldn't it? I am sure I would be unhappy and lonely if I didn't have any friends. I like to be around people, but there are also times when I like to be alone. Sometimes when I am alone I like to read; sometimes I like to think; and sometimes I like to let my imagination wander. Perhaps some of you can tell me what you like to do when you are alone.
2. After the students respond, continue: I would like to read a poem to you about an adventurous child whose imagination often wandered. See whether you can tell why I think this is an adventurous child.

The Secret Cavern

Underneath the boardwalk, way, way back,
There's a splendid cavern, big and black—
If you want to get there, you must crawl
Underneath the posts and steps and all.
When I've finished paddling, there I go—
None of all the other children know!

There I keep my treasures in a box—
Shells and colored glass and queer-shaped rocks,
In a secret hiding-place I've made,
Hollowed out with clamshells and a spade,
Marked with yellow pebbles in a row—
None of all the other children know!

It's a place that makes a splendid lair,
Room for chests and weapons and one chair,

In the farthest corner, by the stones,
I shall have a flag with skulls and bones
And a lamp that casts a lurid glow—
None of all the other children know!

Some time, by and by, when I am grown,
I shall go and live there all alone;
I shall dig and paddle till it's dark,
Then go out and man my pirate bark;
I shall fill my cave with captive foe—
None of all the other children know!

Margaret Widdemer

3. Discussion: Now can any of you tell me why I think this is an adventurous child? (Responses will probably be related to the dark cavern. If students are unfamiliar with the word *cavern,* explain its similarity to *cave*. The students may suggest the "treasures," "chests," "weapons," "flag with skulls and bones," and the "pirate bark.")
4. Why do you suppose there is just one chair? (The child wanted this as a private, secret place.)
5. Do you think the child truly wants to live there all alone when all grown? What tells us in the poem that the child really does like to be around other people? (The child is going to fill the cave with "captive foe.")
6. I am going to read the poem again, and this time I want you to notice what kinds of pictures the poem helps you to see. (Read the poem again. Children often close their eyes while creating images. The atmosphere must be such that the students are relaxed and feel free to close their eyes or put their heads on their desks, if they wish.)
7. Now let's talk about the mental pictures the poem helped us to see. (The students will probably describe the cave, the colorful treasures, and so forth. Try to elicit responses about the feelings they experienced while listening. Some students may think that the dark cave seems "spooky." The sensation of "dampness" may also be mentioned by the students. The sound of the paddle of the boat as it swishes in the water is a possible response. At this point the students may be eager to paint or draw the scenes that you and they have pictured.
8. Writing Activity: Just think of all the pictures and feelings we have been talking about. By choosing certain words, the poet was able to help us see these pictures. Let's see whether we can think of a picture we might like to paint using words. We've had so many good ideas about the poem, about secret places and being alone, that I think we would all enjoy painting some pictures with words. You might like to

describe a place you know—a cave, a treehouse, a quiet place, or perhaps your own room. We will need two sheets of paper. We will call one our "idea paper." We will jot down on this paper ideas that come to our minds. Then we may want to think about our ideas for a while and decide how we'd like to put them together. Some of you may want to write a paragraph that will make a picture for us, or help us to "hear" certain sounds. Some of you may want to write a poem using your ideas. Perhaps some of you already have a short story in mind. I see that everyone has his "brush" (holding up pencil) and his "canvas" ready (hold up paper), so let's start "painting." (The teacher who takes this time to write creatively along with the students will see many satisfying results. The experience seems to become more enjoyable and worthwhile to the students when the teacher is writing also. After their poems or paragraphs are finished, the students may want to exchange papers for proofreading or to form into small groups to read them aloud. Compositions could be recopied for a bulletin board or a composition booklet. The central objective is to make certain the experience has been enjoyable for the students and that they feel that their compositions are noteworthy.)

Although it is necessary for the teacher to prepare before presenting poetry in the classroom, her attitude and personal characteristics have been found to have more influence on the students than the method of instruction used (Travers, 1984). Students developed a liking for and a better understanding of poetry when the teacher interacted with them, showing enthusiasm, sympathy, and encouragement. The successful teacher of poetry is flexible when selecting poems, respects the views of the students, and keeps the emphasis on the enjoyment of poetry.

In addition, the teacher must provide for ever-increasing depths of appreciation. It is not enough to expose students only to the poems they can feel and readily understand. We must also introduce to them "a sense of a margin beyond, as in a wood full of unknown glades, and birds and flowers unfamiliar," as Andrew Long said in his introduction to the *Blue Poetry Book.* Following are some specific ideas and suggestions of poems to use to help students understand the concepts:

1. Enjoyment of rhythm, melody, and story.
   a. Rhythm
      Barbers' Clippers, by Dorothy Baruch—child listens for rhythm in this unrhymed poem.
   b. Melody
      Sea Shells, by Amy Lowell—hear the sea in the alliteration of *s.*

c. Story
The Little Elfman, by John Kendrick Bangs—hold a conversation between a child and a puppet elf.

2. Appreciation of seeing one's own experiences mirrored in poetry. *Choosing Shoes,* by Efrida Wolfe—children describe the way they felt when they went shopping for shoes and then compare experiences.
3. Projection into a world other than that in which one lives. *Radiator Lions,* by Dorothy Aldis—a child who lives in a home that is owned not rented may be helped to understand George's predicament, living in an apartment, housing unit, etc.
4. Understanding of symbolism and hidden meanings. *Boats Sail on the Rivers,* by Christina Rossetti—see clouds as ships and rainbow as a bridge.
5. Sensitivity to patterns of writing and literary style. *Merry-Go-Round,* by Dorothy Baruch. If this poem is put on a chart, young children can note that the shape of the lines as well as the words convey the movement of the merry-go-round.

How May a Verse Choir Encourage the Classroom Use of Poetry?

The oral reading of poetry has long been a tradition in the British Isles. In some areas, the choir is as highly organized as an orchestra, and the performances given are as effective as that of a singing choir. The voices are limited to certain voice qualities, and high and low voices are balanced for special effects. These high performance standards are not the objectives of the elementary school verse choir. Instead, our goals are enjoyment, the satisfaction of self-expression, and appreciation of the poetry selections used.

In achieving these primary objectives there are a number of parallel benefits. Shy children feel that they are contributing members of the group. They are able to participate in a public appearance without any agonizing emotional pressures. The greatest benefits are in the area of speech. The values of precise enunciation and careful pronunciation are obvious to the most slovenly speakers. The slow or fast speaker is made aware of the effect of such speech on the listener. Not only is the quality of voice tone brought to the level of awareness, but also those whose voices are unpleasant receive needed attention.

From the beginning the approach should be one of enjoyment. With any group, start with familiar material so that there is no problem of memorization. A favorite with all ages is *Hickory Dickory Dock.* After writing it on the chalkboard, the teacher might point out that the poem has the rhythm of a clock ticking. Then add the words *tick-tock* three times at the beginning and end.

Tick-tock, tick-tock, tick-tock
Hickory Dickory Dock
The mouse ran up the clock.
The clock struck, One!
The mouse ran down.
Hickory Dickory Dock.
Tick-tock, tick-tock, tick-tock

The teacher might say, "Now watch my arm. I will move it as if it were a clock pendulum or metronome. When I go this way, say *tick,* and this way say *tock.*

Let's practice it once to see how much we can sound like a clock." After one round of practice, go ahead: "That was fine! Now we will have one row be a clock and tick all the way through the verse while the rest of us say it. Notice that we must pause after the *tick* to allow time for a *tock* sound. We might say the last *tick-tock* very softly as if the clock were stopping."

Later you might wish to discuss with your students ways to emphasize the word *one*. Sometimes emphasis is secured by asking only one person to say the word, sometimes by clapping hands or ringing a bell, and sometimes simply by telling everyone to say it louder.

Another verse with a dramatic effect is one with a "wind" idea in it. Ask the entire group to hum to sound like a wind blowing, then while some continue to hum, ask them to speak the verse as the humming quietly fades away at the end. Most children will know *Who Has Seen the Wind?*

Who has seen the wind?
Neither I nor you;
But when the leaves hang trembling
The wind is passing through.

Who has seen the wind?
Neither you nor I;
But when the leaves bow down their heads
The wind is passing by.

Christina Rossetti

Before saying a verse together it is wise to note the punctuation. If a group pauses at the end of each line, an unpleasant singsong effect destroys the meaning of the poetry. Sometimes this can be avoided by a slight pause after words that should be emphasized, such as *seen* in the first line or *leaves* in the third.

Usually the signal "Ready, begin" is used for primary children. A hand signal can serve the same purpose. The opening of a closed fist might be the sign to start.

Choral Readings with Refrains. The simplest type of choral reading is one using a refrain. One student may be selected to read the "solo."

The Christmas Pudding

(Read faster and faster with each line.)

Solo: Into the basin put the plums,
Refrain: Stirabout, stirabout, stirabout.
Solo: Next the good white flour comes,
Refrain: Stirabout, stirabout, stirabout.
Solo: Sugar and peel and eggs and spice,
Refrain: Stirabout, stirabout, stirabout.
Solo: Mix them and fix them and cool them twice,
Refrain: Stirabout, stirabout, stirabout.

Lillian Taylor

Additional selections may be found in Appendix A.

Another simple form is the two-part arrangement. Half of the children say one part and the other half the other part. Question-and-answer poetry is often used for the two-part arrangement.

A third arrangement is the line-a-child pattern. Each child has a chance to speak one or more lines by himself. In some poems certain lines can be spoken by individual children and other lines can be spoken in unison.

The Song of the Pop-Corn

Unison: Pop-pop-pop!
1st Child: Says the pop-corn in the pan;
Unison: Pop-pop-pop!
2nd Child: You may catch me if you can!
Unison: Pop-pop-pop!
3rd Child: Says each kernel hard and yellow:
Unison: Pop-pop-pop!
4th Child: I'm a dancing little fellow,
Unison: Pop-pop-pop!
5th Child: How I scamper through the heat!
Unison: Pop-pop-pop!
6th Child: You will find me good to eat.
Unison: Pop-pop-pop!
7th Child: I can whirl and skip and hop.
Unison: Pop-pop-pop-pop!
Pop!
Pop!
Pop!

Louise Abney

Choral Readings Involving a Group

The most difficult of all choral reading is that involving the total group. Much practice is required in speaking together; in drilling on articulation, enunciation, inflection, and pronunciation; and in blending the voices into workable balance while maintaining satisfactory timing. Sometimes it is wise to divide a class into high and low voices.

Solo parts should be used to encourage all students rather than to display a few stars. Frequently solo parts would be spoken by small groups of three or four whose voices are similar.

After students are interested in choir work, they will accept some special speech exercises, such as rolling their heads for relaxation, or such tone exercises as saying, *ba, be, bi, bo, bu* toward the front of their mouths. If the teacher starts with these, most children think they are ridiculously funny and no worthy results are achieved.

A verse choir should perform because it motivates both effort and interest, but the teacher must avoid the temptation to use material beyond the appreciation level of the students or material unworthy of memorization. A sixth-grade graduation class might prepare a patriotic verse, *I Am an American,* from *Book of Americans* by Stephen Vincent Benet. Inviting visitors from another room to hear a choir perform is as motivating as more elaborate presentations.

Scripts suitable for choral presentations are provided in Appendix A.

Which Verse May Be Used with Young Children

Young children delight in action verses and finger plays. These verses are a part of every culture; the Chinese have them, the American Indians have them, and new ones are invented daily. Friedrich Wilhelm August Froebel, the father of the kindergarten, collected many of his time and called them mother's-play. You may recall the delight you felt as your mother moved your toes and said, "This little piggie went to market, this little piggie stayed home." We suspect that one of the most interesting experiences of childhood is that of self-discovery, and these verses reflect the charm of that experience.

Thumb Man

Thumb man says he'll dance,
Thumb man says he'll sing,
Dance and sing my merry little thing,
Thumb man says he'll dance and sing.
Where is thumb man?
Where is thumb man?
Here I am.
(Fist forward with thumb standing.)
Here I am.
(Other fist forward, thumb standing.)
How do you do this morning?
(Wriggle one thumb in direction of other.)
Very well, I thank you.
(Wriggle other thumb.)
Run away, run away.
(Hands behind back again.)

(Can be sung to the tune of *Are You Sleeping?*)

The poem is repeated with each of the digits of the hand, using the following names: *pointer, tall man, ring man,* and *little man.*

In working with action plays, it is better to use too few than too many. The fun seems to be in repetition of the familiar favorites. The teacher first demonstrates the entire verse, then asks one or two students to come to the front and do it with her. After that, each line is recited by the group and repeated until a few have mastered it. Needless to say, parents delight in watching a verse choir use these materials.

After these become old favorites, children will want to make up their own. To do this, start with a movement such as holding up an arm with the fist closed.

"This is an airplane searchlight" (arm held up, wrist bent).
"It turns to the left" (open the fist).
"And the airplane came home" (movement of both hands of airplane landing).
"On a dark, dark night."

Other movements might be holding hands together to indicate something closed, fingers raised as candles on a cake, fingers "walking" to indicate movement either on the table or for an insect on the bend of the arm or opposite palm, fists pounding to indicate marching, building, or loud movements. Soon total body action is needed and eventually one reaches simple pantomime.

When using nursery rhymes, children's names may be substituted for those of the rhyme characters. Let each child select the person he or she wants to be, to avoid its selection being used in a way that might hurt the child. Let children join in on a repeated refrain. This may also be done in such a story as "Little pig, little pig, let me in!" "No, no, no, not by the hair of my chinny-chin-chin." Poems involving the use of body and hand motions appear in Appendix A.

Supervisors and principals sometimes use finger play as a means of establishing acceptance by little children. A principal who can teach a new one in the kindergarten will always be welcome. Froebel saw in this common interest a mystic relationship. Perhaps he was right. But it is obvious that these simple verses help children to speak better, notice sounds in words, learn about rhyming endings, and gain social recognition in a way that is pleasant to both the child and the teacher.

Action stories may be developed after the pattern of the old nursery rhyme in which one child says, "I went upstairs," and the other child replies, "Just like me." A leader tells a part of a story and the remainder of the group does the action, saying at the same time, "Just like this."

Leader: Goldilocks went for a walk in the forest.
Group: Just like this.
Leader: She stopped to look at a bird.
Group: Just like this.
Leader: The bird said, "Cheer up! Cheer up!"
Group: Just like this, "Cheer up! Cheer up!"

Other rhymes of this nature may be "played" as the beginning of creative dramatics.

What Values Are There in a Teacher's Poetry File?

A poetry file assures the teacher of having interesting material available. Most teachers prefer to put into the file a few old favorites that they know will be used. Without a file it sometimes takes hours to locate such well-known verses as E. L. Thayer's *Casey at the Bat* or Joaquin Miller's *Columbus.*

After teaching the same grade for some time, many teachers prefer to put favorite verses into a notebook classified by the months. The beginning teacher usually finds a card file most convenient. Then as the teacher borrows and clips, she selects those that are most useful. She will then have a collection from which selections are readily available for incorporation into class activities.

There are many ways to organize such a collection. One heading might be *Holiday and Seasonal Poems.* Later these might be divided under the titles *Halloween, Christmas, Hanukkah, Valentine's Day, St. Patrick's Day, Winter, Summer, Spring,* and *Fall.* Although there are many poems about holidays, it is sometimes difficult to find one appropriate to your group. Another broad category for a poetry file might be that of *Curriculum Enrichment.* In time, this too could be divided into the various subjects.

One of the major reasons for asking children to write poetry is to release strong feelings. Poems that express these feelings for children probably act the same way. There are some children who will find these poems delightful "because they say exactly the way I feel." As a category for a poetry file, they might be listed under *Expression of Strong Feelings.*

One Day When We Went Walking

One day when we went walking,
  I found a dragon's tooth,
A dreadful dragon's tooth,
  "A locust thorn," said Ruth.

One day when we went walking,
  I found a brownie's shoe,

A brownie's button shoe,
  "A dry pea pod," said Sue.

One day when we went walking,
  I found a mermaid's fan,
A merry mermaid's fan,
  "A scallop shell," said Dan.

One day when we went walking,
  I found a fairy's dress,
A fairy's flannel dress,
  "A mullein leaf," said Bess.

Next time I go walking—
  Unless I meet an elf,
A funny, friendly elf—
  I'm going by myself!

Valine Hobbs

Probably the most charming of all poems for children are those that allow adults to regain insight into the child's world, to rediscover the simple ways of life again. Such poetry is childlike rather than childish. In your poetry file you will want a section on *Enrichment of Daily Life*. Those who work with primary children will especially want material by Dorothy Aldis. Another author for this age is Aileen Fisher, who wrote this favorite:

Coffeepot Face

I saw
my face
in the coffeepot.
Imagine
A coffeepot face!
  My eyes
were small
but my nose was NOT
and my mouth
was—every place!

Aileen Fisher

Verses that suggest a way to act will always be popular with teachers. Some of these suggest standards of conduct, others are gentle reminders, and a few use a bit of ridicule to guide behavior.

Little Charlie Chipmunk

Little Charlie Chipmunk was a talker
Mercy me!
He chattered after breakfast
And he chattered after tea
He chattered to his sister
He chattered to his mother
He chattered to his father
And he chattered to his brother
He chattered till his family
Was almost driven wild
Oh, Little Charlie Chipmunk
Was a very tiresome child.

Helen Cowles le Cron

You will find many verses that are worthy of a poetry file simply because they are fun and add humor to life. These include limericks, nonsense verses, and those making clever use of words. The whimsical couplets of Ogden Nash are recorded with musical background. Children especially enjoy his *The Panther* (which ends with "Don't anther") and his *The Octopus*.

A bit of wisecracking doggerel like this has its place in your file:

Modern Light

Twinkle, twinkle little star
I know exactly what you are
You're a satellite in the sky
And why my taxes are so high.

Another group of verses in your file should consist of poems that help the child relate himself to all nature. In the fall children will sense the rhythm of nature when you read to them Rachel Field's *Something Told the Wild Geese*. Children who have found animal tracks made in sand or snow may listen with appreciation to *The Tracks* by Elizabeth Coatsworth. The following poem employs delicate and sensitive imagery:

Soft Is the Hush of Falling Snow

I like the springtime of the year
When all the baby things appear;
When little shoots of grass come through
And everything is fresh and new.

But, oh, I like the summer, too.
When clouds are soft and skies are blue
Vacation days are full of fun
I like being lazy in the sun.

But when the fall has once begun
I'm glad that summer then is done
I love the frosty biting air
The harvest yield seen everywhere.

But winter is beyond compare
For though the world seems black and bare
It's rest time for the things that grow
And soft is the hush of falling snow.

Emily Carey Alleman

Poetry that will help us understand other cultures is needed. Poems of this type are included in Appendix A.

Sharing poems related to the same topic will help children see the way different points of view come to be. You might say to your class, "In these poems each writer is talking about houses. Do they agree in any way?" Then share with them *Sometimes a Little House Will Please* by Elizabeth Coatsworth, *Our House* by Rachel Field, *Our House* by Dorothy Brown Thompson, and *Song for a Little House* by Christopher Morley.

Teachers will find that the building of such a file increases their own appreciation of poetic expression. However, what has been said concerning individual differences of pupils applies to teachers as well. If you do not truly feel some pleasure and delight in sharing poetry with children, possibly it will be well for you to spend time on those aspects of the curriculum about which you are enthusiastic. In a few cases, you may learn with the children or from the children. Start where you are, even if the only poetry that stirs you in any way is *The Star Spangled Banner* or *Home on the Range*. That is a beginning. We have included many poems in Appendix A as a first step in building your poetry resource file.

Should a Teacher Read to Children?

Reading aloud to children is beneficial for all those involved. Kimmel and Segel (1983) discuss several reasons for reading aloud to children of all ages. Hearing a story read promotes a student's desire to read independently and fosters improvement of his independent reading skills. At every level, there are books that students enjoy hearing. Some books that may be difficult to get into are more interesting when read by someone else. By reading aloud, the very poor reader can enjoy great literature that he or she may never have the opportunity to discover alone. Children's reading interests and tastes are broadened by exposure to many pieces of literature. By reading to children and modeling a love of reading as enjoyment, the chances increase that your students will become lifelong readers.

Reading aloud is a shared experience that acts as a bridge between those involved. The quiet moments with a parent while Huckleberry Finn drifts down the Mississippi or with an entire class as the teacher leads it through Walla Walla, Washington, with the travels of *Prune* by Ramon Ross, or *Alice in Wonderland,* or Dorothy's wonderful land of Oz establish kindred spirits and high morale.

In many schools throughout the nation teachers read selected books to children. In the intermediate grades the first fifteen minutes after lunch is usually set aside for this purpose. While the pupils relax after strenuous play, the teachers read from old and new classics. Appendix A includes some favorite books for reading aloud.

Preparation for Oral Reading

There are only a few hints that the teacher needs to remember to be a good oral reader. First, enjoy the story yourself. If it is a book that you do not mind rereading as each new group of children comes to your room, you can be certain not only that the book is worthy of your efforts but also that your appreciation will be sensed by the children. Second, interpret the mood and differentiate between the principal characters in dialogues; be a bit dramatic when the plot is exciting, but do not explain the action while reading. Let some of the new words be interesting enough for the children to discover their meaning from the context; if there is a moral, let the listener discover that, too. Third, because of time limitations, scan a new book and note the good stopping places. Sometimes a "wrong" stopping point spoils a story just as it does a movie to come in late or to have the film break in the middle of a scene. Finally, always keep in mind that your purpose is to guide the children toward an appreciation of good literature and excellent writing. This period is not a time to spend with material of only passing interest or mass production quality.

Reading to Young Children

Reading a picture book to little children requires special preparation. The books for kindergarten and primary grade children must be selected with care. Although little children respond to almost any material presented by a teacher whom they love and respect, always remember that the materials you read establish the standards the children will use for later reading. A book such as *Petunia* by Roger Duvoisin presents animals with childlike characters with which the child easily identifies. Humanized machines in books such as *Mike Mulligan and His Steam Shovel* and *The Little Engine That Could* tie together the worlds of fantasy and reality. The humanized animals of the old, old favorite *Peter Rabbit* continue to charm children because of their intimacy with all living things. Rhyme adds charm but is not necessary. To be avoided at this level are stories with dialect; fairy tales of giants, dragons, and cruel stepmothers; and stories that are overemotional or overexciting.

The story should be short or in episodes that cover easily divided parts. Establish standards as to behavior during story reading. Routines should be known to all so that stories are expected at certain times or at a certain signal. Children should not be expected to stop an especially interesting activity without a "getting ready" or "finishing up" time. At the beginning, some teachers prefer to start the story hour with only a part of the group.

To regain a wandering child's attention, call him softly by name, or smile directly at him to bring his attention back to your voice. In some groups, the more mature students may need to work together. This may be the beginning group for the story hour while others rest or color. The teacher usually does as much telling as reading, using the pictures in the book to guide the questions and interest of the listeners.

Although it may be handled well by some teachers, a child's retelling of the stories read seldom holds the attention of other students. A story book brought from home should be identified as "Billy's book." After the teacher has examined the material, she may feel that the stories are appropriate for the group. Otherwise, a chance to see and talk about the pictures usually satisfies everyone.

To help some develop better habits, two students may be chosen to sit on each side of the teacher. These children in turn help show the pictures in the book. A special honor on a birthday or at the arrival of a new baby at home might be to select an old favorite for the teacher to read that day. It is well to remember that some students have never listened to a story read to them before coming to school.

One of the major purposes of presenting a book to a child of this age is to enable the student to select a book to peruse with pleasure without your help. Watch students as they thumb through a new set of library books. They will pick one up, glance through a few pages, then discard it for another. In many classrooms, it is wisest to put books on the library table only after they have been read to the children. With this experience, the child can make a meaningful selection. Here are nine suggestions for reading a picture book:

1. Gather the students closely around you either on low chairs or on the floor.
2. Sit in a low chair yourself.
3. Perform unhurriedly.
4. Handle the book so that students can see the pages at close range.
5. Know the story well enough so that you do not need to keep your eyes on the page at all times.
6. Point out all kinds of minute details in pictures so that pupils will look for them each subsequent time they handle the book.
7. Encourage laughter and spontaneous remarks.
8. Make illustrations as personal as possible by relating them to the pupils' own experiences.
9. Impart your own enjoyment of the book.

Many teachers feel that there should be no interruptions the first time a story is presented. With a picture book, the reader and listener are involved in a rhythm of learning the words and seeing the pictures. The reader does not intrude anything, such as explanations of word meanings or personal reactions. For some students and some books, this is the only way a story should be read. In many cases, the first reading of a story should proceed in this way so that the total book experience will be felt by the child. For other books and other children, careful attention to detail and involvement through personal association with story incidents enrich the reading. Experience will determine the most effective procedure for a new teacher. In Appendix A we have included a list of books that may be used for oral reading.

How May Book Reports Be Effectively Used in the Classroom?

Book reporting has not been a very popular activity with many students. There are several reasons why this may be so. At one time it was common practice to require students to read a prescribed number of books from a specific list. The books were frequently inappropriate, and the motivation was coercion. The required uniform review was an artificial writing assignment that was dull for the writer and for those reading it or listening to it. It was not uncommon that students would copy from one another or from book summaries found in libraries.

The purpose of the report was reflected in its form. Teachers using the "FBI approach" asked questions to determine whether the student had really read the book. This approach contributed to the unpopularity of the activity.

Another approach that is often inappropriate for the classroom is that of account keeping. This listing of books often encourages a competitive spirit. Many readers are going to feel embarrassed if others read ten books while they read only two. Classroom activities should foster a love for reading, not a spirit of nervous competitiveness. A spirit of ease with reading was developed by a third-grade teacher who stimulated a high interest in books that her students were to select independently. A rule accepted by the group was that once a book selection was made, that book was to be completed. One child, for example, selected an excellent but long and difficult book. She was still reading this while other students were on a second or third book. Because a public record was kept, this had a negative effect on the child. The next book she selected was short and had many pictures. Because the teacher knew that the element of competition is difficult to eliminate, she attempted to correct this factor by allowing a number of points for each book so that the more difficult and longer ones were allotted

Classroom activities should foster a love for reading not a spirit of nervous competitiveness. Putting the book reports on a computer often adds to the enjoyment of writing them. (Photo by Linda Lungren)

more points. Thus, these books were no longer avoided by the students.

There are many worthwhile purposes for book reports. First, reports are a way of learning from the reading of others. When a child has had a reading adventure or learned some interesting information, others like to share it. Second, reading can be motivated by a report. One student's stamp of approval on a book will encourage others to want to read it. "Even the boys will like Laura," exclaimed one student after reading *Little House on the Prairie*. Third, reports meet a social need. Sharing the fun of *Freddie, the Detective* is as important in the conversation of fourth graders as discussing the current bestseller is among adults. Fourth, specifics need to be noticed in order to appreciate a book thoroughly. Such specifics can include an author's use of words, descriptive passages, or illustrations. Fifth, reports give recognition to students. For many students reading a book is an achievement. Each one is a trophy that attests to greater mastery of a complex skill that has been put to use. Sixth, reports tell the teacher about the student's interests and needs. Misinterpretation or confusion revealed in a report indicates special needs that guide the teacher in planning work with the student. Although literature is largely for enjoyment and appreciation, the reading process can be observed and can be improved so that further experiences in literature will prove more satisfying and rewarding.

In all grades, both oral and written reports are used. Oral reports require careful direction and planning to be worth the attention of the class. Time required to prepare cartoon strips, dioramas, dressed characters, flannelboard figures, and other such accessories for book reports is often questioned. Some students have both the time and interest needed to complete such activities. These visual devices add to the effectiveness of a presentation. A balanced approach in terms of the overall needs of a student must play a part in any consideration by the teacher.

Primary school children may give book reports as a part of the sharing period. Or, an opening exercise one morning a week might emphasize books they find interesting. At such times teachers make suggestions like the following: Show only the cover of a book and tell why the reader liked it. Show one picture and incite curiosity as to what is happening in the story. Show a seashell, leaf, model airplane, spaceship, or rock that some books explain. Show a flannelboard figure or a picture for a part of a story read by a child. Form a book club and follow a simple outline in making reports. Such an outline might include the following:

1. What kind of a story is it? Is it true?
2. What is it about?
3. Is it about this country or some other? When did it happen?
4. What are the pictures like?

5. Is the book easy to read?
6. Who wrote the story? Do we know any other stories by that person?

These items are only suggestions. Certainly these points are not appropriate for every book. Any item-by-item checking can become monotonous. We merely want to help students become conscious of the many qualities that books have and the substance that develops real appreciation of literature. The forms on the following pages have been used by some teachers.

Intermediate children have a wider range of possibilities with respect to book reports, both because of greater maturity in oral language and in writing facility, and also because of greater breadth of reading interests. The purposes of reporting are to interest others in expanded reading, to share information, to communicate the pleasure of ideas from reading, and to emphasize the achievement of reading a book that was significant for one reason or another. Often children themselves have useful suggestions for accomplishing these purposes. The person who read the book pretends to be one of the characters. The audience is to guess the name of the book from what is said or done. A series of clues may be given, and the listeners and observers may write the name of the book opposite the number of the clue. These guessing games give all children a chance to participate. A group of children may also present a panel. They may discuss a book they have all read, or a subject such as "Dog or Horse Stories I Have Liked."

A good way to emphasize authorship is to have a "Lois Lenski Day" or a "Newbery Award Day (or Week)." Students may be curious to find the qualities that made certain books worthy of awards. Such qualities as characterization, picturesque words, descriptive passages, ingenious plot, appropriate illustrations, imaginative humor, and range of experiences take on meaning and importance as children learn to recognize them. The group might create an award for a favorite book.

An oral synopsis of a story is good practice in arranging events in sequence and in learning the way that a story progresses to a climax. It also helps children who are interested in writing stories of their own (see Figure 8–1).

Broadcasting a book review over the public-address system or radio is a challenge for careful preparation and ingenuity in planning sound effects, background music, or dramatic reading. Clear enunciation and good voice modulation are also important.

Telling a story, telling about a new book, or reading a small excerpt to another class may be good for the student who wants to share the experience, and it may stimulate the audience to learn more about the book or others by the same author.

During an informal book club session, the students meet in small groups and talk about books they have read. The object is to whet the book appetites of the group.

An oral comparison of two books related in theme is a good exercise in critical evaluation. The problems of the black girls in *Shuttered Windows* by Florence Means and *Mary Jane* by Dorothy Sterling might be compared; so, too, the humor in the *Paul Bunyan Stories* might be compared with that in *Pippi Longstocking*.

Such projects as constructing a miniature stage, making preparations for a television show, planning and decorating a bulletin board, dressing dolls as book characters, impersonating book characters, and planning quiz programs about books may all, on occasion, stimulate interest in both oral and written reports. Displaying such related objects as a cowbell for Heidi, wooden shoes for Hans Brinker, a Japanese doll, travel pictures, or pioneer relics is a good device for vitalizing both reading and reporting. In social studies the study of a country can be personalized through a story character, thus providing a broader understanding of both the literature and the geography of the country.

Written reports may take many forms. Letters of appreciation may be written to authors or librarians. A letter to a friend or relative recommending a book should actually be mailed. Advertisements may be written for the school paper, a bulletin board, or a book jacket. Short reviews may be written for "We Recom-

1. READ FOR FUN (*Used in Grade 2*)

Name ______________________________ Date ______________

Book title ____

Main character ____

____

People who like

________ animal stories

________ stories about children

________ stories about ______________________________

________ adventure stories

________ funny stories

________ exciting stories

will like this book.

Did you enjoy this book?_________________________________

It was

________ easy to read.

________ hard to read.

________ just right.

2. BOOK DISCUSSIONS (*Grades 3 and 4*)

Name of book ____

Author ____

Illustrator (if any) ____________________________________

Name some of the characters: ____________________________

____

____

Tell which character you liked best: ____________________

____

____

The part of the book I liked best was ___________________

____

____

____

Do *one* of these things:

1. Tell your class part of the story.
2. Make a picture.
3. Make something suggested in the book.

My name is ______________________ Room No. ______________

Figure 8–1. Oral synopsis form.

mend" bulletin boards or for "Before You Read" or "My Opinion" scrapbooks. Sometimes the local paper will publish well-written book reviews. Some classes keep a file of brief summaries that is consulted when a child wants a certain type of book. These are usually limited to a few sentences. Some children like to keep a "Personal Reading Notebook" in the form of a diary (see Figure 8–2).

Teachers have developed many techniques to encourage children to read widely. A bulletin board on which each child has a small book in which to record the titles and authors of each book read is quite popular. Sometimes this is done on a bookshelf and each child has a cardboard-bound book cover in which to do this recording so that the bulletin boards are not occupied for a long period of time. One class capitalized on the interest in space by putting the name of each new book read on a small paper satellite. The caption read "We Are Really Orbiting."

Students sometimes are inclined to limit their reading to a single interest. To encourage a more balanced reading program, teachers sometimes use a reading wheel divided into areas of biography, foreign lands, animals, science, adventure, or folklore. As each student reads a book, his or her name is placed in the proper area on the wheel. The object is to have one's name in each area. Many publishing companies provide a free wall chart designed to encourage a well-rounded program in reading. The *News-Journal* of North Manchester, Indiana, has several forms of "My Reading Design" that also serve this purpose.

Another plan to widen the reading interest involves the use of a map. The object is to "Take a World Cruise" or "See America First." Books appropriate to each region are suggested. Sweden might be represented by *The Sauce Pan Journey* or France by *The Big Loop*. After a book about one country or area is read, the child moves on to the next until the tour is completed.

Bulletin boards or charts frequently motivate the reading of a book. The teacher might make a list under the title "These Are Ms. Smith's Favorites." A group of children might list others under such titles as "We Recommend for First Purchase," "Interesting Travel Books," "Books to Grow On," or "Books About This Area."

In most situations the reading is more important than the reporting. The teacher needs to know the quality of the children's reading to be sure they are getting the most from each reading adventure. This can be done in classroom situations through observations of children reading independently, in teacher-pupil conferences, and in some of the discussions and reporting that they do. There is no need for a report on every book. Some children need more of these reporting experiences than other children. In the final analysis, the best reports may be a child's heartfelt spontaneous statement, "Ms. Cunningham, do you know of another book like that?"

How Do Teachers Become Effective Storytellers?

Like reading aloud, storytelling is a shared experience. However, the act of storytelling can be even more intimate as gestures and close eye contact bring the students and the storyteller together. With practice, the teacher can become a good storyteller, reviving the ancient oral tradition of literature. There are no basic rules to ensure the proper telling of a story. Some of the greatest story craftsmen cannot agree as to the best methods to use. Storytelling is as individual an art as acting or playing a musical instrument. Each person must develop his or her own techniques, style, and selection of stories to suit personal taste and abilities.

There are a few basic considerations, however, on which most storytellers agree.

1. The story must be appropriate to the audience. The very young child likes simple folk tales, but does not respond to stories that are completely make-believe, with goblins, elves, and fairies. Young children do not understand the completely abstract. There must be some elements in the story that relate to personal

Here are some ways in which information about the things in my book have helped people: ______________

Below are some unsolved problems or questions (about things in my book) that scientists are still working on:

I recommend this book because ______________

Name ______________ Date ______________

MY BOOK REPORT

Title ______________

Author ______________ Number of pages ______________

Illustrator ______________

The biographer (one who writes about a real person) tells the following childhood incident in the life of his subject:

The subject of the biography is ______________

The following people were important in helping this real person to grow into a famous adult ______________

A problem that this person had to overcome was ______________

This person overcame his problem in this way: ______________

This person had the following characteristics that I admire: ______________

I think the most exciting adventure that this person had was ______________

Figure 8–2. Personal reading notebook form.

experiences. In the story of *The Three Bears,* we have chairs, beds, bowls of soup, and activities that are familiar. Associating them with bears adds mystery and adventure, but the events are familiar, everyday experiences. The child accepts the unreal because it is close enough to the real known world.

Little children love rhymes and jingles, and many old story favorites have a marked rhythmic quality. In stories, this rhythm is the result of repetition of words and phrases in a set pattern. Such phrases as "Not by the hair of your chinny-chin-chin" or "Then I'll huff and I'll puff and I'll blow your house in" always bring delighted responses.

Children also like to play with words. That is the way words become more meaningful and a lasting part of their vocabulary. Children cannot keep from repeating "a lovely, light luscious, delectable cake": as the teacher reads *The Duchess Bakes a Cake*. In telling some stories, the teller prepares the listeners by saying, "This story contains some wonderful new words. One of them is ________, which means ________; another is ________, which means ________. Listen for them." One or two words presented before a story would be enough. The story will do considerable teaching by providing context for the words.

Make-believe is most important to children in the years from six to ten, because it helps them understand the world about them and increases their imaginative powers. In the stories that they read and hear, the youngsters are the heroes, at least for the time being. They know they are pretending, but as the story unfolds, each child wishes to become Jack the Giant Killer or Cinderella.

2. The storyteller knows that some stories are good to tell and other stories are better to read. The rich dialogue and description of *Winnie the Pooh* and *The Jungle Book* should remain intact. A story for telling must be simple and direct. The plot must be strong and develop rapidly. In storytelling there is no place for long analyses of characters or situations. The mental pictures must be supplied by a few words or a phrase. Each incident must be vivid and clear-cut in the listener's mind. The climax must be emotionally satisfying. This can be a surprise, the solution of a problem, or something achieved.

The charm of simplicity can best be learned through experience. We know that children respond to cumulative repetition, such as one finds in *The Gingerbread Boy*. They want the characters to talk. Descriptions are simple because children supply so much with their own imaginations. Good must triumph, but it is all right for the bad people to be very bad as long as in the end they are punished. Some prefer stories of animals to those with people in them. For many, the gentle stories about raindrops, flowers, and insects are a new discovery, in contrast to the rapid pace of television and movie cartoons. A story that lasts six or eight minutes is quite long enough, and many favorites take less time than that.

The Three Little Pigs is an example of a good story for telling little children. Each step is an event. No time is spent in explanation or unnecessary description. The story tells what the characters did and said and the events are linked in the closest kind of sequence. There are no breaks and no complexities of plot. Each event presents a clear, distinct picture to the imagination.

Ordinarily it is wisest not to change traditional stories. If you question any element in a story, it is usually best to select another story. There is a trend in the direction of removing many of the horror aspects from the old folk material. The three bears are now friendly bears. They are provoked by Goldilocks because she enters their home without permission. The wolf now chases Red Riding Hood's grandmother into a closet instead of devouring her. In the original version of *Three Billy Goats Gruff* the troll had his eyes gouged out and was crushed to death. In the modern version he is merely butted into the river and swims away unscathed, never to return. The first two of the three little pigs are no longer eaten by the wolf, but make an exciting escape to the house of the wise pig.

Any idea that may cause the young child to lie awake at night is best omitted from the program. It is well to discuss make-believe with children. Let them be assured that there are really no dragons and that wolves are unlikely visitors in the suburbs or the city.

Another common theme in many of the old tales is the cruelty of stepparents and other family members related by remarriage. Stereotypes that stigmatize family members, old age, or social groups have no place in the story hour.

A discussion before reading some of these stories can take care of such questionable elements. The story of a good stepmother like Abraham Lincoln's provides a balance to *Cinderella.* There are many good and kind old ladies to offset the cruel old hag in *Hansel and Gretel.* Teachers should remember that the horror that an adult senses in a story such as *Snow White* is quite different from a child's point of view. Torture and even death have only incidental significance for many children. Death is frequently an acceptable solution to a problem. Children play cowboys and Indians, good guys and bad guys, with violent shouts, agonizing mock deaths, and melodramatic hardships one moment and listen with rapt attention to a poem of delicate beauty the next.

Sometimes children themselves suggest changes in these stories. This frequently happens as they dramatize a story. Another interesting variation on the traditional material is to put the characters into a new situation. Make up a story of visiting the three bears during summer vacation or let Cinderella go to school.

3. A storyteller knows that preparation is needed to make a story vivid to listeners. After a careful reading, put the story aside and think about it until you can picture it clearly in all details. Check any doubts by reading the story again. It is better for a beginning storyteller to know a few stories well than to attempt so many that none can be told with complete confidence. The "tell it again" quality of stories is a great safeguard for beginners. Any storyteller is almost sure to tell a story better each additional time it is told. A beginner might plan an introduction, plan the sequence of the events, plan an ending, and then practice telling it aloud without an audience.

4. A storyteller knows that the audience must be comfortable and free from interruptions during the story, and that the story must end before the audience becomes weary or bored. Wait a few moments before starting a story so that there is a hush of expectancy in the room. If some children are inattentive or noisy, pause until quiet is restored. If many grow restless, it is quite obvious that you have the wrong story. Do not blame the children; just say, "I guess this isn't the right story, so let's stand up and stretch." Then go on with some other group activity such as marching, singing, or finger play. Start another story only when there are expectancy and readiness for wholehearted listening.

Certain devices can be used to hold the attention of listeners. When Hans Christian Andersen entertained the children of Denmark with his stories, he used to cut out silhouettes in order to make his characters more vivid. In ancient China, the storyteller would cast shadows to illustrate the characters in his tales of magic and ancient ways. Movie cartoon favorites use a combination of silhouette figures and movement to hold attention. In many classrooms, flannelboards, films, slides, and pictures provide the storyteller with the means of achieving similar types of movement, magic, and characterization.

As children listen to the storyteller, their visual attention is focused on character and movement as figures representing the main characters are moved about on the flannelboard.

Flannelboard stories should be looked on as a means of stimulating the imagination and improving the quality of oral language of children. Many teachers find that permitting children to make their own flannelboard stories and then tell them helps expand their language power, self-confidence, and creative talents. Another prospect is the emotional release that can be observed in some children as they plan, cut out, and manipulate figures to illustrate some story they especially like or that they create.

Although the term *flannelboard* is used here, the device may be made with felt or coat lining. Those made for children's games are sometimes sprayed with "flocking." A store that specializes in window-display materials will have this available for sale. If flannel is used, get the heaviest available. Coat lining is usually obtainable from a dry goods store. If you have a large bulletin board that you wish to cover, use felt or coat lining. Each figure needs to have a large piece of flannel or felt glued to the reverse side. Then as it is placed on the board, the storyteller should run his or her fingers over the figure, causing it to adhere to the board. Some teachers use rough sandpaper or flocking on the figure. For some figures, bits of flannel about an inch square in three or four places serve to hold better than one large piece.

Children seem to respond better to cutouts made of bright and heavy construction paper than to drawn figures. Apparently cutouts allow more scope for the imagination. However, illustrations cut from books and made into figures for the flannelboard also appeal to them. In a sense, this exercise simply transfers the book illustrations to the flannelboard. Faces and clothes can be drawn with ink or wax crayon or made of bits of construction paper pasted to the figure.

Some stories need scenic backgrounds—a big woods, a lake, or a castle. Rather than make these of paper, it is easier to draw them with crayon on a large piece of flannel. Then the figures will stick to the scenery as the story is told. Regular outing flannel is good for this purpose.

Most flannelboards are made of plywood or heavy composition cardboard about two feet wide and three feet long. The felt or flannel should be about three feet by four feet in order to allow adequate overlap on the back of the plywood. Staples from a regular paper stapler will hold it well. Do not glue the flannel to the board, as the glue reduces the static charge that causes the figures to adhere. The size should be large enough to hold the figures, but not so large that it is uncomfortable to carry or awkward to store. Some teachers like to have handles on the board; while others hinge them so they will fold. It costs about as much to make a board as to buy one. The only advantage to a homemade one is that you have exactly what you want. Please refer to Appendix A for a flannelboard favorite.

The following techniques should be used as a story is told with the flannelboard:

1. Place the flannelboard where it will remain securely in a place that can be seen by all students. The chalkboard is good if the group is in a small circle seated before it. An easel is better if the board must be seen by an entire room. If children are seated on a rug, they must be farther away from the teacher then when she used a picture book. Those in front will be under a strain looking up if too near the board.
2. Arrange the figures to be used in the sequence needed for telling the story. It is best to keep them in a folder away from the sight of the listeners. Otherwise, some of the surprise and suspense are lost as they are introduced. A manila folder used in file cabinets makes a good container. Staple a pocket on one side of the folder to hold the figures and staple the story to the other side.
3. There is a tendency to look away from the listeners to the figures as they are placed on the flannelboard. Of course, this is necessary. Try to use this movement to direct the listeners' eyes but turn back to the audience as you tell the story. Otherwise, you will find yourself talking to the flannelboard, thus creating a hearing problem for your audience.
4. Plan your follow-up before you tell the story. Are you going to evaluate the story? Are you going to ask the children to retell parts of the story? Are you going to have them create a favorite story? When a story ends in the classroom, it is a little different from the ending of a play in the theater or a television program. The audience is still with you. Instead of going home or turning on another station, you must plan the transition to the next school task.

In the Orient there are still storytellers who earn a living walking along the street. They signal their approach by tapping two pieces of wood together.

Each child offers a small coin and is given a piece of hard candy. While the child eats the candy, the storyteller entertains with some of the famous folk stories of the land or the latest adventures of Mickey Mouse. As the story unfolds, the storyteller illustrates it by a series of color prints from books or hand-drawn pictures. These *Kamishe-bai,* or picture stories, might well be used in our own country.

Stick figures and simple puppets used as characters in a story or as the teller of the story will hold the attention of those children who need something to see as well as to hear. An important object in a story such as a lamp, old coffee mill, glass slipper, shaft of wheat, apple, miniature rocker, spinning wheel, or toy sword may be used. If the story involves a fable, the teacher may provide an explanation of the core of an apple, the way a seed or feather is formed, or the shape of a flower or leaf, because the fable was a means of explaining a fact of nature. And one should not neglect the chalkboard or simple stick figures to illustrate a scene or character.

In addition to a pleasant voice, clear speech, adequate vocabulary, and a relaxed appearance, today's storyteller needs the resources of inner grace that come from sincerity and a respect both for the audience and for the art of storytelling. When you have a clear visual picture of each character and scene, know the plot thoroughly, can establish a mood for listening, and are able to end the story so that your audience is satisfied, you are a good storyteller.

Throughout this chapter we have suggested that you supplement your curriculum with a variety of reading materials. Appendix A has been included at the end of this text to provide you with a sample of the suggested materials.

Summary

A rationale and procedures for integrating literature throughout the curriculum provided the unifying theme of this chapter. Procedures for selecting appropriate literature and sources for obtaining classroom literature were highlighted. Awareness and inclusion of issues involving sex, death, and stereotypes in children's literature were discussed as were other features of selection. Strategies for involving parents in the literature program were also explored. Storytelling, poetry, verse, and oral/choral reading are other topics that received attention.

Suggested Classroom Projects and Questions for Discussion

Projects

1. Review ten books that might be read by students in a single grade to improve their understanding of a foreign land. Include a list of examples of art and music which would enhance an understanding of the country.
2. Make a collection of twenty-five poems that will appeal to children in a single grade. Indicate in general ways to introduce and use such poetry.
3. Make a collection of ten poems appropriate to the purposes of a verse choir at a grade level.
4. Select three stories or ballads that might be dramatized by children.
5. Make a bibliography of dramatic material to use in the intermediate grades.
6. Indicate the skills needed and ways they may be developed with regard to the dramatic presentation of a play.
7. Collect a group of ballads or stories that might be read aloud while a group presents the action in pantomime.
8. Compile a list of activities that can be used as alternatives to the traditional written book report.
9. Prepare a story to tell. Tape and critique yourself. Share the story with a group of children.
10. Begin a file of your own response guides. Develop extending activities for two books, using the format provided in *Response Guides for Teaching Children's Books* by Somers and Worthington (1979) or a similar one.

Questions

1. Have you had an experience that would justify the following statement?

   As children, most of us were turned off and away from literature by teachers' instructions to read selections of prose or poetry to find their "true" meaning—dissecting, analyzing, and finally giving succinct summaries of what the authors were attempting to communicate to us. We came to view literature not as an encounter with life as it is or might be, but as a formal, dull learning experience in which the teacher engaged in literary criticism with an uninvolved audience.

2. How can we prevent embarrassment for a child who must read books much below the reading level of others in the class?
3. How should such topics as death, divorce, and propaganda be treated in children's literature?
4. How concerned should parents and teachers be when they discover children reading books that they consider inappropriate? What countermeasures would you suggest?
5. What sources of information concerning new books for children are available in your teaching community? What responsibility must a teacher assume for finding this information?
6. What influence would this poem have on the parents of the children you teach?

My Mother Read to Me

Long ago on winter evenings,
I recall, my mother read;
There beside our old base-burner
Just before my prayers were said.

Here she gave me friends aplenty,
Friends to fill my life for years;
Meg and Jo and Sister Amy
For little Beth I shed my tears.

Scrooge and Tim and Mrs. Wiggs
Robin Hood and Heidi too,
Young Jim Hawkins and his treasure
Saved from Silver's pirate crew.

Can it be that one small lady
Could, just by her magic voice,
Change a room so, in a twinkling
To the scenes from books so choice?

Poor we were, as some might count us,
No fine house, our clothes threadbare,
But my mother read me riches
From the books she chose with care.

Now in times of fear and struggle
When woe and want about me crowd,
I can use reserves of courage
From the books she read aloud.

E. H. Frierwood

7. What were some of the poems you memorized in elementary school? Why did you memorize them?
8. Why do teachers feel more secure presenting a poem by a recognized poet than one containing ideas and rhyme that children enjoy?
9. Do you feel that a more analytical approach to poetry should be made in the intermediate grades than is suggested in this chapter?
10. How would you handle the criticism that reading aloud to a class is entertaining children instead of teaching them?
11. How do you think book reports might be individualized?
12. How can we find time in the school day to provide opportunities to tell stories and listen to them?

Chapter 9

Effective Spelling Instruction

(Photo by Linda Lungren)

OBJECTIVES

After reading this chapter, the student will be able to:

1. understand how spelling strategies are learned and developed.
2. understand what constitutes a spelling program, including which words should be taught and when.
3. know how to implement teaching strategies to develop competent spelling by students.
4. recognize problems associated with learning and teaching spelling.

What Is the Place of Spelling in the Language Arts Program?

> My dear Hemmingway,
>
> Please join us at the appartment. Gertrude Stien will be their, to. We will dine, ect.
>
> Yours,
> Scott

Although the composition of this note is fictitious, the spelling errors are among the many famous examples of F. Scott Fitzgerald's abominable spelling. Fortunately for Ernest Hemingway and Gertrude Stein, their names (and egos) are famous enough to withstand the infamy of Fitzgerald's spelling.

Fortunately for him and for readers of American literature, F. Scott Fitzgerald had a good editor! Unfortunately, in everyday written communication most of us must depend on our own ability to spell in order to make ourselves understood. Poor spelling miscues readers and hampers effective communication. Since a language arts program concerns itself with the comprehension and manipulation of language, both spoken and written spelling instruction are a vital component in any such program.

Correct spelling may be considered the counterpart of legible handwriting in effective written communication. Poor spelling and poor handwriting interfere with comprehension, which is the major criterion of communication. Furthermore, poor spelling may result in lost employment opportunities (Medway, 1976) and social embarrassment. Although overemphasis on spelling may be detrimental if it constricts a child's written output, the inculcation of a positive attitude is an important step in motivating the child to spell correctly.

Your task as a teacher is to guide the student's growth in the ability to spell the language. It has been assumed by many that if the teacher supervises the student's use of a spelling book or workbook, this objective will be realized. Sometimes this has resulted in efforts to master the content of the book, much as if it were a geography text, rather than to develop individual spelling skills. Spelling levels differ as much as reading levels, and because far less attention can be given to formal spelling instruction, it must therefore be well planned, individualized as much as possible, and effectively implemented.

Spelling Skills

Some of the major skills needed to spell are the following:

1. The ability to relate phonemes (sounds of the language) with the graphemes (letters) used to represent them in writing. This means being able to understand the relationship between the beginning sound of *put* and the letter *p* and knowing that the sound of the group of letters at the end of *seeing* is represented by *-ing*.
2. The ability to recall and represent consonant-vowel patterns as used in English spelling.
3. The ability to recognize sound variations represented by vowels and such consonants as *g* in *garage*.
4. The ability to use the dictionary to ascertain correct spelling and pronunciation of words.

In addition, a knowledge of the origins of words can be of assistance in learning to spell. For example, the word *know* shows its Scandinavian source and contains a letter no longer pronounced. According to some linguists *kn* is a phoneme.

Although it is true that children do not need to know the meanings of words in order to spell them (Fitzsimmons & Loomer, 1978), spelling is seldom used for the purpose of creating nonsense words. A person who wants to spell a word starts with an idea of what he or she wishes to express in writing. The idea must be associated with its speech symbol, or word, such as *pain* or *cake*. After selecting the word, the speller thinks of the separate sounds in it. These sounds are identified with the letters of the alphabet that represent them. Then the speller reproduces the letters in the sequence that will spell the word in its approved form, so that the letters *c-a-k-e*, rather than *kak*, *cak*, or *kake*, are used. As the speller matures and spells more sophisticated words, other skills relating to the meaning of the words come into consideration. These include understanding word roots and the changes produced by ***bound morphemes*** (prefixes and suffixes), knowing how to use a dictionary, and seeking to conform to the widely accepted standards of correctness that facilitate communication.

After one has mastered the spelling of a word, parts of this sequence are performed without conscious effort. If you learned to use the typewriter, you will recall how you progressed from a conscious effort involved in striking each letter to an automatic "cluster" of whole words and phrases. Similarly, the fluent writer expresses abstract ideas or involved concepts without groping for words letter by letter. A dictionary and thesaurus may be kept at hand to enrich one's output and to ascertain the spelling of difficult words.

What Is Developmental Spelling?

By knowing at what level a student functions in a particular skill, the teacher is better able to ascertain the appropriate methods to facilitate mastery of that skill. The theory that spelling is a developmental process, wherein spellers pass through various cognitive stages to arrive at a system for correct spelling, is quite useful for "placing" a child's ability to spell. There has been a great deal of interest in this area in recent years (Read, 1971; Beers & Henderson, 1977; Henderson & Beers, 1980; Bissex, 1980; Gentry, 1981 and 1982) which has led to the generation of five developmental stages of spelling.

Developmental Stages of Spelling

Stage 1: Precommunicative. The precommunicative stage is characterized mainly by a total lack of any letter-sound correspondence knowledge. An example of this stage might be a sign similar to the following posted on the door to the room of a four-year-old warning his sister to knock before entering his room.

This writing sample from a precommunicative speller (Figure 9–1) indicates that:

1. The child understands that words are composed of letters.
2. He knows how to write a variety of letters, if not the whole alphabet.
3. He favors uppercase letters, but may mix upper- and lowercase randomly.
4. He may understand left to right progression in spelling.
5. He has no idea which letters correspond to which sounds.

The writing of the precommunicative speller appears to be a random stringing together of letters. As the child moves toward the second stage, the ***semiphonetic stage,*** he or she develops an awareness of the rudimentary phonemic principles.

Stage 2: Semiphonetic. The semiphonetic stage is characterized by the beginnings of an understanding that letters represent the sounds that form words. This stage is sometimes called "prephonetic."

Figure 9–1. Writing samples from a precommunicative speller.

RUCMN (Are you coming?)
LEFNT (elephant)
BZR (buzzer)
ERZ (ears)
KT (cat)

These "words" illustrate two points:

1. The semiphonetic speller is aware of a letter-sound correspondence but does not map the entire word. A few letters represent the entire word.
2. The child exhibits the use of the *letter name* strategy wherein a letter is used to represent an entire word or syllable when the sound corresponds to the name of the letter (most commonly: *R* [are]; *U* [you]; *LEVTR* [elevator]).

Although the writing of a child progressing from precommunicative to semiphonetic spelling may appear unstructured, there is some evidence that the writing process that produces these gibberish manuscripts is anything but random. Hall and Hall (1984) examine this process by working with and observing the efforts of five-year-olds who understand letter names and who are approaching an understanding of letter-sound relationships. As the children created a story based on a preselected picture, they were asked how they would write each sentence as they said it. The children represented the entire thought by producing a single letter or small group of letters. Put together on a page, the letters appeared to be totally random but when supplied with the "key" (the child's thought process), this precommunicative ramble was in fact a systematic representation of a story.

Example of Very Early Writing

Figure 9–2 shows a story by Toni, one of the children:

In the translation of Toni's writing, the italicized word in each sentence is represented by the selected letter:

S = *It* was *his* birthday.
G = She gots a *dress*.
CC = He's *sitting* at the table.
S = Then he had a *cake*.
K = Then the *door* opened.
MOM = Then his *mommy* came in.
MOMB = Then he said, "*Mommy,* it's my *birthday.*"
CP = There's *spoons* and *plates*.
C = He is *sitting* on the chair.
K = There's a *cloth* on the table.
K = The *kitty* gots ears.
HD = There's a *handle* on the door.
LK = The *kitty's looking* that way.
K = *The kitty's* sitting on a chair, too.
MOM = Then his *mama* came in.
B = The *chair* gots handles.

Figure 9–2. A story is shown by Toni, one of the children. [In the translation of Toni's writing, the italicized word in each sentence is represented by the selected letter.]

Stage 3: Phonetic. The phonetic stage is characterized by a letter representation of all the surface sounds of a word. This is illustrated in the following example.

DOU LEV ON FRST STRET NER THE BNK?

In this example the phonetic speller demonstrates:

1. The ability to map out the entire sound structure of a word, representing each surface sound with a corresponding letter: Since a student in this phase is not a true speller, these letter-sound assignments reflect traditional orthography only incidentally.
2. Some ability to space words and generate conventional-looking sentences.

Stage 4: Transitional. The transitional stage is characterized by nontraditional orthography that is quite readable: vowels in every syllable, use of learned words, common English letter sequences. The following is an example of this stage.

THE MONSTUR IS GOING TO OPNE A BANGK FOR MONSTURS ONLEE.

In transitional spelling:

1. The child begins to rely more on visual and morphological (word part) presentations than on phonological information.
2. An adherence to basic principles of English orthography is in evidence. The use of a vowel in every syllable, the silent *e,* vowel digraphs (*ai, ea, ay*), nasals, and inflectional endings become common in the transitional speller.
3. Correctly spelled words that have been taught to a child are used frequently.

Stage 5: Correct. Correct spelling is characterized by a knowledge of common English orthography (spelling) and its basic rules. The child who has mastered this stage has:

1. A firm understanding of the basic rules of the English orthographic system, including ways to handle structural components of words (prefixes, suffixes, contractions, and so on), silent and doubled consonants, and homonyms.
2. Learned to spell correctly a core of words commensurate with his or her grade level.
3. The ability to identify misspelled words and correct them by making the word "look right."

Spelling is an area in which there is little systematic relationship between growth and the amount of time spent in teaching. It appears probable that growth in ability to spell is related to extensive reading, maturational factors, and the specific needs for oral or written communication. There appears to be a positive relationship between spelling strategies and cognitive development that reflects growing language proficiency as children mature (Zutell, 1979; Bissex, 1980). A successively large number of children spell a given word correctly in each grade. However, the progress does not appear to be closely related to the presence or absence of the word in the formal curriculum. By incorporating proven spelling principles and techniques with students' individual developmental needs, you will do your students the favor of helping them become that most marvelous of civilized creatures—good spellers!

What Are the Instructional Implications of Developmental Spelling?

For teachers of young children, or children first beginning to spell or in any of the "precorrect" phases of spelling, certain methods for building upon their existing skills and easing them on their way through the development of subsequent spelling skills are dictated by the developmental approach to spelling. By careful monitoring and intervention teachers may determine a child's level of spelling development and provide instruction as indicated. Gentry (1982) suggests these guidelines:

Precommunicative	1. alphabet knowledge
Semiphonetic	1. directionality of print 2. spatial orientation 3. matching oral language to print
Phonetic	1. word families 2. spelling patterns 3. phonics 4. word structure
Transitional	extended word study, including use of a textbook and formal spelling instruction
Correct	As in the transitional phase, further spelling instruction is indicated in the correct phase. Structural analysis, etymology, and other vocabulary-stimulating activities will provide opportunities for continued spelling instruction.

Once the transitional and correct phases of spelling have been reached, a teacher can build a good spelling program that is consistent with modern psychology and can gain additional time in the curriculum with the following program:

1. Be aware of the words used frequently in everyday speech as revealed by a word list and make occasional checks that these are being mastered.
2. Ask the children to keep a notebook of words they have misspelled and once a week give a lesson pertaining to these words. A class list may serve as well. Students should print "difficult" words as encountered on chart paper which is visible to the entire class.
3. Have planned worksheets available for use by those who are not able to make letter-sound association; divide words into syllables, identify base words, use abbreviations, apply generalizations, and so forth. These should be ungraded, since they are appropriate to some children's needs in each of the intermediate grades.

Modern textbooks reflect the careful thinking and planning of many individuals. Used in the light of a developmental approach, these textbooks will serve the teacher well. Teachers should feel free to change the words in the assignment to meet the needs of their students. The fact that grade placement of words follows no absolute rules should encourage teachers to select the lessons in any sequence that seems wise. Above all, they must remember that the average textbook deals with the minimum needs of children. Only the teacher can meet the spelling needs represented by children's desires to express their ideas in words that are uniquely their own as they develop their spelling skills.

Providing an environment that encourages children to write for the purpose of expressing their ideas rather than for the purpose of spelling every word correctly enhances a child's need and desire to spell.

Geedy (1975) reports that learning may best be effected by making word meanings important to the child. "The best learning occurs when spelling is related to purposes real to the child. Teachers must create situations where children *need* to know how to spell" (p. 235). These "situations" are, of course, writing exercises that are creative, fun, and *purposeful* (Gentry, 1982). Activities involving the children in creating stories based on school happenings, personal experiences outside school, pictures selected by the teacher or the students, or music played in the classroom are excellent ways to begin the writing experience. Asking the children to write lists of things to do, places to go, wishes, dreams, recipes, diaries, messages, plans, songs, and poems all lead to better spelling skills by instilling a *need* to know how to spell certain words. Reading teachers often speak of a "reading-rich environment." Spelling needs the same sort of nurturing environment for it to develop into the useful communications tool it is meant to be.

English Orthography: Puzzle or Pleasure?

The English language has twenty-six symbols (letters) to represent over forty phonemes (sounds). Is it any wonder we have trouble with the orthography of this somewhat eclectic language? Because English has evolved by taking words from various languages at various historical times and changing them, we are faced with a diversity of spellings for the same sounds and, conversely, differing pronunciations for the same configurations of letters.

There are, however, many helps as well as hindrances to correct spelling within the structure of the English language. When a child reaches the "correct" phase of the spelling process, formal instruction becomes helpful and, indeed, necessary. By being aware of the phonetic consistencies and inconsistencies, teachers may help young spellers turn the idiosyncrasies of English orthography to their advantage.

Help: Phonetic Consistencies

Phonetic aids do exist in the spelling of the English language. An analysis of the 3,381 monosyllables in our language and the separate syllables of 2,396 polysyllables in words from the many spelling lists shows that the English language is 86.9 percent phonetic. As early as 1952, Hanna and Moore reported that our system of writing was basically alphabetic and that for almost every sound there is a highly regular spelling:

> Eighty per cent of all the speech sounds contained in words used by elementary school children were spelled regularly. Single consonants are represented by regular spellings about 90 per cent of the time.
>
> The vowel sounds cause the most spelling difficulty but even here the short *a* is spelled with an *a* about 90 per cent of the time as is the short *i* at the beginning of a word. Short *e* is spelled with an *e* about 89 per cent of the time, short *o* with an *o* 92 per cent, and short *u* with the letter *u* 72 per cent of the time.
>
> The long vowel sounds cause much more trouble in spelling than short vowel sounds. All the long vowels may be written in a variety of ways.

Others have indicated that some of the frequently used words of our language do have phonetic consistency. Of the first thousand words on the Rinsland spelling list, we find that the sound *a* is spelled as follows, with the figures in parentheses representing percentages:

a = able (57)
ay = lay (23)
ai = laid (13)
ei = reindeer (3)
ea = break (3)
ey = they (1)

The sounds of the consonants are more consistent.

Phoneme		*Grapheme correspondence*	
b	=	bad	(100.0)
d	=	dog	(99.5)
f	=	fun	(85.3)
f	=	phone	(10.5)
j	=	age	(58.4)
j	=	jump	(31.5)
k	=	came	(60.0)
k	=	keys	(15.9)

Phoneme		*Grapheme correspondence*	
l	=	lit	(89.7)
l	=	ball	(10.3)
m	=	me	(100.0)
n	=	no	(99.8)
p	=	pin	(100.0)
r	=	run	(100.0)
s	=	sit	(67.3)
s	=	city	(25.1)
t	=	time	(99.8)
v	=	vine	(99.4)
z	=	his	(75.5)
z	=	zero	(17.4)

However, even with apparently consistent consonants such as *b, d,* and *p,* there are spelling problems in words where the letter is silent, as in *bomb, debt, doubt,* or *subtle.* The letter *d* is silent in *handkerchief, handsome,* and *Wednesday,* and in *soldier* it has a *j* sound. The *p* is silent in *raspberry, receipt, cupboard, corps,* and in words like *psalm, pneumonia,* and *psychology.*

Hindrance: Phonetic Inconsistencies

A serious spelling problem is posed by the phonetic inconsistencies in the way our language is written. Horn analyzed the word *circumference* by syllables and by letter in order to determine the possibilities for spelling the word by sound. He discovered 288 possible combinations when each letter is analyzed. In summarizing this study, he states:

> It is no wonder that a few months after a word has been temporarily learned in a spelling lesson, and subsequently used only occasionally in writing, the child is sometimes confused by the conflicting elements which his pronunciation of the word may call out of his past experience. With so little of the rational character to guide him the wonder is that the child fixes as easily as he does upon the one arbitrary combination which constitutes the correct spelling (Horn, 1954).

This point can be illustrated in its most extreme form by spelling *potato* as "gh-ough-pt-eight-bt-eau" by using these sounds: *gh* in *hiccough, ough* in *though, pt* in *ptomaine, eigh* in *weigh, bt* in *debt, eau* in *beau.*

Everyone knows the uncertainty of the English graphic form *-ough* in such words as *though, through, plough, cough, hiccough,* and *rough.* Only slightly less troublesome to the learner are such ambiguities as *doll-roll, home-come, sword-word, few-dew, break-squeak, paid-plaid.*

Vowels. In our writing of the language, the letter *a* has forty-seven different sound associates. There are three hundred different combinations that express the seventeen vowel sounds.

When the child meets the letter *a* in a word, it may have one of these sounds: *all, allow, nation, want; e* is different in *legend, legal; i* in *fin* and *final; o* in *pot, post, come; u* in *cub, cubic; y* in *cyst* and *tyrant.* The combinations of vowels are still more perplexing; *ea* has such variations as *clean, bread, hearth; ei* in *receive,* in addition to being different from *ie* in *siege,* has a different sound in *neigh* and *weight* and still another in *height.* The *o* combinations give forms like *blood-bloom, cow-crow, shout-should, shoulder-tough, though-rough, couple-court, cough-enough,* and *plough-rough.* Final *e* is generally mute and is supposed to affect the preceding vowel as in *van, vane; rob, robe;* but in *sleeve,* it has no effect and there is a series of words—*come, dove, love, some, have*—in which the vowel is short rather than long.

The short *i* sound is especially difficult. It is spelled at least fifteen ways in common words and only a little more than half the time with the letter *i* alone. Examples are *i* (*bit*), *e, y* (*pretty*), *ie* (*mischief*), *ui* (*build*), *ey* (*money*), *a* (*character*), *ay* (*Monday*), *us* (*busy*), *ee* (*been*), *ei* (*foreign*), *ia* (*marriage*), and *o* (*women*). There are other spellings in less common words. In these words one would expect the long vowel sound: *furnace*, *mountain*, *favorite*, *minute*, and *coffee*.

Another sound, the schwa (ə), is found in half of the multisyllabic words of the ten thousand most common words. It is spelled thirty ways with almost any vowel or vowel digraph: *about*, *taken*, *pencil*, *lemon*, *circus*, *teacher*, *picture*, *dollar*, *nation*. Although the use of the schwa may simplify the pronunciation of the unstressed syllables, the implication for spelling is quite different.

Good auditory perception and careful listening habits are a part of the spelling study procedure. If children use common pronunciation as a guide for spelling, they face many difficulties. If the pronunciation of a word is somewhat blurred in reading, the sound is still near enough to carry the meaning. In spelling, the word must be exact. Any word with a schwa calls for careful visual discrimination in order to learn the pattern used to spell the sound.

Silent Letters. Silent letters are especially perplexing in spelling. If one includes letters not pronounced in digraphs, as in *please* or *boat*, and double letters with only one pronounced, nearly all letters of the alphabet are silent in some words. In reading we can call them ghosts or use them to identify words that may be confused with others, but in spelling all these silent letters must be remembered. There is no phonetic clue to their presence in a word.

Spelling Updates. To alleviate the problems encountered in both reading and spelling, various authorities since the time of Noah Webster have called for changing the spelling of words to coincide with phonetic pronunciation. There does, indeed, appear to have been some very minor movement in that direction, as may be seen by the acceptance of such spellings as *donut* and *drafty*. Making our language more accessible through spelling reform benefits all readers and spellers of the English language. It is felt that such reforms would also help teachers to diagnose reading and spelling problems better (Citron, 1981).

Words: Which Ones to Teach?

Although the study of words in sentences does promote some syntactic and semantic understanding, the use of words in lists has been shown to be more effective when promoting spelling skills (Horn, 1962; Erhi, 1980). Words studied from lists are learned more quickly with greater retention and transfer more readily to new contexts.

Functional Frequency

There are more than 600,000 words in a modern dictionary. Textbook writers must determine how many of these should be included in a spelling program. Their decisions have been guided by the early research of Horn and Rinsland. Horn (1927) examined correspondence of business firms to learn what words were most frequently used by adults. Rinsland (1945) conducted a nationwide study of children's written material.

In addition to these research efforts, other scholars have examined the words most frequently misspelled at each grade level, words that have frequent use in both adult and children's word lists, words common to reading lists, and words that contain special difficulties.

When a group of authors start to write a spelling textbook, they consult all these studies and make a list of their own that reflects their personal philosophy about what should be done with respect to spelling instruction. Those who feel that success motivates students will usually have a rather short list. Those who stress phonics may include words that are not used very often, yet provide phonetics practice. Those who feel that children learn to spell many common words outside school will emphasize the words in the language that cause misspelling. Usually they include about four thousand words. A survey of the most popular spelling textbook series will reveal that there are approximately ten thousand different words to be found in all.

Geedy (1975) summarized the diverse notions concerning criteria for inclusion of words to be studied. "There appears to be greatest agreement in making selections based on children's present needs in writing and frequency of need at a given grade level" (p. 233). Hillerich (1977) suggests that the lists should change as the child's spelling skills mature. To promote feelings of accomplishment and success, spelling words should be selected from word lists containing 50 to 75 percent known words.

Studies by Johnson and Majer (1976) as well as others reveal the interesting fact that a few words of our language are used over and over again. Over one-half of our writing consists of a repetition of the following one hundred words.

a	eat	in	our	there
all	for	is	out	they
am	girl	it	over	this
and	go	just	play	time
are	going	know	pretty	to
at	good	like	put	too
baby	got	little	red	tree
ball	had	look	run	two
be	has	made	said	up
big	have	make	saw	want
boy	he	man	school	was
but	her	me	see	we
can	here	mother	she	went
Christmas	him	my	so	what
come	his	name	some	when
did	home	not	take	will
do	house	now	that	with
dog	how	of	the	would
doll	I	on	then	you
down	I'm	one	them	your

Horn (1927) noted that after the first thousand words the addition of the next thousand added a very small percentage of the words used by writers. Isn't it interesting that a person who learns twenty-eight hundred words knows 97 percent of the words in common use? If students learn the twelve hundred words next in frequency they increase their writing vocabulary only 1.1 percent, or up to 98.3 percent of all the words they will write, which are found among the frequently used words of our language.

High-frequency words are useful when students move into the intermediate grades, and it is further indicated that more emphasis on word meanings as they relate to word forms may help students see the relationships among words (N. Chomsky and Halle, 1968; C. Chomsky, 1970). Variant forms of the same words (for instance, *real*, *really*, *reality*, *realize*) may sound different phonologically, but on a lexical level they may be more easily spelled through understanding their connected meanings.

Phonetic Knowledge

Research by other linguists disagrees fundamentally with the principles of functional frequency in the grade placement of words. Hanna and Hanna (1965) indicated that the selection of vocabulary for a modern spelling curriculum should begin with a linguistic analysis of American English. The study words should illustrate the principles, generalizations, and correspondences considered appropriate for a child at a given time.

Table 9–1 illustrates the suggested progression of linguistic patterns.

Student Work as Word Source

A final criterion for determining which words should be selected for study should, of course, be the students themselves. An analysis of student writing samples based on words presented in eleven commercial spelling programs revealed that students varied greatly as to which words they misspelled. Many of the words included in the lists were spelled correctly, whereas many others the students themselves used were misspelled. This indicates that students' own writing may be the best source for compiling spelling lists (DiStefano and Hagerty, 1983). Certainly, as suggested ear-

Table 9–1
Spelling Patterns Recommended for Elementary Level

Pattern	*Examples*	*Exceptions*
C-V-C (short vowel)	cat drip dent	
C-V-C + *e* (long vowel, silent *e*)	save hive drove	love have give come
C-V-V-C (long first vowel)	rain leaf coat need	relief break brief bear
C-V + *r* (controlled, preceding vowel)	far bird clear bore	heard burn third
C-V (long vowel)	go be by	to do too

Source: Lamb, P. (1977). *Linguistics in Proper Perspective*, 3 ed. Columbus, Ohio: Charles E. Merrill Publishing Company, pp. 67–72.

lier, students should compile their own lists of problem spelling words.

Other researchers (McTeague, 1980; Cotton, 1982) conclude that spelling words should be drawn from the classroom material and units of study rather than from "random" lists taken from commercially prepared programs.

Teachers need to know the spelling needs of their students and formulate word lists appropriate to these needs. A combination of prepared word lists and students' own "need to know" words presented alternately or periodically may best satisfy the needs of everyone.

Horn (1960) devised the following criteria for evaluating possible spelling words:

1. *Frequency of use*—How often is the word used in writing?
2. *Difficulty*—How difficult is the word at various grade levels?
3. *Geographic distribution*—Is the word used only regionally or throughout the entire country?
4. *Permanency*—Is the word a fad, a trend, slang? Or is it a permanent part of the language?
5. *Spread*—Is the word "spread" across various kinds of writing?
6. *Cruciality*—If the word were misspelled, would it result in miscommunication?

Words: When to Teach Them

Equal in importance to the problem of which words should be taught is the question of *when* a word should be taught. This problem might be emphasized by asking yourself, "At what grade level should the word *school* or *elephant* be taught?" Textbook authors have been guided by the answers to these two questions: "When do students want to use this word? How difficult is it to spell?"

It is a complex task to decide about the difficulty of a word. If we were to take a single word, such as *elephant*, and give it to ten children in each grade in school, we would learn that some in each grade would spell it correctly and others would misspell it. If the following figures indicated those who spelled it correctly in each grade, we would have the beginning of a scale to measure its difficulty.

Grade	*Number Spelling Word Correctly*	*Number of Students Surveyed*
2	2	10
3	4	10
4	7	10
5	9	10
6	9	10
7	10	10
8	10	10

On the basis of both need and possible error, it would seem that these students needed help on the word during the third and fourth grades. It may be that the word is too difficult for second graders and would challenge no one in a seventh-grade class.

New Iowa Spelling Scale

The first spelling scale was designed in 1913. In 1955 Harry A. Greene designed the New Iowa Spelling Scale, which was revised in 1977 by Loomer. It is still widely used because it provides not only a list of frequently used words, but also information on the difficulty of the words (how many children at what grade level can spell the word correctly).

The extent of the New Iowa Spelling Scale indicates the amazing scope of modern research. Approximately 230,000 pupils in almost 8,800 classrooms in 645 different school systems were involved. Because each pupil undertook to spell 100 words, a total of over 23 million spellings comprise the data for this scale. With respect to the words *elephant* and *school* the scale provides the following information:

Percentage of Class Spelling Each Word Correctly

Grade	*Elephant*	*School*
2	0	32
3	5	68
4	24	86
5	55	92
6	57	97
7	74	99
8	82	99

It is evident from the preceding table that the correct spelling of the word *school* occurs much earlier and more completely than does the correct spelling of the word *elephant*. However, we still do not know how interested the child in your room is in using the word *elephant*.

Although the New Iowa Spelling Scale may serve as an indicator, there still remain uncertainties about the grade placement of individual words. When we recognize that the linguistic maturity of children differs, it is apparent that a formal graded list will be unrelated to the needs of certain children in a classroom.

The first lesson in a spelling textbook may be as difficult as the last. Thus if there are units designed for Halloween, Hanukkah, or Christmas, it is good judgment to skip to those units at the appropriate time. Similarly, the words in a fourth-grade speller may actually be more difficult for a specific child than those in a fifth-grade lesson. Spelling lists must be examined so that word selections reflect the individual needs of the child or group of children being taught.

How Should Spelling Be Taught?

We have noted the efforts that have been made to find *which* words should be taught and *when* they should be taught. The problem of *how* words should be taught has been of equal concern. In the late nineteenth century, Rice (1897) suspected that the methods of spelling instruction were not very efficient. He conducted experiments that convinced many schools that they were spending too much time on the direct teaching of spelling. Although we know it must be taught systematically, there is still controversy over whether it is best to teach spelling in association with other school work or to have a specific period each day. The amount of time spent in the spelling period has been reduced to about seventy-five minutes a week—or fifteen minutes per day—and the child who has demonstrated spelling mastery is permitted to engage in other instructional activities.

Test-Study Plan

For over fifty years research has proved the test-study plan to be the most efficient method of organizing a week's worth of spelling (Gates, 1931; Blanchard, 1944; Fitzgerald, 1953; Horn, 1960; Petty, 1969; Stetson & Boutin, 1980).

In this plan the students take a pretest of the weekly assignment the first day. This separates the words they know how to spell from those that need drill. Exercises and other activities to encourage writing the words that were misspelled are used during the week, and a final test of all the words is given at the end. A chart of progress is kept by each student, and words missed are used during the week, and a final test of all the words is administered at the end. Each student keeps a chart of progress, misspelled words are added to the next week's lesson, and review lessons are given at intervals to assure a respelling of words studied.

A variation of this plan is the *study-test* plan, in which fewer words are given each day, but they are words known to be difficult for most of the class. There are daily tests as well as one at the end of the week on all words. Two drawbacks to the study-test approach are that (1) teachers may be less able to know whether instruction is in fact needed, and (2) students may spend time studying words they already know.

The following procedures for spelling instruction are typical of many school programs.

Planning for the Teaching of Spelling

Plan A

First Day

1. Introduce the words in the new lesson in a meaningful way.
2. Discuss meanings of words.
3. Use words in sentences.
4. Note which words are phonetic.
5. Note likeness to words previously learned.
6. Note any unusual spellings.
7. Form visual images and sequence of letters in each word.
8. Write the words.
9. Develop word lists, which are on continuous display.
10. Integrate use of these words throughout the curriculum.

Second Day

1. Use words in a worksheet.
2. Do the exercises in the spelling book.
3. Write sentences using the words.
4. Write a story suggested by the words.
5. Play bingo or other games which call for use of the words.

Third Day

1. Test and check words with the children.
2. Design plans for further study (games, worksheets, word practice).

Fourth Day

1. Study the words missed on the test and words from individual card files.
2. Give additional words to children who have mastered the list by the third day. (This may be done earlier in the week.)
3. Teach additional words by making derivatives.
4. Work with individuals and small groups with special needs.

Fifth Day

1. Give the final test. It is advisable for each child to have a booklet in which to write the words.
2. Check the tests with each child.
3. Test children on additional words learned.

Plan B

1. Present the lesson on Monday.
2. Test on Tuesday, giving additional words to children who need no further study on the regular lesson.
3. Study the words and use them on Wednesday and Thursday.
4. Give the final test on Friday.

Plan C

Give a pretest on Monday and then plan the following days according to the results of the test. Make tests more interesting and valuable by variety in method. For example, test certain other abilities:

1. Circle or underline vowels in certain words.
2. Mark long or short vowels in certain words.
3. Select the words of more than one syllable.
4. Divide words into syllables and mark accents.
5. Write abbreviations of words.
6. Alphabetize the words.
7. Change all singular words to plurals.
8. Show contraction or possession.
9. Introduce words similar to those in the word list to apply generalizations.

Teaching Spelling

The following plans provide examples of lessons for a second-grade class.

Structural Analysis: Grade 2—Lesson 1

Objective

To develop ability to recognize variants formed by adding *-es* to root words.

Procedure

1. Write the following: "I found a mother fox. She had two baby foxes." Have the sentences read; then point to the first and ask, "How many does the next one tell about? What letters are added to *fox* to make it mean more than one?"
2. Write the following: "Harold rolled the potato across the floor. Harold rolled the potatoes across the floor." Have the sentences read silently and ask, "Which sentence means that Harold rolled more than one potato across the floor?"
3. Write the following: "I wish I had some cake. Patty wishes she had some cake." Point to *wishes* and ask, "What ending is added to *wish* to make *wishes*? Does *-es* make *wishes* mean more than one?" Explain that we say "I wish," but we say "Patty wishes" or "he wishes." Read the sentences using the word in the incorrect ways: "I wishes" and "Patty wish."

Objective

To develop the ability to attach inflected and derived forms of known words in which the final *e* is dropped before an ending.

Procedure

1. Write the word *ride* on the board and have it pronounced. Erase the final *e* and add *-ing*. Call attention to the dropping of the *e*. Have *riding* pronounced.
2. "What is the root word of *riding?*" Write *ride* opposite *riding*. "How many vowel letters do you see in *ride*? What vowel sound do you hear? Does dropping the silent *e* and adding *-ing* change the sound of the root word? Can you hear *ride* in riding?"
3. Write *coming* on the board. Ask pupils to tell what ending they see and to what root word *-ing* was added. Write the root word.
4. Use the same procedure with *rule–ruling–ruler; bake–baking–baker; dive–diving–diver.*
5. Lead the children to formulate the generalization that when a word ends in final *-e*, the *e* is usually dropped before adding an ending (-er, -est, -ed, -ing).

SEATWORK

Write the root words after each word:

making ________
liking ________
mover ________
giving ________
driver ________
caring ________
having ________

Inflected -er and -est Forms: Grade 2—Lesson 2

OBJECTIVES

To promote ability to recognize inflected forms by adding *-er* and *-est.*
To express ideas in comparative terms.

PROCEDURE

1. Write these words on the board and have them pronounced: *short, long.*
2. Add *-er* to make it *shorter.* What word is this?
3. Erase *-er* and add *-est.* Now what word is this?
4. Repeat with *long.* (*longer, longest*)
5. Draw three lines and write these sentences and fill in the blanks:
   first The ________ line is the longest of all.
   second The ________ line is shorter than the second.
   third The ________ line is the shortest of all.
6. Write the following words on the board, have each pronounced, and have pupils use them in sentences: *cool, cooler, coolest; fast, faster, fastest; deep, deeper, deepest.*

SEATWORK

1. Write these sentence on the board and have the children copy the sentences and add the comparative endings.
   I am tall _ _ than you are.
   She is slow _ _ than I am.
   The wind is getting cold _ _.
   He is the fast _ _ _ boy on our team.
2. Write *-er* endings and *-est* endings for
   fast *long* *cold*
   tall *deep* *slow*

Observing, Listening, Writing: Grade 2—Lesson 3

Objective

To teach the children how to spell words through observing, listening, and writing.

Materials

Spelling story. (On board.)
Pencils. (In desks.)
Paper. (Distribute before children come into the room.)
The story: *Our News*
There are thirty-six at *school* today.
We will *read* a new book.
We have a *new* turtle.

Method

Have the children:

1. Put name on paper and fold into four columns.
2. Look at the story and be able to read it.
3. Read the story, one sentence at a time.
4. Frame the words (e.g., *school, read*).
5. Put a box on the board with letters in it.

   (e.g.)

s	o	o
h	l	c

6. Ask the children: "What spelling word do we have that has all of these letters?" (e.g., school)
7. "What letter goes first?" (for example, *s*)
8. "Can you use it in a sentence?" (Call on a student.)
9. "What can you tell me about the word?"
10. "Let's close our eyes and think of the word. Think of the silent *h*, double vowel, and size. Spell it to yourself."
11. "Look at the board to see whether you spelled it right."
12. "Close your eyes and spell the word for me." (Call on a student.)
13. "Write the word in your first column. Write it in the second."
14. "Let's spell the word once."
15. "Who can read this word for the class?" (Point to *read.*)
16. "Can you use it in a sentence?"
17. "Let's look at the word carefully. What can you tell me about it?"
18. "Let's close our eyes and think of the word. Think of the two vowels, silent *a*, three short letters, and one tall letter. Spell it to yourself. ____. Can you spell it?"

19. "Let's look at the word and spell it once again."
20. "Write it on your paper."
21. "Write it in a second column."
22. "Write it by memory in a third column."

Systematic Spelling Instruction

Commercial spelling programs often use independent study of word lists and exercises to accomplish their goals. Although independent work is effective with higher-achieving students, skill-deficient children may require a more structured, teacher-directed approach. One such approach, designed to be adapted to any word list found in commercial spelling programs, is the *Archer Method of Effective Spelling Instruction* (Archer, 1982).* Based on a carefully controlled sequence of *testing*, *study*, *direct instruction*, *sentence dictation*, and *review*, this method stresses total student participation in the acquisition of new spelling words. Each phase of the lesson is carefully scripted so that teachers know how much and what kind of instruction to include at each phase and when to repeat a lesson or move on, based on student performance. The components of the Archer method are included in the "Unit Daily Lesson Plans" in Table 9–2, and a sample script for a direct instruction lesson on Common Elements is illustrated in Table 9–3.

For some teachers and classrooms this programmed approach to spelling may be too rigid, but the various components are easily adapted to a variety of purposes. The study procedure called "Copy-Cover-Write-and-Check" provides children with a systematic, effective method for studying new words.

Copy, Cover, Write, and Check

1. Copy the words from a master list (the chalkboard, printed list, and so on).
2. Cover the word with an index card.
3. Write the word from memory.
4. Uncover the master word and check the spelling. If it is misspelled, it must be crossed out and rewritten correctly.
5. Repeat the procedure two more times, covering all examples of the words each time.

Sentence dictation provides a method for using the new words in context and also allows for practice of careful listening, punctuation, and spelling of nontargeted words. Dictation as a method of instruction has been a staple of the teaching methods in many countries for many years. In France, "la Dictée" is a fact of life. Whole passages of literature are dictated to students who benefit by being exposed to sophisticated thoughts, vocabulary, and syntax as well as spelling and punctuation in an interesting, rather than an isolated, form (Stotsky, 1977). For beginning spellers, a combination of the Language Experience Approach to creating stories and dictation using the students' own stories may provide a stimulating context for spelling.

Self-Corrected Test

Horn (1954) concluded that the self-corrected test seems to be the single most important factor in promoting spelling achievement. Allowing students to have immediate feedback and correction reinforcement on spelling errors makes them better able to master the new words than if the tests were graded by the teacher or another student. Seeing, hearing, pronouncing, and then correcting the errors provide on-the-spot insight into what errors were made and perhaps why they were made. The immediate reinforcing of the proper spelling implants the word correctly in the child's mind.

The usual method of administering the corrected

* The material that follows is from Archer, A. (1982). *Basic Skills Curriculum/Spelling Program: User's Manual.* San Diego: San Diego City Schools. Used with permission.

Table 9–2
Unit Daily Lesson Plans

Pretest	*Practice 1*	*Practice 2*	*Practice 3*	*Posttest*
Pretest on all words	Direct Instruction on half of words	Direct Instruction on remaining words	Word Dictation on all words	Posttest on all words
	Word Dictation on half of words	Word Dictation on half of words	Sentence Dictation	
Study Procedure (copy, cover, write, check on errors)	Sentence Dictation	Sentence Dictation		Writing of sentences containing spelling words
	Review	Review		
	Repeat if necessary	Repeat if necessary	Repeat if necessary	

Table 9–3
Script 5: Common Element

Note: On your lesson plan certain letters are underlined in the spelling words. These are the elements that will be stressed.

Write the first word on the board or overhead transparency and underline the letters that are underlined on the lesson plan.
Point to the first word.
WHAT WORD? rain
(Point to underlined letters.)
IN THE WORD RAIN, THE SOUND /a/ IS MADE BY THE LETTERS ai.
WHAT LETTERS MAKE THE SOUND /a/ IN RAIN? a-i
SPELL RAIN WITH ME. r-a-i-n
SPELL RAIN BY YOURSELVES. r-a-i-n
(Cover the word.)
WRITE RAIN. (Students write word.)
BE SURE THAT IT LOOKS LIKE RAIN.
(Uncover word.)
CHECK RAIN. IF YOU MISSPELLED THE WORD, REWRITE IT.
(Repeat these procedures for each of the words to be taught.)

test is to dictate the entire list of words and then correct them all at once by pronouncing the word, writing it on the board, and spelling it aloud at the same time. Students check the word, letter by letter. If it is incorrect, they cross it out and rewrite it correctly next to the misspelled version. Hillerich (1984) discovered that slightly better results may be obtained from correcting each word *immediately* rather than waiting to correct after the entire list of words has been dictated. Either of these methods produces better instructional results than a teacher- or peer-corrected test. If cheating on spelling tests is deemed to be a concern, insist that students write in pen and correct in red pencil; however, if spelling tests are presented as an instructional procedure rather than a means to a grade, children will realize the purpose of the test and cheating will not be a problem.

After the papers have been corrected, a short discussion of the common errors is valuable. Review the steps used in individual study by asking the following:

1. Did you pronounce and *hear* the word correctly?

2. Did you try to spell by sound when the sound did not agree with the letters?
3. Did you forget the letters in one part of the word?

Each misspelled word should be written correctly in the pupil's individual review list or workbook. Teachers should praise pupils who initiate their own review work and thereby establish one of the habits of good spelling.

The Self-Study Method

The self-corrected test procedure gives each student an individualized list of words she needs to master. Now, each student must be taught to learn these misspelled words efficiently. Teachers know students do not automatically use the most effective study methods. In fact, proper study methods should be reviewed at the beginning of each grade.

Horn (1960) recommends teaching the following self-study procedure:

1. Pronounce the word correctly. Correct pronunciation is an important factor in learning to spell. Enunciate each syllable distinctly while looking closely at the word.
2. Close your eyes and try to recall how the word looks, syllable by syllable. Pronounce the word in a whisper while you try to visualize the word.
3. Open your eyes and make sure you have recalled the word correctly. Repeat steps 2 or 3 times.
4. When you feel you have learned the word, cover it, and write it without looking. Check your written word with the correct, covered word.
5. Repeat this writing procedure until you have correctly spelled the word three times. Check the correct spelling after each writing.

Spelling Errors: Cause and Effect

The student and the teacher should recognize the fact that testing in spelling is done to guide learning. Errors should help the students direct their study efforts. After the children have correctly rewritten each misspelled word in the review list, the class and teacher should analyze words to diagnose the nature of the errors. Certain assumptions can be made about the spelling errors children commit. They make errors according to their own assumptions about spelling rules. By collecting samples of children's errors, evaluating them, and discussing them with the child, a teacher may determine which approach may be most effective to help the child correct his or her basic assumptions (Ganschow, 1981).

An analysis made by Wolfe (1952) of spelling errors in a fifth-grade class indicated that 36.3 percent were phonetic mistakes. Phonetic errors seem to indicate a need for emphasis on visual and auditory imagery, but it is apparent that there are elements of unreasonableness in the way our language is spelled. Vowel substitution formed 8.1 percent of the errors—*sence* for *since*, *togather* for *together*, *eny* for *any*, *lissen* for *lesson*. Vowel omissions formed 6 percent—*busness* for *business*. Doubling or nondoubling caused 5 percent—*refuell* for *refuel*. Consonant substitution, endings, and diphthongs caused the remaining errors—*pance* for *pants*, *feels* for *fields*. Vowel and consonant substitutions were not grouped with phonetic errors, but are related—*pagun* for *pagan*, *leater* for *later*, *stolden* for *stolen*, *finely* for *finally*.

The frequent *causes* of spelling errors are summarized in Table 9–4.

An analysis of the errors made by a class will reveal a wide variety of spellings of a single word. Study exercises are planned to place emphasis on parts of words without identifying them as "hard spots." It is apparent that other irregularities also cause spelling trouble.

To, Too, Two. Some persistent spelling errors demand specific attention. *To, too,* and *two* are often confused. The error is usually of the following type:

I am to tired to play.

Children seldom make such errors as the following:

Table 9–4
Frequent Causes of Spelling Errors

Error	*Cause*
acurate for *accurate*	Faulty observation
docter for *doctor*	Group pronunciation or faulty teacher pronunciation (Break into syllables and point out difficult spots.)
laffun for *laughing*	Inaccurate auditory and visual perception
horse for *hoarse*	Inaccurate visual perception
athalete for *athlete*	Pronunciation error
ate for *eight*	Incorrect meaning association
bying for *buying*	Incorrect root word association
non for *none* *opn* for *open* *Wensday* for *Wednesday*	Too dependent on phonics (Children must be helped early in spelling to note orthographic irregularities of our language.)
beyoutey for *beauty* *exampull* for *example*	Overemphasized pronunciation (Words should be spoken naturally.)
cents for *sense*	Incorrect meaning association
except for *accept*	(Such words should be taught in pairs.)
askt for *asked* *berrys* for *berries* *largist* for *largest*	Unfamiliarity with common word endings (These should be taught as they apply to many common words.)
dissturb for *disturb* *preevent* for *prevent* *bysect* for *bisect*	Unfamiliarity with common prefixes
possum for *opossum* *bucher* for *butcher* *juge* for *judge*	Failure to note silent letters that appear in some words (Help children to form correct mental images.)
bill for *bell* *brin* for *brain* *alog* for *along*	Lack of phonics or faulty writing habits
allright for *all right* *goodnight for good night*	Unfamiliarity with expressions that must be written as two words (Specific teaching is required.)

The game is two easy.
To more days until Christmas.

In order to reinforce proper identification and use of *to, too,* and *two,* ask the children to make charts of this type:

Too = more than enough:
The window is too high.
Too = also:
Jack went too.
Use *to* like this:
I rode to town. I went to see the game.
two = 2 (1 + 1):
We found two pennies.

Note that each is a different part of speech. Too is an adverb, *to* is usually a preposition, and *two* is an adjective.

Exercise. The drill found in Table 9–5 will provide meaningful contrast. The class is divided into teams and captains are chosen. The captain gives each pupil on his or her team one of the words listed in the table. The pupil writes a sentence on a slip of paper, using the word that has been given with *to, two,* or *too*. For example, a pupil on Team 1 may be requested to compose a sentence using *loudly,* as well as *to, too,* or *two*. The pupil may write, "We sang too loudly." He then writes "Team 1" and his name on his slip and gives it to his captain. The captain tells him whether or not the usage is correct. The entire sentence is examined for capitals, periods, and correct spellings.

Each team may now choose a pupil to write a sentence on the board. Is each sentence correct? If so, the team scores a point. Then a second pupil is chosen from each team. When any pupil makes an error, that team fails to score. The team that scores the highest wins the game.

When a team has a perfect score, the teacher may dictate sentences of greater complexity to that team, and the other teams continue the game. The following sentences may be dictated for further practice:

Table 9–5
The Teaching of Spelling

Team 1	*Team 2*	*Team 3*	*Team 4*	*Team 5*
loudly	cold	hot	exciting	sneeze
quietly	run	help	wrestle	whistle
stoves	town	movies	camp	swim
marbles	dogs	puppies	the circus	sing
young	heavy	automobiles	carrots	thin
jump	bad	fast	school	books
dark	the beach	slippery	icy	warm

1. You have far too many apples to go in that basket.
2. I have two pencils too many.
3. I came to school too late to see the exhibit.
4. Were you too late to go with Tom to town?

IT'S, ITS. Another frequent error is confusion between *its* and *it's*. Make charts of this type to help students see the difference:

It's is a contraction meaning "it is."
Examples: *It's a new desk. It's too sweet.*

Its is a possessive, like *his* or *your:*
Example: *The bird hummed its tune.*

Have your children make up sentences to illustrate each definition.

Exercise. The following exercise may be written on the chalkboard for further practice. Have the children write the numbers 1 to 23 on a sheet of paper. Either *its* or *it's* is supplied for each blank in the stories according to its appropriate usage.

What Is It?

A RED BREAST

_1_ breast is red. _2_ song is "Cheer up!" _3_ home is a nest of grass and twigs. What is it? _4_ a robin.

MAN'S BEST FRIEND

_5_ called man's best friend. _6_ eyes are kind. _7_ tail wags when _8_ friendly and happy. _9_ teeth are sharp, but _10_ heart is all gold. What is it? _11_ a dog.

FENDERS BEND EASILY

It has four wheels. _12_ motor hums. _13_ tires screech. _14_ steering wheel is round and smooth. _15_ fenders are easily bent or battered. What is it? _16_ an automobile.

GOOD FOR BONES AND TEETH

__17__ something to drink. __18__ color is creamy white. __19__ good for bones and teeth. Butter is made from __20__ fat. __21__ best when __22__ cold. What is it? __23__ milk.

A useful extension of this idea is for each pupil to write a "What Is It?" story. The teacher may give a category such as *toys* or *animals* with a requirement that the possessive (*its*) be used, for example, at least two times in the story. The personal application of a principle is one of the most effective means of ensuring learning and retention.

CAPITAL LETTERS. Capital letters are a cause of spelling confusion. Have the children note the words that are capitalized in their social studies books, then make up a classroom chart similar to the following.

Capitalization Chart

Do Capitalize

1. The first word of each sentence:
   This afternoon we went to the game.
2. The names of months of the year, days of the week, and holidays:
   February *Wednesday*
   Halloween *New Year's Day*
3. The names of particular streets, schools, and buildings:
   Adams Avenue *Central School*
   Riverview Street *State Office Building*
4. The first word and all important words in the titles of books, movies, stories, magazines, and poems:
   Skid *My Visit to the City*
   Charlotte's Web *The Star Spangled Banner*
5. The names of people and pets, the titles and initials of people, the word *I:*
   Miss Mary A. Cunningham *My dog, Dingle*
   Reverend Collins
   Denise, Daryl, and I
6. The names of countries, states, cities, mountains, and rivers:
   New York City, New York *Rocky Mountain*
   Colorado River
   Warren, Ohio
7. The first word in the greeting or closing of a letter:
   Dear Nancy, *Sincerely yours,*
   Gentlemen: *Yours very truly,*
8. Words referring to the deity:
   God *Holy Ghost* *Jehovah*
   Lord *Savior* *He*

Do Not Capitalize

1. The names of seasons:
   spring *winter*
   summer *autumn*
2. The names of games, birds, trees, flowers, vegetables, fruits, and animals:
   baseball *carrots* *robin* *chickens*
   oak *apples* *rose* *maple*

The following exercises may be useful in reinforcing the concept of capitalization.

Practicing Capitalization

1. Have students write the answer to such questions as the following:
   Where do you live?
   What is your father's name?
   What school do you attend?
   What countries would you like to visit this summer?
   When is your birthday?
   What is your favorite subject in school?
   How would you address a letter to your principal?
   What is the title of your favorite book?

2. a. Change the small letters to capitals:

   my cousin lives in denver. her name is linda lou. she attends jefferson school. each wednesday they have a class in spanish. last year she went east for her vacation. she heard the president in rhode island. her favorite book is the little house in the woods.

Children who find the preceding too difficult might be helped by omitting the initial letter of each capitalized word. (This also avoids showing an error.)

   b. Copy this letter and supply appropriate capital letters:

115 south hill street
san diego, california
january 6, 1990

dear jim,

our girl scout troop just made an overnight trip to palomar mountain. it was fun since i slept in my own sleeping bag. please write and tell me how the evanston little league made out.

your friend,
sharon

MNEMONICS. A mnemonic device is one that aids the memory. Such devices are highly personal; although they may help some children, they may be merely an additional burden to others, because in order to remember one thing the child must remember the association among several things.

Following are a few association ideas that may help some children who are having specific spelling difficulties:

all right	*All right* is two words like *all wrong.*
cemetary	Watch the *e*'s in *cemetery.*
principal	The *principal* is a prince of a *pal.*
principle	A *principle* is a *rule.*
separate	There is a *rat* in *separate.*
balloon	A *balloon* is like a *ball.*
familiar	There is a *liar* in *familiar.*
parallel	*All* railroad tracks are *parallel.*
almost	*Almost* is always spelled with one *l.*

capitol There is a *dome* on the capitol.
bachelor The *bachelor* does not like *tea*. (Common error is *batchelor*.)
yardstick A *yardstick* is in one piece.

A mnemonic association that works for one person does not always work for another. The associations you think up for yourself are better than the proclaimed masterpieces of others. The more startling an association is, the better it will be remembered:

```
        l
        e
        t
        t
stationery
        r
```

hear: You have to use your *ear* for this one.
independent: We made quite a *dent* in England in 1776.
gram mar Anyone can spell the first half. Copy the second part from the first, in reverse order.

The hardest spelling rule concerns when to double a final consonant and when not to. Note how a single consonant (not double) favors a long vowel sound and how a double consonant favors a short sound. Examples will make it clear:

mated	(matted)	bated	(batted)
rated	(ratted)	dined	(dinned)
pined	(pinned)	planed	(planned)
loped	(lopped)	writing	(written)

When stress is on the first syllable, the consonant is less likely to double, as in *traveled*.

An association between related words will clarify some spellings. One can remember the *a* in *grammar* by relating it to *grammatical*. One can remember the *a* in *ecstasy* by relating it to *ecstatic*. These blanks can be filled in properly by noticing the vowel in the associated words.

dem_cratic	democracy	ill_stration	illustrate
pres_dent	preside	ind_strial	industry
prec_dent	precede	imm_grate	migrate
comp_rable	compare	ab_lition	abolish
comp_sition	compose	comp_tent	compete
hist_rical	history	si_n	signal
janit_rial	janitor	bom_	bombard
manag_rial	manager	mali_n	malignant
maj_rity	major	sof_en	soft
cond_mn	condemnation	mus_le	muscular

How Are Spelling Generalizations Formed?

In psychology the word *generalization* describes the process of discovery in learners as they notice identities in different situations. If one teaches generalizations made by others, these become the traditional spelling rules. Good spelling teachers plan situations in which the elements of identity needed for a generalization may be discovered by the learner. For example:

Teacher: Quick is an interesting word. The *qu* sounds like *kw*. What other words do you know that start like *quick?* (These words are listed on the board.) Do you notice anything about these words? Yes, they start with *q*. Let's look in our dictionary and notice the words that start with *q*. What do you notice about spelling words that start with *q*? Yes, the initial *q* is followed by *u,* except in a very few foreign words that are sometimes used in English.

On the subject of teaching spelling rules, E. Horn expressed his reservations over sixty-five years ago. He stated that in order to justify teaching a spelling rule, "one must show . . . that the rule can be easily taught, that it will be remembered, and that it will function in the stress of actual spelling. Evidence seems to cast doubt on all three of these assumptions." With Horn's advice in mind, later in this chapter we present suggestions for handling generalizations.

Lesson Plans

The following two lessons will illustrate the development of generalizations with children.

Lesson One: Simple Generalization

Generalization: "Many new words are developed from root words by simply adding *-s*, *-ed*, or *-ing* to a root word, without any other change."

Aims

1. to show that by adding *-s*, *-ed*, and *-ing* to many words one can spell three or four more words after learning to spell the root word only.
2. to extend gradually the concept of generalization so that pupils can use it as an aid in discovering correct spellings.

Materials

The words were chosen from word lists for second and third grades.

play	rain	help	spell
want	garden	burn	clean
need	open	paint	pull

This list was chosen for the simple meanings at the grade three level and because they are basic words to which the suffixes *-s*, *-ed*, and *-ing* can be added to make new words without any other change. Thus, if children learn to spell *play*, they should be able to generalize and spell *plays*, *played*, and *playing*.

Procedure for the Week

MONDAY

1. Present root words as follows: "Here are the new words to be learned this week. Some of them you already know because you had them in the second grade. Who can point out one that we know?"
2. Have a child point out one known word and spell it. Continue somewhat as follows: "This week we have chosen some words that we already know how to spell because we are going to learn to use a spelling trick that will save us time and work. We will take the word *play*. Let

us call this a root word. *Root word* means the simplest form of a word. In talking, writing, and spelling, we use many forms of a root word by adding one or more letters to it to make new words that we need. Let us see what happens to *play* when we add an *s*. What word does this make?"

3. Use both forms of the word in sentences and demonstrate on the board: "Barbara and Bill play with the dog," "Barbara plays with the dog," and so on.
4. Ask pupils to demonstrate with other words in a list, until you are sure they understand. Have the pupil tell what they do as he changes the word at the board. Ask a student to spell the new word without looking at the board.
5. Use the remainder of the period for supervised study period. *Pronounce*, *use*, and *study* each word.

Tuesday—Review

1. Have the root words written on the board. Give ample opportunity for recall of the new spelling trick. Select several pupils to go to the board and change a word by adding *-s,* spelling it as they do so.
2. Point out again that we only had to add one letter to make a whole new word, which we could spell without studying.
3. Suggest that there is another trick by which we can add another ending and get another word. (Perhaps some child will be able to show this step.)
4. One of these endings is *-ing*. Using *play,* add *-ing* to show that the new word now becomes *playing*. Example: "Bobby is *playing* with James."
5. Call for a volunteer at the board to change *help* to *helping*.
6. Go through the whole list, showing by pupil demonstration how each word may be changed and used.
7. In the same manner add *-ed* and get *played, rained,* and so forth.
8. Ask all pupils to make a chart as follows. Pronounce several of the words. Have pupils spell the other forms.

	New Words Formed		
Base Word	+ *s*	+ *ing*	+ *ed*
1. play	plays	playing	played
2. rain	rains	raining	rained

9. Announce that there will be a test on Wednesday. Suggest that maybe only the root word will be given and the students will be asked to build three new words from it.

10. How many new words should we be able to spell by Friday (count) (thirty-six new words) (forty-eight words counting root words)?

Wednesday

The trial test may be a game. Explain that different forms of the words will be given, such as play*ed,* jump*ing,* or help*s*. Each pupil must spell the word correctly and then write the root word following the form pronounced. Give children time to correct the mistakes and rewrite the words. (*Note:* Do not give words that end in *k* for examples of the *-ed* ending. The pronunciation is not clear enough. It sounds like *t*. Example: *bark, barked.* Explain this later to the pupils.)

Thursday

1. Reproduce the chart on the board.
2. Give only the root word. Have individual children fill in the spaces under careful guidance. (Choose those who had errors on Wednesday.)
3. Have pupils spell orally all four forms.
4. To show a working knowledge, give about three new base words, such as *learn, fill, hunt,* and have the children discover the derived forms from them.
5. Select only words to which the generalization will apply.
6. Caution the children that there are some words that have other changes before *-s, -ed,* or *-ing* is added. To explain an instance in which other changes in words are necessary, select the word *grow*. Try the generalization. Show pupils that they do not say *grow-ed,* but use *gr__w*. See whether some child can supply the *e*. Such exercises develop *thought spelling*.

Friday—Final Test

1. At this time, as many of the derived words as desired may be used.
2. After the derived word is pronounced, the group could be asked to give orally, then write, the root words beside the others as an aid to spelling.
3. Check papers. Make note of pupils who do not understand the process. Repeat this type of lesson soon for these pupils.

Individual needs may be met in these ways:

1. Pupils who are able to learn more words could be allowed to take their readers, find words with these endings, and write the root word, followed by other derived words. These should be checked individually.
2. A few extra words from the second- or third-grade list could be given, such as *add, hunt, wheel, seat*.

3. Those pupils who did not learn the trick should be given copies of the chart and several of the easy words to work on the following week for extra practice.

After a generalization is discovered, it is important that a maintenance program be planned to use this knowledge.

Maintenance Procedures

1. Every subsequent list of words should be studied for new words, derivatives of which are formed by adding *-s, -ed,* and *-ing*.
2. A number of words in the third-grade list are formed with other generalizations, which will be learned later. The teacher should explain this to the pupils as they discover them.
3. One group of words that may confuse them—such as *know, hear, grow, bring, buy, fall, find*—may be used to show how new words are formed by adding *-s* and *-ing,* but a different word is used to form the past, such as *knew* or *heard,* instead of simply adding *-ed*.
4. Extending the pupils' experiences to include the spelling of derived forms as they learn the base words will prepare them to write more fluently and with fewer errors in written English situations. Individual discovery of spelling creates an interest in the various forms of words they use and causes pupils to scrutinize more carefully the arrangement of letters in all words. The feeling of success in achievement (learning the spellings of forty-eight new words in a week) has a tonic effect on attitude toward learning to spell.
5. This generalization is a valuable one at this level for there are many words to which it applies.

Other words that can be used for this generalization are the following:

Second-Grade List		***Third-Grade List***		
ask	look	add	land	park
call	last	count	learn	part
end	show	fill	light	pick
milk	snow	jump	nest	pull

The following lesson might be taught in the fourth grade and above to establish the silent *e* generalization.

Lesson Two: Silent *E* Generalization

Generalization: "Many words ending in silent *e* drop the *e* before adding suffixes beginning with a vowel (lov*ing,* lov*ed,* lov*able*) but retain the silent *e* when the suffix begins with a consonant (lov*ely,* car*eful,* sam*eness,* hom*eless*).

General Aims

1. to provide children with adequate methods of word study, so that they may gradually solve their spelling difficulties individually.
2. to increase a child's written vocabulary.
3. to stimulate pride in correct spelling in all written situations.

Specific Aims

1. to introduce the use of the generalization: "Many words ending in silent *e* drop the *e* before adding *-ing* or *-ed*."
2. to extend gradually the use of the silent *e* generalization to include the use of other common suffixes, such as *-er*, *-est*, *-able*, beginning with a vowel.
3. to emphasize the fact that in adding suffixes, such as *-ly*, *-ful*, *-ness*, *-less*, beginning with a consonant, do not drop the final *e*.
4. to develop the concept of learning to spell by the use of insight or transfer of training as well as automatic memory.
5. to emphasize the economy of time and effort in becoming a good speller when insight is used.

Materials

The following word list was selected from a word list for third and fourth grades:

skate	hope
dance	bake
close	chase
share	divide
vote	smoke
move	love
place	trade
line	

Approach

A very easy group of words ending in silent *e* was chosen from the third- and fourth-grade list so as to present as few spelling difficulties as possible in mastering the root words. Attention here should be focused on what happens to the root word ending in silent *e* when the endings *-ing* and *-ed* are added to make new words. When this is clearly understood, the fun of discovering new words and their spellings by adding these endings to other silent *e* words should follow.

Procedure for the Week

MONDAY

1. Teach or review meaning of *root word, syllable, vowel, consonant, silent letter, derived.* Illustrate and ask for examples to make sure pupils understand.
2. Begin the lesson in the following way: "Most of you already know how to spell some of these words, for several of them you learned in the third grade. The others are easy. Let us look carefully at these words. What final letters do you see in all of them? Yes, it is *e.* (Bring out the fact that it is silent by having words pronounced.) This week we are going to learn how to spell twenty-four or more new words without studying them. To do this, we will use a spelling trick on these root words. Before we are ready to learn the trick, we must be sure we can spell the root words. Remember, they all end in a silent *e.*"
3. Study base words. Make sure pupils can spell them.

TUESDAY

1. "Yesterday we noticed some things that were alike in all these root words. What are they?" (Each ends in *e.* Final *e* is silent.)
2. "You often learn to use new words by adding new endings to root words. (Illustrate with *skate-s.*) Each ending changes the meaning and the spelling of the word. Let us see what happens when we add the ending *-ing* to *skate.* This is the trick." Write *skate* on the chalkboard. Erase *e;* add *-ing.* "What new word does this make? What happened to the final *e* when we added *-ing?*"
3. Write *skate* on the board and say, "Let us see what happens when we add the ending *-ed.*" (Erase *e* and add *-ed,* calling attention to the return of the *e* when we added *-ed.*) Illustrate on board the need for dropping final *e,* to avoid skat*eed.*
4. Repeat same procedures with *dance, close, share.*
5. Let pupils make new words with *vote, move, place* by adding *-ing* and *-ed.* Carry on with pupils at chalkboard and in seats. Bring out the fact that the trick works for all words in the list.
6. Let pupils try phrasing the generalization for all of these words. A simple wording is this: "Most words ending in silent *e* drop the *e* before adding *-ing* or *-ed.*" Write this on the chalkboard and leave for further reference.
7. Let several pupils come to the board to illustrate by stating the rule and spelling the word formed.
8. Address class somewhat as follows: "This week's spelling words should not be difficult. When you learn the base words, you can easily spell

the derived words by following the rule. How many words will we have in our final test?" (Three times the number of root words.)

Wednesday

1. Turn to the list of base words on the chalkboard. Have one child pronounce all the words. Review the application and statement of the generalization.
2. Pass out duplicated sheets and say: "Complete this chart by adding *-ing* and *-ed* to the words you learned Monday. The new words are called derived words. The first one is done for you. Perhaps you will need to read the generalization before you start to work."
3. Call attention to the increase in pleasure and the decrease in work that comes from spelling by transfer.
4. Check the work of poor spellers as they proceed.

Thursday

1. Pass out duplicated sheets again. Explain to children that you will pronounce the root words or their derivatives and they are to put them in the correct spaces. See that the children are following directions.
2. Be sure that the children think of the generalization as a way to increase their ability to spell without study.

Friday

1. Test on generalization: "dropping the final *e*." Have pupils prepare three columns on their papers.
2. Mastery test: Spell root word and both derivatives for each as pronounced.
3. To give practice in recognizing word variants by identifying the base word, the following lesson might be used: Write the following words on the chalkboard. Have pupils copy in a single line on paper. Then opposite these words write the word from which the derived word was formed. (Example: *glancing–glance*.)

faced	saving	smoking
sneezing	poked	graded
taking	prancing	stating
chased	loving	becoming
noticing	taken	blamed

4. Children may show that sometimes derived words can be made by adding other suffixes such as *-er* or *-est,* or *-able,* to *love, nice, move,* and so on. Continue to show how many new words they can spell by using this generalization.

5. In order to avoid the development of incorrect ideas concerning the addition of *-ed* to all base words when we wish to make students tell what happened yesterday rather than today, it is advisable to call attention to other ways of changing a root word. We say *lost* not *losed, took* not *taked, drove* not *drived,* etc. These changes should be noted, not as exceptions to our present generalization ("Most words ending in silent *e* drop the *e* before adding *-ing* or *-ed*"), but rather as unusual changes in root words in order to change the meaning of the word.
6. There are a few exceptions that may well be noted. We do not drop the silent *e* in such words as *see, free, agree,* when we add *-ing,* although we do so when we add *-ed* in order to avoid *freeed.*

Further Study—Reinforcement Activities

Activities of the following type should follow in order to reinforce the learning.

1. Extension of the use of generalization—for words ending in silent *e* to include *all* common suffixes.
   a. Use small groups of words ending in silent *e* to which common endings or suffixes, such as *-er, -able,* or *-est,* can be added. (Note that *-ed, -ing, -er, -est, -en,* and *-able* all begin with vowels.)

love	lov*ed*	lov*ing*	lov*er*	lov*able*
use	us*ed*	us*ing*	us*er*	us*able*

   Pupils should be encouraged to note other words ending in final *e* that they use often in their writing to add to spelling lists.

   b. Use groups of words to show that final *e* is *not dropped* when adding common endings such as *-s, -ly, -ness, -ful, -less,* and *-ment.* (Note that these suffixes begin with consonants.) Use only the forms of words that pupils understand readily and can use in meaningful sentences. The following words are appropriate.

voice	voice*s*	voice*less*	
care	care*s*	care*less*	care*ful*
love	love*s*	love*ly*	
bare	bare*ness*	bare*ly*	
brave	brave*s*	brave*ly*	
sore	sore*s*	sore*ness*	
base	base*s*	base*ment*	

   Ask pupils to suggest others that they use.

c. Formulate a statement of the generalization for suffixes beginning with a consonant.

2. Maintaining and developing skill in the use of the generalization as a spelling aid.
   a. Pupils should be exposed to many new situations with root words in which they are asked to discover spellings of derived words. They should say orally the derived form for a given use of a base word, try to spell it by substituting other letters or adding syllables, then write it. "Checking guesses" is an important step in this procedure. The play with words combines ear, eye, and thought spelling so that pupils have several types of associations to aid in recall. Games based on such procedures can be devised. Saving effort and time and having fun with words should be stressed.
   b. When selecting words for spelling lists in third, fourth, fifth, and sixth grades, make sure that representative root words or their derivatives are used each week. The new word list should be analyzed for the purpose of detecting words with which pupils have learned to deal through generalization, for example, include a *-y* word; one ending in silent *e;* others to which *-s, -ed,* or *-ing* can be added without change.
   c. Within the grade list, group together those root words ending in silent *e*. Pupils may add to these roots common endings beginning with a vowel or consonant through using the generalization. For example, nic*er,* nic*est,* nice*ly;* care*ful,* car*ing,* care*less,* car*ed;* clos*er,* clos*est,* close*ly,* close*ness*. A hectograph chart may be useful for illustrating base words and their derivations:

Base Word	Derived Words									
	-ing	*-ed*	*-er*	*-est*	*-s*	*-able*	*-ies*	*-ful*	*-ness*	*-ly*
nice			nicer	nicest					niceness	nicely
care	caring	cared			cares			careful		
close			closer	closest						closely
state	stating	stated			states					stately

   d. Other words in the list for fourth grade that can be used for the application of this rule should be noted.
   e. Note important exceptions, such as *tie, die, lie, tying, dying, lying.* (Final *e* preceded by *i* is dropped and the *i* changed to *y*.) Teach these individually because they are common words often used. See whether children can think of others.
   f. *Emphasize* the value of using generalizations by having pupils select

certain derivatives or root words formed from words in the list that they agree to add to the list *without study*. Provide opportunity each week for pupils to practice use of generalization with these unlearned words. A limited number of such words should be pronounced and spelled in the *final* test each week.

g. A correlate lesson with reading will extend the use and understanding of this generalization dealing with the spelling of one-syllable words. Change the emphasis of the reading aid: "In words of one syllable containing two vowels, one of which is a final *e*, the first vowel is usually given long sound." Apply it as an aid in spelling one-syllable words when they are pronounced. Take such a word as *safe:* ear spelling would stop at *saf,* but applying the reading rule for final *e* spelling would help the children to remember to add the silent *e*—*safe,* also *side, shake, cave,* and so on.

For Reference: Most Common Spelling Generalizations

In the middle and upper grades a number of generalizations may be *drawn inductively* from experience with words. Generalizations similar to the following are *not* to be memorized by your students.

1. Plurals of most nouns are formed by adding *-s* to the singular: *cat, cats,* and so on.
2. When the noun ends in *s, x, sh,* or *ch,* the plural generally is formed by adding *-es: buses, foxes, bushes, churches*.
3. A noun ending in *-y* preceded by a consonant forms its plural by changing the *y* to *i* and adding *-es: body, bodies*. Words ending in *-y* preceded by a vowel do not change *y* to *i: boy, boys*.
4. Plurals of a few nouns are made by changing their form: *woman, women; mouse, mice; ox, oxen*.
5. An apostrophe is used to show the omission of a letter or letters in a contraction: *aren't, we'll*.
6. An abbreviation is always followed by a period: *Mon., Feb*.
7. The possessive of a singular noun is formed by adding an apostrophe and *s: father, father's*.
8. The possessive of a plural noun ending in *s* is formed by adding an apostrophe: *girls, girls'*.
9. A word that ends in silent *e* usually keeps the *e* when a suffix beginning with a consonant is added: *nine, ninety; care, careful*.

10. A word that ends in silent *e* usually drops the *e* when a suffix beginning with a vowel is added: *breeze, breezing; side, siding; move, movable.*
11. A one-syllable word that ends in one consonant, preceded by a short vowel usually doubles the consonant before a suffix that begins with a vowel: *fat, fattest; big, bigger, biggest.*
12. A word of more than one syllable that ends in one consonant preceded by following one short vowel usually doubles the final consonant before a suffix beginning with a vowel, provided the accent is on the last syllable: *commit, committed, committing; forget, forgetting.*
13. A word ending in *y* and following a consonant usually changes the *y* to *i* before a suffix is added unless the suffix begins with *i: cry, crying.* A word that ends in a *y* and follows a vowel usually keeps the *y* when a suffix is added: *buy, buys, buying.*
14. The letter *q* is usually followed by *u* in a word.
15. The letter *i* is usually used before *e* except after *c,* or when sounded like an *a* as in *neighbor and weight.* Exceptions: *neither, either.*
16. Proper nouns and adjectives formed from proper nouns should always begin with capital letters: *America, American.*

Phonic generalizations that apply two-thirds of the time or more are as follows:

1. If the only vowel letter is at the end of a word, the letter usually stands for the long sound (*he, she, me*).
2. The *r* gives the preceding vowel a sound that is neither long nor short (*horn, more, worn*).
3. When a vowel is in the middle of a one-syllable word, the vowel is short (*rest, grass, glad*).
4. The first vowel is usually long and the second is usually silent in the digraphs *ai, ea,* and *oa* (*nail, bead, boat*).
5. Words having double *e* usually have the long *e* sound (*seem, tree, week*).
6. In *ay* the *y* is silent and gives *a* its long sound (*play, say, day*).
7. When the letter *i* is followed by the letters *gh,* the *i* usually stands for its long sound and the *gh* is silent (*high, fight, might*).
8. When *y* is the final letter in a word, it usually has a vowel sound (*dry, my, fly, happy*).
9. When there are two vowels, one of which is final *e,* the first vowel is usually long and the *e* is silent (*bone, home, write*).
10. When *c* and *h* are next to each other, they make only one sound, usually pronounced as in *church* (*catch, child, watch*).
11. When *c* is followed by *e* or *i,* the sound of *s* is likely to be heard (*cent, city, circle*).
12. When the letter *c* is followed by *o, a,* or *u,* the sound of *k* is likely to be heard (*camp, came, code, cute*).

13. When *ght* is seen in a word, *gh* is silent (*fight, thought, might*).
14. When a word begins with *kn,* the *k* is silent (*knew, knot, knife*).
15. When a word begins with *wr,* the *w* is silent (*write, wrist, wrong*).
16. When two of the same consonants are side by side, only one is heard (*happy, called, guess*).
17. When *ck* appears together in a word, only the *k* is pronounced (*black, brick, sick*).

Many old rules must be evaluated carefully not only as to their accuracy but also as to the child's ability to use the rule in practice. It was once taught that when two vowels are found together in a word, as in *each,* the second vowel is silent but helps the first to "say its own name" or have the long vowel sound. If you check the words in spellers, you will find numerous exceptions to this rule (*break, height, through*).

It is not true that one can spell correctly by "spelling the word the way it sounds." In fact, thiss staytment iz enuff to mayk won shreek. However, some phonetic generalizations should be mastered in the intermediate grades. The polysyllabic words in the Rinsland list contain twenty-three thousand syllables. Of these, fifty are key syllables spelled consistently the same way. The fifty are listed in Table 9–6.

Table 9–6

Key Syllables of Spelling Consistencies

Initial syllable	*Medial syllable*	*Final syllable*
*re*ceive	an*i*mals	go*ing*
*in*to	Jan*u*ary	start*ed*
*a*round	sev*er*al	mat*ter*
*de*cided	dec*o*rated	on*ly*
*con*tains	af*ter*noon	hous*es*
*ex*cept	el*e*phant	vaca*tion*
*un*til	pe*ri*od	ver*y*
*com*mon	reg*u*lar	pret*ty*
*dis*covered	In*di*an	re*al*
*en*joy	won*der*ful	ta*ble*
*an*other	car*ni*val	af*ter*
*o*pen	gym*na*sium	base*ment*
*e*ven	ar*ti*cle	sto*ry*
*pro*gram	ear*li*est	long*est*
*ac*cident	o*ver*alls	sev*en*

The syllable that occurs most frequently is *-ing,* which is found in 881 words. Thus a child who has learned to spell the *ing* syllable in one word will know it in 880 more. A test might be given asking that only the first syllable heard be spelled, as the words in the first column are pronounced, the second syllable as the next column is heard, and so on.

A test of the following type might be given to intermediate-grade children to discover those who already are able to apply some phonetic knowledge to spelling.

To the students: I am going to pronounce some words that do not have a meaning. You are to spell these words as they sound to you.

bab	lib	ving	clace	spug
dod	mif	med	cray	quam
fim	nam	yim	flest	shork
gog	paber	zet	gloil	
huf	rading	blash	plold	
jil	sim	chad	theet	

When the regular spelling test is given, check the ability to transfer phonetic knowledge in this manner:

Word in Spelling Lesson	***Pronounce This Word and Use in a Sentence***
stop	*stop*ping
*bl*ow	*bl*ack
shrill	d*rill*
nation	vaca*tion*

There are some learners who do not form generalizations with ease and thus need special help in spelling. As suggested by Fernald (1943), if you have a poor speller who is an able student capable of doing better work and who *wants* to spell correctly, use the following steps in learning to spell a word [from Grace M. Fernald, *Remedial Techniques in Basic School Subjects* (New York: McGraw-Hill, 1943)]:

Becoming a Better Speller—Practice Activities

Step 1. Look at the word very carefully and say it over to yourself. If you are not sure of the pronunciation, ask the teacher to say it for you, or look it up in the dictionary yourself.

Step 2. Find out whether the word can be written just the way you say it. Mark any part of the word that cannot be written the way you say it.

Step 3. Shut your eyes and see whether you can get a picture of the word in your mind. If you cannot get a clear picture of the word, you can remember the parts that are written the way you say them by pronouncing the word over to yourself or feeling your hand make the movements of writing the word. If you are learning the word *separate,* all you need to do is to say the word to yourself very carefully and then write what you say. If there are any parts of the word that you cannot write the way you say them, you will probably have to remember them by saying something you can write. Say the letters, if necessary, for these syllables of the word, but not for the rest of it.

Step 4. When you are sure of every part of the word, shut your book or cover the word and write it, saying each syllable to yourself as you write it.

Step 5. If you cannot write the word correctly after you have looked at it and said it, ask the teacher to write it for you in crayon on a strip of paper. Trace the word with your fingers. Say each part of the word as you trace it. Trace the word carefully as many times as you need to until you can write it correctly. Say each part of the word to yourself as you write it. After you have learned words in this way for a while, you will find you can learn them as easily as the other children do without tracing them. (Some teachers ask the child to trace the word in sand or on fine sandpaper in order to achieve a greater touch impression.)

Step 6. If the word is difficult, turn over the paper and write it again. Never copy the word directly from the book or from the one you have just written, but always write it from your memory of it.

Step 7. Later in the day, try writing the word from memory. If you are not sure of it, look it up again before you try to write it.

Step 8. Make your own dictionary. Make a little book with the letters of the alphabet fastened to the margin so that it is easy to see them. Write any new words you learn, or any words that seem especially difficult for you, in this book. Get this book out often and look these words over, writing again, from time to time, those that seem difficult. When you write these words by yourself, do just as you did when you learned them the first time. Say them, looking at them while you say them, and then write them without looking at the word in your book.

What Dictionary Skills Do Children Need?

Children need to appreciate the tremendous effort that has gone into the production of the dictionary they use. Let them discuss what it must be like to live in a country that does not have a dictionary for reference. There are many such countries.

The idea of a dictionary is not new. The Assyrians prepared a dictionary of their language nearly twenty-six thousand years ago. Other people, notably the

Greeks and Romans, prepared dictionaries, but these included only the rare and difficult words found in their language. With the coming of the Renaissance, during the fourteenth and fifteenth centuries, a great deal of attention turned to the early literature of the Greeks and Romans. This brought about the preparation of lexicons and glossaries containing the translated meanings of foreign words.

It was not until about the middle of the eighteenth century that any attempt was made to catalogue the common words in the English language. The most complete work was done by Samuel Johnson, who brought out his famous dictionary in 1755. Johnson spent nearly eight years in getting his book ready and did make an effort to include the most accepted spelling and definition for each word that he used.

The first American dictionary of 70,000 words came from the pen of Noah Webster in 1806. The Merriam brothers brought out their dictionary in 1864 with 114,000 words. The second edition (1934) contained over 600,000 entries. The last revision of the second edition contained a little more than 750,000 words, of which over 100,000 were new entries. In 1962 the radically new third edition appeared, causing considerable controversy among scholars because of its inclusion of many words and expressions previously considered to be substandard or slang. The third edition contains 100,000 "new" words, but the total number of entries is less than that of the second edition. The fact that many words were dropped explains the lack of increase in the number of entries.

The following twenty-five years brought a newcomer to the dictionary field, the dictionary designed for elementary classroom use. Until recently, each classroom, regardless of the age of the pupils, usually had a large *Webster's Unabridged Dictionary* on a stand or shelf for use by the entire class. A few of the more enterprising pupils might have had small dictionaries of their own, but these were rather drab, uninviting books with diminutive type, few illustrations, perplexing definitions, and a selection of words ill suited to the pupils' needs. The newer dictionaries have hundreds of illustrations of plants, animals, and objects, with their scale indicated by a numerical fraction. The point size of the type has been increased, the format has been made more attractive, the definitions have been clarified, and illustrative sentences have been added. All words are carefully appraised before inclusion in an effort to eliminate rare, obsolete, or obsolescent words. A good modern dictionary is one of the most valuable books a pupil can have. It is as essential as any textbook.

Picture dictionaries have been developed for use in the primary grades. The picture-word association does help some children as they look up words for spelling.

In all classroom work with the dictionary, the words to be alphabetized, located, or discussed should be carefully chosen to contribute some real purpose in the pupils' writing or reading. The children, as well as the teacher, should recognize the need or use.

Some fourth graders will be more ready to begin with more advanced work than will some sixth graders. The teacher should determine each child's ability and then work with small groups having common needs. She should vary and repeat practice at intervals until the children achieve mastery of a given skill. Besides a list of words, the dictionaries for schools frequently contain other information: the story of language, flags of nations, foreign words, biographies, geographical names, pronunciation, syllabication, and even instructions on how to use the dictionary.

Teaching Dictionary Skills

Steps in teaching the use of the dictionary are discussed here in an approximate sequence of difficulty, but teachers may vary the order of presentation and omit or add material to meet the needs of their classes.

Alphabetical Sequence. The first dictionary skill to be taught is the location of a word. Some children may not know the alphabet sequence because it has not been used frequently prior to this time.

Check to be sure that the children know the sequence of letters in the alphabet, and then practice until they can find words in the dictionary by their first letters. To avoid the necessity of having some children recite the alphabet before they can locate a word, discuss the relative placement of letters. Have the children discover that when the dictionary is opened in the center we find the words that start with *l* and *m*. If it is opened at the first quarter, we find the words with *d* and *e*, and at the third quarter we find the *r* and *s* words. Discuss how this will help them to locate a word more rapidly than just starting at *a* and going through the alphabet. Here are some suggested exercises for practice in alphabetical sequencing and locating words in the dictionary.

1. Ask the children to suggest a word. Have them open their dictionaries near the place the initial letter would be found without thumbing through the pages. Then have one pupil stand in front of a group and open the dictionary at random while the other members of the group guess the initial letter of words on that page.
2. Have a student locate in the dictionary a word from that week's spelling list. Each student would then take turns at saying a test word from the spelling list. The "leader" would say whether the test word appears before or after the chosen word in the dictionary. The objective is to guess the word in the least number of tries.
3. To teach pupils how to arrange words in alphabetical order, have them alphabetize brief lists in which no two words begin with the same letter. When this has been mastered, alphabetize by second letters (*sat* before *seven*); by third letters (*share* before *sheep*); and so on.
4. For additional practice, ask children who finish work early to arrange the books in the classroom library alphabetically according to authors, write an index page for a class book, make a card catalogue for a collection of pictures, or find in a telephone directory the telephone numbers of absentees.

Guide Words. The second skill to be learned is the use of guide words. After discussing the advantage of being able to find a word quickly, show the group that at the top of each page in the dictionary there are two words. The one at the left is the same as the first word on the page. The one at the right is the same as the last word on the page. These are called guide words. Here are some activities for working with guide words.

1. Give a page number to the class. Have the children turn to that page and read the guide words. Then write on the board a word that the group wishes to find. Above this, write the guide words on the page where you happen to open the dictionary. Have the group decide whether you must look nearer the front or nearer the back of the book. Continue the process in this manner until you find the right page and word. To check understanding, write a word on the board. Have the pupils find the word, keeping count of the number of times pages are turned to find the word. Thus, opening the dictionary to the correct initial letter would count as one turn. The next turn would seek to find the approximate vicinity of the word. Each successive approximation would count as a turn until the word was found. The children with the least number of turns might be recognized by hand raising or by having their names written on the board as "Word Finders" or some such heading. This type of work should be repeated many times under supervision and then independently.
2. Chalkboard drills may be used to develop skill in the use of guide words. Start by writing on the board a pair of guide words taken from the dictionary. Below them write a group of

four or more words, some of them selected from the dictionary page. Have the children select and check the words that belong on the page of the dictionary. For example:

kent	khaki	*kindred*
	kennel	
	kine	
	kidnap	

This kind of work should be repeated on successive days. At first it should be done under teacher guidance at the board. Later the children may do it independently at their own desks. Individual children may create exercises of this nature for the class to do.

3. The following game is helpful as a review: Divide the group into two teams. Write a word on the board. Ask children to find the word and hold up their hands when they have found it. The first child to find the word scores one point for his or her team. The first team to finish scores one point. (Check by page number.) The game should be limited by using a certain number of words (ten) or by playing for a certain number of minutes.
4. Another exercise is built on word meanings. The teacher prepares a list of words that the children will need to know, locates each word in the dictionary, and notes the guide words for each word. When the game begins, the teacher writes a pair of guide words on the board and gives a brief definition of the word that the group is to find. The pupils find the page and scan it for the right word. For example:

   Guide words: *springboard* and *spurt*
   Definition: a short run at full speed
   Answer: *sprint*

Definitions. The third major area of dictionary skills relates to definitions. Explain to students that whenever a word is found in their reading that cannot be defined from context, they should use the dictionary. Many words have only vague meanings. Use the dictionary for more exact meanings. Explain the difference in meaning between the following pairs of words: *climate* and *weather; less* and *fewer; hotel* and *restaurant.*

Some words get so overworked that we call them "tired" words. The dictionary can suggest other words to use for words such as *said* or *big.*

Considerable thought is required in selecting the right meaning from several given in the dictionary. For a few children it will be a discovery that words have more than one meaning. Introduce this work with the word *run.* Have the group think of several meanings, writing each new meaning on the board before looking it up in the dictionary. Underneath the definitions suggested by the children, write those definitions from the dictionary that were not mentioned. Then ask the children, either as a class or independently, to write a sentence incorporating *run* to illustrate each definition. Have the pupils select another common word, such as *safe, strike, husband,* or *signal,* and discover how many different meanings for it they can find and illustrate.

Interesting lessons can be planned to show how the illustrations in the dictionary clarify meaning. The arithmetic in the ratio should be studied so that the phrase *one-sixth actual size* has meaning. An interesting discussion can be planned around the topic "Which words can be illustrated and which cannot?"

An understanding of prefixes and suffixes is another aid to word meaning. When the children understand that *trans-* means "across" or "over" in *transportation, transfer, translate,* and *transcontinental,* they have a meaning clue to other words with this prefix. They can discover that the dictionary gives the meanings of many prefixes.

A discovery or inductive lesson is easy using the dictionary. Have the students read a series of definitions of words starting with another prefix, *sub-,* then decide what meaning the prefix gives to the words.

One of the basic clues to meaning is the ability to identify the root word. Start by supplying a root word and have pupils list other members of the same family: *kind* (*kindly, kindness, unkind, kindliness*). Discuss the fact that these words are similar in meaning as well as in appearance. Children need help in learning the way the dictionary deals with word families. The root word is listed at the margin in heavy type; other members of the family are not listed marginally but are explained under the root word. In spelling and reading, root words should be identified and sometimes checked with the dictionary. This is important when the word is to be divided into syllables. Even though we divide the word as we pronounce it, the basic root is seldom divided in writing. Some children will enjoy knowing about a few common Greek and Latin roots that will help them guess word meanings. These were used by a fifth-grade class:

Latin		*Greek*	
annus (year)	annual perennial anniversary	*aster* (star)	aster astronomy asterisk
aqua (water)	aqueduct aquaplane aquarium	*cycle* (ring or circus)	bicycle motorcycle cyclone
audio (listen or hear)	auditorium audible audition	*graphein* (to write)	autograph telegraph graph
avis (bird)	aviary aviation aviator	*logos* (word)	catalogue dialogue log
ducere (to lead)	conduct educate aqueduct	*metron* (measure)	meter thermometer speedometer
via (way)	viaduct trivial deviate	*phone* (sound)	phonics telephone phonograph

The interest in looking up words and learning definitions should also be developed by selecting sentences from the children's reading material, for example, "The initial expense was about thirty dollars." Have the children find *initial* in the dictionary. Discuss the meanings given, and choose the one most applicable.

A list of "difficult" words from the children's readings should be compiled by the teacher and/or pupils and tested at the end of each week in one of the following ways:

1. Give the words and ask the children to supply the definitions.
2. Give the words and ask the children to use them appropriately in sentences.
3. Supply both words and definitions in scrambled

order and have the children match them appropriately.

4. Supply the words in scrambled order along with the sentences from the readings that incorporated the words, leaving blanks where the words are to be filled in.

Have the children keep a record of their own "problem words," words missed on the preceding exercises. These should be presented to the teacher at designated intervals (for example, each month). The teacher can then compile individualized word lists to strengthen vocabulary skills. Such words may also be used in "vocabulary bees" or as team exercises.

The most frequent use of a dictionary is to locate the correct spelling of a word. This is not easy when it is a word that the child cannot spell at all. Take as an example a word that a child has asked you to spell for him, such as *usable*. The group will be sure of the first two letters. Have the children look up the word as far as they are sure and then glance down the page until they find the word. Even after looking up a word it is possible to make a mistake. Before the spelling is copied from the dictionary, the definition must be read in order to prevent such errors as the use of *complement* for *compliment, maze* for *maize, sent* for *scent,* or *accept* for *except*.

Sometimes a word is located through the trial-and-error method. Words with difficult beginnings, such as *cistern,* after they have not been located under *s,* must be sought under other letters having the same sound. It takes real detective work to track down some words, such as *kneel*.

Other spelling help in the dictionary concerns abbreviations, capital letters, and plural forms, but children must be shown how to locate each of these items.

PRONUNCIATION. Another area of dictionary skills concerns pronunciation.

Syllabication. The first step in pronunciation involves dividing words into syllables. These rules are usually taught in third-grade reading. This is a good time for children to discover that the dictionary can act as a check on their syllabication. A few listening lessons in which children tell how many syllables they hear when words are pronounced will reveal that the number of vowels we hear in a word tells us how many syllables there are in it.

Accent Marks. While dividing words into syllables, point out to the students that we pronounce some syllables with more force or accent than others. Then show how the dictionary indicates this stress with the accent mark. Children will be interested in words in which a change in accent may indicate a change in meaning, as in "Use the movie machine to *pro ject'* the picture" or "He found that building the dam was a difficult *proj' ect*."

Some dictionaries indicate a secondary as well as a primary accent, as in *mul' ti pli ca^ tion*. To check understanding of accent, give the children sentences containing blanks and a choice of the same word already syllabicated and accented in two different ways. The pupils decide which form to use in the blank and then write a sentence of their own using the other form. For example: "The chairman will (*pre' sent* or *pre sent'*) the speaker."

Diacritical Marks. Another skill involves the use of diacritical marks as an aid to pronunciation. The pronunciation key at the bottom of each page (or on the endpapers of the book) is a basic reference. Although this key may differ from dictionary to dictionary, its use remains the same. If the children can read the key words, there is no great need to be able to identify all the markings. The sound association can be made between the key pronunciation word and the one in the dictionary.

Instruction needs to be given involving marking long and short vowels; students will also discover that vowels have other sounds as well as the long and short sounds. Illustrate how these are indicated in the key words on each page in the dictionary.

Have available such assignments as the following as spare-time work for students:

Underline the word or words that have the *same* vowel sound as the word on the left.

ă as in *at*	*rattle, sale, athlete, clasp, gas*
ā as in *age*	*pale, name, display, radio, pat*
â as in *care*	*square, maple, fair, compare, dare*
ä as in *art*	*harvest, tame, star, depart, arm*
á as in *ask*	*grass, vast, grant, brave*

Teach the children to use the phonetic respelling given in the dictionary as an aid to pronunciation. Have the group make a list of words in which:

c sounds like *s* (*cent*)
c sounds like *k* (*act*)
c, x, or *s* sounds like *sh* (*ocean, anxious, sugar*)
l, w, k, or *b* is silent (*calf, wrong, know, comb*)

Teach the children that for some words there is more than one pronunciation and that the preferred one is given first.

Appendix B has been designed to provide additional activities for teaching children how to use the dictionary effectively.

Games provide extra motivation for some of the practice that children need to master spelling. If you have access to computers, word processors, typewriters, or other electronic mechanical spelling machines, they can all be employed to motivate children to spell. (Photo by Linda Lungren)

How May Spelling Games Be Used for Motivation?

Games provide extra motivation for some of the drill that children need to master spelling. Although it is unlikely that spelling will ever have the fascination of baseball for some children or golf for some adults, interest in words and their spelling can be heightened by using a spelling game.

Games call for considerable planning to be successful. In introducing the game, first give the name, then ask some children to "walk through" each step as you describe it. After that, have a trial run to be certain that everyone understands. Establish a few rules during the practice period. Choosing partners or teams can create considerable social tension. This can be avoided by using row against row or counting and having "odds" versus "evens."

The timing of a game is important. Just before recess is usually a good time, because it avoids the necessity of a difficult transition from an exciting game to an uninspiring game in a history book. Do not make a game last very long unless it is a special privilege. Ten to fifteen minutes should be the maximum. To be of value the game should provide drill on needed words or skills.

College students using these games will find this list of words that were missed by the finalists in the National Spelling Bee a challenge.

Famous Last Words

The following list consists of thirty of the words on which national championships have been won or lost since the National Spelling Bee began in 1925. Can you spell them?

abbacy	interning	abrogate
knack	acquiesced	luxuriance
albumen	oligarchy	asceticism
onerous	brethren	plebeian
canonical	promiscuous	pronunciation
chrysanthemum	deteriorating	propitiatory
dulcimer	psychiatry	flaccid
sacrilegious	foulard	sanitarium
fracas	semaphore	gladiolus
stupefied	intelligible	therapy

A Fateful Fifty

The fate of fifty contestants in National Spelling Bee championship finals in recent years was determined by the following fifty words. On each of them a boy or girl finalist missed, and a championship chance was lost. See whether you know them.

aeriferous	febrile	agglomeration
fission	aggression	foment
aplomb	glacial	archetype
guttural	assonance	herbaceous
bier	homiletic	catalyst
imitator	consensus	imposter
coruscation	indissoluble	cuisine
insouciant	disputatious	jocose
effeminate	manumit	efflorescence
mattock	elision	medallion
emendation	meretricious	ennoble
minatory	exacerbate	obloquy
pallor	saponaceous	peripatetic
scintillate	peroration	shellacked
pomegranate	urbane	requiem
quandary	vilify	wainscot
rue	yawl	

Additional activities for extending skills in spelling are suggested in Appendix B.

Challenging Every Child to Spell

In every intermediate classroom there are children who do not respond to formal spelling instruction or who are far beyond the spelling level of the class. The suggestions that follow may be used in light of the teacher's knowledge of the children's needs.

These may be assigned by the teacher or self-assigned by the student as is appropriate to the situation. The child who scores 100 percent in the week's assignment in spelling instruction or who is far beyond the class might profit by doing one of these activities. The child who never succeeds with the words in a spelling assignment may find motivation for proper spelling through an interesting writing experience. Correct spelling is a refinement of writing, and a writing approach to spelling makes sense to many students.

Write a news report of an event in the school or classroom.

Find other meanings for words in the spelling list and write a sentence illustrating the meaning.

Write a paragraph about a secret wish, or a wish you made but do not really want, such as being a baby again or a dog.

Write a story of the first Thanksgiving (or any holiday) you remember.

How did people first learn to use fire, the wheel, or glass? Make up a story answer or find the material in a reference book.

Take an old story or fable and make it modern, such as "Christmas (or Hannukah) with the Three Bears."

What was the bravest thing your father or mother ever did?

Make up a story of a dog hero (or any pet).

Write a description of a bird or flower.

Make a list of first-aid items that should be in every automobile.

Look up in an encyclopedia or almanac and report

how long these animals usually live: dog, horse, bear, elephant.

Write a description of someone in the room; let the class guess who it is.

Try to write twenty compound words.

How many words can you list that end with *-le* (or *-age*, or any other common ending)?

Report on a radio or TV program that you think your class would enjoy.

Make up a Paul Bunyan story.

Make a list of words that have *tele-* in them (or any other base Latin or Greek form).

Cut out a newspaper story and do one of the following: Underline each adjective (noun, adverb, and so on). Underline each compound word. Underline the topic sentence. Make an outline of the story.

Correct the English used in a comic strip or book.

Discover different ways in which the same meaning is expressed in different parts of the English-speaking world; for example, in England: *lift* for *elevator; cinema* for *movie; petrol* for *gasoline; sweets* for *dessert* or *candy;* in Canada: *spool of cotton* for *spool of thread; tap* for *faucet;* in Australia: *sundowner* for *hobo.*

Report on the origin of some of the words we use.

Collect and discuss words that have come to us from other peoples. For example:

African languages	zebra, chimpanzee
American Indian languages	hominy, persimmon, squaw
Arabian	admiral, alfalfa, magazine
Australian	kangaroo, boomerang
Chinese	silk, pongee, tea, ketchup
Dutch	skipper, sleigh, waffle, boss
French	cafe, bouquet, aileron, dinner
German	hamburger, waltz, kindergarten
Greek	theater, botany
Hebrew	amen, hemp, shekel
Hindu	calico, jungle, chintz, dungaree
Hungarian	goulash, tokay
Irish	brogue, colleen, bog
Malay-Polynesian	gingham, bantam, tattoo
Persian	scarlet, caravan, lilac, seersucker
Portuguese	veranda, marmalade, yam
Scandinavian languages	ski, squall, smelt, key
Scots	clan, reel (dance)
Slavonic	sable, polka, robot
Spanish	barbecue, bronco
Turkish	tulip, coffee, fez
Welsh	flannel, crag

Collect and discuss words that have been derived from place names. For example:

italics	Italy
cashmere	Cashmere (Kashmir, India)
morocco (leather)	Morocco
calico	Calcutta
milliner	Milan

Discuss new words invented to meet new needs: for example, *airplane* (1870); *vitamin* (1930); *jeep, radar, microcomputer.* Explore the "new words" section of the dictionary.

Find out how the days of the week and the months of the year got their names.

Discuss and list the origin and meaning of the names of members of the class. (Example: John = Hebrew *Yohanan,* "God Is Gracious.") Appendix B contains many references to books of word origins. These may be of help to you in preparing such activities.

Electronic Variety

If you have access to computers, word processors, typewriters, or other electronic mechanical spelling machines, they can all be employed to motivate children to spell. Nothing will take the place of teacher-directed, -assisted, and -evaluated instruction (Nolen, 1980), but certainly creative variations on any theme make an old topic fresh for many students. (For a detailed discussion of computers and the language arts program see Chapter 14.) The simple enjoyment of seeing or hearing words appear from pressing buttons motivates many students to progress after they may have otherwise become bored or tired.

Tape recorders have long been used successfully in reading instruction and may be employed in myriad ways to facilitate spelling. Teacher-made tapes to accompany worksheets or for individual self-correction are excellent means of reaching students who are outside the skill range (either above or below) of the other children.

One innovative technique developed by Martin (1983) involves spelling to music! The process requires two tape recorders and two tapes—one blank and one with prerecorded Baroque or Classical music (for example, Handel's *Water Music*). After pronouncing and defining the words with the child, she or he plays the music as loud as or louder than her/his voice, then proceeds to spell, pronounce, and define the words on the list, two at a time, onto the blank tape. After every two words the tapes are shut off, and the two words are reviewed and corrected if necessary. The child then continues recording the words, two by two, to the music until all the words on the list are recorded. The completed tape is taken home and listened to before going to sleep and first thing in the morning every day until test day. Once the child understands the process, the entire recording session only requires ten to fifteen minutes. Results from this approach include better spelling, certainly, as well as more fluent articulation of thoughts, improved sequential memories, better speaking voices, and a feeling of high self-esteem.

Spelling need not be a dreary, nose-in-the-workbook period of drudgery. Students need to be aware of the importance of and need for good spelling. It should be an integral part of their language arts program and a daily part of their lives so that good spelling becomes a good habit they will not break.

Summary

Strategies for integrating systematic spelling instruction into the daily curriculum were presented. Appropriate words to be taught, generalizations allowing for spelling ease, causes of spelling difficulties, scales for measuring spelling growth, and the role of the dictionary in the spelling curriculum were all highlighted for discussion. Also included in this chapter were many spelling games appropriate for the daily curriculum.

Suggested Classroom Projects and Questions for Discussion

Projects

1. Experience for yourself what your students go through when approaching spelling problems. Try this with your colleagues and friends.

The following words are considered spelling demons. Decide whether the spelling is correct or not. If a word is correct, mark a check by it; if it is incorrect, rewrite it correctly.

1. achieve
2. alright
3. analize
4. anoint
5. battalion
6. cooly
7. definately
8. dependant
9. descendant
10. disappate
11. dissapoint
12. drunkeness
13. ecstacy
14. embarrassed
15. indispensable
16. inimitible
17. inoculate
18. irresistable
19. irridescent
20. liquefy
21. neice
22. occassional
23. occurence
24. perseverance
25. proceed
26. putrify
27. reccomend
28. recieve
29. sacreligious
30. seize
31 seperate
32. supercede
33. superintendant
34. tyranny
35. ukelele
36. vilify
37. wierd

Now compare your responses with the answer key. In the word list were there common misspellings? What are the patterns of letters that persistently cause confusion? What explanation might be given for the erroneous spelling? How did those who spelled each word correctly remember the standard sequence of letters? Did anyone follow a rule to spell correctly? How may individual errors be analyzed in a manner that will avoid repetition of the error?

Key: 1. OK 2. all right 3. analyze 4. OK 5. OK 6. OK 7. definitely 8. dependent 9. OK 10. dissipate 11. disappoint 12. drunkenness 13. ecstasy 14. OK 15. OK 16. inimitable 17. OK 18. irresistible 19. iridescent 20. OK 21. niece 22. occasional 23. occurrence 24. OK 25. OK 26. putrefy 27. recommend 28. receive 29. sacrilegious 30. OK 31. separate 32. supersede 33. superintendent 34. OK 35. ukulele 36. OK 37. weird

2. Are there words in your listening or reading vocabulary that are not in your speaking and writing vocabulary? Why? Which vocabulary is largest? Why? Make a list of some of these words for yourself. Do the same for your students (or have them do so). Make a bulletin board display to illustrate the differences.
3. Compare the glossary in an intermediate science or social studies text with a dictionary. What changes have been made in language, syntax, and so on?
4. Make a tabulation of errors from one final test of a class. Detect common needs suggested by the errors.
5. Recall an association you have used to help remember the spelling of a word. These are called mnemonic devices. Sometimes the more absurd they are, the easier they are remembered. For example, one could say *dessert* has *ss,* but *desert* has only one *s,* because one would rather have more of it. Or remember the stationery you write on has *er,* just like *letter.* Make a collection of these devices used in your class.
6. Prepare a file or collection of examples of "invented" or precommunicative, semiphonetic, phonetic, and transitional spelling. You may wish to cooperate with teachers in other grade levels to exchange samples. Use the collection to prepare a presentation for parents' organizations to encourage them to become more actively aware of the spelling needs of their children.
7. One of the simplest spelling games is Endless Chain. A third grader might start with three-letter words. The first child spells *cat.* The next child must then start with a three-letter word starting with the last letter of the previous word, which in this case is *t,* so he might spell *ten.* The next child's word must then start with *n,* such as *not.* When a child cannot think of a word or misspells the one selected, the chain is broken. Sometimes each child writes the words being spelled orally in order to get a visual image. A college class might start with five-letter words. For variety the words may be adjectives (any number of letters) or names of places (thus involving capital letters). Experiment with this game and see how many words you can make into a chain in two minutes.
8. Think of the number of words you spell correctly that were never in a spelling lesson. How did you learn to spell them?
9. The following examples of phonetic irregularities in the way we spell might be used to help parents understand the spelling problem. What other uses might be made of such information?
   a. What common word could you get by pronouncing the letters *ssworps?* (*Sure. Ss* as in *mission, wo* as in *two,* and *rps* as in *corps.*)
   b. *What common word could you get by pronouncing the letters psolocchouse?* (*Circus. Ps* as in *psychology, olo* as in *colonel, cch* as in *Bacchus, ou* as in *famous,* and *sc* as in *science.*
   c. *Sugar* is the only English word beginning with *su* sounded as *shoo.* ("Are you sure?")
   d. What common word could you get by pronouncing the letters *ghoti?* (*Fish. Gh* as in *rough, o* as in *women,* and *ti* as in *fiction.*)
   e. What word has five consecutive vowels? (*Queueing.*)
   f. What word has five *e*'s and no other vowels? (*Effervescence.*)
   g. Pronounce *Pothzwabyuckeling.* (There's nothing to pronounce! Every letter is silent: the *p* as in *pneumonia, o* as in *leopard, t* as in *ballet, h* as in *catarrh, z* as in *rendezvous, w* as in *wrong, a* as in *dead, b* as in *dumb, y* as in *today, u* as in *four, c* as in *czar, k* as in *knock, e* as in *blue, l* as in *would, i* as in *cruise, n* as in *condemned,* and *g* as in *gnu.*)
10. Make a study of the way the orthography of various words has evolved over the years.

Questions

1. Why do children have difficulty understanding the relationship between spelling and communication?
2. Why are students unmotivated by continuous failure?
3. Why is a word easy for one student and difficult for another in the same grade?
4. Should some students become spelling tutors to help the less able? What would such students learn from the experience?
5. Why is the term *remedial* inappropriate with respect to teaching a developmental skill?
6. What are some words that would be used in the vocabulary of children in your locality that are not frequently used nationally?
7. Why do classroom teachers frequently favor a workbook in spelling? What advantages and what disadvantages characterize such a program?
8. Why is it better to use one or two instructional games at a single grade level?
9. How can a teacher give recognition to the successful students without discouraging those less competent?
10. For some children, understanding a generalization such as "Adding *s* makes more than one" or "Each syllable has a vowel" is quite difficult. How would you teach one of these generalizations?

Chapter 10

Handwriting Instruction

(Photo by Linda Lungren)

OBJECTIVES

At the end of this chapter, the student should be able to:

1. understand the differences between manuscript and cursive writing.
2. understand how to track and evaluate manuscript writing for all children.
3. understand how to track and evaluate cursive writing for all children.

While at school last week I received the following handwritten note.

[illegible]

Mike

Could you read my note? As you can see, the handwriting was so poor that the message was barely discernible. I did recognize the name of the sender and attempted to call his home to receive further communication. No answer! Toward the end of the day, the sender and I were at the same meeting. When he saw me, he asked whether I had received his tennis invitation. Without the verbal expansion of his written communication, I would have missed a very good match. In case you are wondering, the note said:

Diane,

If you're free today at 4:00, I'd love to get together for a match. It looks like a great day for tennis. Give me a call if you're available.

Mike

Why write legibly? *To communicate.*

What Is the Best Way to Teach Elementary Age Children to Write?

Since communication is the goal of handwriting, most teachers plan instruction toward conformity to a recognized standard. In addition, it is the responsibility of the classroom teacher to encourage students to develop a positive attitude toward handwriting and to nurture enthusiasm about skill attainment. Teachers influence the writing of students by example, by planned lessons, and by establishment and maintenance of standards.

As one visits classrooms, it appears that a variety of techniques is very successfully employed. Some are supported by complex developmental theories (Hagin, 1983; D'Angelo, 1982; Peck et al., 1980; Addy and Wylie, 1973; Anderson, 1965). Others are the result of informal classroom experimentation (Hanover, 1983; Tompkins, 1980). Although discussion with teachers suggests a conviction to their program as the one that will produce the highest quality of writing, it is not apparent from existing research that any single foolproof method consistently produces superior results.

Therefore, after evaluating available commercial programs you will need to employ the approach to teaching handwriting that is most compatible with your other classroom programs.

The History of Handwriting Instruction

Much that we teach about handwriting is the result of tradition. In the past, "copperplate" writing (examples engraved on copper plate for printing by the early masters) was extensively used. Business schools taught Spencerian script, which was a beautiful, ornate writing, closely related to that devised by the Dutch teachers. Systems based on "arm movement" became popular in schools. These consisted of a carefully organized series of exercises designed to train the individual to write rhythmically. The writing arm rested on the forearm muscle, and finger movement was avoided. One of the reasons for the wide acceptance of this method was that much of the fatigue associated with long periods of writing was avoided. The exercises consisted of a series of continuous ovals and "push-pulls" or were designed to give practice in writing individual letters and their parts. Students were encouraged to complete sets of exercises to high enough quality to receive certificates of merit and pins awarded by the publishers.

Some have criticized exercises of this type as being so unrelated to actual writing as to be isolated skills: one may learn how to make ovals but not necessarily how to write. A discouraged teacher is likely to accept such criticism and justify the neglect of writing practice. On the other hand, there is a great deal of evidence that writing drills did produce excellent and even beautiful handwriting or calligraphy. Many students were actually self-taught by the manuals because their teachers were not masters of the system. Although all students did not become calligraphers, neither did all become excellent readers, mathematicians, musicians, or artists. Nearly all systems used today involve a modification of those used in the past.

The reform movement in penmanship instruction that was started in England by William Morris (1834–96) is still growing. This is an effort to return to the forms used at the time of the Renaissance. In the schools of England one finds systems based on this influence. That of Marion Richardson is an extension of the use of "print-script" writing in the primary grades. It is called Italic writing. This is a form of print first used by Aldo Manuzio in Italy during the Renaissance; Virgil was the first author printed in this type (1501). The current revival is based on the desire to find a script that is both beautiful and legible but that still expresses individuality. No claim is made concerning speed. Italic writing uses a flat pen held at a forty-five degree angle, which gives a thick descending line and thin ascending line. The oval, rather than the circle, is its basic movement. Many of the letters appear connected and may be so if the writer wishes.

Experiments with the typewriter in the elementary school date back to at least 1927. All such studies have indicated that children enjoy the experience and achieve some skill in the use of the machines. Kindergarten teachers report that as a prewriting experience it is an effective way to teach letter names and aspects of visual discrimination. Students in the upper elementary grades profit from summer schools that have courses in typing or word processing. The typewriter

Sing a song of sixpence,
Pocket full of rye;
Four & twenty blackbirds
Baked in a pie.
When the pie was opened
The birds began to sing
Wasn't it a dainty dish
To set before a King.?

Figure 10–1. An exercise in modern italic script as used in many European schools.

and the computer appear to provide a bridge between their advanced ideas and the lack of physical maturity for a large amount of handwriting.

It would be impractical to assume that typewriting skill would replace the need for learning to write either print script or cursive writing. The ability to write a neat, legible hand with reasonable speed and without strain is essential in the modern curriculum.

Modern trends in handwriting instruction reflect current understanding of factors in child growth; however, none can be said to be universally acceptable or based on such absolute information that future change is impossible. In comparison with the past, these changes may be observed:

1. Cursive writing is losing its place as a recognized part of the early primary program. The simpler print script writing is preferred (Groff, 1975). Print script is being accepted as desirable writing in all grades.

2. Children no longer trace letter forms except under special circumstances.
3. Children who show a strong preference for writing with the left hand are no longer required to learn to write with the right hand.
4. The use of the rhythmic aids is discouraged. The size and shape of the various letters are so different that an absolute conformity to set rhythm is unnatural.
5. Accessory drills that presumably contribute rhythm and freedom in muscular movement are minimized. Ovals and related exercises are used much less than in the past.
6. There is less emphasis on speed in writing.
7. Fountain, ballpoint, and felt pens are used in classroom practice.
8. Such incentives as penmanship certificates and pins are not widely used, although still available.

What Is the Difference Between Script and Cursive Writing?

Print script writing (also called manuscript writing) started in England. In 1919 Miss S. A. Golds of St. George the Martyr School, London, published a copybook called *A Guide to the Teaching of Manuscript Writing.*

In 1922 a course taught by Marjorie Wise of England at Columbia University introduced print script to the American schools. Since that time the use of this simple form of lettering has been accepted in nearly all of the United States.

The term *cursive* means "running" or "connected"; the terms *print script* and *manuscript* refer to writing in which each letter is separately formed, as in printer's type. The major differences are contrasted in Table 10–1.

The use of print script in the primary grades has been accepted for the following reasons:

1. Primary school children learn only one alphabet for reading and writing.
2. With its three basic strokes—circles, arcs, and straight lines—print script is easier for the young child to learn.
3. Print script is more legible than cursive and with practice may be written rapidly.
4. Children who master print script do a great deal more writing of a creative nature than those who must master the cursive form.

Table 10–1
Differences Between Print Script and Cursive Writing

Print Script	*Cursive*
Letters are made separately.	Letters are joined.
Pencil is lifted at the end of each letter or stroke.	Pencil is lifted at the end of each word.
Letters are made with circles, parts of circles, and straight lines.	Letters are made with overstrokes, understrokes, connected strokes, and ovals.
Letters are spaced to form words. Space between letters is controlled by the shape of the letter. The *i* and the *j* are dotted, and the *t* is crossed immediately after the vertical stroke is made.	Spacing between letters is controlled by the slant and manner of making connective strokes. The letters *i* and *j* are dotted and the *t* is crossed after the completion of the word.
Letters closely resemble print and are therefore legible and easy to read.	Letters are unlike those on the printed page.
Small letters and capitals are different except for *c, o, s, p, v, w, x,* and *z.*	Small letters and capitals are different.

How Much Time Should Be Allocated for Handwriting Instruction?

The Association of Supervision of Curriculum Development (Cawelti and Adkison, 1985) analyzed the amount of time that the average fourth-grade teacher devotes to language arts instruction and found that an average of five hours or less per week was so spent. Within this allocation of time, how many minutes can realistically be used for instruction in handwriting? Although there is no definitive answer, most teachers agree that in the early grades (K–4) formal handwriting instruction should be given each day in ten- to fifteen-minute sessions. Once students have reached grades five and six, two or three fifteen-minute sessions per week should be sufficient. In grades seven to twelve all teachers should insist on legibility as a must for all written assignments.

What Variables in Handwriting Instruction Have an Impact on Primary and Intermediate Students?

Because we are concerned with visual and muscular development and physical maturity in handwriting, there are some factors in the growth patterns of children that should be considered in our teaching.

Primary

The primary school student frequently lacks the muscular coordination needed for writing. The strength that is developed is in the large muscles and nerve centers rather than in the small muscles of the fingers. We accept the dominant handedness of little children, which is usually observable at the age of three but may not be fully developed until the age of eight. Because farsightedness is normal in young children, we must avoid long periods requiring close work with small details, remembering that patterns of progress differ widely during the primary grades.

Instructional implications based on these factors would include the following practices. The little child is encouraged to work with clay, finger paint, or other materials that require finger coordination. Large muscles are used by forming chalkboard letters about three inches high. When children are practicing writing at their desks, either lined or unlined paper may be used. Some evidence suggests that the kind of paper used at the primary level has no effect on the later quality of handwriting (Halpin, 1976). Standard writing equipment is recommended, but children should be allowed to use the instrument with which they are most comfortable. Lamme (1983) found that children wrote equally well using primary pencils, mechanical pencils, pens, and felt-tip pens.

Speed should never be emphasized. Copy work, which forces constant refocusing of the eye, should be avoided. This especially applies to work on the board that the child copies on paper. No effort should be made to keep the entire class together for instruction. Each child should set his or her own progress pattern, and the aptitudes or skills of boys and girls should not be compared. Early manuscript efforts are usually characterized by great deliberateness.

Intermediate

During the intermediate grades, the students gain greater control over both large-muscle activities and eye-hand coordination involving the small muscles. These are the years that influence lifetime habits with regard to musical instruments, skill with tools, and handwriting. The longer attention span of these children results in a willingness to accept drill and repetition if they understand the final goal. As students approach adolescence, the rapid growth of their hands may affect their handwriting. At this stage handwriting can be improved by exercises involving ovals and push-pulls. Older children sometimes express their egos through highly individualized writing, such as ringing the *i's*, or adding hearts instead of dotting them, making triangles or loops below the lines, or crossing the *t's* in unconventional ways. Insistence on standard practices is left to your discretion and the rules of the school in which you are teaching.

As students mature, their handwriting becomes smaller. Depending on school policy, a standardized writing scale may be introduced in the fourth grade. Adherence to the scale should not be mandatory; it should be viewed as a guideline by which students may judge their own handwriting and correct discernible defects. At this time, speed is gradually encouraged and writers' clubs that provide rewards for good penmanship may be established. The transition from print script to cursive writing should be deferred until a later time for those students who experience difficulties. However, such students should still receive instruction in *reading* cursive writing.

Are There Experiences That Prepare the Child for Writing?

Three kinds of experiences lead to writing readiness:

Manipulative Experiences. The first group of experiences can be described as manipulative. These are designed to strengthen muscles needed for writing and to gain control over tools used in writing. Children develop the small muscles of the hands through playing with toys, dialing the telephone, setting the table, changing a doll's clothes, putting puzzles together, cutting with scissors, finger painting, and clay modeling. They draw or scribble with chalk at the chalkboard or with crayons on large sheets of paper. It is well to remember that scribbling is writing and it is the child's first means of identifying himself with the writing process until the student is ready to be taught the letter forms. In the eighteenth and early nineteenth centuries Johann Pestalozzi (1746–1827) asked children to draw geometric forms on slates as he told stories. These were actually exercises in writing readiness.

Oral Expression. The second group of experiences is designed to increase the child's ability in the use of language. It is futile for children to learn to write before they can express their ideas orally. Beginners must have many experiences that stimulate their desire for self-expression. As they listen to stories and poems, look at pictures, dictate stories and letters, or make up songs, they should be encouraged to comment freely. As children see their ideas written by the teacher in a letter or an invitation, writing becomes a magic tool for extending speech. With this recognition comes not only an understanding of the usefulness of writing but also a strong personal desire to perform the writing task.

Practice in Writing Movements. The third group consists of experiences designed to give practice to the basic movements of writing itself. These are usually started at the chalkboard, where only large muscles are involved. The purpose is to understand certain letter forms and the way they are created. Circles are first drawn by the children. They are given directions as to the starting place. Then they are asked to look at the number 2 on the clock. When a circle is made it is best to start where the 2 would be if you were making a clock. Children draw clocks, doughnuts, balls, soap bubbles, and Halloween faces, or they "set" a table with a circle for the plate and lines for the knife, fork, and spoon. Some like to attempt such advanced circles as a string of beads, a bunch of grapes, a Christmas tree with ornaments, an umbrella, or a cat.

Combinations of circles and straight lines can be made by drawing a square wagon with wheels, making a turkey with tail feathers, or making stick figures with round heads. As children transfer this activity to paper, some supervision is necessary to establish certain habits. All lines are made from top to bottom and left to right. All circles are started at the two o'clock position or where one would start to make the letter *c* and move toward the left.

As soon as possible, even at the readiness period, writing should say something. Students should be encouraged to label their picture of a cat with the word; the letters *c a t* might be copied from a teacher-made example. The children should know the names of these letters before writing them and should realize that they have made a word when they finish. Thus knowing the letter names and the ability to read what is written are parts of writing readiness.

Is There a Developmental Sequence for Handwriting Acquisition?

The teacher must always be cognizant of the personal variation that exists in skill acquisition and provide individualized attention when necessary. Thus, the following sequence of skills acquisition should be interpreted as a guideline only, to be fashioned and modified according to the needs of each child.

Kindergarten

By the end of kindergarten, most children may be expected to possess the following knowledge about handwriting:

1. The child should know that writing is a form of communication. It is a language shared through signs. Signs, names, and other written symbols have meaning.
2. In some cases, a child will be able to write in print script his or her first name.
3. There will be some familiarity with the forms of print script writing as the teacher uses it in recording children's stories, labeling pictures, or writing names.

Grade 1

By the end of first grade, many students will be able to do the following:

1. Write in print script form all letters, both capitals and lowercase.
2. Write their names and addresses in print script.
3. Write simple original stories in print script.
4. Understand and practice proper spacing between letters of a word and between words of a sentence.

Grade 2

By the end of second grade, a student should be able to do the following:

1. Use print script writing in daily lessons.
2. Understand and use margins, headings on papers, and spacing.
3. Write a friendly letter in print script.
4. Know the correct use of the terms *capital letter, period, question mark,* and *comma* as used between city and state and in dates.
5. Write print script with apparent ease.

Grade 3

By the end of third grade, students should be able to do the following:

1. Use both print script and cursive writing to meet their daily needs.
2. Write their own names and the name of their school, city, and state in cursive style.
3. Analyze and improve their own written work.
4. Write with reasonable speed.

Grade 4

During fourth grade a student should be able to do the following:

1. Write a friendly letter (one or two paragraphs) in cursive.
2. Write notes to friends and classmates in cursive.
3. Use cursive to write original stories, poems, and reports.
4. Show evidence of retaining print script writing as a supplementary tool.
5. Meet the grade standards as indicated on a handwriting scale.
6. Recognize and correct errors in letter formation.

Grade 5

By the end of fifth grade, the student should be able to do the following:

1. Write a business letter.
2. Take notes in class.
3. Plan and present written reports.
4. Use pen and ink neatly.
5. Attempt cursive writing on stationery without lines.
6. Meet grade standards with regard to legibility and speed (fifty to sixty letters per minute).

Grade 6

By the end of sixth grade, the student should be able to do the following:

1. Proofread and rewrite many first writing efforts.
2. Take pride in submitting neat, orderly papers in all class work.
3. Meet grade standards of legibility and speed.

Grades 7 and 8

By the time students are in the seventh or eighth grade they will have developed a personal style of writing. The language teacher should devote some time to writing instruction each week, especially for the students who have not developed a legible personal style.

Teaching Manuscript Writing

How Should a Pencil Be Held?

During early instruction some children may need to be shown how to hold their writing instrument correctly.

You may want to give your students the following instructions. "Put your pointer (index) fingertip near the end." Demonstrate position. "Put your middle fingertip next to it" (again demonstrate). "Put your thumb underneath" (again demonstrate).

Once the child has mastered the writing position, you can present models similar to those shown in Figure 10–2 and 10–3. All writing that is made available to the child for copy should be properly spaced and aligned.

Occasional comments by the teacher may be used to strengthen the child's impression of well-spaced letters and perfectly straight lines. However, in the early stage of writing instruction the child needs to concentrate chiefly on getting a clear visual image of the letters written and on learning the correct order of making the strokes. After the child has learned to form the letters properly, there will be plenty of time for him to master the art of letter arrangement.

How Should Papers Be Held When Writing?

The paper should be positioned in front of the child in such a way as to facilitate maximum ease in forming letters. The position may vary slightly from child to child, but in general will be parallel with the lines of the desk (as shown in Figures 10–4 and 10–5). The paper should be positioned at a slant for both cursive and manuscript writing. The right-handed child should slant the paper from left at the top to right at the bottom. The left-handed child should slant the paper from right at the top to the left at the bottom. The paper is moved as the child writes. Standard writing equipment is made available, along with chalk, crayons,

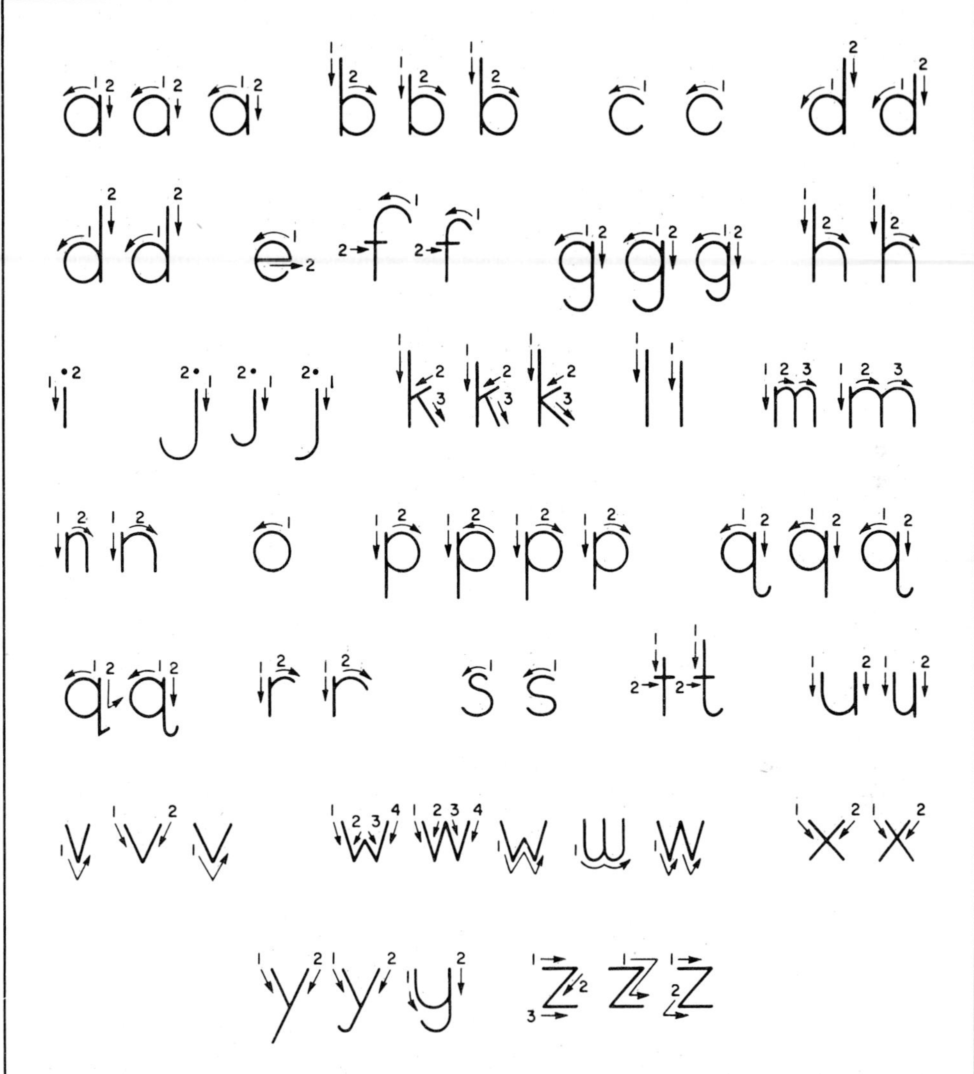

Figure 10–2.

and other writing utensils. The child should experiment with the various writing tools to ascertain which affords the most comfortable grip that can be sustained with a minimum of fatigue. Ordinarily, a child can write easily while seated in a properly fitted chair and desk. Some small children write better if they can stand while writing. This is especially true if they are writing on large or oversized easel paper.

Early handwriting instruction should use whole words that have real meaning for the children. These

Figure 10–3.

are usually words they are interested in and that are easy to write. It will probably be necessary to contrive ways to bring in words like *queen, quite, quail, fox, fix, box, excuse, zebra, zoo, buzz,* and *dozen,* in order to teach the letters *q, x, z,* which are not frequently used. The entire alphabet must be taught.

A study by Coleman (1970) indicated that the lowercase letters presented the following order of difficulty

Figure 10–4. Position for left-handed students.

for beginners: *l, o, i, f, x, s, t, v, r, g, a, b, h, j, p, n, m, z, q, k, y, d, c, e, w, u*. The letters *p, q, b,* and *d* give trouble because of their obvious structural similarities. Many programs present the letters in similar groups. One text teaches *o, a, d, q, g, b, p, c,* and *e* as Group One. The letters that use straight lines are Group Two: *l, t, i, f, j, n, m, r, h, u, w, y, r, z,* and *k*. The letter *s* is taught as a continuous series of curves. The capital letters are usually taught in association with children's names. Those identical in shape with their small letter counterparts pose few problems. These are *O, C, S, V, X,* and *Z* in most programs.

Figure 10–5. Position for right-handed students.

Making an ABC book also gives practice with capital letters.

The following are frequent errors: rounding straight lines and angles, making letters upside down and backward, forming lines so that they do not meet at the proper places, and making incomplete letters. These errors can be prevented by careful initial teaching, although all children make some errors when absorbed in thinking about what they are writing. With respect to closure errors, it is easier for children to join the circle and straight line strokes if the *c* rather than the complete oval is used for parts of the letters *a, d, g,* and *q*.

A factor that governs the formation of some print script letters is ease of transfer to cursive writing. The reason for starting the letter *e* with the straight line, then the circle, is simply that this is the way the cursive letter is formed. It may well be that it is wiser to consider the letters in one alphabet as distinct from the other.

As the teacher writes, she should call attention to details, naming the letters and commenting on the size, shape, and direction of strokes. She should watch the child write the word, comment favorably on letters that are well-formed, and give additional instruction when it is needed. If a particular letter proves difficult, the child should give it additional practice. When introducing letters in a word or isolating a difficult letter for study, the teacher may give more time to demonstration and discussion: "The *t* is a tall letter. We start at the top, go down, and try to make it very straight. We cross it near the top from left to right. The *t* is not quite so tall as an *l*, but it is taller than *i*, or *m*, or *n*" (depending on which letters the children already know).

As the child becomes proficient at printing the letters, teachers might help with spacing by suggesting that the student place the index finger of the hand not being used for writing after the last letter of the completed word and then print the first letter of the next word to the right of the finger. Although this may provide initial assistance, the child must be encouraged to develop spacing visualization as quickly as possible. To avoid finger dependence, appropriately spaced models should be placed on the bulletin board and chalkboard.

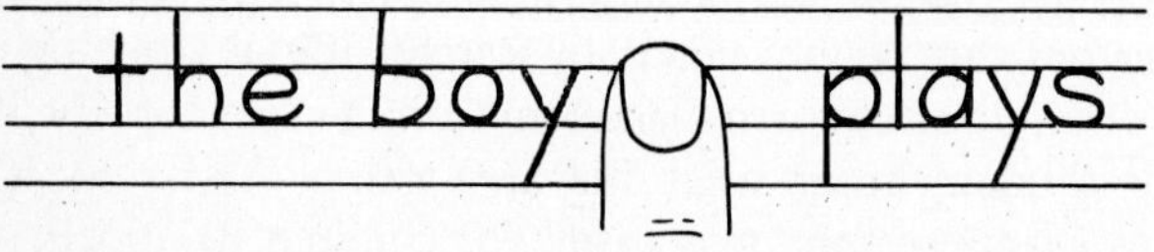

At this point it is well for you as a teacher to bear in mind that when children begin to write they cannot remember everything they have been told. Only two things are essential: (1) they must form the letters in fair approximation to the copy, and (2) they must make every stroke in the correct direction as they form their letters. If one cannot do both, he or she probably is not ready to write and would profit more from nonwriting activities at this time.

The effectiveness of the practice of tracing, except in special problem cases, has been questioned (Ackov & Greff, 1975). If children cannot make the strokes without the tedious, time-consuming muscular drill involved in tracing, they are hardly ready for handwriting instruction. And if the children, in tracing, put all of their attention on the segment of line that they are attempting to follow at the moment, they lose sight of the letter or word as a whole, and so at the end of the lesson may be able to write no better than at the beginning.

Kirk (1978) discusses the cognitive differences the children encounter during copying and tracing activities. The child may begin manuscript writing by tracing letter models but must eventually be guided to copying activities that encourage the development of cognitive transfer as well as muscle development.

In learning to write, as in other kinds of growth, all children pass through the same general stages of development. The rate of progress and the time at which each level of achievement is reached vary according to the individual differences of the children themselves. It is not uncommon for a child to start slowly and then pick up speed as he or she matures, or for another to start rapidly and then slow down later. Nevertheless, at any given time, there will be enough children with similar needs to make some group instruction possible. In writing, as in reading, groups must be small enough to permit close personal teacher supervision of each child's work. This is true whether the writing is done on the board or on paper.

A good lesson in handwriting contains five elements: (1) visualization, (2) analysis, (3) practice, (4) comparison or evaluation, and (5) correction.

Note the following examples in teaching children to write their names:

1. *Visualization.* The teacher has prepared a three by five card with the name of each child. "I wonder how many of you can read each other's names. As I go through the cards, the person whose name I say will call on another child to read it. After all have been read, I will give you your name cards."
2. *Analysis.* "How many have an *e* in their name? Trent, show us how to make an *e*. This is one letter that does not start at the top. Do any of you have an *s* in your name? Stacy, show us how to make an *s*. Look at each letter in your name. Are there any letters you think we should practice?"
3. *Practice.* "Now go to the board and put an *x* at the eye-level line where you will start. Write your name once. When you have finished, go over your name card and check that each letter is correct."
4. *Evaluation.* "How many have all the letters on the line? How many have all the letters right? How many have the space between letters right?"
5. *Correction.* "Now let's write our names once more and make them better. You may keep the name card at your desk and use it whenever you wish to write your name."

Modeling A Lesson—Manuscript Writing

Anita Archer (1985) presents a synthesis of these elements for manuscript writing.*

Step 1. Teacher MODELS formation of the letter providing verbal cues as he/she models.

Teacher	*Child*
"Today we are making *p*. What letter? Who has that sound in their name?"	*p*
"Watch me make *p*. I start at the beltline and go straight down. Touch down. Now I lift my pencil and go back to the beltline. Touch around. What letter did I make?"	*p*
"Watch me again. I start at the beltline to make *p*. Touch down. Touch around."	
"Where do I start *p*?"	"At the beltline."
"Watch. Touch down. Touch around."	

Step 2. Teacher LEADS children in formation of the letter.

"Say it with me as I write *p*. Touch down. Touch around. Touch down. Touch around."	"Touch down. Touch around. Touch down Touch around.
"Now it's your turn to do it with me. Put your hand on your paper. Place your pencil on the beltline. Where is your pencil?"	"On the beltline."
"Get ready. Say it as you make *p*. Touch down. Touch around.	Children make *p* "Touch down. Touch around."
Teacher leads children in making additional letter *p*.	

* Archer, A. (1982). *Basic Skills Curriculum/Spelling Program: User's Manual.* San Diego: San Diego Schools.

Step 3. Teacher TESTS children in formation of the letter. (Supervised Practice)

Teacher	Child
"Now it's your turn to make *p*. Remember to start at the beltline. Touch down. Lift your pencil and then touch around."	
Make one line of *p*.	Children make *p*.

Step 4. Teacher provides FEEDBACK to children on their letter formations.

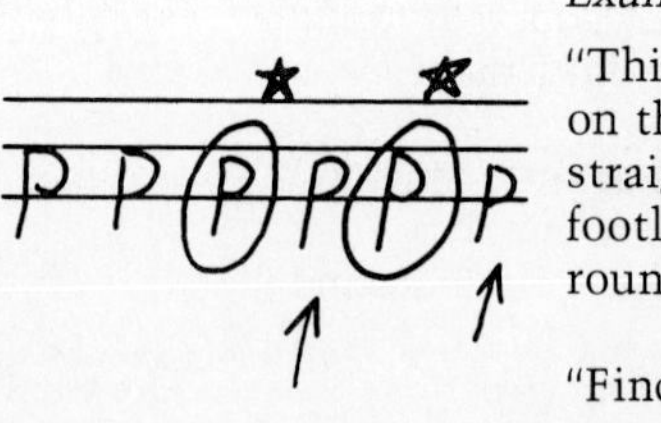

Example feedback	
"This is your best *p*. It starts on the beltline. It goes straight down below the footline and is nice and round."	
"Find another good *p*."	Child locates good *p*.
"Why did you pick this *p*?"	"It is nice and straight and this part is round."
"Why didn't I circle this *p*?"	"It isn't straight."

(Note: This type of analysis can be done with an entire group by examining examples of well-formed letters and poorly formed letters. However, the child must then apply that analysis to his or her own writing by circling well-formed letters. The teacher may also use an acetate sheet with well-drawn letters to provide feedback to the child. The acetate is placed over the letter(s) for analysis and comparison.)

Step 5. Teacher dictates REVIEW letters. Students write those letters. Teacher can provide feedback by writing the letters on the board after children have completed the letter formations.

Step 6. The teacher dictates words containing known letters. The children write the words.

The teacher then writes the words on the board and the students check the letter formations and the spacing.

Handwriting Worksheets

In the first grade, many lessons in handwriting will require the teacher to prepare a worksheet. Normally these worksheets should meet the following standards:

1. The learner's attention is focused on a few handwriting difficulties.
2. The worksheet contains enough guidance so that possible errors will be avoided.
3. Although the drill is on a single element, the practice results in the feeling that something has been written.
4. There is enough practice to give a sense of purpose to the lesson, but not so much that there is physical strain.

The first thing on the worksheet should be the letters or word demonstrated by the teacher. There may be arrows or other markers to show where the writer starts each letter and to show the direction of the strokes. The first stroke may be in red, the second in yellow, and the third in blue.

The second part of the worksheet may consist of practice on one or two letters. An example should be given and spaces should be made indicating how many "copies" of each letter are required.

Finally, these letters should be put together to form a word or sentence. Sometimes only part of a word is given, with blanks left for the missing letters. Other worksheets may indicate by a picture what word is to be written. As soon as the child is ready, the writing should become personal. The worksheet may start a letter by having printed on it:

Dear Santa,
Please bring me . . .

Handwriting Practice

After the children have had practice forming letters and combining them into words and sentences, the students should be engaged in a great deal of personal writing, using model alphabet charts as a guide. Homemade greeting cards provide writing practice. These cards may then be sent to a child who is ill, or they may be used for birthdays, Christmas or Hannukah greetings, Mother's Day remembrance, or Valentine's Day. Labeling also provides excellent writing practice. Children can make their own flash cards for drill in reading. But best of all are the stories written to illustrate a picture or to entertain the group. Such stories will be discussed later under the topic of creative writing.

There are standardized scales to evaluate print script writing. However, few children can use them. A chart that asks the child to check the following elements will serve for most of the evaluation needed at this grade:

Did you make each letter the way it is on the chart?
Are your letters on the line?
Are your down strokes straight?
Are your round letters like a circle?
Did you leave enough space between words?

Suggestions for Generating Interest in Handwriting Instruction

There are a number of devices that teachers can use to add interest to the writing practice. Here are some examples.

1. Ask the children to listen carefully to a word description to see whether they can identify a letter that is on the alphabet chart. The teacher says, "I am thinking of a small letter that is made with a circle and then a tall stick." The child who identifies *d* goes to the board and writes it. The teacher then describes another letter.

   The teacher asks, "Who can find the letter that comes before *m*? What is its name?" The child who identifies the letter may write it on the board. A variation is to ask, "What letter comes after *m?*

2. Each child in turn goes to the front of the room and gives his or her name and initials. "My name is Mildred Cunningham. My initials are M. C." Then she writes them on the board. Or a child may write a classmate's initials on the board and the class can identify the person.
3. A magic slate with transparent acetate sheets can be bought at a novelty store. Insert a sheet of paper with the letters, words, or numbers you wish the child to practice. The children trace over these with a crayon—or, better, write under the examples. These can be used many times because the crayon marks can be wiped off.
4. One teacher starts her group by saying, "We are going to make pumpkins today. Watch how I make one." The teacher uses the guide words "Once around." After the children have made a row of pumpkins, the teacher says, "Let's put our pumpkins beside a fence post. Now look again," the teacher says, "because you have made the letter *a.*"
5. Another teacher talks about the letters that are done only on one floor such as *a, c, e, m.* Other letters are upstairs letters like *d, b, h, l.* Basement letters are *g, j, p, y.* Sometimes children do a better job of alignment if they are told, "Let's see whether we can keep our letters sitting straight on a self."
6. After the children have spent several lessons on lines, circles, their names, and single words, one teacher starts with a sentence such as "I am a toy." After the unlined paper is distributed, the children are asked to fold the paper in half lengthwise, then fold the bottom half to the center fold. This provides folded lines to follow. The children write the sentence on the bottom fold and then draw a picture in the top half to illustrate their sentences.

If Children Can Print, Why Must They Learn Cursive Writing?

Although some school systems make no effort to teach any form of writing but print script, the majority do introduce cursive writing in either the late second grade or the third grade. This change is more the result of response to cultural tradition than to educational merit. The reason for changing from print script to cursive may simply be the child's, parents' and/or teacher's desire. Many children attempt to imitate "adult," or cursive, writing and need direction to do it correctly. Parents may think that cursive writing is better than print script. Finally, there is a strong traditional force within the teaching group. Upper-grade teachers using cursive writing often seem unwilling to change. Thus the child must change to conform to the teacher's writing pattern. Another factor in this situation is that cursive seems to be a teaching specific that indicates educational growth. Teachers often like to introduce something new; the home reaction is generally that "children in Ms. Hess's class are certainly making progress."

Surely it makes sense for the child to use print script as often as possible after mastering this skill. Children may more readily express their ideas in the written form throughout the second and third grades if they use print script. Some may be ready to make the transition from print to cursive when very young, late in the second grade, whereas others may not be ready for this transition until later in their school career. Even those beginning an early transition should not be rushed. Children should continue to write spelling words and answers to test questions in the form of writing that is better for them. Even after cursive has been mastered, there will be occasions throughout all grade levels to use print script skills in such exercises as filling out forms, writing invitations, and designing greeting cards or posters. Many adults mix their writing to include both script and cursive styles.

The major aspect of readiness for training in cursive writing is the ability to read words written in it. Members of the family frequently teach a child to "write" rather than "print" his/her name. Teachers start using cursive to present assignments and words in the spelling lessons. Children play games with their sight vocabulary in both printed and cursive forms. Other factors, such as desire to write, adequate physical development, and the ability to use print script, should be considered. Children who are just beginning to understand how to read should not face the additional problem of learning a new way to write.

A few children will make the transfer in imitation of the writing of parents or older children. The change is made with very little guidance, and penmanship instruction is only a matter of perfecting the new forms. These children do not need to follow any of the instructional patterns suggested here.

The transfer to cursive should conform to the principle of moving from the simple to the complex. Experience indicates that the small or lowercase letters should be introduced first, in the following order: *l, e, i, t, u, n, m, h, k, w, o, b, v, x, y, j, f, s, p, r, c, a, d, g, q, z.*

Capital letters should be taught in association with the children's names. Rather than drill on all of them in the third grade, it is best to practice them in usage with an example and teacher guidance.

The best equipment to use is an ordinary lead pencil at least six inches long, with soft (No. 2) lead. In general, the paper should be ruled. Because some children have a tendency to write too small, wide-ruled paper is generally recommended. The following represents a typical sequence of introducing note paper of given specifications for each grade:

Grade 1	At first, unruled paper (without lines), 12- by 18-inch, folded; later, 1-inch ruled paper
Grade 2	9- by 12-inch, ruled ½-inch alternating light and heavy lines; ruled 1-inch light, later
Grade 3	At first, ½-inch alternating light and heavy lines; later, ⅝-inch, one space for tall letters
Grade 4	Reduce to ½-inch as children are ready
Grades 5, 6	Rules ½-inch, reducing to ⅜-inch; ⅜-inch spacing

It is good classroom management to have a jar of sharpened pencils ready (prepared by a monitor) so that a pencil with a broken point can be exchanged for a new one without class interruption.

Slanted cursive writing is best introduced as a completely new form of writing. Before distributing paper to the class, you might make remarks such as this:

"Many of you have noticed that your mothers and fathers do not use print-script writing. They may be using a form of writing called 'cursive.' (The teacher writes *cursive* on the chalkboard.) Some of you have written your names or other words in cursive. Let's see how cursive writing differs from the print script that we have been using. I will write the name of our town on the board in this new writing. You will see that the letters are slanted and joined. We have been writing with our papers directly in front of us. It will be easier to write this new way if you slant your paper. For those who are right-handed, the paper should slant to the left, with the bottom corner pointing toward your heart. If you are left-handed, the paper should slant to the right."

The exact positions for each person will differ according to arm lenth. These variations may be suggested to each individual as you observe children's cursive writing attempts.

Introducing Cursive Writing

Why write? may be the topic of conversation that is needed to transfer students from manuscript to cursive writing instruction. Once the rationale for the transition has been established, a series of lessons on proper letter formation may be undertaken:

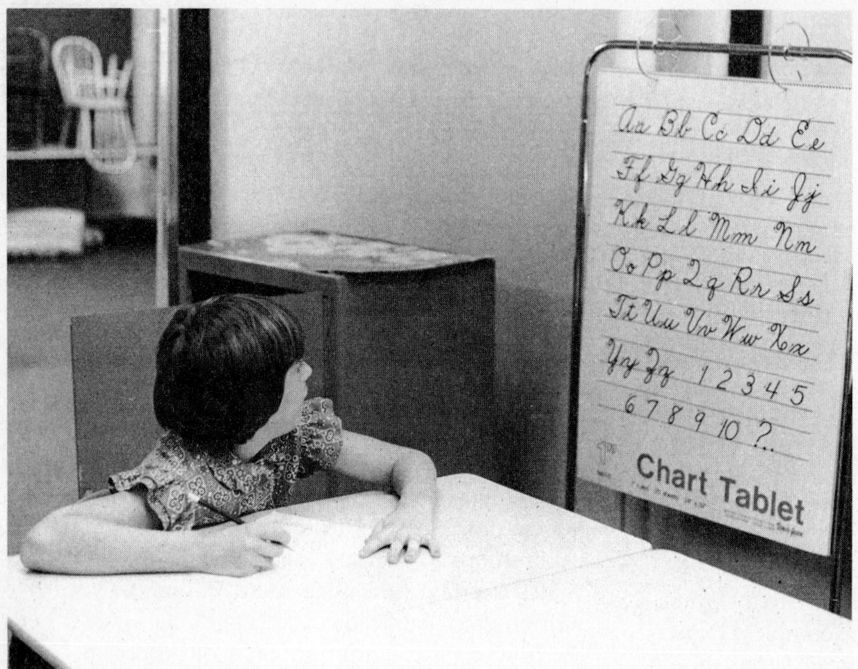

It is the responsibility of the classroom teacher to encourage students to develop a positive attitude toward handwriting and to nurture enthusiasm about skill attainment. (Photo by Linda Lungren)

1. Begin by introducing guidelines. The teacher might say: "Watch while I make some lines on the board. Notice how each line slants the same as the other lines. I want them to slant only a little. I am going to leave a space between each pair of lines. Now you may make three pairs of slanted lines. The first letter we make will be the letter *l*. I will start at the bottom on the first slanted line, make a curved line to the top of the second slanted line, and then make a curved line along the same slant in the middle of the two slanted lines. At the bottom, finish with a small upward curve. Now you try it. Make an *l* with each guideline. Now, make three guidelines and this time we will make two letter *l*'s that join. We might say, 'Up, around, straight down; up, around, straight down.' " (Observe that the letters are neither too wide nor too thin.)
2. Demonstrate the letter *l*, using only half a slanted line as a guide. Use the same three steps. Follow this with the letter *i*.
3. Introduce the letter *t*. Start by making guidelines on two-thirds of the writing space. The cross on the *t* is one half the distance between the top and bottom writing lines. The children should now start to use these letters in words. The teacher may say: "I am thinking of some words that use the letters we have practiced. If I put the guidelines for the words on the

board, I wonder how many of you will be able to write the word. Copy the guidelines on your paper before you write the word. Yes, the words are *ill* and *tell*. Can you think of another word that we can write with these letters? Yes, we could write *tile*. What guidelines will we need? See how many other words you can think of using *i, e, l,* and *t*. We'll compare lists after I have helped some children with their writing." Some children will think of only two or three. Possible words include *little, let, lie, lit, tie, title, tell, it, ill, tilt, eel* and *tee*.

4. Introduce the letter *u*. Start by making two short guidelines in groups of three. Use guide phrases such as "Up, down, around; up, down, around." The letter *n* is made with groups of two small guidelines. This letter begins with a hump that starts a space before the first guideline. Guide words such as "up, over, down, up, over, down, up" may be used. The letter *m* is made with groups of three guidelines. The first stroke is the hump, a space before the first guideline. Now a number of words may be written. "Instead of starting with guidelines, write the word, then put in the slanted guidelines to see whether you have the proper slant. I wonder how many words you can make using *i, l, t, e, m, n,* and *u*." Practice on these letters should continue for several days.
5. Introduce the letter *h*. This is a combination of *l* and *n*. As a guide you need a long line and a short line. Write words: *hit, hen, hill, him, the, then, them*. The letter *s* presents a special problem. Some prefer a square as a guide rather than a slanted line. The upstroke goes to the corner of the square, and the downstroke follows straight down before making the curve.
6. Introduce the term "bridge." The new letters are *w, o, b,* and *r*. In illustrating the *w*, start by making groups of three lines as for *m*. The teacher may say: "We will make the letter *w* by starting as if we were making the letter *u*. At the end, we go up once more and then make a bridge. This bridge sags a little. (The letter *o* does not need a guideline but the bridge should be stressed.) For the letter *b*, we need only a long line as a guide. We first make the letter *l* then close the ending by coming around as you would make an *o* and end with a bridge."
7. Introduce these words to write: *will, bill, we, be, wet, bet, tub, new, bum*. Practice several days on words with the bridge. Note that when *e, i, r* follow a letter with a bridge, they start in a different way. Combinations to be practiced at this point are *os, or, ox, ve, br*. The next letter to study is *k*. This letter is like *h*. It starts as if you were writing *l*, then instead of a letter like *n*, you go around and makes a little circle, then comes down to finish the letter. If you cover part of the letters *k* and *h*, you should see *l*.
8. Introduce the letters *a, g, d,* and *q*, which contain the oval, the most difficult aspect of transfer from print script to cursive. One reason for insisting that the children start their circles at the two o'clock position (as in the letter *c*) when learning print script is to aid in this transfer. Start by having the children make a series of "eggs that tip" or "leaves on a stem." If short slanted lines are used, start at the top of these guidelines, make the oval by returning to the starting point, then follow the guideline down to make the connecting stroke.

The Connected Print Script Approach

Another method that might be described as "connected print script" would be handled in the following manner: Ask the child to print a word like *good*. Then have the child trace the word he or she has printed, without raising his or her pencil. This, of course, means that he or she will connect the letters. As the child retraces, provide directions such as: "Around, down, make the tail on the *g*; now, without raising your pencil, go up and over to the top of the letter *o*, around the *o*, and without raising your pencil, slide over to the other *o* and around it, *goo;* without raising your pencil, slide over to the round part of the letter *d,* go around and up on the stick stroke, down again, and add a tail stroke, *good.*" Next let the child try to write the word *good* without retracing the print script.

Only letters that connect almost automatically should be taught by this connective method. The following primary words have letters that are easy for children to connect:

1. act
2. add
3. all
4. at
5. auto
6. call
7. cloth
8. cloud
9. cold
10. cup
11. cut
12. dad
13. did
14. dig
15. do
16. dog
17. dot
18. dug
19. glad
20. go
21. goat
22. gold
23. good
24. got
25. ha
26. had
27. hail
28. hall
29. hat
30. hill
31. hid
32. hit
33. hog
34. hold
35. hole
36. hood
37. hop
38. hot
39. hug
40. hunt
41. hut
42. it
43. lad
44. laid
45. lap
46. late
47. laugh
48. lip
49. little
50. load
51. log
52. lot
53. oat
54. o'clock
55. oh
56. old
57. out
58. pa
59. pad
60. paid
61. pail
62. pat
63. path
64. pig
65. pill
66. pool
67. pop
68. pot
69. pull
70. put
71. tag
72. tail
73. tall
74. tap
75. till
76. to
77. too
78. tool
79. tooth
80. up

The letters *b, e, f, r, k, s, z* must be taught as specific difficulties because of the lack of form correspondence between the print-script and cursive representations. The cursive that results from the connective method is vertical. Slant is obtained by turning the paper. Some teachers prefer to introduce the connective method by using dotted lines to show the cursive form on top of the print script. Children trace over these dotted lines as they master the new form.

The teacher starts with words containing letters that are alike in cursive and print scripts as shown in Figures 10–6 and 10–7. These would contain the small letters *i, t, o, n, m, e, h, l, u, d, c* and the capital letters *B, C, K, L, O, P, R, U.* A word is written in print script on the board as an example for the children to observe. The word *it* would be printed at a slant. The teacher then adds a "reach stroke," going to the first letter and from the first to the second. An ending stroke for the word is added. Then the teacher says: "Now I am going to do it without patching (guiding dots). Reach for the *i.* Now make the *i* lean right back against the reach line. Reach high for the *t.* Lean the *t* in the middle and dot the *i.* Let's do it again but this time you tell me what to do. First we will put in patch lines; then we will do it without patching." After this, each child practices at the board.

This type of lesson is repeated with *in, me, he, let, nut, do, cut, ice, mud, hut, den, cent, nice, home, mile, come, then, did.* Each lesson contains these steps: the word is written first in slanted print script, reach strokes are patched in, the word is written without patching, and children steer the teacher's chalk through the word before writing it under supervision. Practice cards that illustrate these steps for all the other letters are provided. In the independent writing of the children during this period, both cursive and print script appear. Both are expected—and permitted.

When parents ask about teaching their children to write at home, the teacher may explain thus: "If children are urged to write before they are ready they frequently develop feelings of tension, grip the pencil too tightly, and build up a dislike for writing. Then, too, many young children's muscles are not developed enough yet for successful writing. Writing at school is supervised to avoid poor habits, such as gripping the pencil too tightly, incorrect letter formations, and poor position."

If, however, children are eager to write and seem ready, parents might provide them with a variety of writing equipment (pencil, crayon), allowing them to select the one best suited, along with unlined paper. Print script letters may then be taught according to the school's alphabet specifications obtained from the child's teacher. Instruction should deal mainly with lowercase letters; capital letters should be treated only when beginning proper names.

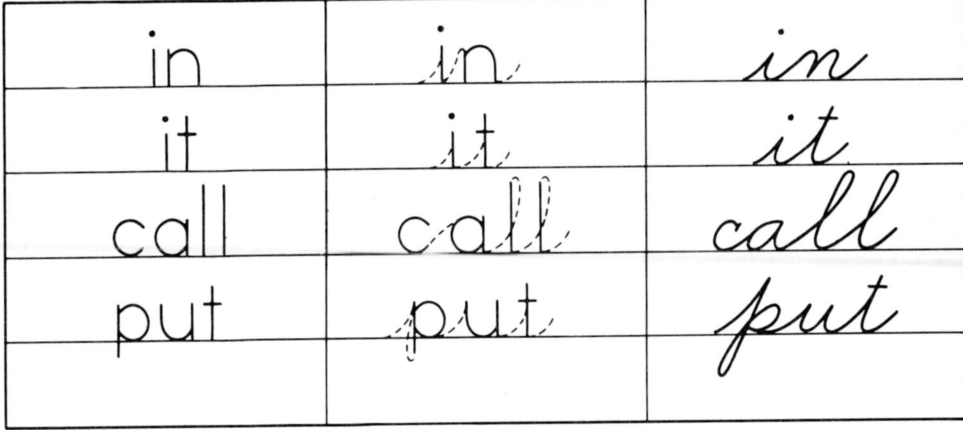

Figure 10–6.

D'Nealian Handwriting Program

The D'Nealian handwriting program is a method which is based on the connected print script approach as shown in the D'Nealian models of manuscript and cursive. Most letters are made with a continuous stroke. As shown in Figure 10–8, either the *uphill stroke* ⌡ or the *overhill stroke* ∫ is used to change many manuscript letters to cursive letters; *f, r, s, v, z* are the major exceptions.

Handwriting Scales

Handwriting scales are available in nearly all commercial programs. Children find these difficult to use in analyzing their own writing. There is no reason why any class or school cannot collect enough writing samples to develop its own standards or expectancies for each grade. The standardized scales can be used by teachers as they make judgments concerning the samples selected. Probably the most scientifically constructed scale is that devised by Leonard P. Ayres and published by the Educational Testing Service of Princeton, New Jersey. A major consideration is general quality of writing rather than specific style. It is difficult to determine if the writing being judged is vertical or backhand. Most individuals making such appraisals are also influenced by the formation of certain letters, such as capital *R* or small *r*. Noble and Noble and the Palmer Company have scales that diagnose specific writing problems of children practicing methods published by these firms. The Zaner-Bloser Company makes available a small dictionary of letter forms that each child uses. This dictionary presents the letters of its system with a space for children to make their own examples. These can be used to record progress. As children compare present writing with past work, they can note progress or weakness. This comparison serves much the same purpose as a standardized scale. Many schools purchase an alphabet strip to place over the chalkboard as a constant point of reference for children as they write. This technique can be effective if it is made significant to the children. Some teachers have pictures drawn to go with each letter. In the lower grades the drawing of an apple for *a* will suffice, but the upper grades may require more challenging words such as *avocado* or *astronaut* to illustrate the letter *a*. Unfortunately, the space over the chalkboard may be an awkward point of reference. For some children the details of the letters are lost because of vision problems. Figure 10–9 shows a num-

a c d g h i j l m
a c d g h i j l m
a c d g h i j l m
n o p q t u v w x y
n o p q t u v w x y
n o p q t u v w x y
b e f r k s z
b e f r k s z
a clown doll
a clown doll
a clown doll

Figure 10–7.

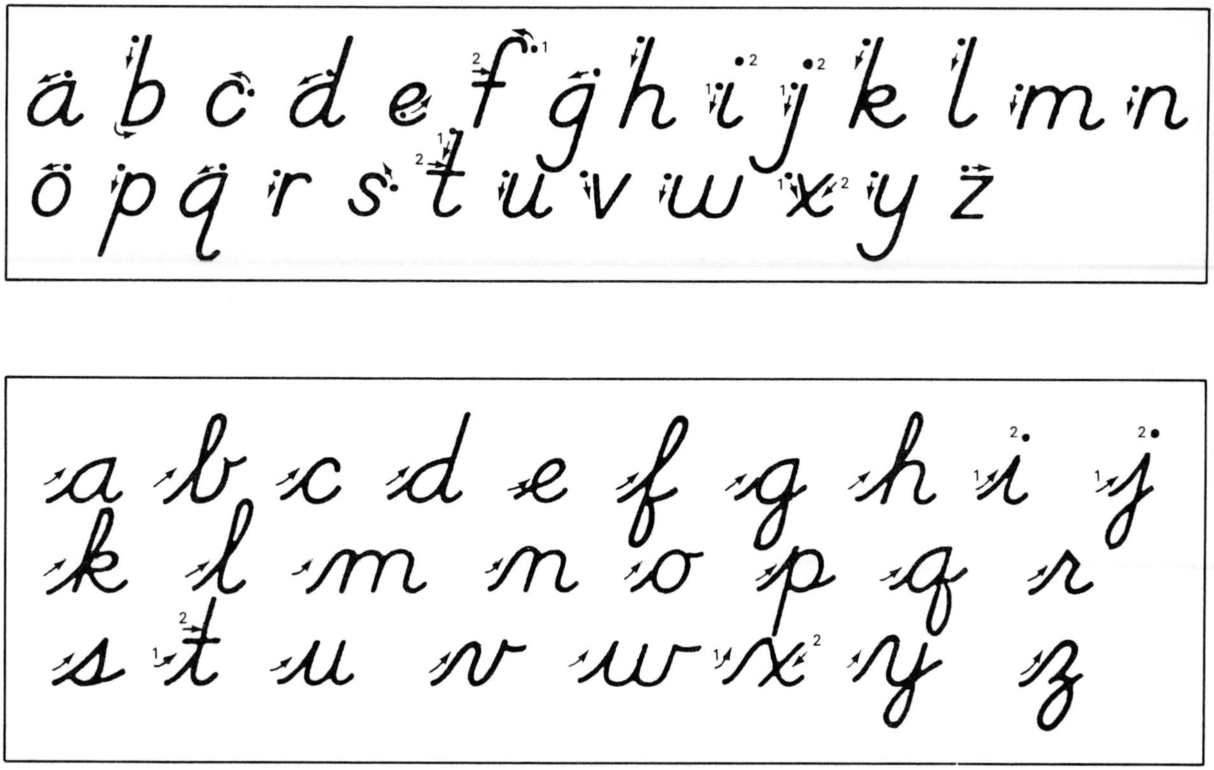

Figure 10–8. D'Nealian samples. (From Thurber, D. N. (1981). *D'Nealian Handwriting*. Glenview, Ill: Scott, Foresman and Co. © Scott, Foresman and Company.

ber of programs which provide individual desk cards used by the children when they need to recall how a letter is made. In practice, these are more effective than the alphabet strip.

Evaluation of Student Handwriting

Writing samples should be collected from all children at least four times during the year and kept in a collection of other examples of their work. Some teachers ask the child to write, "This is a sample of my writing on October 1." This inscription is folded back so that it is not visible when the child later writes, "This is a sample of my writing on January 1." Direct comparison can be made to determine whether skills are being maintained or improved. Both examples of writing are folded back when the child writes a third or fourth time on the same paper. Such a sample is especially helpful when talking with a parent about a child's work.

The form on p. 266, prepared by the Shaeffer Pen Company, is an example of an individual diagnostic device. It is designed to help children establish goals for their work in handwriting as well as establishing meaningful standards.

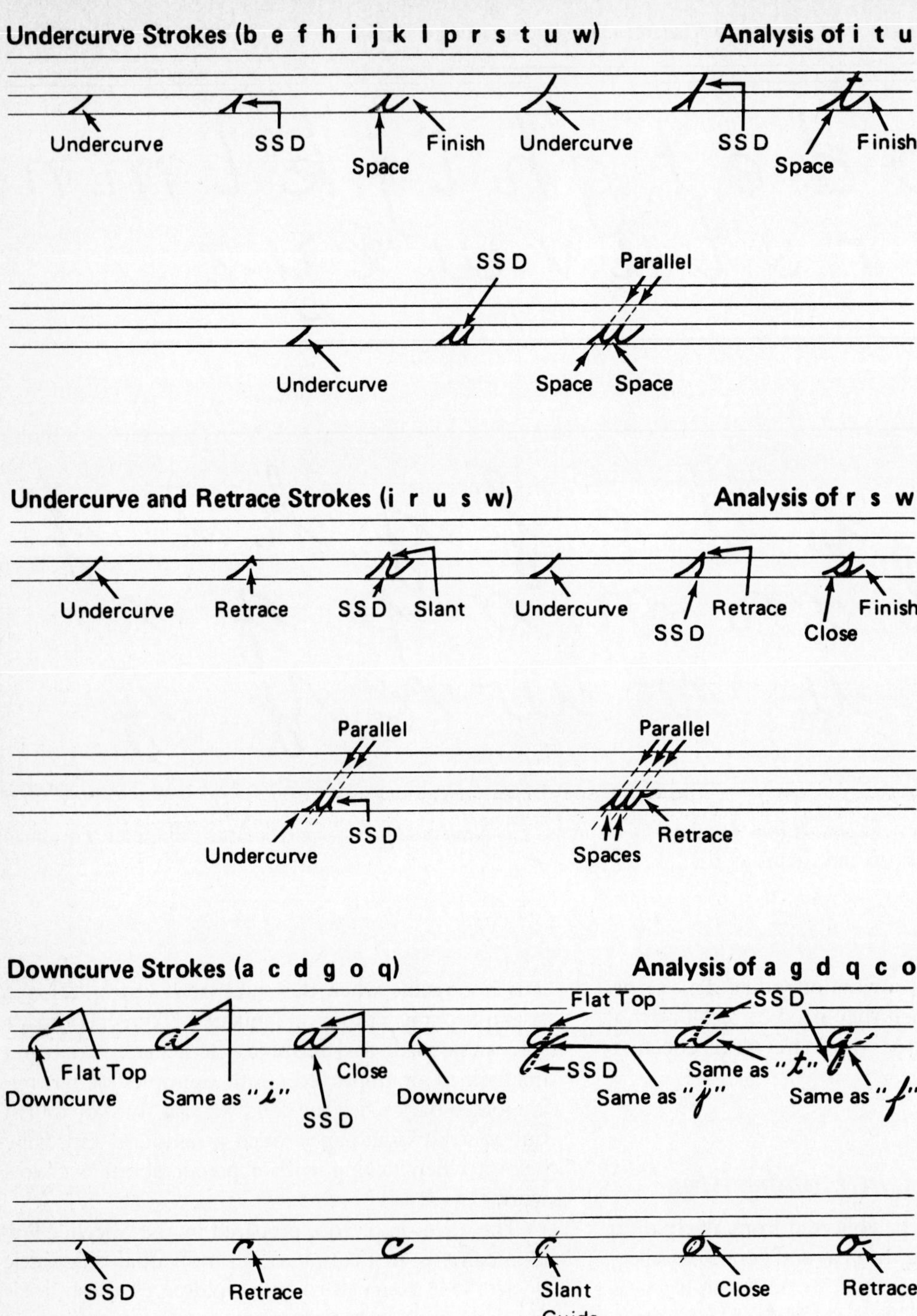

Figure 10–9. (A) (B) (C) (D) (E) (F)

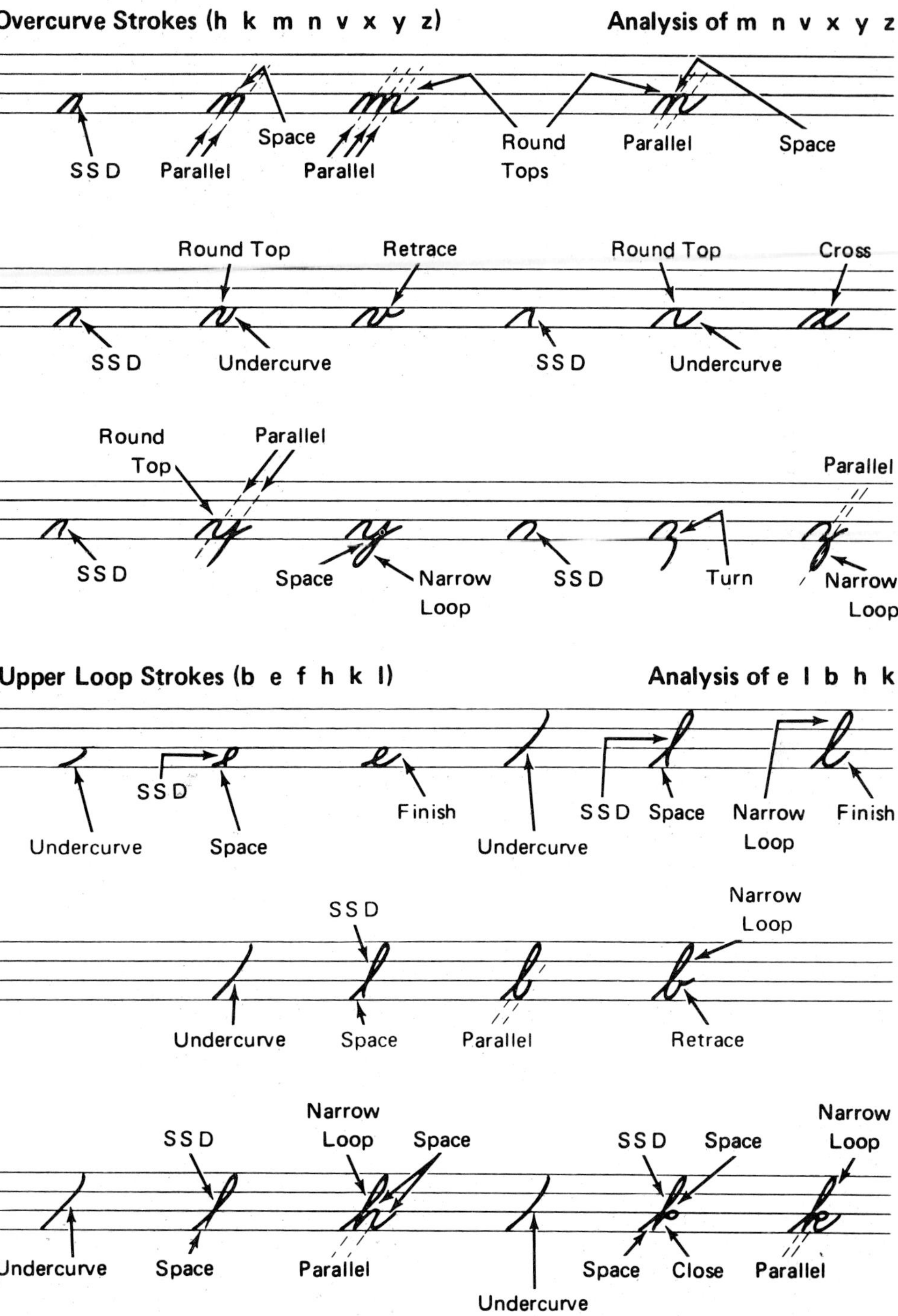
Overcurve Strokes (h k m n v x y z)
Analysis of m n v x y z
SSD
Parallel
Space
Parallel
Round Tops
Parallel
Space
Round Top
Retrace
Round Top
Cross
SSD
Undercurve
SSD
Undercurve
Round Top
Parallel
Parallel
SSD
Space
Narrow Loop
SSD
Turn
Narrow Loop
Upper Loop Strokes (b e f h k l)
Analysis of e l b h k
Undercurve
SSD
Space
Finish
Undercurve
SSD
Space
Narrow Loop
Finish
SSD
Narrow Loop
Undercurve
Space
Parallel
Retrace
SSD
Narrow Loop
Space
SSD
Space
Narrow Loop
Undercurve
Space
Parallel
Undercurve
Space
Close
Parallel

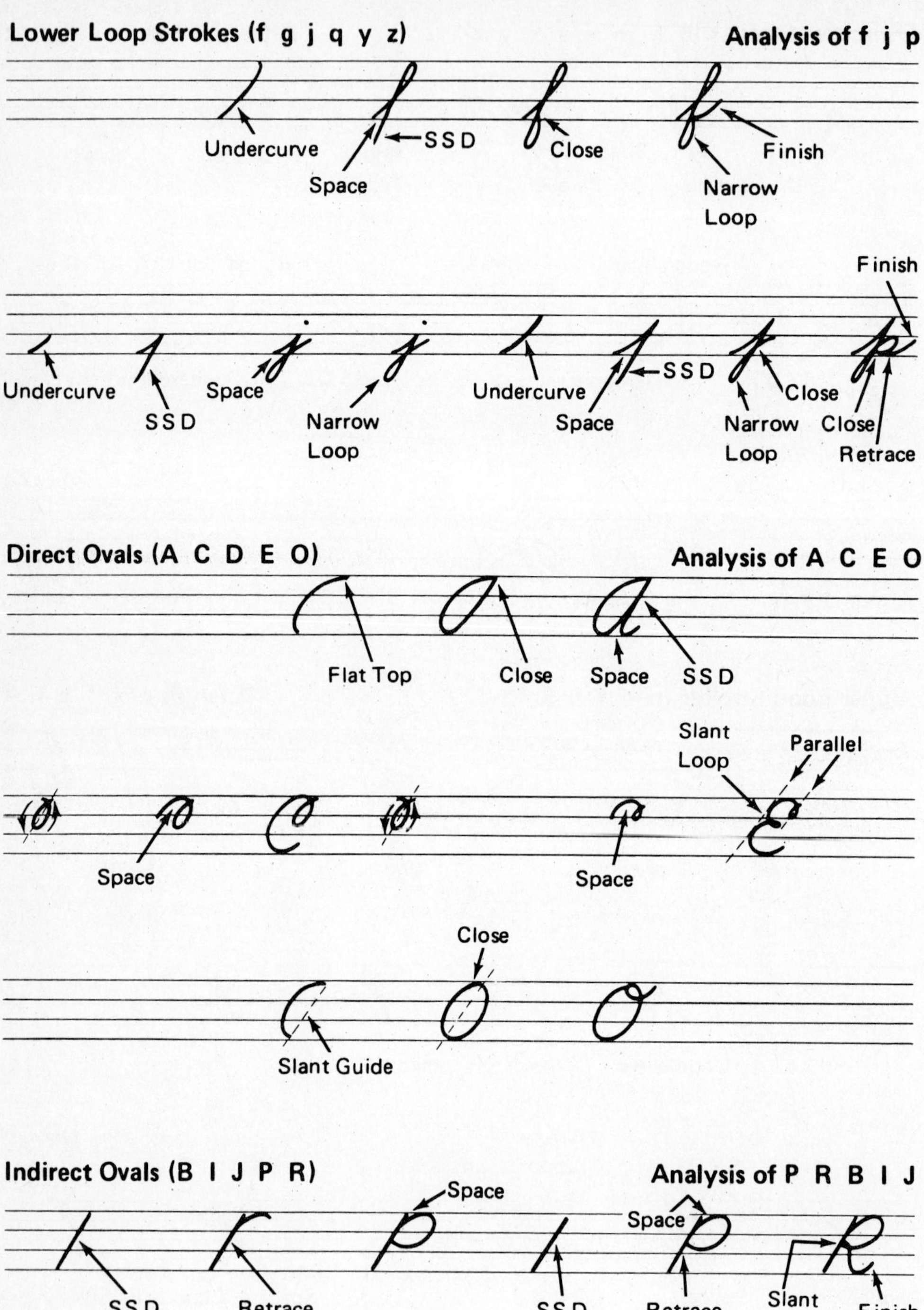
Lower Loop Strokes (f g j q y z)
Analysis of f j p
Undercurve
SSD
Space
Close
Finish
Narrow Loop
Finish
Undercurve
SSD
Space
Narrow Loop
Undercurve
SSD
Space
Close
Narrow Loop
Close
Retrace
Direct Ovals (A C D E O)
Analysis of A C E O
Flat Top
Close
Space
SSD
Slant Loop
Parallel
Space
Space
Close
Slant Guide
Indirect Ovals (B I J P R)
Analysis of P R B I J
Space
SSD
Retrace
Space
SSD
Retrace
Slant Loop
Finish

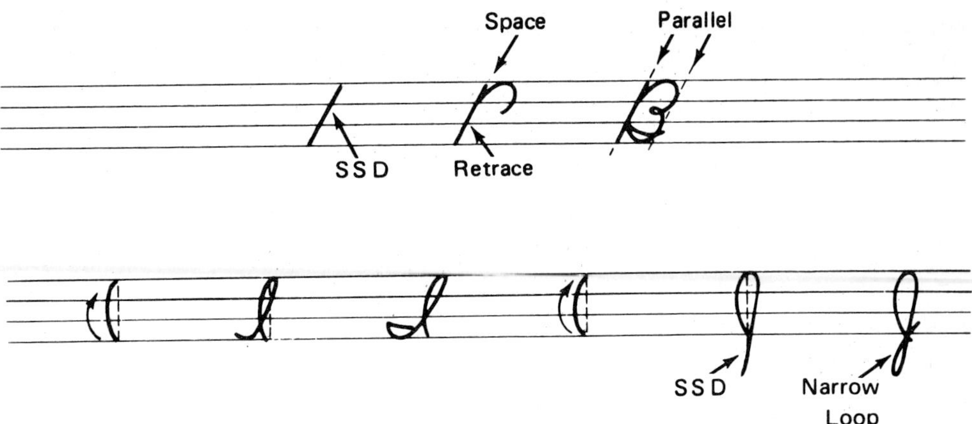

Loop-Stem Straight Strokes (H K M N U V X Y) **Analysis of H K M N U V X Y**

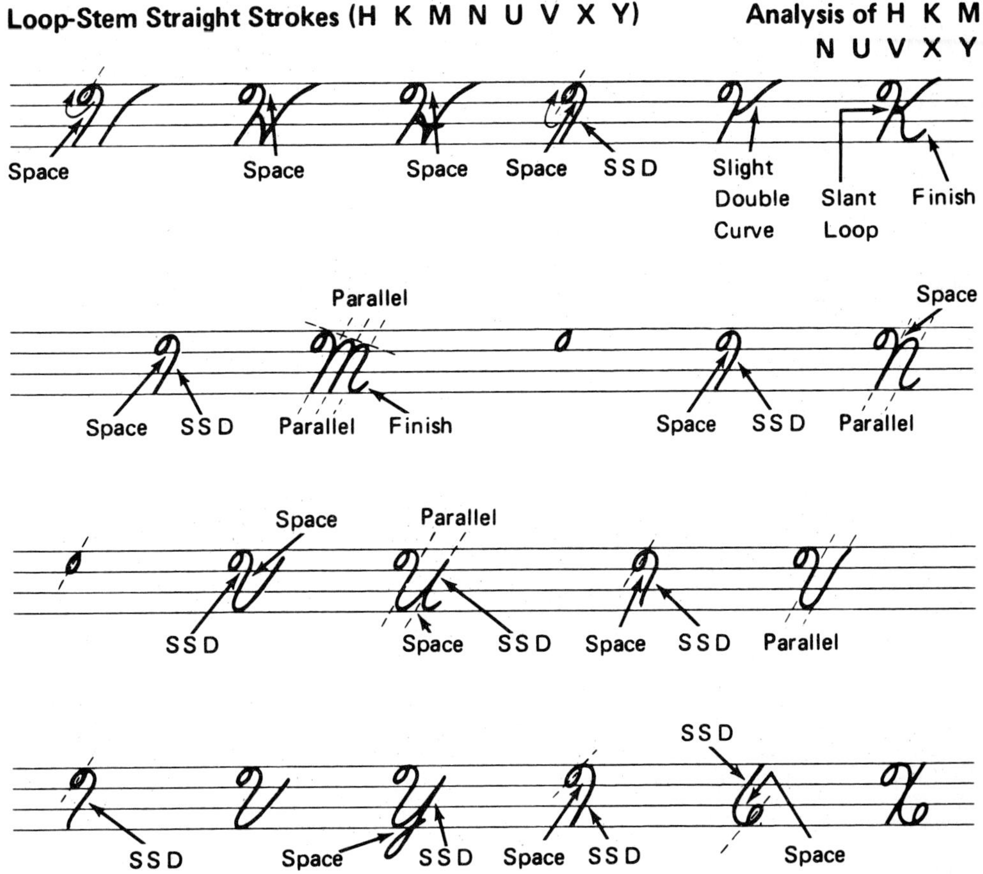

Loop-Stem Curved Strokes (Q W Z) **Analysis of Q W Z**

Compound or Double Curved Strokes (D F L Q S T) **Analysis of D L S**

Boat Ending Strokes (B F G I S T) **Analysis of F G T**

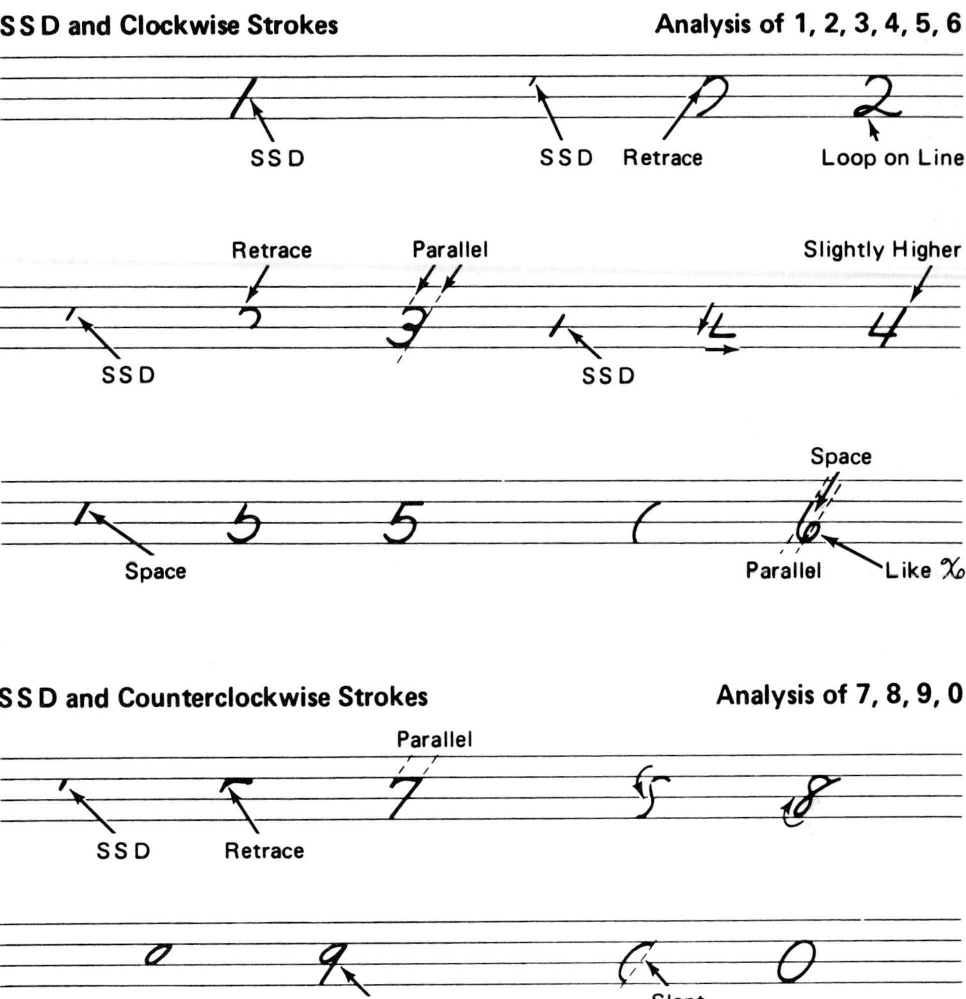
SSD and Clockwise Strokes
Analysis of 1, 2, 3, 4, 5, 6
SSD
SSD
Retrace
Loop on Line
Retrace
Parallel
Slightly Higher
SSD
SSD
Space
Space
Parallel
Like
SSD and Counterclockwise Strokes
Analysis of 7, 8, 9, 0
Parallel
SSD
Retrace
SSD
Slant
Guide

Pupil Self-Analysis Sheet*

A. Here is how I write when I am in a hurry:
(Write: "This is a sample of my writing")

____

____

B. Here is how I write when I do my best writing:
(Write: "This is a sample of my best writing")

____

____

C. I would mark my fast writing (circle one grade):	Excellent	Good	Fair	Poor
I would mark my best writing:	Excellent	Good	Fair	Poor
D. Here is my analysis of my handwriting:	EXCELLENT	GOOD	FAIR	POOR
1. SLANT .... Do all my letters lean the same way?	____	____	____	____
2. SPACING .... Are the spaces between letters and words even?	____	____	____	____
3. SIZE .... Are all small letters evenly small and tall letters evenly tall?	____	____	____	____
4. ALIGNMENT ...... Do all my letters touch the line?	____	____	____	____
5. SLANT .... Are *l, f, h, g, y, k, b* well formed?	____	____	____	____
6. STEMS .... Are all my downstrokes really straight?	____	____	____	____
7. CLOSINGS .... Are *a, d, g, o, p, s,* closed?	____	____	____	____

* Pupil Self-Analysis Sheet. Courtesy of Sheaffer Eaton Division of Textron Inc., Iowa.

8. ROUNDNESS ...... Are *m, n, h, u, v, w, y* rounded?	___	___	___	___
9. RETRACES .... Are *t, i, d, p, m, n* retraced?	___	___	___	___
10. ENDINGS .... Do my words have good ending strokes without fancy swinging strokes?	___	___	___	___

The forms shown in Figures 10–10, 10–11, and 10–12 are used for evaluation in many schools and may be of help to both teachers and students.

An additional exercise that may improve a child's handwriting involves evaluating the handwriting of a "partner." Either a standardized scale or one developed by the school or teacher may serve as the model comparison. The purpose of such an exercise is to alert the child to what constitutes correct letter formation. This is a cooperative effort; no grades are assigned. The teacher is able to circulate among the students, giving assistance as required.

In the handwriting period there will be times when the entire group will be working on the same problem—perhaps that of word endings or alignment. Because all have a like purpose, group diagnosis is effective. Samples of the writing can be shown on a screen by means of an opaque projector. Because the purpose is to seek a means of improvement rather than provide graded evaluation, most children will welcome the attention and suggestions concerning the next step they should take for improvement. First, attention should be directed toward one or two specific points. After this type of diagnosis has been used for some time, any aspect of the child's writing may be the basis for suggestion. A plastic transparent overlay will help some children examine specific letters. These are available with most handwriting systems. Another device is to cut a small hole in a piece of paper and examine the child's writing one letter at a time. Frequently only those who have special handwriting problems participate in the classwork, whereas those who have no special needs use the time for independent writing.

Tips for Good Writing

Regardless of the system used, the following five elements enter into the handwriting program; a chart of these made for the classroom can act as a constant reminder:

Formation. Each letter should be made and joined correctly according to whichever penmanship system is followed. Examples of letters that cause trouble can be shown on this chart.

Size. This is to remind students of the need for uniformity in size regardless of the type of letter.

Slant. The problem here is usually one of consistency.

Alignment. Letters that go above or below the line get mixed with other writing and thus are very difficult to read.

Spacing. Even spacing is necessary for rhythmic reading.

The final judgment concerning handwriting should be based on the child's daily written work. Occasionally, before and after children complete a written assignment, make a class inventory of writing needs. Ask the students to look at their papers while you

Total points possible = 4 points
Minimum proficiency = 2 points

HANDWRITING EVALUATION—FORM 1

NAME ______________________________ DATE ______________

Handwriting will be evaluated on a 4 point scale as follows:

The quick brown fox jumped over the lazy dog.

4 points

satisfactory		need improvement
✓	letter formation	
✓	slant	
✓	spacing	
✓	alignment and proportion	
✓	line quality	

The quick brown fox jumped over the lazy brown dog.

3 points

satisfactory		need improvement
	letter formation	✓
✓	slant	
✓	spacing	
	alignment and proportion	✓
✓	line quality	

The quick red fox jumped over the lazy brown dog.

2 points

satisfactory		need improvement
	letter formation	✓
	slant	✓
✓	spacing	
	alignment and proportion	✓
✓	line quality	

The quick red fox jumped over the lazy brown dog.

1 point

satisfactory		need improvement
	letter formation	✓
	slant	✓
✓	spacing	
	alignment and proportion	✓
	line quality	✓

If letter formation is such that words are unintelligible as in the last sample, assign no more than one point, disregarding other criteria.

Figure 10–10.

HANDWRITING EVALUATION—FORM 2

NAME ______________________________ DATE ____________________

yes no 1. Are the letters slanted in the same direction?

slant — yes slant — no

yes no 2. Are the letters well spaced? (Not too close or too far apart.)

spacing — yes s pa ci n g — no

yes no 3. Are the words well spaced? (Not too close or too far apart.)

words well spaced — yes

words notwell spaced — no

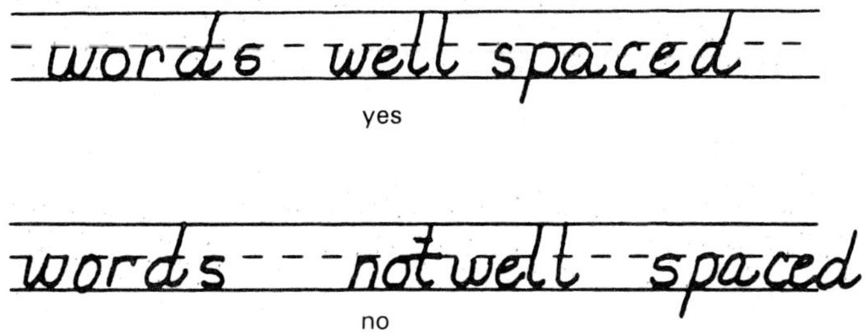

yes no 4. Are the tall letters the correct height?

bdfhkl — yes bdfhklt — no

yes no 5. Are the small letters the correct height?

aceimns — yes OrUVwxZ — no

yes no 6. Are the descender letters the correct height?

gjpqy — yes gjpqy — no

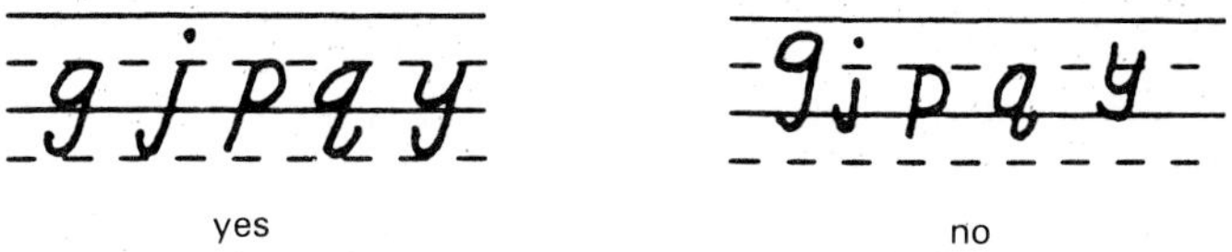

Figure 10–11.

HANDWRITING EVALUATION—FORM 3

NAME ________________________________ DATE ______________________

yes no 1. Are the letters slanted in the same direction?

slant (yes) slant (no)

yes no 2. Are the letters well spaced? (Not too close or too far apart.)

spacing (yes) spacing (no)

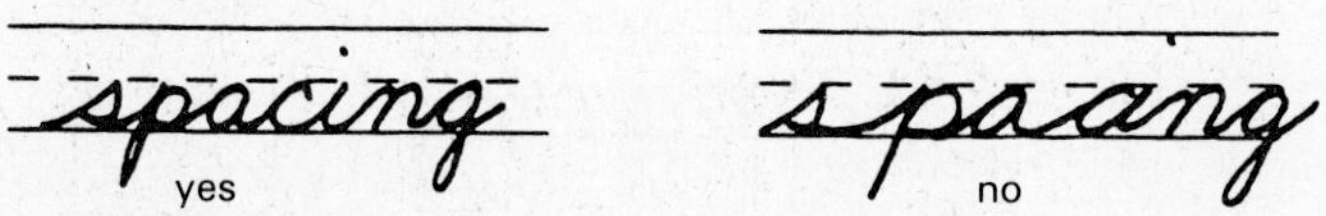

yes no 3. Are the words well spaced? (Not too close or too far apart.)

good spacing (yes)

poor spacing (no)

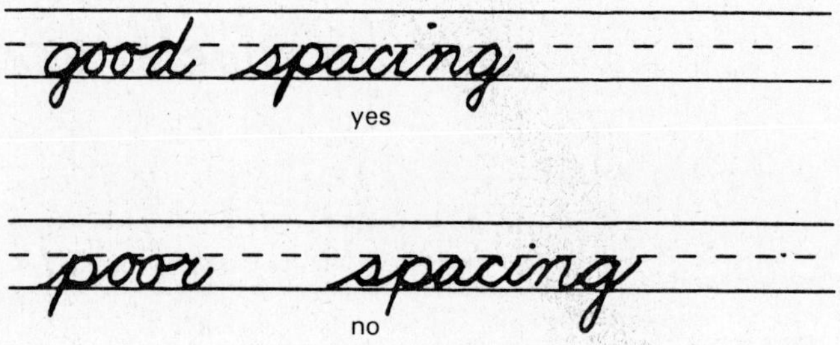

yes no 4. Are the tall letters the correct height?

b d f h (yes) k l t h (no)

yes no 5. Are the small letters the correct height?

a c e i m (yes) (no)

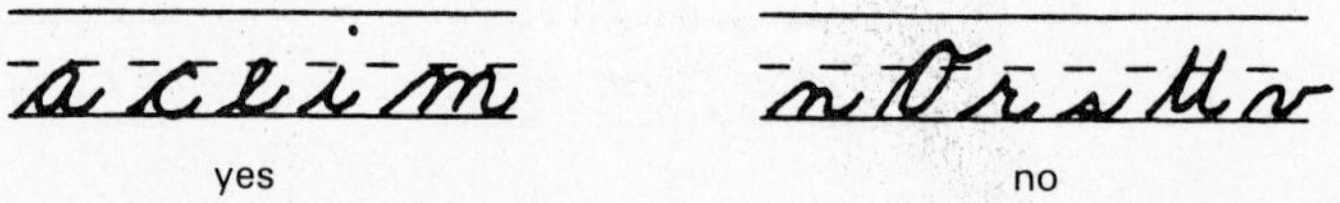

yes no 6. Are the descender letters the correct height?

j p q y (yes) z j p q (no)

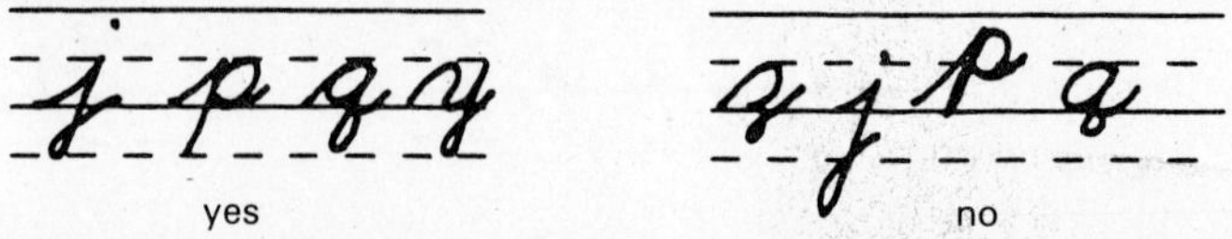

Figure 10–12.

record by number (not name) the results on the chalkboard. Use the following inventory of writing habits:

Alignment
- How many had
  - correct top alignment?
  - uneven top alignment?
  - correct bottom alignment?
  - uneven bottom alignment?
  - writing under the line?
  - writing over the line?

Letter Spacing
- How many had
  - correct letter spacing?
  - uneven letter spacing?
  - letter spacing too close together?
  - letter spacing too far apart?

Word Spacing
- How many had
  - correct word spacing?
  - uneven word spacing?
  - word spacing too close togeher?
  - word spacing too far apart?

The secret of continuous improvement is to establish a feeling of achievement. This can be done by setting specific attainable goals. When a goal is achieved, celebrate it fittingly.

Write the small letters of the alphabet correctly four times, joining the letters to each other as shown in Figure 10–13. The teacher (or a committee) can be the judge until an acceptable exercise is received from each member of the class.

Write sentences using words with difficult letter joinings, such as *bring, arrow, written, following, uncommon, bewitched, disturbance, suited,* and *delighted.*

Write sentences using these words: *there, their, they're, here's, hears, were, we're, wear, your, you're.*

Copy a short poem.
Write a good thank you letter.
Write the alphabet in capital letters.

Write the addresses of three friends as they would appear on an envelope.
Write five quotations.
Make a directory of the class showing names, addresses, and telephone numbers.
Keep the minutes as a secretary of a meeting.

The following sentences contain *all* the lowercase letters of the alphabet. When they are written a few weeks apart, students may evaluate their progress.

1. The violinist and the zither player were equally fine, so the judge marked both excellent.
2. At the zoo, the children saw an ibex, a jaguar, a kangaroo, a flamingo, and a very queer bird called a pelican.
3. The writer moves the hand quickly but smoothly across the page, watching the sizes of the letters and joining them expertly.

1. In the lowercase alphabet, every letter, except *c* and *o,* must have a *straight* downstroke, slanting from right to left.

   The downstrokes are straight. *straight*

   The downstrokes are not straight. *not straight*

2. The *space* between two letters should be wide enough to hold an *n* without the upstroke:

   "n spaces" between letters *space*

Spaces are too narrow. *space*

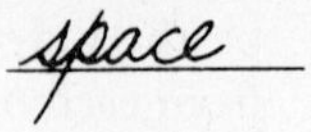

Spaces are too wide. *s p a c e*

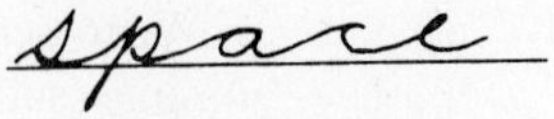

3. All downstrokes must be parallel.
   Downstrokes are parallel. *parallel*

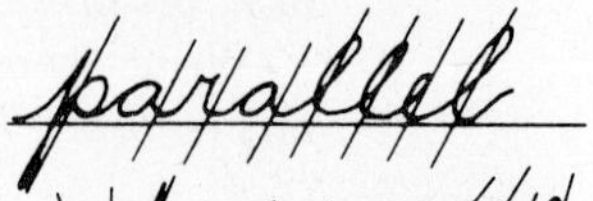

   Downstrokes are not parallel. *not parallel*

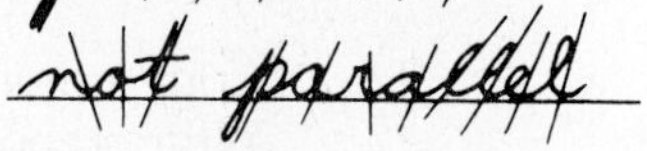

4. All letters must rest ON the line.
   Letters rest ON the line. *on the line*

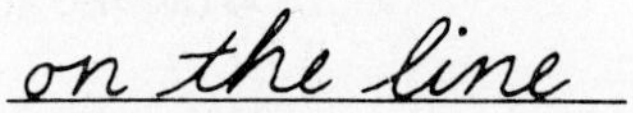

   Letters do not rest on the line. *not on the line*

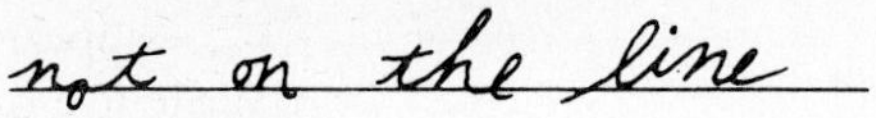

5. Letters must be of uniform and proportionate size.

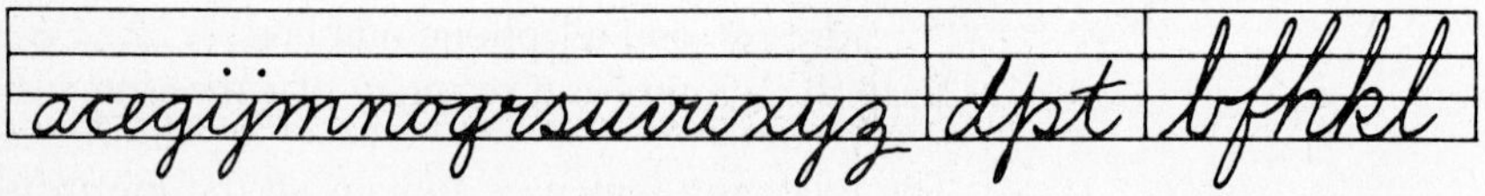

acegijmnoqrsuvwxyz	dpt	bfhkl

6. The *total* slant of the writing should be parallel to the diagonal of the paper, whether by right-handed or left-handed writers.

Figure 10–13. Rosenhaus's Guiding Rules for cursive writing of the small alphabet. [From Max Rosenhaus, "You Can Teach Handwriting with Only Six Rules," *The Instructor,* March 1957, p. 60.]

Example: Cursive Writing Lesson Plan

The following example of a cursive writing lesson is appropriate for fifth and sixth graders.

General Objective

To maintain proper spacing between letters.

Specific Behavioral Objective

Given instruction in the formation of the small letters with rounded tops, the children will be able to develop all such letters correctly, allowing for correct spacing between letters.

Motivation

The teacher shows the class a piece of written work in which many words are illegible (postcard or envelope returned because of illegible address; spelling, composition, or social studies papers). On the lined chalkboard, she copies some of the incorrectly written words and writes the correct form next to each. She discusses with the children the causes of the difficulty encountered in reading the words and guides them to the conclusion that the main cause is essentially the pointed tops in certain letters. They also note that other elements, including poor spacing, make words difficult to read.

The teacher writes the letters *m, h, v* on the chalkboard and adds, at the students' suggestion, other small letters which should have rounded tops, as *n, y, x*. The teacher and students decide which of these letters to reanalyze and practice in order to help them improve the writing of all small letters with rounded tops.

Procedures

Teacher: Writes the letter *y* on the lined chalkboard and discusses it as she writes it.
Reviews with the children posture and position of paper and pencil.

Students: Copy the letter, compare it with the teacher's model, note any deviation, rewrite it correctly if necessary, and then write it three or four times more.
Dictate to the teacher, for writing on the chalkboard, words in which the letter occurs at different places, for example, *you, by, eye*. Copy these words and check specifically for the correct formation of the letter *y* and the spacing between letters.

Teacher: Moves about the room to assist a few children individually.

Students: Dictate to the teacher, for writing on the chalkboard, a sentence that includes the practice letter and possibly other letters in the related group, for example, "The boys help each other in many ways." Copy the sentence from the chalkboard once or twice, depending upon individual speed.

Evaluation

The teacher helps the children to compare their letter *y* in the sentence with their practice writing of the letter. They also note the rounded tops of the related letters in the group. In addition, they compare a piece of writing from their folders with their practice paper to note the improvement in the writing of these letters.

Assignment

The children plan to pay particular attention to the writing of the letters with rounded tops in copying their reports for the class newspaper.

Lesson Review

Occasionally a student may need a review of cursive letter construction.

The following lesson is appropriate for intermediate-grade children.

Finishing Strokes

Ending the last letter of each word with a good finishing stroke makes our handwriting look much better. Most of these strokes swing up with a slight upward curve to the height of the letter *a*. The curve of the final stroke is downward on the letters *g, j, y,* and *z*.

Part 1

Look at yesterday's sample of your best handwriting. Look for the final stroke or "tails" on every word that you wrote on this sample. Put the number of tails that you left off here.__________ Count every tail that is poorly shaped or that reaches above or below the height of the letter *a*.

Part 2

Now put your name on the right of the top line of your paper. Put the date just below your name. On the third line just to the left of the center, put the title, "Handwriting." Skip the next line. Using good finishing strokes, write the following sentence three times:

Paul said, "The big brown fox quickly and slyly jumped over the lazy dog."

Skip a line and then write the following words, ending them with good tails:

month	because	windy	high	kite	string
west	held	fell	oak	broke	away
will	where	an	hold	east	air

Part 3

Again, look at yesterday's sample of your handwriting. Copy those words needing tails and put good tails or finishing strokes on them. Look closely at the ending of each word to see that you are improving your final strokes.

Using Good Slant in Handwriting—Lower Loop Letters

Proper slant in handwriting is very important in the making of lower loop letters. Be sure the slanted part of these letters is straight. The lower loop letters are *g, j, p, q, y,* and *z*.

PART 1
Take the written work. Put the guide sheet under it. See whether the lower loop letters have the correct angle of slant. How would you grade your slant? Is it excellent, good, fair, or poor? ___________

Now look at the finishing strokes. Put a check by those that do not reach as high as the letter *a*.

PART 2
Today we will practice good slant on the lower loop letters. Put your name on the upper right on the top line of your paper. Put the date just below your name. On the third line just to the left of the center, put the title "Handwriting." Skip the next line.

gag pipe pig

Carefully write a line of each of these lower loop letters:
g, j, p, q, y, z
Here are some words that have lower loop letters. Write each two times:

gag pipe gang jig pig

Write this sentence two times: "The big pig danced a jig."

PART 3
Now look at all of the writing you have done today. See whether all of your lower loop letters reach halfway below the line. See whether they have straight backs. Circle those that are poorly formed. Practice writing those words that you circled. How would you grade today's work? Is it excellent, good, fair, poor? ___________

Spacing in Handwriting

After one word has been finished, a space is left before the next word is written. This space is just about as wide as the small letter *a*. This space should never be larger or smaller than this.

PART 1
Look back at the sentences you wrote in earlier lessons. See whether the spacing between words is about as wide as the small letter *a*. Are you leaving too much space or too little? How would you grade your spacing on these sentences? Is it excellent, good, fair, or poor? ___________

PART 2
Put the heading on your paper. Now here are some sentences for you to write. Be careful to leave a uniform space between your words. Write each sentence twice:

The quick brown fox jumps over the lazy dog.
Whatever is worth doing at all is worth doing well.
Well begun is half done.
Here is a sample of good spacing:

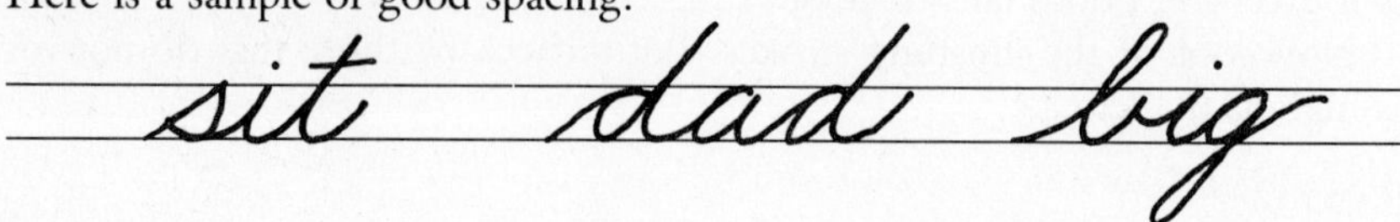

Part 3

Skip a line and write the following:

"Here is another sample of my best handwriting. I am careful with finishing strokes, slant, letter size, and the spacing between letters."

Compare this writing with the writing in the first lesson. Is it better, just as good as, or poorer than, this first lesson? __________

The following are other suggestions with respect to handwriting instruction in the intermediate grades that come from experienced teachers:

1. Make the paper on which the final writing will appear have special significance. Make mimeograph copies of a flag, holiday picture, or school letterhead on good-quality "mimeo" bond paper. Explain that the number of copies is limited and that the paper should not be used for the exercise until students feel they are prepared. Sometimes attractive stationery will serve the same purpose.
2. Hold a writing clinic with one or two of the best writers acting as "doctors" for specific letters.
3. Exchange handwriting samples with other schools, both in the United States and in other countries.
4. Suggest to parents the value of a good writing instrument as a gift.
5. Make art designs formed of alphabet letters.
6. Have an "Each One Teach One" week, during which each student teaches one letter and its formation to another student or small group. Let the students devise worksheets or lessons for this activity. One fifth grade produced a textbook titled "How to Write Well."

Techniques to Improve Legibility

Because of the diversity of what is considered acceptable handwriting, it is important to assess each student's performance individually. The major emphasis of handwriting instruction should be legibility coupled with ease of production.

The most significant handwriting problem is illegibility. Illegible handwriting is due to seven errors: (1) faulty endings; (2) incorrectly made undercurves; (3) mixed slant; (4) failure to give letters in a group proper slant; (5) incorrect information of the initial stroke of such letters as the capitals *W, H, K;* (6) incorrect endings in final *h, m, n;* and (7) failure to make the downstroke of *t* and *d*.

End strokes as spacers between words improve the legibility of writing more than any other single device.

Some claim that attention to this factor can improve legibility by 25 percent.

Ability to make the undercurve of the letter *l* alone improves the shape of many related letters and brings about the orderly appearance of written paragraphs.

The letters that extend below the line should show the same slant as those above the line. The principle of parallel slants brings about harmony in handwriting.

When *h, m,* or *n,* appears at the end of a word, there is a tendency to slur the last two strokes. Emphasis on precision in making the last downstroke in writing these letters and in the final upstroke removes a common fault. The letters *t* and *d* constitute a special application of the *l* principle. Once the relationship of these letters to the *l* principle is recognized, errors in letter formation are eliminated.

The letters *e, a, r,* and *t* cause the most confusion. Such combinations as *be, bi, br, by, bo, oe, oi, os, oc, oa, ve, va, vo, vu, we, wi, wa, ws,* and *wr* also cause trouble. The demons of handwriting are *a* that looks like *o, u,* or *ci; l* that becomes *li; d* that appears as *cl; e* like *i* or the reverse; *m* and *n* like *w* and *u; t* like *l* or *i;* and *r* like *e* or *n.*

To make children aware of certain legibility difficulties, ask them to do the following:

1. Write the words *add, gold,* and *dare* and analyze the letters *a, d,* and *g.* What happens if the letters are not closed at the top?
2. Write the words *no, nail, make,* and *name* and analyze the letters *m* and *n.* What happens if the top is not rounded?
3. Write the words *it, tin, nine,* and *trip* and analyze the letters *t* and *i.* What happens if the letters have open loops?
4. Write the words *late, let,* and *lend,* and analyze the letters *l* and *e.* What happens when the loops are not open?
5. Write the words *up, under,* and *run* and analyze the letter *u.* What happens when the tops of *u* are not pointed?

Some writing habits must be changed to increase legibility. Children who write *gt, ot,* or *ju* with short connecting strokes should be told to "swing between each letter" or "spread your letters out like an accordion." At first the distance should be exaggerated, then modified to proper spacing. If a child continues to write all letters close together, let that student practice his spelling words on a regular sheet of ruled tablet paper but with the lines vertical rather than horizontal. There should be one letter between each pair of lines.

A tight grip on the writing instrument may produce tense, slow writing. The writer can be helped by wadding a sheet of paper into a ball, which is held by the lower fingers against the palm of the hand. Such a practice seems to direct the pressure from the pen.

Speed is the great enemy of legibility. We can think as fast as 250 words a minute and write about 25. Yet eventually some rhythmic speed must be attained.

Drills to increase speed may be one of these types:

1. Write one letter.
2. Write difficult letter combinations that tend to decrease speed of writing, *b, w, v,* followed by *e, i, r.*
3. Write an easy word or words.
4. Write words with thought associations: *clap hands, green grass, blue sky.*
5. Write one- or two-minute time tests.

Suggested sentences containing twenty letters are:

1. Working for speed is fun.
2. She will meet you at home.
3. Write all papers neatly.

Suggested rate per minute:

1. Fourth grade, with pencil: forty-five letters or more.
2. Fifth grade, with pen: fifty-five letters or more.
3. Sixth grade, with pen: sixty-five letters or more.

If a child persists in poor writing, it may reflect an emotional problem. In such cases it is wise to forget about handwriting instruction until the basic problems of the child are cared for. Remember that the basic cause of illegible handwriting is often carelessness.

The solution is to make handwriting so important that the learner will care enough to do it well.

What Provisions Should Be Made for a Left-Handed Child?

It is seldom very satisfying to be a member of a small minority or to be considered different from other people. The left-handed person faces both of these problems. From 4 to 11 percent of the population is left-handed. The range of these figures may be explained by the extent of tolerance of left-handedness in the segment of the population surveyed. Where no effort has been made to convert the left-handed individual to right-handed writing there are higher percentages of left-handers.

To expect or require a left-handed person to become right-handed makes no more sense than to expect a right-handed person to develop left-handedness. Many outstanding people have been left-handed: Leonardo da Vinci, former President Harry S. Truman, Judy Garland, and James V. Cunningham. Historically there has been prejudice against left-handed people. The terms *sinister*—from Latin *sinistral,* meaning "left-handed"—and *gauche*—French for "left"—reflect the negative characteristics that have been attributed to the left-handed. Sinistrals in school should have the same individual respect that we advocate for all children.

Writing Difficulties Encountered by the Left-Handed Person

Some of the difficulties faced by the left-handed person learning to write a system devised by right-handed individuals can be experienced by a right-handed person who attempts a few left-handed exercises. Draw a series of squares, first with the right hand and then with the left. Note that the "pull strokes" with the right hand are "pushing strokes" with the left. These strokes involve different muscles according to the hand

One result of imitating right-handed writing is that the student develops an awkward writing position. Start writing instruction for a left-handed student by adjusting the position of the paper and arm. (Photo by Linda Lungren)

used. Then observe a right-handed individual writing. He starts at a midbody position and writes in a natural left-to-right movement, away from the body. An attempt to imitate this will reveal why a left-handed child copying a right-handed teacher will write moving away from his midbody position toward his natural direction, or right to left. The result is mirror writing, which is completely legible to the writer but cannot readily be deciphered by the rest of us unless it is held up to a mirror. Correction is made by explaining to the child that he must conform to the left-to-right pattern so that others can read what he writes. Ask him to copy individual words and letters, always starting at the left side of the paper. This will take considerable time because he is being asked to learn to write words that seem backward to them.

Another result of imitating right-handed writing is that the child develops an awkward writing position. In order to hold a pencil or pen in exactly the way a right-handed person does, left-handed children may twist their hand around to a backward or upside-down position. Some actually write upside down.

It is very difficult to help these children once such awkward writing positions are well established. The first requirement is that both the child and the parents want to correct it. Without this desire, the results of any teaching effort will be limited. For the child it is almost a punishment. Some will write quite well in the "backward" position, but for many it will mean uncomfortable writing for a lifetime.

Writing Instruction for the Left-Handed

Start writing instruction for a left-handed child by adjusting the position of the paper and arm. Place two tape markers on the desk or writing table. Have the child rest her left arm between these two tapes. This will prevent the arm from swinging out. Another tape can be used to indicate the proper position for the paper. Provide a long pencil or ballpoint pen as the writing instrument. Have the child hold this about an inch and a half from the point. The first exercises should be tracing over letters and words written by a left-handed individual. A considerable amount of writing should be done at the chalkboard; it is practically impossible to use the upside-down position there. The teacher might even guide the hand movements to assure the correct response. These children should have a card of letters written by a left-handed person for personal reference at their desks. If children who have reached the fifth grade are using an awkward position, it is sometimes best to let them continue. Urge instead that they learn to use the typewriter as soon as possible. Some school systems have special summer classes in typing for such left-handed children. Here the left-handed have an advantage over right-handed people; the standard typewriter keyboard was designed by a left-handed person.

There is little experimental evidence to guide a teacher in developing a writing program for the left-handed child. Teachers with experience suggest the following procedures:

1. Group left-handed students together. This makes it easier to supervise instruction and prevents a tendency to imitate right-handed individuals.
2. Begin instruction at the chalkboard, where close supervision can be given. Early detection of an error can prevent the formation of a bad habit. Stress left-to-right movement and the starting place when writing each letter. Circles should be made from left to right in print script, even though this may seem awkward at first.
3. When left-handed children start writing on paper, it may be wise to have them place an arrow as a "traffic signal" at the beginning of their writing to assure the teacher that they are starting at the correct place and proceeding in the correct left-to-right direction. A left-handed child may be a good helper to another left-hander.
4. The child learning to write print script with the left hand places the paper directly in front of him, just as the right-handed individual does. It will be necessary to move the paper frequently while writing; this is the task of the right hand. Accordingly, the writer should be seated at the left-hand side of a table, or alone at an individual desk, rather than sharing a table with a right-handed child. Once these first steps have been mastered, the left-handed child might continue writing print script throughout the grades. In the second grade the child's print script may develop a natural slant if the paper is slanted, as will occur later for cursive writing, so that the left hand follows a natural arc while moving from left to right. However, some feel that the left-handed child should be started on cur-

sive immediately. Why should such children be required to learn two different systems developed for right-handed people?

5. The natural arc of the left hand as it rests on the desk should determine the position of the paper for cursive writing. The upper-right corner of the paper will be in line with the centerline of the body. Children can be told that the bottom corner should point "toward your heart." In shifting the paper the right hand presses down on it, holding it firmly until the line is finished, and then moves it up for the next line. The left hand slides lightly along the line of writing while the paper is kept stationary.
6. The pen or pencil is held with the thumb, index, and middle fingers. It should slant toward the writer's left shoulder. The pen should be held a little higher than it would by a right-handed writer, so that the child can see the writing and avoid running the left hand over the written material. Some teachers place a small rubber band around the pen to indicate where to grip the instrument.
7. A ballpoint or felt-tipped pen is a good writing instrument. The ballpoint does not dig into the paper with the upstrokes, and the ink dries immediately. Avoid cheap ballpoints that are too short or those that must be held in a tight grip because the sides are too smooth. A strip of adhesive tape on the barrel helps to keep a pen from slipping.
8. Copy for the left-handed writing exercises should be directly in front of the writer, not on the chalkboard. At first some children need to have their hands guided through the proper movements. If a single letter is reversed in any writing, take time to work on that letter alone.
9. Let the child determine his or her own letter slant after you have established the proper position of the paper for him. Most left-handed children seem to prefer a vertical form of writing. A few find a backhand more natural. Because our objective is legibility and ease of writing, slant should not be predetermined for the left-handed.
10. Special attention may need to be given to the letters *O, T, F,* and *H* to prevent the use of sinistral strokes. Because upward strokes are difficult for some left-handed writers, they may be eliminated on the letters *a, c, d, g, o,* and *q* when they begin a word.

What Type of Handwriting Instruction Should Be Provided for Learning-Handicapped Students?

Although there is much to be discovered about the most effective means of teaching learning-disabled students, the teacher should be sensitive to timing and sequencing of lessons. This may be achieved by using materials that provide good visual feedback, such as tracing and copying exercises using colored green (start) and red (stop) dots as directional cues. It may also be helpful to make oval rather than round shapes for ease of letter formation. Increased letter size and spacing will aid the child with letter and word discrimination. Association of letters with objects of interest to the child and introduction of only one letter per lesson will also provide more carefully paced instruction. Instruction in small groups of only four to six children per group will allow for more individualized attention to special needs. Joined print script or written script may be most easily mastered by perceptually disabled students because of its connected lines, which more clearly indicate that words are units with fixed ordering of letters. Unfortunately, this approach may cause problems with letters such as *m* and *n,* which have one and two humps when printed, and two and three humps when written.

Although the information about manuscript and cursive writing is given to all children in the same manner, presentation may have to be adjusted for learning-handicapped students. Sensitivity to the needs of all of your students will increase your ability to make these adjustments.

Are Children Learning-Handicapped If They Write Reversals?

Most teachers of young children have found that in learning to read and write some types of reversals are not uncommon. Types of reversals include letter confusions (*b, d, p, q*), whole word confusions (*saw/was, no/on*), and whole phrase confusion (*there are often/often there are*). Until approximately nine years of age these types of reversals of letters and words may occur. As children get older substitutions become more prevalent than reversals among competent readers.

Too often reversals are confused with *dyslexia,* which is a reading disability classified as a neurological dysfunction. Although reversals can be a symptom of dyslexia, they usually are not. Reversals are very normally made by beginners. With practice, maturity, and guidance they will disappear.

Activities that provide correct models, left-to-right directionality, and habit formation will decrease the occurrence of continuous reversals. Activities of this type include the following:

1. Tracing and simultaneously naming difficult letters and words. Once tracing and naming is complete, ask the children to write the letter from memory.
2. Identifying and counting the number of problem letters or words in a passage. This provides practice with the visual image.
3. Writing all *p*'s and *b*'s in red because they loop on the right and all *d*'s and *q*'s in green because they loop on the left.
4. Having children print dictated words on the chalkboard.
5. Using a typewriter or microcomputer to type the words.
6. Having children make word cards (about 8½ by 3 inches). Encourage them to trace these troublesome words with the index and middle fingers (both at once) while they sound the parts of the word. Next have them write the word from memory. Have them keep files on these word cards (an old shoe box will do as a file box).
7. Using flash cards for practice of troublesome words.
8. Having the pupil manipulate letters to form words commonly reversed. Use a magnetic board with three-dimensional letters.
9. Writing in pairs, words sometimes reversed. (*was/saw, net/ten, war/raw, trap/part*). Use one word in a sentence and ask students to point to or write the word used.
10. Using a colored letter at the beginning of words commonly confused. Discontinue this practice as soon as the word no longer presents any difficulty for the child. This encourages the child to give a little extra attention to the troublesome word.

Summary

The question of whether handwriting has a developmental sequence began a discussion of the similarities and differences in teaching manuscript and cursive writing. Time as a factor in the writing process was interwoven throughout all sections of the chapter. The focus, however, was on strategies for teaching both types of writing at the appropriate grade level. There was also a discussion of teaching handwriting to learning-disabled students. Model lessons, worksheets, practice activities, scales, and evaluation criteria were also presented for both right- and left-handed children.

Suggested Classroom Projects and Questions for Discussion

Projects

1. Assemble enough samples from one classroom or school to construct a handwriting scale. This might be a scale

for judging the manuscript writing of children in the third grade, the writing of left-handed individuals of the same age, or boys in the sixth grade.

2. Plan a display that will explain the handwriting program of your school to the public.
3. Make a comparison of the various handwriting programs now on the market. What are the essential differences with regard to philosophy, equipment, letter-formation drills, and special features?
4. Make a case study of an individual with a handwriting problem.
5. Plan a worksheet that will provide for the steps in a writing lesson suggested in this chapter or evaluate a worksheet in a commercial workbook designed to teach handwriting skills.
6. Make a collection of handwriting samples written by children in other countries. Contrast the style and quality of handwriting demonstrated.
7. Introduce the term *calligraphy* and display illustrations of various styles.
8. Find an example of Spencerian writing or, if possible, a person who can write this script. Defend the modern point of view that such art is not needed in writing.
9. Design a classroom bulletin board entitled "Writing Is Sharing" that includes models of legible writing.
10. Ask children to collect models of illegible handwriting. Analyze the problem as a class.

Questions

1. How can children be taught to appreciate the importance of learning to write skillfully?
2. What information do you find in children's encyclopedias that might be used for classroom research on the alphabet?
3. Why is it important that early writing practice produces words?
4. What additional activities can you suggest to make handwriting interesting to students?
5. What advantages and disadvantages does a left-handed teacher have?
6. Would it be wise to have all left-handed children in the intermediate grades meet together for handwriting instruction?
7. In the Orient, writing instruments such as the ink brush are regarded as objects of art. Should we try to develop an attitude that writing is an art form?
8. How can a typewriter be used as a teaching machine?
9. Would it be desirable to require all teachers to pass a blackboard writing test before granting them certification to teach?
10. Why are young children quickly labeled learning-handicapped when they have reversals in their writing?

Chapter 11

The Conventions of Writing: Grammar, Usage, and Mechanics

(Photo by Linda Lungren)

OBJECTIVES

After reading this chapter, the student should be able to:

1. understand the need to teach formal rules of grammar.
2. understand how teaching creative writing is compatible with teaching the conventions of standard English.
3. understand *which* conventions of grammar and mechanics should be taught in the elementary grades and *when* they should be taught.
4. understand the most effective ways to teach these.

Onceuponatime

> therewasnosuchthingastransitionaldevices withinandbetweensentencesspacesbetween wordsandsentencesdidnotexistandpunctuation marksweremanyyearsinthefuture itcameto passthatsomescholarcontrivedtheideaof separatingonesentencefromanotherwithablank space it was not too long after this that another scholar hit upon the next logical step of separating the words within the sentence with blank spaces while this did much to end some of the confusion it was still a little difficult to tell where one sentence ended and another began to resolve this the period was invented. closely on the heels of the period came the capital letter to begin the sentence. We were on our way. At this point in the evolution of the sentence it was up to a fiendishly clever or sadistic scholar to introduce internal punctuation marks; the world, by the way, has not been the same since.

The world of language is truly dynamic. As teachers we must share our students' joy in understanding the remarkable power of language.

As teachers of language arts we are always in a quandary concerning when and how to teach grammar. Should it be taught separately? Should it be integrated into the writing process? How much time should be spent teaching grammar? How should grammar be evaluated? This chapter addresses these issues.

Why Is It Necessary to Teach Formal Rules of Grammar and Punctuation?

For many teachers, the question "Why teach the formal rules of grammar and mechanics, including punctuation and capitalization?" can be answered by one word—accountability. Curriculum guides direct teachers and students through countless exercises, and many standardized and district competency tests evaluate the levels to which students have acquired knowledge of grammar and mechanics. In fact, so much emphasis is placed on teaching these conventions of written English that they often become isolated from other components of the language arts curriculum, thus taking on an intrinsic value. The purpose here is not to suggest how to teach the conventions of written English (which is explained later in this chapter) but to discuss why they should be taught. We can begin to answer this question by examining the type of English that is taught in virtually all language arts programs.

Have you ever heard a student say something like the following?

> Me and him is good friends!

On a very superficial level, this probably sounds very discordant to your trained ear as a proficient language user. However, to the student who said it, it probably sounds just fine, and the student may be inclined to tell you so.

Several points can be made about this hypothetical student-teacher interaction that will help us answer the question of why to teach grammar. One involves examining the idea of correct usage, and the other focuses on the terminology necessary to discuss the components of classroom English.

As we first examine the idea of correct usage, we must look at the English that is taught in classrooms. This form of language is called Standard, also referred to as public English. Because English is spoken by approximately 400 million people in many different parts of the world, a standard and universally accepted form of usage has been agreed upon so that all English speakers may easily understand one another. In language arts programs, this Standard English is considered correct usage. Thus, to most teachers, teaching grammar means teaching what is correct. However, Duffy (1969) suggests that this notion of correctness may actually interfere with what we, as teachers, are trying to accomplish. Children come to school with a rich store of language and an ingrained sense that what they use is, indeed, correct. Therefore, it is counterproductive to view language differences as being either correct or incorrect. Instead, from a linguist's perspective,

Me and him is good friends!

represents grammatically sound language structure. What it does not represent is conventional usage that has been agreed upon and thus made standard by speakers of American English.

The concept of levels of usage can be introduced to students easily. Instead of attempting to convince them that what they say is incorrect and what we teach is correct, we can show them that what is appropriate when speaking privately with friends on the playground may not be appropriate when talking to the superintendent or when writing a business letter. As suggested in Chapter 6 role-playing activities help students understand the difference between public (Standard) and private levels of usage. These activities might include classroom simulations of the following:

1. A conversation between a student who is new to the school and a group of students he wants to accept him.
2. A conversation between a student who has just won an award for a heroic deed and the mayor of the city.

Johnson (1984) suggests that we view Standard English as an alternate form of language rather than as a replacement for nonstandard pronunciations and grammatical patterns that students may bring to the classroom. He advocates using strategies of second-language teaching, which include the following:

1. Understanding a child's native language or dialect.
2. Pointing out the differences between the child's English and that of the classroom without implying value judgments on either.
3. Providing structured listening experiences in Standard English.
4. Directing students to produce and read scripts representing varying levels of usage.

Thus, when we teach the conventions of English, we heighten students' awareness and understanding of the different levels of usage.

Now, let's look again at the question, "Why teach these conventions of English?", and at the comment of our hypothetical student,

Me and him is good friends!

We have already discussed the potential futility of telling this student that this sentence does not sound right, because in all probability it does sound right to that student. Another approach would be to explain that in Standard English, certain words can only be used in certain ways. For example, *me* and *him* can only be used as objects, not as subjects. Also, we can explain that this statement has a compound subject, which requires a plural verb. However, this conversation would be meaningless unless the student understood some terminology associated with English usage. In other words, the terminology of English grammar and mechanics must be taught in order for students and teachers to have commonly understood labels through which to study Standard English. Our hypothetical student would have understood the teacher only after having knowledge of subjects, verbs, and objects within complete sentences.

How Are the Teaching of Writing and the Conventions of Standard English Compatible?

Some educators contend that a clear distinction exists between "creative" and "practical" writing. They often refer to stories and poems as acts of creativity, whereas they label reports, essays, and business letters as practical, and thus more formal, modes of discourse.

Although such a viewpoint is understandable, it also makes sense to acknowledge that any time a person conveys thoughts through written language, regardless of the form, that person has engaged in an act of creativity. In fact, there are very few acts more creative than a child's placing symbols (letters) in various configurations to produce meaning.

One point that is appropriate to make here is that creativity in writing cannot exist if ideas cannot be communicated. Even if children write a particular piece for their eyes only, they must employ sufficient conventions in their writing so that they can read it. Most teachers have seen students write with random capitalization and punctuation and with invented spellings that even the writers have difficulty deciphering. Obviously very little can be considered creative in this situation.

However, beyond this level of noncommunication, it is more realistic to let audience and purpose dictate the degree of correctness and formality needed in a written work. Instead of viewing "creative" and "practical" writing as being separate and mutually exclusive, they can be viewed simply as two aspects of the writing process that, according to purpose, receive different emphasis at different times. Perhaps the distinction might instead be viewed as being between "practical" and "personal" writing.

Correct form seems intrinsically a function of realistic writing because other people are practically concerned. This is the type of writing in which the authors work more as reproducers of known facts, conditions, or ideas presented in their own words. Here the emphasis may be on the mechanics of writing, spelling, penmanship, neatness, punctuation, and similar external items without injury to the child's creative expression.

On the other hand, when students express in one way or another their feelings or their intellectual reactions to an experience, something they have seen, heard, or otherwise come in contact with through the senses, this expression of personal reactions uniquely represents the quality of originality because no one other than the individual writer can produce it. It is his or her own contribution. This type of writing is that of artistic self-expression. It is personal, individual, imaginative, and highly perishable. To keep it alive there must be complete freedom to experiment and complete assurance of a respectful reception of the product regardless of its nature.

Although in a sense the two aspects of writing develop separately and serve different purposes, students gradually carry over what they have learned of techniques in practical writing and apply it where it suits their purpose in personal writing. The emphasis is first and last on saying something that is worth saying, and saying it effectively. A balance between the two types must be maintained, and to give all writing the same treatment is to suppress or inhibit the creative spirit of children.

Confidence in the craftsmanship of writing and expression also releases creativity. Great writers and artists have also been expert craftsmen. Certainly no great painter has emerged by ignoring the disciplines of his craft. By mastering these disciplines artists are able to project their own personal qualities more effectively. Our objective is to use the child's desire to create and to make disciplined craftsmanship acceptable.

One of the acknowledged tasks of the elementary school years is to further the pupil's self-concept. Few experiences in school can so effectively destroy a positive self-image as the teaching of composition. Excessive correction has thwarted the pencil of many a beginner. In other cases, no correction at all has been offered for fear of cramping self-expression. When to correct and when not to correct children's writing has been a dilemma for many teachers. Correction of any writing is best done orally by teacher and pupil in an editing conference, taking turns reading aloud. Thus they apply the oral-auditory facility established long before the newer learning of writing and reading.

When writing is an opportunity to reveal one's own feelings and imagination without fear of criticism and with the assurance of respectful listeners, the pupil's picture of himself/herself is enhanced. Not being on the defensive, one can appreciate the good writing of others, both peers and professionals. Pupils can enjoy what is worthy in the teacher's eyes because they too are worthy as writers. Both the listening audience and those who see the corrected public writing fortify one's pleasure and pride in writing and in oneself.

Which Conventions of Grammar and Mechanics Should Be Taught in the Elementary Grades and When Should They Be Taught?

Conventions of Punctuation and Capitalization

Have you ever wondered how the punctuation marks came to be? In pages of Chinese writing there is no punctuation, and as recently as 1945 no punctuation was used in the Korean language. However, when the Koreans decided to write horizontally rather than vertically, they recognized the need for such marks.

The ancient Greeks and Romans frequently wrote without separating the words, let alone separating sentences. It was the orators who made the first separations in order to emphasize the thoughts they were expressing. Originally punctuation was built on a single series of pauses. The comma was for a one-unit pause, the semicolon for a two-unit pause, a colon for a three-unit pause, and a period for a four-unit pause. The question mark was a sign to raise the voice at the end of the word. The explanation point was a little dagger drawn to resemble the real dagger used to fasten important notices to buildings.

Human beings learned to talk about a million years ago and have been using alphabetic writing for several thousand years, but punctuation in the modern sense came into use in our language less than three hundred years ago, and the system is far from perfect. In the system as it stands, the marks are used as follows:

1. For *linking,* use
   ; semicolon
   : colon
   —linking dash
   - linking hyphen
2. For *separating,* use:
   . period
   ? question mark
   ! exclamation point
   , separating comma
3. For *enclosing,* use:
   , . . . , paired commas
   —. . .— paired dashes
   (. . .) paired parentheses
   [. . .] paired brackets
   ". . ." paired quotation marks
4. For *indicating omission,* use:
   ' apostrophe
   . omission period in abbreviations (or dot)
   — omission dash
   . . . triple periods (or dots)

In the primary grades the child first learns about the *period.* Three uses of the period are taught:

1. At the end of a sentence: *The books are here.*
2. After an abbreviation in titles of persons and things: *Dr. James.*
3. After initials in proper names: *J. H. Hill.*

The teacher stresses the period in the first reading the child does and in the first sentence written on the board. "This little dot is called a period," she explains. "It tells us to stop because this is the end of a statement." The other uses are taught as an aspect of spelling.

Two uses of the *question mark* are taught:

1. At the end of a direct question: *Is this your balloon?*
2. After a direct question but within the sentence: *"Will you be ready?" the man asked.*

The first use of a question mark can be understood and used by beginners in the first grade. The second should not be presented until late in the third grade. This form is less difficult: *He asked, "Will you be ready?"*

Lord Dunsany once complained that there were so many *comma rules* that printers could write one of his sentences like this: "Moreover, Jones, who, as indeed, you, probably, know, is, of course, Welsh, is, perhaps, coming, too, but, unfortunately, alone." In some handbooks one can still find hundreds of rules for the comma. Fortunately for the teacher, eleven seem to be enough to meet the needs of elementary school children.

Four of these eleven rules are those that concern the writing of a letter:

1. To separate the date from the year: *June 5, 1985.*
2. To set off the name of a city from a state: *Winfield, Kansas.*
3. After a salutation in a letter: *Dear Linda,*
4. After close of a letter: *Your friend,*

Additional comma rules taught in the elementary grades include the following:

5. To set off short direct quotations: *"We are ready," called the boys.*
6. After clauses of introduction: *While they were eating, the bell rang.*
7. Between parts of a compound sentence joined by a short conjunction: *Mr. Hill took Paul, and Jim went in Ms. Thrope's car.*
8. Before and after appositives: *The principal, Mr. Bellus, talked to the parents.*
9. Before and after parenthetical expression: *You told your mother, I suppose, about your report card.*
10. Before and after a nonrestrictive clause: *That boy, who has the dog, is in the fifth grade.*
11. To separate the words in a series: *Sue, Rick, and Billy are cousins.* (Immediately we run into the problem of the comma before *and*. Using one in that position helps to clarify the meaning.)

The *colon* is quite simple to teach, because there are only four ways it is used:

1. After the greeting in a business letter: *Dear Sir:*
2. Before a long series: *Mother bought the following: oranges, lemons, bread, jam, and cake.*
3. To separate the hour from the minutes: *2:30 A.M.*
4. To denote examples: *A proper name should be capitalized: Mary.*

The *apostrophe* receives a great deal of attention in spelling. It is used in the following ways.

1. With the letter *s* to show possession: *Mary's coat, boys' coats.*
2. To show where letters have been omitted: *don't* (do not), *o'er* (over).
3. To show the omission of number from a date: *Class of '84.*
4. To show the plural of letters and figures: *A's, 2's.*

Quotation marks are a special problem for students. Few adults ever use quotation marks unless they are professional writers. The reader is the best textbook for these marks. After a story has been read, go back and have children take the parts of the story characters. Then while the narrator reads all material except quotations, the characters read their proper lines. Then examine how the material was punctuated so that each person knew what to read. If the class is engaged in story writing, examples of all the varieties of use should be illustrated on the chalkboard as a reference. These are two basic usages that all children need to learn:

1. The unbroken quotation with the descriptive element preceding the quotation: *He cried, "Get a new man on first base!"*
2. The reverse of the preceding: *"Get a new man on first!" he cried.*

In order to use a *semicolon* properly, it is necessary to understand conjunctions. *Conjunctions* may join either words or groups of words. When a conjunction is preceded by a comma (as when joining two clauses), a semicolon may be used instead of the comma and conjunction. It confuses children to present the semicolon as a compromise between a comma and a period.

Mary was happy, but Joe was sad.

may also be written:

Mary was happy; Joe was sad.

Clauses joined by a semicolon must be related and independent; however, the situation must also be related in that it affects both Mary and Joe. One may write:

The sea is beautiful at sunset; the water reflects the brilliant glow of the sky.

But not:

The sea is beautiful at sunset; the cry of the seagulls makes me homesick.

Textbooks contain other rules for the semicolon.

The *hyphen* is usually considered an orthographic feature rather than a punctuation mark. It is a growing practice to avoid the hyphen except where a word is divided at the end of a line. Many words formerly hyphenated are now either "solid" (one word, like *flannelboard*) or two words, like *decision making*. Webster's *Third New International* is a safe guide to follow in hyphenating. Students in the elementary school are not encouraged to use the dash, because they will tend to overuse it.

Parentheses seldom appear in children's writing.

Classroom Activities—Primary Years

1. Punctuation

Interesting exercises in punctuation can be made by taking material from readers and reproducing it without any punctuation. The child is told how many sentences there are. The exercises can be made self-correcting by putting the title of the book and page number at the bottom of the exercise.

6 Sentences	10 Capital Letters
5 Commas	4 Quotation Marks

she reached into the big box and pulled out a santa claus suit and held it up it was bright red with real fur trimmings billy could see that there was a cap and a set of whiskers and even boots to go with it isn't that lovely she said to billy the minute i saw it i thought of you im sure it will fit just perfectly she held it up to him

Because some of the punctuation rules are applied primarily in letters, writing a group letter and then copying it from the board is a good way to introduce the comma rules involved. Practice with letter headings is equally good.

2. Capitalization

Rules for Capitalization	*Examples*
1. The beginning of a sentence.	We saw a show.
2. Names of months and holidays.	January, Halloween

Rules for Capitalization	*Examples*
3. Names of particular streets and schools.	Hamilton School, Biona Ave.
4. First word and important words of a title.	My Visit to the Farm
5. Names of people, and pets and initials of people.	Beth, Spot, A. J. Boyd
6. Names of countries, cities, rivers, and mountains.	Mexico, Cincinnati, Eel River, Mt. Hood
7. Only names in the greeting; only the first word in the closing of a letter.	Dear Jan, Yours very truly,
8. References to God.	God, Lord, Savior, Buddha

After presenting the preceding rules and examples, ask children to correct the following by adding the missing capitals and punctuation.

1.
astor hotel
new york ny
july 21, 2013

dear teacher

2.
966 riverview
Corbin, Kansas
june 6 1988

dear mother

3.
gunnison colo
dec 5 1994

dear santa claus

3. *Charts and Bulletin Boards*

Charts and bulletin boards that act as constant reminders are valuable in the classroom. Your students should be involved in the making of these charts. The following samples are suitable for display on bulletin boards:

WATCH YOUR COMMAS!

713 Olde St.
Festus, Missouri
Sept. 16, 1986

Dear Mary,

Your friend,
Marty

One teacher makes punctuation marks come alive through dramatization. A question mark with a face and legs, a comma with a smiling face and wearing a hat, and a chubby little period are placed on a bulletin board, each with a caption telling one thing they do. These characters—Chubby Little Period, Jolly Question Mark, Mr. and Mrs. Comma, and Tall Exclamation Point—are introduced via the bulletin board. Each figure with its rule and title is shown. Other rules of punctuation are added as introduced.

4. Teacher-Student Dialogue

The teacher describes how these "punctuation characters" are used.

> I have the little people made up into plywood puppets. They are kept on hand in the schoolroom at all times. We use them to point up discussion of punctuation in many ways—in language class, social studies, written work, spelling. For example: in oral reading, we talk about "Chubby Little Period being at the end of a sentence to tell us that we stop here for a short time before going on." "Mr. Comma helps us by telling us this is the place to pause when we are reading a sentence."
>
> I use this lesson in teaching how to begin and end sentences. In this lesson I also introduce the good English habit "Use a question mark (Jolly Question Mark) after each sentence that asks a question."
>
> Using the wooden "Chubby Little Period," I say,
>
> Chubby Little Period
> Runs and sits,
> The end of the sentence
> Is always his place.
>
> A sentence is written on the board. Using the puppet, I then demonstrate the period's place.

Classroom Activities—Intermediate Years

1. Punctuation Quiz

Intermediate-aged students enjoy a television quiz program in which each punctuation mark appears and is questioned concerning its activities or in which there is a *What's My Line?* or *To Tell the Truth* format, with the punctuation marks appearing as guests. The master of ceremonies starts by saying, "Our guest does four things (or eleven if it's the comma). We must name all of them to identify him completely.

2. Trick Sentences

Older students enjoy trick sentences like the following:

Harry, when Harold had had *had,* had had *had had; had had* had had the teacher's approval. (Omit italics and punctuation when writing this sentence on the chalkboard.)

3. Punctuation Practice

Have students provide punctuation and capitalization for the following:

The fight over the boys came home.

This is the story of walter who has not heard the story through it walter gained lasting fame a beautiful girl and a glorious name he also gained one autumn day on the grassy field in gridiron play the team was losing the clock moved fast any play might be the last of the game injured walter then called his own signal explaining men ill take the blame if we dont score he ran a full ninety yards or more

Another procedure that illustrates the importance of punctuation in written communication calls for deliberate misplacement of punctuation in a passage with consequent loss of meaning. The same passage can be reproduced several times with varying degrees of distortion. The pupil sees how difficult it is to get meaning from a passage so treated. In the following exercise the first copy completely obscures the meaning, the second copy is frustrating but not impossible, and the third is reproduced correctly.

Billy listened, carefully as the teacher. Explained how punctuation helps. The reader commas periods exclamation marks and questions marks? All help a reader get meaning. From the printed page. Billy wondered what would happen. If the printer got the punctuation marks mixed. UP it was hard for him to imagine. What this would do to a story.

Billy listened carefully as the teacher explained. How punctuation helps the reader. Commas periods, exclamation marks and question marks all help. A reader get meaning from the printed page. Billy wondered. What would happen if the printer got the punctuation marks mixed up. It was hard for him to imagine what this would do. To a story.

Billy listened carefully as the teacher explained how punctuation helps the reader. Commas, periods, exclamation marks, and question marks all help a reader get meaning from the printed page. Billy wondered what would happen if the printer got the punctuation marks mixed up. It was hard for him to imagine what this would do to a story.

To emphasize that punctuation marks reflect the pauses and emphasis of speech, reproduce a page from a book such as *Island of the Blue Dolphins* or *Charlotte's Web* or from a story in the reading textbook without punctuation marks. As the teacher reads the story with appropriate stress, pause, and juncture, the students put in the appropriate punctuation. When they check their marks with the original text, the point can be made that punctuation at times is a personal interpretation and that the student and author may disagree and both be correct. In a discussion as to why the author punctuated as he did, rules may be reviewed or clarified.

Conventions of Grammar and Usage

Before we can discuss what should be taught in the area of grammar and usage, we should carefully define our terms. From a linguist's point of view, *grammar* refers to the terminology used to describe patterns of speech in a particular language. "Him and me is good friends" is as gramatically correct as "He and I are good friends." *Usage,* on the other hand, refers to word usage based on standards of acceptability. Therefore, although "Him and me is good friends" represents an appropriate grammatical pattern in the English language, it is unacceptable as Standard English word usage. It is this concept of word usage with which we, as teachers, should be concerned.

We can now more accurately phrase our original question to ask, "What standards of word usage should be taught?" Our language is dynamic and ever-changing. People are constantly influencing the norm or standard of acceptability. Although many staunch supporters of an unwavering etiquette for language use may cringe at the thought, an example of this dynamic element of language is the phrase "just between you and I." Traditionally, the nominative case *I* could not be used as an object of the preposition *between;* although this would be unacceptable today in most classrooms, common usage is pushing it closer to the realm of acceptability in speech.

In the primary grades, the goal of language arts programs should be to structure activities that will engage students in the use of all four language skill areas: listening, speaking, reading, and writing. The objective is to allow children to hear and to utilize their language in a risk-free setting. Fluency and self-confidence in language skill users are of primary concern. By grade three, students can be introduced to grammatical terminology that will help them to understand the requirements of standard usage better. Also, by the time they are in third grade, students can understand the notion that written language requires stricter attention to these established standards than does oral language.

Flood and Salus (1984) discuss two concepts that should be introduced to children in the elementary grades. One is the concept of *referentiality.* When young children write, they often assume that their readers know what they, as writers, are thinking. For example, a young child might write

> *He played ball with his friend. It disappeared. He tried to find it. I went home.*

We can guess what the *it* refers to, but we cannot be quite so sure about the second *he* or the *I.* Teachers can raise these issues with students and help them be aware of the need to let the reader know exactly whom they are talking about.

According to Flood and Salus, another important concept for elementary students to understand is that of *subject-verb agreement.* In order to clarify this concept, teachers need to introduce nouns and verbs and their singular and plural forms. In the intermediate grades, adjectives, adverbs, prepositions, and conjunctions can be introduced as keys to sentence expansion and standard usage.

How Can the Conventions of Grammar and Mechanics Best Be Taught?

Although it sounds like a cliché, research supports the notion that the only way students learn to write is by writing. Furthermore, young children should write often and in a risk-free environment, for time spent writing is itself more conducive to improvement in written language use than is time spent learning the concepts and terminology that define the relationships within writing (Flood and Salus, 1984). When young children write, they are functioning primarily as experimenters. Emphasis on learning terminology and grammatical definitions in the early grades has a tendency to stifle this experimentation and children's desire to explore the various ways to use their language. Denise, a first grader, wrote:

> This is Jean and Linda.
> They are looking at the kittens.
> The kittens are in the basket.
> The basket is yellow and red.
> The kittens are cute.

But in the same school another first-grade class was writing these stories:

> This is in the Dineoshire's Days. A sea manstre is going to land and eat. a trtaile is under his tail. In those days the were no people.
>
> Jeffrey

> This is the sivl war wen the Americans fot the inglish. The Americans wun the wor becas the American's they did not giv up.
>
> By Bobby

It is obvious that two different philosophies are at work here. In one there has been an emphasis on form, in the second on ideas. The natural question to ask is when these students should be expected to spell and write correctly. Teachers who permit the second type of writing say that late in the second grade or sometimes the third grade the children seek correct form. These new standards are the result of wide reading and the gradual mastery of writing mechanics. It is true that unless the principal and parents understand the purposes of the teacher there will be criticism. But it should be recognized that children are not going to attempt words like *monster* or *turtle* if they face criticism with respect to spelling and writing.

As young writers develop confidence, a greater awareness of good composition qualities will improve their written expression as illustrated in the following examples:

Unity: staying with the subject
Continuity: developing topic statements by addition and illustration
Form: sense of order; organization
Sentence structure: the levels of subordination
Diction: choosing fresh, colorful, precise words
Tone: developing individuality of style

Story Syntax

The following sentences exemplify progress in unity, sentence structure, and diction.

UNITY. The following beginning and closing sentences of a composition indicate "staying with the subject":

Grade Six

> To have a vacation without any accidents this summer, we should be careful in everything we do. Remember, most accidents can be prevented.
> By being careful and using common sense, you will have a very safe summer.

SENTENCE STRUCTURE. The following sentences exemplify logical subordination:

Grade Four

> When I look at Brownstone Falls in Mellen, Wisconsin, I think of purple rocks and water falling down them.
> When Range VI went to the moon he did not bring back pictures because he met space men and they took his camera.

Grade Six

> Summer would be a lot more fun if people would obey summer safety rules.

He replied, "I feel that the American people have a wrong impression of my country of Peru, for my country is a contrast of old and new, of gaiety and sorrow."

DICTION. The following sentences contain fresh, colorful words:

Grade Four

It was very quiet on the marsh, no fish leaping, no birds singing.
The wind makes the flowers nod their heads and twist around and rise off the ground.

Grade Five

Cars are speedy now, whizzing by at one hundred miles an hour.
Whispers come from a motor purring softly.
As a boy I could look down the terraced hillside, to the green valley snuggled between the mountains; or I could look upward to the lofty peaks, their diamond snow shimmering in the blinding sun.

Students use figurative speech as early as fourth grade. For instance:

Clouds look like big cotton balls in the air.
A rhinoceros is big and bold. He has horns like sharp fat long tacks.

Just as oral language develops when children experiment with words in a positive, nonthreatening environment, their facility with written language increases when we allow them to develop fluency in a risk-free setting.

In about the second grade, children begin to distinguish between personal and practical writing. Yatrin (1981) proposes that teachers capitalize on this growing awareness by focusing on the elements of audience and purpose. This approach, which she refers to as *functionalism,* joins creativity and correctness, which are two aspects of language arts programs that are too often separated. Within a framework of real-world writing, teachers can provide instruction in grammar and mechanics for the same reasons that real-world writers use these conventions of English: to ensure effective communication.

What does this functional approach mean in the classroom? The following principles of functionalism apply to classroom writing instruction:

1. **Classroom writing should, as much as possible, approximate the kinds of writing that can be found in the world outside the classroom.** This includes lists, notes, messages, and letters. Students can exchange notes with the teacher, other students, and their parents. After writing a short note to the teacher, a young child can be encouraged to read the message aloud. The teacher can then respond with a note to the child, which she or he can read either silently or aloud. Parents can be encouraged to write notes regularly and put them into the child's lunch sack or book bag. One teacher staples a manila folder to a bulletin board and writes NOTES TO (TEACHER'S NAME) on the front. During the year she encourages students to write thoughts, feelings, and ideas to her and put them into the folder. Of course, she always responds promptly with a written reply.

Letters can also be a regular part of the curriculum. Pen pals do not have to be far away. Students can exchange regular letters with students in another school in their district or even with another classroom in the same school. Of course, if you know someone who teaches in another part of your state or another part of the country, you can encourage students to establish pen pals there. It is always fun to exchange letters with people from diverse areas.

Several publications provide students with real world opportunities for letter writing. They include:

Albert, B. (1983). *Clubs for Kids.* New York: Ballantine Books.
Feinman, J. (1983). *Freebies for Kids.* New York: Wanderer Books.
Grady, T. (Ed.) (1983). *Free Stuff for Kids.* Delphaven, Minn.: Meadowlark Press.

2. **Each time children write, they should do so with a specific audience and purpose in mind.** In

the world outside the classroom, writers write primarily to communicate with others. In the case of personal writing, they may write to clarify or express thoughts, ideas, and feelings. However, whether writing for someone else or for themselves, writers always have a purpose for writing; if that purpose is to communicate thoughts and ideas, they also write to a specific audience.

Too often, classroom writing denies children a sense of either audience or purpose. Most of the time the teacher is the only audience to whom students write, and they are thus more preoccupied with achieving the correctness necessary for a particular score than with perfecting their communication skills.

Students are more likely to see a need for refining these skills if they are motivated by a desire to communicate their thoughts and ideas to someone else. Of course, the classroom teacher cannot just wait for opportunities for real-world writing to present themselves. If someone from the community comes to a classroom to speak, the teacher can capitalize on this fortuitous event by having students respond to that individual in writing. If a parent comes into the classroom to help supervise a special occasion, again the teacher has a ready-made audience and purpose for writing a thank you note. However, these instances do not occur on a daily basis.

Most often, teachers must devise instances of writing that address issues of audience and purpose. The following is not a complete list, but it represents a variety of ideas that have been used successfully at all grade levels.

Class Books

Class books can contain stories, poems, jokes, and personal narratives. Students love seeing their collected works bound in book form for their classmates to read; during a school's open house, parents are especially pleased to see that their child's work has been "published." For younger children, these books can consist of a class collection of language experience stories that have been illustrated. In the intermediate grades, students can write books not only for their peers and parents, but also for younger children in other classes. These books can be theme-oriented, consisting of writings about a special occasion (Happy Birthdays) or a certain content recently studied (the Discovery of America).

Personal Communications

Personal communications can be business and friendly letters, thank you notes, invitations, greeting cards, and directions. The degree to which this communication is personal will dictate the degree of attention to standard usage required.

11 Agassiz Avenue
Albany, N.Y.
Jan. 6, 1989

Dear Grandmother:

Christmas is so full of surprises. I never expected to have a pair of mittens made by my own grandmother. The colors are just right for my coat. It must have taken you a long time to make them. I'll think of you whenever I wear them.

We gave a Christmas play at school. I was an angel. Daddy says they must have made a mistake to give me a part like that. He is always teasing.

With love,
Jim

An incentive for letter writing is provided by a child's having his own stationery. The paper should be lined. Parents might be encouraged to buy such material as birthday presents for children. The Cub Scouts and Brownies have such stationery for their members. If the teacher gives a gift as a birthday present, it is wise to have a local printer create the type of writing paper the children need. Children might make their own "crests" in art class.

A chart illustrating the terms used in letter writing should be mimeographed and given to each intermediate child. An example of a friendly letter is shown with these parts identified: heading, salutation, body, complimentary close, and signature. A business letter